HANDS
ON THE
PAST

Other Books by C. W. Ceram

Yestermorrow (1961)
The March of Archaeology (1958)
The Secret of the Hittites (1956)
Gods, Graves, and Scholars (1951)

HANDS ON THE PAST

Pioneer Archaeologists Tell Their Own Story

Edited by

C. W. CERAM

SCHOCKEN BOOKS • NEW YORK

First SCHOCKEN PAPERBACK edition 1973

Library of Congress Catalog Card Number: 66-19372
Manufactured in the United States of America

FOREWORD

'Archaeology is at the same time
a science and an art'.

Encyclopaedia Britannica 1950

LIKE EVERY OTHER ENCYCLOPAEDIA DEFINITION, this one is incomplete. Archaeology is, as well as being a science and an art, moreover an adventure, an adventure of spirit and deed. Not only in the nineteenth century, the 'classical' period of great archaeological discovery, but also today, in the mid-twentieth century, the archaeologist has to combat physical forces – in the form of jungle and desert, or of visionless officials, or other obstructions of every sort. Therefore Part One of our book is concerned mainly with modern tomb-robberies and with the struggle of the archaeologists to protect these monuments.

Although the archaeologists' accounts of these kind of adventures, the accompaniment to their serious scientific researches, are very exciting, more exciting by far are the spiritual adventures which the scholar can experience in the quiet of his study – as did Champollion, when he deciphered hieroglyphic script.

We shall find both kinds of adventure in this anthology. The book is not put together like a novel, to be read from cover to cover in one session. The purpose of every anthology is to give as complete as possible a survey of a spiritual landscape; but only a geometrician measures out a landscape systematically, whereas the inquisitive viewer picks out the places amenable to him for a short stay.

The choice of extracts is purely subjective; how could it be otherwise, the material on this subject being as extensive as it is? The primary principle involved was to choose what was *interesting*, but to give it in doses which eventually combined to bring into view the whole picture of archaeological discovery. It would be out of place here to take into account literary merit. Many scholars were very poor narrators of their discoveries, but one or two of these badly written accounts have been included because of the importance of the material. Much had to be omitted because it was available only in a strictly scientific form and quite unreadable for the layman. But a few things have also been 'excavated' which had been lost to the scholar himself for many years.

This book is confined almost entirely to the authentic writings of the archaeologists themselves. In preparing it a basic rule of archaeology was rigorously adhered to – that nothing was to be altered. Every omission is indicated. The very variable spelling of names created quite a problem; but in this case too the original spelling of the names was preserved as far as possible and all the variants in spelling of each name have been entered in the index, where the one in common usage today has been indicated.

My purpose is not to provide a comprehensive anthology, since Jacquetta Hawkes has already done this in her two-volume work, *The World of the Past*, New York 1963 and London 1964. To show the whole scope of archaeological research, also where it has erred, a few of the completely abstruse, nonsensical statements have been included (such as the fantastic analysis of the meaning of the pyramids by Smyth, or the no less fantastic interpretation of hieroglyphic script by Kircher) which illuminate more fully than any description, the amount of wrong directions and by-ways scientific research has had to travel before an acceptable solution was found.

In the introductory chapters, therefore, a few articles have also been included to illuminate the subsidiary problems of archaeology – for example, the exemplary excavations-agreement of Olympia, as well as the archaeologists' experiences with reconstruction, forgers and antique dealers.

Our book covers the period of the first systematic excavations up to the present day, when the excavator with a spade has suddenly had his work made easier and more effective by complicated technical advances. We have restricted ourselves regionally to Europe, North Africa, the Near East and both the Americas. Prehistoric discoveries have not been included because they do not come within the scope of the book.

In conclusion I should like to thank Dr Anne G. Ward, who wrote the biographical notes and who takes the credit for these; she performed a very hard task in an exemplary manner.

C. W. CERAM

CONTENTS

ILLUSTRATIONS

Part One

IN PLACE OF AN INTRODUCTION

The ideal archaeologist

CHARLES LEONARD WOOLLEY

The prime duty of the field archaeologist is to collect and set in order material with not all of which he can himself deal at first hand. In no case will the last word be with him; and just because that is so his publication of the material must be minutely detailed, so that from it others may draw not only corroboration of his views but fresh conclusions and more light. Should he not then stop at this? It might be urged that the man who is admirably equipped to observe and record does not necessarily possess the powers of synthesis and interpretation, the creative spirit and the literary gift which will make of him a historian. But no record can ever be exhaustive. As his work in the field goes on, the excavator is constantly subject to impressions too subjective and too intangible to be communicated, and out of these, by no exact logical process, there arise theories which he can state, can perhaps support, but cannot prove: their truth will depend ultimately on his own calibre, but, in any case, they have their value as summing up experiences which no student of his objects and his notes can ever share. Granted that the excavator is adequate to his task, the conclusions which he draws from his own work ought to carry weight, and he is bound to put them forward; if they are palpably wrong then his observations also may justly be held suspect. Between archaeology and history there is no fenced frontier, and the digger who will best observe and record his discoveries is precisely he who sees them as historical material and rightly appraises them; if he has not the power of synthesis and interpretation he has mistaken his calling. It is true that he may not possess any literary gifts, and that, therefore, the formal presentation of results to the public may be better made by others; but it is the field archaeologist who, directly or indirectly, has opened up for the general reader new chapters in the history of civilized man; and by recovering from the earth such documented relics of the past as strike the imagination through the eye, he makes real and modern what otherwise might seem a far-off tale.

Digging up the Past, 1954

How to buy antiquities

CHARLES LEONARD WOOLLEY

Before the modern archaeologist puts his spade to the earth, all his possible findings are carefully allotted by treaty, and piracy of antiquities has been reduced to a minimum by careful legislation. But however far-sighted the legislators, human nature and the value of ancient artifacts have made even the most painstaking laws liable to abuse.

Rascality where antiquities were concerned was not always confined to the dealers.

I was in Naples, staying with a friend of mine, an Englishman who had lived all his life in Naples, and one day there came along a plumber who had a little house and a small business at a place called Pozzuoli, which is on the outskirts of Naples to the north, and he said he had heard I was there and that he had something of interest to report. He had been enlarging his house, and in digging the foundations he had come upon a number of blocks of marble, some of which were covered with inscriptions and one was carved. He had shown this to his local priest who thought the things were interesting and important, and he wanted to know whether I would come and look, and buy anything that I wanted.

I went along, and there was, among a number of inscriptions, a very large marble slab, about 6 feet high or rather more, and about 5 feet across, with a group of life-size figures carved, one in high relief and two in lower relief. The one in high relief was obviously a member of the Imperial Family of the Emperor Augustus, and the other two were soldiers, and I realised that it was a fragment of an extraordinarily important and beautiful monument.

I said to the man, 'This is absolutely first-class! It's worth a great deal of money, but I can't buy it.' He said, 'Why not?' So I explained, 'In the first place, I could never get it out of the country, and in the second place I haven't got the money to pay for a thing of that sort.'

He said, 'Well, what am I to do?' and I told him, 'There is only one thing you can do. Nobody can smuggle a thing of that size out of

Italy, and if you try you will get into frightfully serious trouble. Go to the Naples National Museum and report what you have found. They will send a proper man along, and they will then take the things and value them, and pay you three-quarters of the sum. They keep one-quarter for the Government, but you will get quite a large sum of money, and that is the best thing you can do.'

He didn't like it – he didn't want to get the Government in at all; but in the end he thought perhaps he had better do what I had told him, and he went and reported it. And the second man in the Museum, who was an Inspector of Antiquities, came to the house. He saw these things and said, 'What a lot of fuss you are making about nothing. Those inscriptions are of interest to us, but they have no commercial value, so I'll take them away and there is no payment for them.'

The plumber asked, 'What about this carving?'

'That!' he said, 'Good heavens! It's absolute rubbish, not worth anything at all – you would be very lucky if anybody gave you £5 for a thing like that. I don't want it, I will leave it in your hands. The Museum is not interested in a thing of that sort!' And he went off with the inscriptions.

The plumber came to me a few days later and told me the story. 'It is very disappointing,' he complained, 'I thought I was going to get quite a large sum of money, and I am getting nothing at all.'

'Well,' I said, 'I can't understand it. That is a very valuable object.'

He said, 'Well, I don't know about that, but yesterday a man did come along' (and he gave me a description of the man and his name). 'He offered me £10 for it – shall I take it?'

I said 'No', and made certain enquiries. The man was an antiquity dealer, and was the brother-in-law of the Inspector, and the whole thing was a put-up job. So I saw the plumber again and explained to him what the law was. I said:

'If they don't want it, they ought to give you a permit for export. I have told you I can't afford to pay the value of the object, and you have got to remember that if you sell it abroad a third of the sum goes to the Government in tax. I can only afford to pay you £60, but you can tell them it has been sold for £100, and I will pay them the £33. That is all the money I can lay my hands on, and it is nothing like the value of the object, but if you would like to sell it to me on those terms and if you get the permit to export, I'll take it.'

He said that was very nice of me, and he would be delighted to do it. So he went round to the Museum, saw the Inspector of Antiquities and said, 'About this stone you don't want, will you give me permission to export?'

The Inspector said, 'You ignorant peasants: You are such fools! You think because a man comes along and offers you a pound or two more than another, and says he wants to export it you are going to profit; but actually you're not, because you have to pay a third to the Government. Now I suppose someone has offered you £15 – well, the most you'll get is £10.'

'Oh no,' said the plumber, 'I am going to pay you £33.'

The Inspector said, 'What?'

He repeated, 'I am going to pay you £33, a third of the price of the thing.'

The Inspector said, 'Look here, you are not going to have authority to export at all. The Museum is not going to take over your sculpture; it is going to remain in your hands, and it is valued at £4,000. I shall put it on the list of National Monuments. You are going to be responsible to the Government for the safeguarding of a £4,000 object. It is at your risk if anythings happens to it.'

The poor man came round to me in tears. He said, 'You have ruined me', and he told me the whole story.

This was in front of my friend, who listened carefully and then said, 'Well, I think, you know, we have got to take a strong line.'

I said, 'Right, I would do anything. The Inspector is an absolute scoundrel, I would do anything to down him.'

He said, 'That's all right if you will give me a free hand – will you?' To which I agreed.

Now at that moment in Italy, the Government party had in Parliament a majority of one. Suddenly the Prime Minister received a letter sent from Naples and signed by a well-known citizen of Naples, saying that it was requested that the Government would appoint a Royal Commission to remove a certain Roman sculpture from the list of National Monuments on which it had been placed by the local Inspector of Antiquities, which made it a thing immovable. The Commission were to remove it from the list and give authority to the peasant owner to export it; failing which, as the result of the sudden and unexpected demise of the three sitting members of Parliament for Naples (who all supported the Government), opposition members would be elected and the Government would fall. The fact was that we had got that secret society called the Camorra to back us, and the Camorra could do anything.

Within three days a Royal Commission came down and hurriedly altered the list of the National Monuments of the South of Italy, and gave permission to export the Pozzuoli stone. And it went off, and is now in Philadelphia – (I was working for Philadelphia at the time). Nobody looking at it in the Museum now would ever imagine that there had been that drama behind the scenes. Actually the Italians themselves did not know what had happened.

About a month later I went into the office of the Inspector of Antiquities, and on the table was a copy of the most recent issue of the Government publication reporting discoveries of antiquities in the country, and there was a large photograph of this particular Augustan monument. When the Inspector came into the room – he was out when I first went in – I said, 'Oh, Doctor Gabrici, what a lovely thing this is! I'll go and have a look at it – is it down in the Gallery yet?'

He said, 'No.'

'Is it in one of your stores still?' He said, 'No.'

'Where is it?' He said, 'It has been exported.'

I exclaimed, 'Why, Doctor Gabrici, you couldn't allow a thing like that to go – it's a National Monument! It's a treasure! Whatever induced you to allow anyone to take it out of the country?'

And he looked at me, and I looked at him, and he didn't know what to say. He didn't know whether I was responsible, and I wasn't going to tell him; but he never gave an explanation of why it had gone, which was his own fault entirely.

As I Seem to Remember, 1962

How to steal antiquities

CARLO MAURILIO LERICI

In 1958 at a meeting of the Rotary Club of Rome the speaker drew attention to the work recently undertaken by the Milan Polytechnic which involved the application of geophysical methods in archaeological research. After speaking of the results achieved by thus exploring a necropolis in the Cerveteri area, he was unable to hold back his own views on the facts which the technicians of the Polytechnic had noted – facts which shed light on the illegal and destructive excavational activities taking place in that same area side by side with the lawful work carried on by the State or by authorized bodies. Then an eminent university personality took advantage of this opportunity to give a spirited defence of the work of the tomb-robbers. He used seemingly paradoxical arguments that were not without a basis of truth, claiming that these people actually forward the cause of culture because it is thanks to them alone that thousands of collectors and scholars have been able to assemble these testimonies to our ancient civilizations under their own roofs. Indeed everyone knows that were it otherwise these pieces would still be unknown because they would have remained buried or been kept in the archives of Italian museums which are overloaded with material that is condemned either to remain for ever unseen or to be squandered or disposed of in other ways.

To this argument which is intended to justify clandestine excavation somewhat from a moral point of view we can add another based on material considerations.

For the most part tomb-robbers come from among the unemployed or under-employed and it is only the need to earn that makes them attempt the undertaking. This is moreover confirmed by the fact that during periods of seasonal agricultural work which require the maximum utilization of auxiliary manual labour, clandestine archaeological research is reduced to a minimum, whereas it is at its height at periods of greater unemployment. There can therefore be no doubt that in many cases there exist motives of necessity among people without means of support – motives which can explain if not justify the phenomenon.

It is true that the law gives the representatives of the Department of Antiquities powers to compensate discoverers of archaeological material with a reward. It is equally true that this reward, however modest, is higher than that which the tomb-robbers can get from the receivers, but they do at least pay straight away, whereas the State's practice is better left unsaid. This is known well enough to the few who have abided by the law, declaring and handing over valuable objects such as collections of coins, bronzes or ceramics, and who, years later, are still waiting to be compensated.

A first attempt to estimate the damage caused

Let us now consider some specific events that have taken place recently.

The reference to examples drawn from the Lazio territories should not lead one to suppose that illegal research is exceptionally prolific in those areas. One should remember that so far the Milan Polytechnic have only been able to carry out their surveys with freedom in the territories subject to the Department of Antiquities of Southern Etruria, which, from the start, has facilitated and encouraged the application of geophysical methods. The numerous bits of information which have reached us from every part of Italy have shown how in many archaeological zones the team of the Milan Polytechnic could have come up with discoveries of a far more important nature than those which it has so far been able to document. But it must unfortunately be stated that local representatives of the Department of Antiquities have not in every case received the Polytechnic's intervention favourably.

In 1957 a team of surveyors from the Milan Polytechnic whose purpose was to give to Southern Etruria's representative of the Department of Antiquities a practical demonstration of new methods of archaeological research based on the use of geophysical apparatus, undertook a campaign in the area of Monte Abbatone. This area was alloted to them by the representative and within it as we all know lies one of the large Etruscan necropolises of Cerveteri.

It was on this campaign which took place during the first term of 1957 that some hundreds of chamber tombs were identified, the greater part of which, although they had been broken into at a much earlier period, still contained material for excavation disregarded by the previous excavators who had only taken away precious objects such as jewels or bronzes. When it came to preparing a topographical measured plan that would show the groups that had been identified and explored it was considered advisable, for the first part which had been explored so far, and which took up about 20 per cent of the total area of the necropolis, to include also the groups that had been opened in the last few years by clandestine excavators. These were easily recognizable because the entrances to the chambers were still open and the numerous fragments of pottery left on the spot pointed without a shadow of doubt to the recent date of many of the fractures. It was thus possible for the first time to prepare a document of exceptional interest in that it allowed one to measure the precise extent of an illegal excavational activity that had taken place during the period since the last war – that is a period of between ten and fifteen years. . . .

Obviously the groups in question were those most easily recognizable even to the superficial observer, who would either examine the vegetation and the typical outcrop that grows on the topsoil of the very contours of the original tombs, or who would concentrate on groups so close to the surface as to be easily 'felt' by tests on the soil made with a long iron point shaped like a kitchen-spit which, as it can pierce down into the soil, enables one to search for the entrance passages or for the surrounding ditches along which the point will penetrate with ease.

The development of the campaign that followed during the years 1957, 58 and 59 led to the identification of over 550 chamber tombs and at the same time it was easy to establish the fact that the proportion of pillaged tombs in the last few years, as illustrated in figure 1, remains constant throughout the area of this important necropolis. It is therefore reasonable to suppose that the tombs which have been 'worked over' since the war by tomb-robbers number in this area alone between 350 and 400 and that the booty acquired can at least be equalled to the amount salvaged by the Department of Antiquities among the tombs discovered by the team of the Milan Polytechnic. Since the latter includes over 5,500 pieces salved by the Department itself at the accepted total of 12 million (lire) one can presume that the material illegally taken has a considerably higher value. Now this hypothesis drawn up from concrete facts such as those we have given here can give some idea not only of the damage caused in this particular case – that is in an archaeological area that is notoriously poor – but also of that caused in the remaining areas of Italy where the phenomenon repeats itself with the same causes and the same results. The example of the necropolis at Monte Abbatone is notedly repeated in thousands of spots all over Italy where there are ancient necropolises – an inexhaustible repository of material for excavation which led Ceram, the well-known author of *Gods, Graves and Scholars*, to claim that Italy still possesses below ground her own and vaster Louvre.

In the successive campaigns that were carried out in other archaeological zones by the Milan Polytechnic the same observations were in fact repeatedly made and to such an extent that it was practically possible to claim that for the preliminary work of fixing the boundaries of necropolises to be explored by geophysical methods, the testimony of external traces of violation still visible on the site is even more helpful than the examination of aerial surveys of individual zones. Tomb-robbers of all time have thus already taken steps to signal out these zones and in some cases, such as the large necropolis of Monterozzi at Tarquinia, they have gone so far as to scratch in the date of their visits.

In this last zone all the groups have been violated indiscriminately over the centuries and traces of violation repeated in different periods are not infrequent. If the Polytechnic team carried on their research here none the less it is because, as is well known, there are painted groups in this necropolis which in part, at least, are still preserved. We shall see, however, how the work of the pillagers has contributed to their deterioration and often to their destruction.

Figure 2 shows the measured plan of another site in the Cerveteri zone to which the Milan Polytechnic team of surveyors had proposed to extend its activities after having determined the extent of the recent devastation already caused by the tomb-robbers. In the course of just two weeks the team thus singled out about forty groups among which there was one whose original wealth was still intact and of exceptional interest. Unfortunately, for want of a formal authorization from the proprietor, the team was obliged to interrupt its work and naturally enough this interruption was very gratifying to the tomb-robbers, who by now have in all probability completed the raid on the other existing groups.

It is not a matter of one isolated case: in some zones in the province of Grosseto which are notoriously plagued by clandestine treasure-seekers the Polytechnic team did not even receive the authorization of the local representative of the Department of Antiquities to carry out a survey – let alone excavation: incredible but true.

Similarly in the neighbourhood of Viterbo, the little cemetery zone, which is illustrated in figure 3, represents another of the very frequent examples that all the Italian archaeological zones offer and that an entire atlas would not suffice to document. Here again it is a question of recent operations, probably carried out in the years 1959–60, and the innumerable fragments that are still visible testify without any doubt to the kind and variety of the goods that were removed.

But we can now add further evidence which reflects what is perhaps the most serious and alarming aspect of the phenomenon of clandestine research.

These 'freelance excavators', for whose benefit we have been so scrupulously objective and have not failed to bring forward the extenuating circumstances which can be considered a partial justification of their activities, these people demonstrate that they have no notion of the value of the material they excavate or of the precautions that should be taken to avoid its damage and destruction. Archaeologists and specialists in excavation know from their own experience what all this means and they are even more aware that almost the entire collection of archaeological groups, particularly those in burial zones or in temples or sanctuaries – these being the richest in marketable material – show clear traces of repeated violations and of the consequences of the clumsy and hurried work of the pillagers. But without going back to far-off times, let us confine ourselves to recounting what happens today or happened yesterday, that is in the case of the very groups shown in the measured plans illustrated in the figures. From a systematic collection of fragments with recent fractures that was put at the disposal of the Department of Antiquities, some have been reassembled, as is illustrated in figures 4–7 which prove how pieces of great value have been overlooked and dispersed owing to haste. Although some of these pieces when assembled have not allowed for more than a quarter or a fifth of the original to be reconstructed, the expense of restoring them has nevertheless been considered justified. But one can well imagine how much more valuable would be pieces for example such as those illustrated in figures 6–7 which were partially reconstructed from the few fragments discovered in the respective groups that had been violated.

But one of the even more alarming bases for indictment is given us by some painted tombs that had already been discovered in the years 1959–60 in the necropolis of Monterozzi illustrated in figures 8, 9 and 10.

These tombs, which are entirely frescoed, and which have, like all the others in the zone, been stripped of their movable furniture, quite clearly betray from the sound of the walls the immediate proximity of a further sepulchral chamber. Now the excavators have not hesitated to demolish entire frescoed walls with their picks, as those traces that are still visible reveal. Only a few traces remain, but these are sufficient to allow one to estimate the original state of preservation of the painted plaster. This is an example which should make one stop and think, the more because it is not an offence of centuries ago but one that has taken place in the last few years and therefore it is unfortunately particularly current.

It is well known that in the cases of almost all ancient sepulchral groups containing household goods and clothing it is very unusual to discover pieces intact even in the very rare cases of tombs that have not been violated. The movements of the earth as it shifts about, such as those caused by earthquakes which have followed one after another in considerable numbers over the centuries in all Mediterranean areas of historical importance, have caused the breakage of collections of pottery or impasto work, leaving in most instances only the small-sized pieces intact. Now illegal excavators steal everything, even the fragments, but they rarely manage to distinguish the value of the different objects, and the very conditions in which their work takes place, often during the night hours, make selection difficult. They moreover neglect, through ignorance, the precautions for preserving pieces that are most likely to suffer from change of temperature or humidity in the atmosphere. So it can happen that even a portion of the goods they take consequently suffers destruction. If, on the basis of the facts established during the campaigns carried out by the Milan Polytechnic, we were to assess the damage caused by the tomb-robbers by reason of the clumsy methods of excavation and collection alone, we think we would not be far off the mark in claiming that a good half of the excavation material that passes through their hands gets irrevocably ruined.

Then over and above the damage that the national heritage suffers on account of the material that is illegally excavated, sold or exported, there is the no less severe damage caused by these ignorant vandals of archaeology.

If in fact the material that is illegally sold or exported cannot be considered lost to the cultural legacy of civilized men, that which is destroyed out of neglect or ignorance can of itself give us the measure of the immense damage that is caused repeatedly and extensively throughout the archaeological areas of the ancient world. And in the face of this, the damage caused by barbarian raids, by the sackings of history that took place during the great invasions, at the decline of the Empire, in the Middle Ages and up to those that occurred during revolutionary and wartime episodes in the nineteenth and twentieth centuries seems insignificant. Because the vandalism that destroys the buried archaeological heritage of the nation is an everyday problem in the thousands and thousands of places that preserve these testimonies of thirty centuries of history.

How can this be remedied?

The law lays down that anything found in the subsoil is the property of the state and gives the representatives of the Department of Antiquities the authority to reward the owner of the land and the discoverer with a recompense which, in the aggregate, must not exceed half the value of the material discovered. The work of the tomb-robbers and likewise that carried out by the owners of the sites is therefore illegal and for this reason it is, as we know, investigated by the officers of the law. But we know equally well that, given the widespread nature of the phenomenon and the material impossibility of carrying out inspection in all the archaeological zones, the law more or less leaves things as it finds them so that illegal excavations proceed everywhere, the only fluctuations being due either to the seasonal phenomena of greater agricultural employment or to the lesser demands of the market. For obviously even on the open market of antiquities there are fluctuations due to the differing trends of cultural interest; so for example for some ten or twenty years Etruscan objects have been 'doing well' owing to the keen interest of scholars. This interest is clearly indicated by the blossoming of publications, the success of superb newspaper editorials which elucidate the more typical aspects of Etruscan civilization and art, by the art exhibitions shown in the large capitals of Europe, the increasing interest of foreign cultural tourism and finally by the sensational discoveries due to the introduction of the new scientific research methods of the Milan Polytechnic. All this goes to emphasize the gravity of the phenomenon that the law is powerless to suppress.

What is the remedy? Are we to increase the supervision? We should need an army of police and guardians. And then *qui custodet custodes?*

Contact with these relics of ancient civilizations, which often include precious objects and coins that can easily be concealed, little by little exercise a strange charm even over those most in control, and not all are able to resist it. It is as if a mysterious virus found its way into their veins, a virus that succeeds in giving life to a fragment, that brings out a mysterious written document or image, that recalls a moment in the life of an epoch tens of centuries ago – or perhaps a little ornament or ritualistic object which can summon up a human feeling. One has to live for some time in this strange world to understand all this and to come to appreciate the heroic strength of character of the civil servants in the Department of Antiquities who are able to overcome these temptations.

Given the obvious impossibility of seeing that the law is respected, let us put the question again: What remedy is there? Should the law be altered? And in what way?

The facts we have laid out and those that have been the subject of extremely serious and important journalistic enquiries in recent years, lead us to foresee quite clearly, alongside the gravity of the phenomenon, its possible solutions.

There is obviously something that is not quite right in the law concerning excavations and in the ways in which it is interpreted and applied, but that is not all. Even a perfect law leaves things as it finds them when those responsible for seeing that it is respected lack the powers and the goodwill.

Thus we see the State, the legal possessor of as much as exists under the ground, being plundered every day by illegal excavators and by the proprietors themselves because the Department of Antiquities does not have the means for excavations and the authorities are not in a position to prevent this pillage. And the situation, let us bear this in mind, shows every indication of getting increasingly worse because in a great part of the archaeological zones in Italy large-scale programmes of agrarian redevelopment or reform are under way which bring with them the new deep-ploughing machinery that disturbs and often exposes new groups of tombs. Indeed this is already happening and has been happening for over twenty years in all areas along the Tyrrhenian coastline. The primitive ploughshare of the Virgilian peasant who discovered the relics of the ancient warrior buried in his field (*Georg*. I. 493) is today replaced by the work of bulldozers capable of reaching the most deeply buried archaeological stratifications. The world is marching on rapidly in this day and the unprecedented rate of increase in its population forces men to utilize every strip of ground. The necropolises and the archaeological zones that are productive of material for excavation in a country like Italy take up thousands of square miles and are to a large extent doomed to disappear, swept up by the growing exigencies of modern civilization. The large urban centres set the example, spreading themselves over archaeological areas the importance of which tends to be either concealed or played down in the interests of the constructors. We cannot hold on to any illusions here: the task of looking after buried material of historical or artistic value will simply have to be relegated to the Museums or to well-defined zones that allow for adequate supervision and maintenance.

Lecture to the Rotary Club of Rome, 1958

Translated from the Italian by L. A. Tufnell

A strange bargain

CHARLES LEONARD WOOLLEY

Another curious experience occurred to the late Lord Caernarvon, the man who discovered the famous Tomb of Tutankhamen. He was a very keen collector of Egyptian antiquities, and one day he was in his hotel in Cairo and a man came in and asked to see him, and then said, 'You collect antiquities?'

'Yes,' said Caernarvon.

'Well, I've got something wonderful. Wonderful!'

Caernarvon said, 'What is it; show me.'

'Oh,' he said, 'I can't show you here. It's in my house.'

'Well,' said Caernarvon, 'If it is as good as all that I'd like to see it.'

The man said, 'Yes, you can come and see it, but on my terms!'

'Oh, what are those?'

'You have got to come at night, and you have got to submit to being blindfolded and I shall take you to my house, because I don't want you to know where it is. And,' he said, 'you have got to bring with you £300 in gold.'

Now that sounded an impossible condition. To go with an unknown man, blindfolded and with three hundred gold pounds in your pocket, is not a thing that an ordinary man would do. But Lord Caernarvon was completely reckless and fearless. He said, 'Oh certainly, I will do that,' and he added, 'Is that the price you're asking?'

'Yes,' said the man, 'it's £300, and I'm not taking a penny less, but for £300 you can have the thing if you like.'

So that night after dinner three men came in and said to Caernarvon, 'Come along', and they took him outside the hotel, and on the pathway of the street they carefully blindfolded him and they put him into a carriage and drove for a time and then they took him out and took him inside a house and undid his eyes. He said, 'Where are the antiquities?' and they showed him two objects. One was a small vase of polished stone with a gold cover to it and on the cover was engraved a cartouche of one of the earliest known Pharaohs, a Pharaoh of the First Dynasty. It was a marvellous thing. And the other was even more remarkable.

It was a beautifully made flint knife about 8 inches long, beautifully worked and it had a handle of gold embossed with animal figures. It was clearly earlier than the first Pharaohs, of prehistoric antiquity, and Caernarvon simply opened his eyes and said, 'All right, I'll buy it.' He knew that at the price the things were dirt cheap, so he paid out the £300 and they faithfully gave him the things, bandaged his eyes and took him back to his hotel.

He looked at those things when he was back and it struck him that they were familiar; and he thought they must be duplicates of something he'd seen before. So the next day he went round to the National Museum of Cairo and he went to the case where some of the earliest and greatest treasures were kept, a large desk case with red velvet lining, and various objects on it; and he saw a round spot of dark colour on the velvet: the rest had faded where the sun had hit it. There was another long spot which exactly corresponded to his flint dagger; and he realised that the things he had bought were stolen from the Museum.

So he asked to see the Director, old Professor Maspero, a Frenchman, and he said, 'Professor Maspero, I want to ask you, have you had any valuable things stolen from the Museum of late?'

And Professor Maspero said, 'Good heavens, what makes you say that?'

'Well,' he said, 'I've got a suspicion about it. Is it really true?'

And Maspero heaved a heavy sigh and said, 'Yes, it is. We have lost two great treasures.'

'Have you taken any steps to recover them?'

'No,' said Maspero, 'I daren't.'

And Caernarvon knew what that meant; it meant that the things had been stolen by the Sub-Director, who was a German, and to have accused him would have caused an international incident that they couldn't possibly afford.

Caernarvon said, 'I've got these objects. I got them from a man whom I couldn't possibly trace – he was careful about that; I paid £300 for them. Would you like to buy them back? If so, pay me the £300 and you shall have them, because they are not mine.'

And the Professor said, 'Do you really mean that?'

'Yes,' said Caernarvon, 'certainly, I'm prepared to let you have them.'

The Professor said, 'That is more than generous of you: please bring them along.'

So Caernarvon took the two objects to Maspero's office and handed them over and said, 'Now I want a cheque for £300.'

Maspero said, 'Certainly,' and he wrote a cheque, handed it across and said, 'Now of course you will give me an official receipt.'

Caernarvon said, 'Give you a receipt? Not on your life. I'm not going to give you a receipt for stolen goods.'

Maspero objected, 'Without a receipt I cannot give the cheque.'

And Caernarvon said, 'Without the money I'm not going to hand over the objects. Either you give me a cheque without a receipt or I walk away with the two things.'

Maspero said, 'I must have them back, but I must have a receipt.'

Maspero sat for a while and thought. Then he rang his bell and one of the attendants, a sort of sweeper, came in and Maspero said to him, 'Here is a form. I want a signature to it. Go out into the Bazaar and get hold of the first man you like, give him sixpence and get him to sign his name to this.'

And so that was duly done and in twenty minutes the man came back with a signed receipt for £300 and Caernarvon took his cheque and then handed over the objects, which are still in the Cairo National Museum.

As I Seem to Remember, 1962

Legalized art robbery

All too often in the past the masterpieces of classical art have been subject to the depredations of rich collectors who coveted them only for their unique beauty and not at all for their archaeological value. Every attempt has been made to prevent this by suitable legislation, and now it is almost impossible for an archaeologist to lay claim as an individual to any part of the findings of his 'dig' or to any treasure-trove he may find, but when a really determined collector has the power to create his own laws there can be no defence against his appropriations. A startling example of this occurred when Napoleon's victorious army overpowered Italy in 1796; it was followed by a group of commissioners who were ordered by Bonaparte to annexe for France any major work of art which seemed worthy of their attention, and among the terms of the peace treaty offered to the Pope was an article rendering these transactions legal and binding.

Article 8

The Pope shall cede to the French Republic one hundred paintings, busts, vases or statues, to be selected by commissioners who will be sent to Rome, these objects specifically to include the bronze bust of Junius Brutus and that of Marcus Brutus in marble, both on the Capitol, and in addition 500 manuscripts selected by the above-mentioned commissioners.

Correspondance de Napoléon, vol. I, 1858

Translated from the French by V. M. Conrad

The complete forger

CHARLES LEONARD WOOLLEY

Increasing public interest in the artifacts of the ancient world has created a demand which ingenious forgers have been only too ready to supply. Even the greatest archaeologists have had their moments of unfortunate credulity, such as the time when Sir Arthur Evans enthusiastically acquired the so-called Ring of Nestor, which was later minutely analysed by the Swedish scholar Nilsson and proved to be of modern origin. The methods used by the forgers are well documented as they have several times been caught in the act, as Sir Leonard Woolley relates.

Actually, at one time I was completely taken in. I was really shocked. In Crete in the early years of this century I was stopping with Arthur Evans when he was excavating at Knossos, and one day he got a message from the police at Candia asking him to come to the police station, so we went together – he, Duncan Mackenzie, who was his assistant, and myself. And the most surprising thing had happened.

Evans for years had employed two Greeks to restore the antiquities which he had found. They were extraordinarily clever men – an old man and a young one – and he had trained them, and they had worked under the artist whom he employed there, and they had done wonderful restorations for him. Then the old man got ill and at last the doctor told him he was going to die.

He said, 'Are you sure?' The doctor said, 'Yes, I'm afraid there's no hope for you at all.'

'Right', he said. 'Send for the police.' The doctor said, 'You mean the priest.' 'No I don't', he said, 'I mean the police.' He insisted, and they sent for the police, and the police came and asked him, 'What on earth do you want?'

'Now I can tell you,' said the sick man. 'I'm going to die, so I'm all right, but for years I've been in partnership with George Antoniou, the young fellow who works with me for Evans, and we have been forging antiquities.'

'Well', said the policeman, 'I don't know that that concerns me.' 'Yes,' he said, 'it does. Because we've sold a statuette of gold and ivory which was supposed to be a Cretan one to the Candia Government Museum, and that's a criminal offence. George is a scoundrel, and I hate the fellow, and I've been waiting for this moment to give him away. Go straight to his house and you'll find all the forgeries and all our manufacturing plant there.'

The police went, they raided, and they found exactly what he said, and they asked Evans to come and look, and I never saw so magnificent a collection of forgeries as those fellows had put together.

There were things in every stage of manufacture. For instance, people had been recently astonished at getting what they call chryselephantine statuettes from Crete; statuettes of ivory decked out with gold – there is one in the Boston Museum and one at Cambridge, and one in the Cretan Museum at Candia. These men were determined to do that sort of thing, and they had got there everything, from the plain ivory tusk and then the figure rudely carved out, then beautifully finished, then picked out with gold. And then the whole thing was put into acid, which ate away the soft parts of the ivory, giving it the effect of having been buried for centuries. And I didn't see that anyone could tell the difference!

Then they had got Greek coins. These are sometimes very rare and of immense value; recently one Greek coin at a London sale fetched £3,100; another fetched £2,300 – both unique coins. Of course, such coins are generally the treasured possessions of different museums. The two Greeks wrote round to the museums where there were unique coins and asked to be supplied with plaster casts of them. That is a very common request and it is always granted.

They got the plaster casts, and they had discovered how to make a steel mould from the plaster, so they cast steel moulds from the two sides of the coin, making one as an anvil and the other as a hammer-head. They looked up the catalogues of the coin collection from which the cast came, and they found there the exact weight of the coin in milligrams. It would also give the exact character of the alloy, the silver alloy of which the coin was made. So they imitated the alloy, cut off a lump of the right weight exactly, heated it almost to melting point and put it on the anvil and struck it with the hammer in the fashion of the ancient coiner, and produced something so like the original that nobody could have told the difference. They had got about 100 of these forgeries in stock, and how many of such may have found their way on to the market I don't know, but it really was bewildering.

I said to Evans, 'I shall never buy a Greek antiquity!'

He said, 'Well, even I feel rather doubtful now,' and he was a marvellous judge.

As I Seem to Remember, 1962

The Olympia Convention

This is the agreement between the German and the Greek Imperial Government which was concluded and signed on 25 April 1874. This is a significant document, because it was the first modern, legally clear excavation agreement between two governments and became the prototype for the countless other international agreements which became necessary during the course of the history of excavation.

As well as this the excavation of Olympia became an example in another respect. Under the direction of Ernst Curtius and Friedrich Adler (who were joined by a whole team including the friend and assistant of Schliemann at Troy, the architect, Wilhelm Dörpfeld) here the scientific *methods of modern excavation were developed; the results reached their highest peak in our time with the excavation of the great stadium of the Olympic games (where today the torch for the modern Olympic games is lit) and the discovery of the workshop of the most famous of ancient sculptors, Pheidias, under the direction of Emil Kuntze.*

THE AGREEMENT

The Imperial German and the Royal Greek Governments have, guided by the wish to carry out excavations together in the area of the ancient Olympia in Greece, decided to conclude a convention and have agreed upon the following points:

ARTICLE I

Each government will appoint a commissar who will check according to his proportion that the following agreements are kept during the excavations.

ARTICLE II

The site of the old temple of the Olympian Jupiter shall serve as starting point of the excavations, which will be carried out on the site of old Olympia.

A later agreement between both governments will decide whether the excavations are to be extended to other regions of the Kingdom of Greece.

ARTICLE III

Whilst the Greek Government gives permission for the excavations on the site of Olympia, it promises to give the commissars every aid in the carrying out of the work, in the obtaining of workmen and in the fixing of the wages of the latter; also the above-named government will put police on the site of the excavation who will see that the orders of the commissars are carried out, and who can supply, should the need arise, for this purpose, armed force, without in any case deviating from the laws of the land. The Greek Government furthermore undertakes to pay compensation to those persons, proprietors or owners of empty land (whether this be fallow or cultivated) who have any kind of right to it.

ARTICLE IV

Germany undertakes to pay all the costs of the project, that is to say:

The wages of the officials, the wages of the workmen, the erection of store-houses and barracks, should these be needed. Germany furthermore promises to pay damages for plantations and buildings of every kind, as set out in the laws of the land or in the agreements between the Greek Government and the farmers, which are situated on national pieces of ground, in so far as such damages have a really strong ground or the personal rights of private persons can be justifiably claimed. On no account, however, can the compensation exceed the sum of 300 Drachmas (1 Drachma = 7 Sgr. 2 Pf.) per Stremma (1 Stremma = 1000 sq. metres), even if the Greek Government has ceded part of that piece of land to private persons.

Greece, on its part, promises with the aid of all the means in its power, to carry out the eviction or expropriation of those persons who are at this time in possession of pieces of land in which it seems necessary to undertake excavations.

It goes without saying that the work on the excavations can in no case be stopped or delayed on account of eventual objections or protests of private persons or persons at the moment engaged in building on those pieces of land.

ARTICLE V

Germany reserves the right to mark out which pieces of land on the plain before Olympia are suitable for excavating, to employ and to dismiss the workers, and to direct and apportion the work.

ARTICLE VI

Greece holds the rights of possession of all works of ancient art and any other objects which the excavations will bring to light. It will make its own decisions whether or not it will give to Germany, as a souvenir of the mutually undertaken work and in reward for the sacrifices Germany has made to this enterprise, the duplicates or repetitions of the objects found during the course of the excavations.

ARTICLE VII
Germany holds the exclusive rights to make copies and casts of the objects which are discovered during the excavations.

These exclusive rights are valid for five years from the time of discovery of each object. The Greek Government also gives the Imperial German Government the right – though not the exclusive right – to make copies and casts of all the antiques in the possession of the Greek Government or which it will find in the future without the co-operation of the German Government on Greek soil. Excluded from this are only those antiquities which in the view of the competent ministerial advisers could be damaged or might deteriorate during the process of casting.

Greece and Germany reserve the exclusive right to publish the scientific and artistic discoveries of the excavations carried out at the expense of the Germans. All these publications will be published periodically in Athens in Greek and at the expense of the Greeks. The same publications are to be published simultaneously in Germany with figures, plates and pictures which are only to be engraved and made in Germany. This last task is to be taken over by Germany and at the same time she promises to send to Greece fifteen of every hundred copies of the first edition of figures, plates and pictures, and thirty-five of each hundred of the following editions.

ARTICLE VIII
Should the Greek commissar entrusted with the guarding of the excavations unexpectedly object to the work ordered by the German scholars, the Royal Greek Foreign Ministry and the Imperial German Embassy in Athens will together, as a last resort, settle such differences.

ARTICLE IX
The present convention stays valid for ten years from the day of its ratification by the representation of the people.

ARTICLE X
Each of the two contracting Governments pledges to put this contract in front of the appropriate representation of the people as soon as possible; yet neither of the two parties is obliged to bring it into action before it has been ratified by the representation of the people.

ARTICLE XI

This convention should, on the proviso that it has had the permission of the representation of the people, be ratified in two months' time, or sooner, and the ratifications be exchanged in Athens.

As witnesses to this document: Mr von Wagner, Ambassador Extraordinary and authorized minister of the German Emperor in Athens, Professor E. Curtius, specially authorized agent on the one hand, and Mr J. Delyanny, Foreign Minister of His Majesty, the King of Greece, Mr P. Eustratiades, Keeper of Antiquities, on the other hand, all authorized by their respective governments and provided with their seals.

Done in Athens, in duplicate, on the 13/25 April 1874.

E. v. Wagner (L.S.)
Ernst Curtius (L.S.)
Delyanny (L.S.)
Eustratiades (L.S.)

Olympia, vol. I, 1870

Translated from the German by C. M. Kaine

Part Two

THE BOOK OF THE STATUES

The foundation of the British Museum

Sir Hans Sloane (1660–1753) was born in County Down, Ireland. He studied medicine in London for four years and then completed his M.D. degree at the University of Orange in 1683. On his return to England he brought with him a considerable collection of plants, and continued to gather curios for the rest of his life; he spent fifteen months in Jamaica as physician to the Duke of Albemarle, and during this short time he added 800 unknown plants to his collection. His professional and scholastic honours were many. He was elected Secretary to the Royal Society, and in 1716 he became the first physician to receive a hereditary title when he was created a baronet. He was appointed successively Physician General to the army, First Physician to George II, and President of the Royal Society. At his death he offered his books, manuscripts and curios to the nation for the sum of £20,000, and the acceptance of the collection formed the nucleus of the British Museum.

I Sir Hans Sloane of Chelsea, in the county of Middlesex, Baronet, do make this codicil to be annexed to my last will and testament as follows. Whereas I have in and by my said Will given some directions about the sale and disposition of my musaeum, or collection of rarities herein more particularly mentioned. Now I do hereby revoke my said Will as far as relates thereto, and I do direct and appoint concerning the same in the following Manner. Having had from my youth a strong inclination to the study of plants, and all other productions of nature; and having through the course of many years with great labour and expence, gathered together whatever could be procured either in our own or foreign countries that was rare and curious; and being fully convinced that nothing tends more to raise our ideas of the power, wisdom, goodness, providence, and other perfections of the Deity, or more to the comfort and well being of his creatures than the enlargement of our knowledge in the works of nature, I do Will and desire that for the promoting of these noble ends, the glory of God, and the good of man, my collection in all its branches may be, if possible, kept and preserved together whole and intire in my manor house, in the parish of Chelsea, situate near the physic garden, given by me to the company of apothecaries for the same purposes; and having great reliance and confidence that the Right Hon. and other persons hereafter named will be influenced by the same principles, and faithfully and conscientiously discharge the trust hereby reposed in them, I do give, devise and bequeath unto the Right Hon. Charles Sloane Cadogan, Esq:

(Here follows a list of 51 names)

all that my collection or musaeum, at, in, or about my manor house at Chelsea aforesaid, which consists of too great a variety to be particularly described. But I mean all my library of books, drawings, manuscripts, prints, medals and coins, antient and modern, antiquities, seals, &c. cameos and intaglios, &c., precious stones, agates, jaspers, &c. vessels, &c. of agate jasper, &c. chrystals, mathematical instruments, drawings and pictures, and all other things in my said collection or musaeum, which are more particularly described, mentioned and numbered, with short histories or accounts of them, with proper references in certain catalogues by me made, containing thirty-eight volumes in folio, and eight volumes in quarto, except such framed pictures as are not marked with the word (collection) to have and to hold to them and their successors or assigns for ever; to the intent only that the same and every part and parcel of my said collection or musaeum may be vested in the said Right Honourable and Honourable, and other persons upon the trusts, and for the uses and purposes, and subject to the several limitations and directions hereafter particularly specified concerning the same; and for rendering this my intention more effectual, that the said collection may be preserved and continued intire in its utmost perfection and regularity; and being assured that nothing will conduce more to this purpose, than placing the same under the direction and care of the learned, experienced and judicious persons who are above all low and mean views, I do earnestly desire than the king, his royal highness the prince of Wales, his royal highness William duke of Cumberland, the archbishop of Canterbury for the time being, the right honourable Philip lord Hardwick, and the lord high chancellor for the time being, the lord president of the council for the time being, the lord privy seal for the time being, the lord steward of his majesty's houshold for the time being, the lord chamberland of his majesty's houshold for the time being, his grace Charles, duke of Richmond, his grace John duke of Montague, his grace Holles duke of Newcastle, his grace John duke of Bedford, and the two principal secretaries of state for the time being; the right honourable John earl of Sandwich, and the lord high admiral, or the first lord commissioner of the admiralty for the time being; the right honourable Henry Pelham, Esq; and the lord high treasurer, or the first lord commissioner of the treasury for the time being, and the chancellor of the exchequer for the time being, the lord chief justice of the king's bench for the time being, the lord chief justice of the common pleas for the time being, the lord chief baron of the exchequer for the time being, the lord bishop of London for the time being, the lord bishop of Winchester for the time being, the right honourable Archibald duke of Argyle, the right honourable Henry earl of Pembroke, the right honourable Philip earl of Chesterfield, the right honourable Richard earl of Burlington, the right honourable Henry lord Montford, the right honourable Arthur Onslow, esq; and the speaker of the House of Commons for the time being, the honourable lord Charles Cavendish, the right honourable Charles lord Cadogan, the right honourable John earl of Verney, the right honourable George lord Anson, will condescend so far as to act and be visitors of my said musaeum and collection. And I do hereby, with their leave, nominate and appoint them visitors thereof, with full power and authority for any five or more of them to enter my said collection or musaeum at any time or times, to peruse, supervise and examine the same and the management thereof; and to visit, correct and reform from time to time as there may be occasion, either jointly with the said trustees, or separately, upon application to them for that purpose; or otherwise all abuses, defaults, neglects, or mismanagaments that may happen to arise therein, or touching or concerning the person or persons, officer or officers that are or shall be appointed to attend the same. And my will is, and I do hereby request and desire, that the said trustees, or any seven or more of them do make their humble application to his majesty or to parliament, at the next sessions after my decease as shall be thought most proper, in order to pay the full and clear sum of twenty thousand pounds of lawful money of Great-Britain, unto my executors or the survivors of them, within twelve months after my decease, in consideration of the said collection or musaeum: It not being, as I apprehend or believe, a fourth of their real and intrinsic value; and also to obtain such sufficient and effectual powers and authorities, for vesting in the said trustees all and every part of my said collection or musaeum before mentioned in all its branches; and also my said capital manor house, with such gardens and out-houses as shall thereunto belong, and be used by me at the time of my decease, in which it is my desire the same shall be kept and preserved; and also the water of, or belonging to my manor of Chelsea coming from Kensington, subject to furnishing or supplying the lord Bishop of Winchester's house as is now used; and also all that the advowson or presentation or right of patronage of the church of Chelsea: To the end, the same premises may be absolutely vested in the said trustees, for preserving and continuing my said collection or musaeum in such manner as they shall think most likely to answer the public benefit by me intended; and also obtain as aforesaid, a sufficient fund or provision, maintaining and taking care of my said collection and premises, and for repairing and supporting my said manor house, water-work and premises, to be vested in the said trustees for ever: And I do hereby further direct and appoint, that my executors do and shall, upon payment of the said sum of twenty thousand pounds, deliver or cause to be delivered unto the said trustees, or any seven or more of them, for, and in the name of all of them, in the presence of the visitors, or any five or more of them, as well the possession of my said manor house and gardens at Chelsea aforesaid, as also all my collection or musaeum before mentioned and described, and every part thereof in all its branches, whole and intire, as the same shall be bound in my said manor house, according to the said catalogues, and together with the several volumes of catalogues thereunto belonging. And further, my will is, and I do hereby also direct and appoint, that in case his majesty or the parliament do accept the said offer, and do pay the sum of twenty thousand pounds unto my executors or the survivor of them, that then my said executors do, within six months after such payment as aforementioned, and obtaining proper powers for effectually vesting in the said trustees all my said collection, and my said capital house and gardens, with their appurtenances, water and advowson, presentation or right of patronage of the church of Chelsea as aforesaid; together with my heir or heirs at law, and all other proper parties, do and shall join in and execute such acts, deed, or conveyances, as shall be thought requisite and necessary for the more perfect and absolute vesting, conveying, and assuring the said premises in, and to the said trustees and their assigns or successors for ever, for the uses, intents and purposes herein mentioned and intended.

Printed Will and Codicils of Sir Hans Sloane, Bart, 1753

A troublesome legacy

HORACE WALPOLE TO HORACE MANN

One of Sir Hans Sloane's legatees, Horace Walpole, took a somewhat rueful view of the charge laid upon him by the will, as can be seen from his letter to a friend.

Arlington Street, 14 February 1753

I have been going to write to you every post for these three weeks, and could not bring myself to begin a letter with, 'I have nothing to tell you.' But it grows past a joke; we will not drop our correspondence because there is no war, no politics, no parties, no madness, and no scandal. In the memory of England there never was so inanimate an age: it is more fashionable to go to church than to either House of Parliament. Even the era of the Gunnings is over: both sisters have laid in, and have scarce made one paragraph in the newspapers, though their names were grown so renowned, that in Ireland the beggar-women bless you with, 'The luck of the Gunnings attend you!'

You will scarce guess how I employ my time; chiefly at present in the guardianship of embryos and cockleshells. Sir Hans Sloane is dead, and has made me one of the trustees to his museum, which is to be offered for twenty thousand pounds to the King, the Parliament, the Royal Academies of Petersburgh, Berlin, Paris, and Madrid. He valued it at fourscore thousand; and so would anybody who loves hippopotamuses, sharks with one ear, and spiders as big as geese! It is a rent-charge, to keep the foetuses in spirits! You may believe that *those* who think money the most valuable of all curiosities, will not be purchasers. The King has excused himself, saying he did not believe that there are twenty thousand pounds in the Treasury. We are a charming wise set, all philosophers, botanists, antiquarians, and mathematicians; and adjourned our first meeting, because Lord Macclesfield, our chairman, was engaged to a party for finding out the longitude. One of our number is a Moravian, who signs himself Henry XXVIII, Count de Reus. The Moravians have settled a colony at Chelsea, in Sir Hans's neighbourhood, and I believe he intended to beg Count Henry XXVIIIth's skeleton for his museum.

I am almost ashamed to be thanking you but now for a most entertaining letter of two sheets, dated December 22, but I seriously had nothing to form an answer. It is but three mornings ago that your brother was at breakfast with me, and scolded me, 'Why, you tell me nothing!' – 'No', says I; 'if I had anything to say, I should write to your brother.' I give you my word, the first new book that takes, the first murder, the first revolution, you shall have, with all the circumstances. In the mean time, do be assured that there never was so dull a place as London, or so insipid an inhabitant of it as

Yours, &c.

The Letters, vol. III, 1903

The controversial bequest of Lord Elgin

THOMAS BRUCE, 7TH EARL OF ELGIN (*1766–1841*), *succeeded to his title at the age of five. In 1785 he entered the army, where he ultimately rose to the rank of Major-General. In 1790 he began his diplomatic career and was shortly appointed envoy to Brussels and then to Berlin. From 1799 to 1802 he held the post of Envoy Extraordinary in Constantinople, and during this time he secured Turkish permission to record and later to remove many works of classical art from Athens. The sculptures were brought to England in small consignments between 1803 and 1812, and when Lord Elgin himself arrived, he found that he was being violently attacked both for the legality of his appropriations and for the artistic value of the sculptures. He published a memorandum in his own defence, and in 1816 a Parliamentary Committee vindicated his conduct and confirmed the value of his acquisitions by recommending the purchase of the marbles for the British Museum for £35,000 – a sum much lower than their original cost to Lord Elgin.*

In the year 1799, when Lord Elgin was appointed his Majesty's Ambassador Extraordinary to the Ottoman Porte, he happened to be in habits of frequent intercourse with Mr Harrison, an architect of great eminence in the west of England, who had there given various very splendid proofs of his professional talents, especially in a public building of Grecian architecture at Chester. Mr Harrison had besides studied many years, and to great purpose, at Rome. Lord Elgin consulted him, therefore, on the benefits that might possibly be derived to the arts in this country, in case an opportunity could be found for studying minutely the architecture and sculpture of ancient Greece; and his opinion very decidedly was, that although we might possess exact measurements of the buildings at Athens, yet a young artist could never form to himself an adequate conception of their minute details, combinations, and general effect, without having before him some such sensible representation of them as might be conveyed by *casts*. This advice, which laid the groundwork of Lord Elgin's pursuits in Greece, led to the further consideration, that, since any knowledge which was possessed of these buildings had been obtained under the peculiar disadvantages which the prejudices and jealousies of the Turks had ever thrown in the way of such attempts, any favourable circumstances which Lord Elgin's embassy might offer should be improved fundamentally; and not only modellers, but architects and draftsmen, might be employed, to rescue from oblivion, with the most accurate detail, whatever specimens of architecture and sculpture in Greece had still escaped the ravages of time, and the barbarism of the conquerers.

On this suggestion, Lord Elgin proposed to his Majesty's Government, that they should send out English artists of known eminence, capable of collecting this information in the most perfect manner; but the prospect appeared of too doubtful an issue for ministers to engage in the expense attending it. . . .

After much difficulty, Lord Elgin obtained permission from the Turkish Government to establish these six artists at Athens; where they prosecuted the business of their several departments during three years acting on one general system, with the advantage of mutual control, and under the general superintendance of M. Lusieri. They at length completed Lord Elgin's plan in all its parts.

Accordingly, every monument, of which there are any remains in Athens, has been thus most carefully and minutely measured; and, from the rough drafts of the architects (all of which are preserved), finished drawings have been made of the plans, elevations, and details of the most remarkable objects; in which the Calmouk has restored and inserted all the sculpture, with exquisite taste and ability. He has besides drawn, with astonishing accuracy, all the bas-reliefs on the several temples, in the precise state of decay and mutilation in which they at present exist.

Most of the bas-reliefs, and nearly all the characteristic features of architecture, in the various monuments at Athens, have been moulded, and the moulds of them have been brought to London.

Besides the architecture and sculpture at Athens, all remains of them which could be traced through several other parts of Greece, have been measured and delineated, with the most scrupulous exactness, by the second architect, Ittar. . . .

In the prosecution of this undertaking, the artists had the mortification of witnessing the very wilful devastation, to which all the sculpture, and even the architecture, were daily exposed, on the part of the Turks and travellers. . . . The Temple of Minerva had been converted into a powder magazine, and been completely destroyed, from a shell falling upon it, during the bombardment of Athens by the Venetians towards the end of the seventeenth century; and even this accident had not deterred the Turks from applying the beautiful Temple of Neptune and Erectheus to the same use, whereby it is constantly exposed to a similar fate. Many of the statues on the *posticum* of the Temple of Minerva (Parthenon,) which had been thrown down by the explosion, had been absolutely pounded for mortar, because they furnished the whitest marble within reach; and the parts of the modern fortification, and the miserable houses where this mortar was so applied, were discovered. Besides, it is well known that the Turks will frequently climb up the ruined walls, and amuse themselves in defacing any sculpture they can reach; or in breaking columns, statues or other remains of antiquity, in the fond expectation of finding within them some hidden treasures.

Under these circumstances, Lord Elgin felt himself impelled, by a stronger motive than personal gratification, to endeavour to preserve any specimens of sculpture, he could, without injury, rescue from such impending ruin. . . . Actuated by these inducements, Lord Elgin made use of all his means, and ultimately with such success, that he has brought to England, from the ruined temples at Athens, from the modern walls and fortification, in which many fragments had been used as so many blocks of stone, and from excavations made on purpose, a greater quantity of original Athenian sculpture, in statues, alti and bassi relievi, capitals, cornices, frizes, and columns, than exists in any other part of Europe. . . .

The Parthenon itself, independently of its decorative sculpture, is so chaste and perfect a model of Doric architecture, that Lord Elgin conceived it to be of the highest importance to the arts, to secure original specimens of each member of that edifice. These consist of a capital; assizes of the columns themselves, to show the exact form of the curve used in channelling; a Triglyph, and mutules from the cornice, and even some of the marble tiles with which the ambulatory was roofed: so that, not only the sculptor may be gratified by studying every specimen of his art, from the colossal statue to the basso-relievo, executed in the golden age of Pericles, by Phidias himself, or under his immediate direction; but the practical architect may examine into every detail of the building, even to the mode of uniting the tambours of the columns, without the aid of mortar, so as to give to the shafts the appearance of single blocks. . . .

More difficulty occurred in forming a plan, for deriving the utmost advantage from the marbles and casts. Lord Elgin's first attempt was to have the statues and bas-reliefs restored; and in that view he went to Rome, to consult and to employ Canova. The decision of that most eminent artist was conclusive. On examining the specimens produced to him, and making himself acquainted with the whole collection, and particularly with what came from the Parthenon, by means of the persons who had been carrying on Lord Elgin's operation at Athens, and who had returned with him to Rome, Canova declared, that however greatly it was to be lamented that these statues should have suffered so much from time and barbarism, yet it was undeniable, that they had never been retouched; that they were the work of the ablest artists the world had ever seen; executed under the most enlightened patron of the arts, and at a period when genius enjoyed the most liberal encouragement, and had attained the highest degree of perfection; and that they had been found worthy of forming the decoration of the most admired edifice ever erected in Greece; That he should have had the greatest delight, and derived the greatest benefit, from the opportunity Lord Elgin offered him of having in his possession, and contemplating, these inestimable marbles: But, (his expression was,) it would be sacrilege in him, or any man, to presume to touch them with a chisel. Since their arrival in this country, they have been thrown open to the inspection of the public; and the opinions and impressions, not only of artists, but of men of taste in general, have thus been formed and collected. From these, the judgement pronounced by Canova has been universally sanctioned: and all idea of restoring the marbles has been deprecated. . . . From trials which Lord Elgin was induced to make, at the request of professional gentlemen, a strong impression has been created, that the science of sculptors, and the taste and judgement by which it is to be carried forward and appreciated, cannot so effectually be promoted, as by athletic exercises practised in the presence of similar works; the distinguishing merit of which, is an able, scientific, ingenious, but exact imitation of Nature. By no other way could the variety of attitude, the articulation of the muscles, the description of the passions; in short, every thing a sculptor has to represent, be so accurately or so beneficially understood . . .

Under similar advantages, and with an enlightened and encouraging protection bestowed on genius and the arts, it may not be too sanguine to indulge a hope, that, prodigal as Nature is in the perfections of the human figure in this country, animating as are the instances of patriotism, heroic actions, and private virtues, deserving commemoration, sculpture may soon be raised in England to rival the ablest productions of the best times of Greece.

Memorandum on the Subject of the Earl of Elgin's Pursuits in Greece, 1811

The Treasure of Priam

HEINRICH SCHLIEMANN

DR HEINRICH SCHLIEMANN (*1822-1890*) *was born in Neu Buckow in Germany. He was a man of great and varied natural ability, both for scholarship and for business; starting as an assistant in a small shop he amassed a large fortune in trade and was then able to retire and follow out his lifelong ambition to search for the site of Troy. Unlike other scholars of his day, he placed complete faith in the accuracy of the Homeric poems, and by following the topographical descriptions in the* Iliad *he was able to identify the hill of Hissarlik as the site of Troy. His faith in ancient authorities was justified more than once, as it later led him to excavate the citadel of Mycenae, where he discovered an entire pre-Hellenic civilization including a group of royal graves containing an immense burial hoard of gold. He was often misled by his enthusiasm for Homer, and his unscientific methods of excavating would have appalled modern archaeologists, but his discoveries were of the first importance and magnitude. Among his many talents was an outstanding facility for languages; he learned a great many by a plan he devised for himself, which strongly resembles the most recent teaching methods.*

In the new large excavation on the north-west side, which is connected with the one I have just been describing, I have convinced myself that the splendid wall of large hewn stones, which I uncovered in April 1870, belongs to a tower, the lower projecting part of which must have been built during the first period of the Greek colony, whereas its upper portion seems to belong to the time of Lysimachus. To this tower also belongs the wall that I mentioned in my last report as 9 feet high and 6 feet broad and as continuous with the surrounding wall of Lysimachus; and so does the wall of the same dimensions, situated 49 feet from it, which I have likewise broken through. Behind the latter, at a depth of from 26 to 30 feet, I uncovered the Trojan city wall which runs out from the Scaean Gate.

In excavating this wall further and directly by the side of the palace of King Priam, I came upon a large copper article of the most remarkable form, which attracted my attention all the more as I thought I saw gold behind it. On the top of this copper article lay a stratum of red and calcined ruins, from 4¾ to 5¼ feet thick, as hard as stone, and above this again lay the above-mentioned wall of fortification (6 feet broad and 20 feet high) which was built of large stones and earth, and must have belonged to an early date after the destruction of Troy. In order to withdraw the Treasure from the greed of my workmen, and to save it for archaeology, I had to be most expeditious, and although it was not yet time for breakfast, I immediately had '*paidos*' called. This is a word of uncertain derivation, which had passed over into Turkish, and is here employed in place of ἀνάπαυσις, or time for rest. While the men were eating and resting, I cut out the Treasure with a large knife, which it was impossible to do without the very greatest exertion and the most fearful risk of my life, for the great fortification-wall, beneath which I had to dig, threatened every moment to fall down upon me. But the sight of so many objects, every one of which is of inestimable value to archaeology, made me foolhardy, and I never thought of any danger. It would, however, have been impossible for me to have removed the Treasure without the help of my dear wife, who stood by me ready to pack the things which I cut out in her shawl and to carry them away.

The first thing I found was a large copper shield (the ἀσπὶς ὀμφαλόεσσα of Homer) in the form of an oval salver, in the middle of which is a knob or boss encircled by a small furrow (αὖλαξ). This shield is a little less than 20 inches in length; it is quite flat and, surrounded by a rim (ἄντυξ) 1½ inches high; the boss (ὀμφαλός) is 2⅓ inches high and 4⅓ inches in diameter; the furrow encircling it is 7 inches in diameter and 2⅖ of an inch deep. . . .

Next came another cup of the purest gold, weighing exactly 600 grammes (about 1 lb. 6 oz. troy); it is 3½ inches high, 7¼ inches long, and 7⅕ inches broad; it is in the form of a ship with two large handles; on one side there is a mouth, 1⅕ inches broad, for drinking out of, and another at the other side, which is 2¾ inches broad, and, as my esteemed friend Professor Stephanos Kumanudes, of Athens, remarks, the person who presented the filled cup may have first drunk from the small mouth, as a mark of respect, to let the guest drink from the large mouth. This vessel has a foot which projects about 1/12 of an inch, and is 1⅓ inches long, and ⅘ of an inch broad. It is assuredly the Homeric, δέπας ἀμφικύπελλον. But I adhere to my supposition that all of those tall and brilliant red goblets of terra-cotta, in the form of champagne glasses with two enormous handles, are also δέπα ἀμφικύπελλα, and that this form probably existed in gold also. I must further make an observation which is very important for the history of art, that the above-mentioned gold δέπας ἀμφικύπελλον is of *cast gold*, and that the large handles, which are not solid, have been fused on to it. On the other hand the gold bottle and the gold cup mentioned above have been *wrought with the hammer.*

The Treasure further contained a small cup of gold alloyed with 20 per cent of silver, this is the mixed metal called *electrum.* It weighs 70 grammes ($2\frac{1}{4}$ oz. troy), and is above 3 inches high, and above $2\frac{1}{2}$ inches broad. Its foot is only $\frac{4}{5}$ of an inch high and nearly an inch broad, and is moreover not quite straight, so that the cup appears to be meant only to stand upon its mouth. . . .

As I found all these articles together, forming a rectangular mass, or packed into one another, it seems to be certain that they were placed on the city wall in a wooden chest (φωριαμός), such as those mentioned by Homer as being in the palace of King Priam. This appears to be the more certain, as close by the side of these articles I found a copper key above 4 inches long, the head of which (about 2 inches long and broad) greatly resembles a large safe-key of a bank. Curiously enough this key has had a wooden handle; there can be no doubt of this from the fact that the end of the stalk of the key is bent round at a right angle, as in the case of the daggers.

It is probable that some member of the family of King Priam hurriedly packed the Treasure into the chest and carried it off without having time to pull out the key; that when he reached the wall, however, the hand of an enemy or the fire overtook him, and he was obliged to abandon the chest, which was immediately covered to a height of from 5 to 6 feet with the red ashes and the stones of the adjoining royal palace.

Perhaps the articles found a few days previously in a room of the royal palace close to the place where the Treasure was discovered, belonged to this unfortunate person. These articles were a helmet, and a silver vase 7 inches high and $5\frac{1}{2}$ inches broad, containing an elegant cup of electrum $4\frac{1}{3}$ inches high and $3\frac{1}{2}$ inches broad. The helmet was broken in being taken out, but I can have it mended, as I have all the pieces of it. The two upper portions, composing the crest (φάλος), are uninjured. Beside the helmet, as before, I found a curved copper pin, nearly 6 inches in length, which must have been in some way attached to it, and have served some purpose.

At 5 or 6 feet above the Treasure, the successors of the Trojans erected a fortification wall 20 feet high and 6 feet broad, composed of large hewn and unhewn stones and earth; this wall extends to within 3¼ feet of the surface of the hill.

That the Treasure was packed together at terrible risk of life, and in the greatest anxiety, is proved among other things also by the contents of the largest silver vase, at the bottom of which I found two splendid gold diadems (*κρήδεμνα*); a fillet, and four beautiful gold ear-rings of most exquisite workmanship; upon these lay 56 gold ear-rings of exceedingly curious form and 8,750 small gold rings, perforated prisms and dice, gold buttons, and similar jewels, which obviously belonged to other ornaments; then followed six gold bracelets, and on the top of all the two small goblets.

The one diadem consists of a gold fillet, 21⅔ inches long and nearly ½ an inch broad, from which there hang on either side seven little chains to cover the temples, each of which has eleven square leaves with a groove; these chains are joined to one another by four little cross chains, at the end of which hangs a glittering golden idol of the tutelar goddess of Troy, nearly an inch long. The entire length of each of these chains, with the idols, amounts to 10¼ inches. Almost all these idols have something of the human form, but the owl's head with the two large eyes cannot be mistaken; their breadth at the lower end is about $\frac{9}{10}$ of an inch. Between these ornaments for the temples there are 47 little pendant chains adorned with square leaves; at the end of each little chain is an idol of the tutelary goddess of Ilium, about ¾ of an inch long; the length of these little chains with the idols is not quite 4 inches.

The other diadem is 20 inches long, and consists of a gold chain, from which are suspended on each side eight chains completely covered with small gold leaves, to hang down over the temples, and at the end of every one of the sixteen chains there hangs a golden idol 1¼ inches long, with the owl's head of the Ilian tutelary goddess. Between these ornaments for the temples there are likewise 74 little chains, about 4 inches long, covered with gold leaves, to hang down over the forehead; at the end of these chains there hangs a double leaf about ¾ of an inch long.

The fillet *ἄμπυξ* is above 18 inches long and ½ of an inch broad, and has three perforations at each end. Eight quadruple rows of dots divide it into nine compartments, in each of which there are two large dots; and an uninterrupted row of dots adorns the whole edge. Of the four ear-rings only two are exactly alike. From the upper part, which is almost in the shape of a basket, and is ornamented with two rows of decorations in the form of beads, there hang six small chains on which are three little cylinders; attached to the end of the chains are small idols of the tutelar goddess of Troy. The length of each ear-ring is 3½ inches. The upper part of the other two ear-rings is larger and thicker, but likewise almost in the shape of a basket, from it are suspended five little chains entirely covered with small round leaves, on which are likewise fastened small but more imposing idols of the Ilian tutelar divinity; the length of one of these pendants is 3½ inches, that of the other a little over 3 inches.

Of the six gold bracelets, two are quite simple and closed, and are about ⅕ of an inch thick; a third is likewise closed, but consists of an ornamented band $\frac{1}{25}$ of an inch thick, and ¼ of an inch broad. The other three are double, and the ends are turned round and furnished with a head. The princesses who wore these bracelets must have had unusually small hands, for they are so small that a girl of ten would have difficulty in putting them on.

The 56 other gold ear-rings are of various sizes, and three of them appear to have also been used by the princesses of the royal family as finger-rings. Not one of the ear-rings has any resemblance in form to the Hellenic, Roman, Egyptian, or Assyrian ear-rings; 20 of them end in four leaves, ten in three leaves, lying beside one another and soldered together, and they are thus extremely like those ear-rings of gold and electrum which I found last year at a depth of 9 and 13 metres (29½ and 42½ feet). Eighteen other ear-rings end in six leaves; at the commencement of these there are two small studs, in the centre two rows of five small studs each, and at the end three small studs. Two of the largest rings, which, owing to the thickness of the one end, certainly cannot have been used as ear-rings, and appear to have been finger-rings only, terminate in four leaves, and at the commencement of these there are two, in the middle three, and at the end again two small studs. Of the remaining ear-rings two have the form of three, and four the form of two, beautifully ornamented serpents lying beside one another.

Besides the ear-rings, a great number of other ornaments strung on threads, or fastened on leather, had been put into the same large silver vase; for above, and below them, as already said, I found 8,750 small objects; such as gold rings, only ⅛ of an inch in diameter; perforated dice, either smooth or in the form of little indented stars, about ⅙ of an inch in diameter; gold perforated prisms, $\frac{1}{10}$ of an inch high and ⅛ of an inch broad, decorated longitudinally with eight or sixteen incisions; small leaves about ⅕ of an inch long, and ⅛ of an inch broad, and pierced longitudinally with a hole for threading them; small gold pegs $\frac{1}{5}$ of an inch long, with a button on one side, and a perforated hole on the other; perforated prisms about $\frac{1}{5}$ of an inch long, and $\frac{1}{10}$ of an inch broad; double or triple gold rings soldered together and only $\frac{1}{4}$ of an inch in diameter, with holes on both sides for threading them; gold buttons or studs $\frac{1}{5}$ of an inch high, in the cavity of which is a ring above $\frac{1}{10}$ of an inch broad for sewing them on; gold double buttons, exactly like our shirt studs, $\frac{3}{10}$ of an inch long, which, however, are not soldered, but simply stuck together, for from the cavity of the one button there projects a tube (*αὐλίσκος*) nearly $\frac{1}{4}$ of an inch long, and from the other a pin (*ἔμβολον*) of the same length, and the pin is merely stuck into the tube to form the double stud. These double buttons or studs can only have been used, probably, as ornament upon leather articles, for instance upon the handle-straps (*τελαμῶνες*) of swords, shields, or knives. I found in the vase also two gold cylinders above $\frac{1}{10}$ of an inch thick and $\frac{3}{4}$ of an inch long; also a small gold peg above $\frac{4}{5}$ of an inch in length, and from $\frac{6}{100}$ to $\frac{8}{100}$ of an inch thick; it has at one end a perforated hole for hanging it up, and on the other side six encircling incisions, which give the article the appearance of a screw; it is only by means of a magnifying glass that it is found not to be really a screw. I also found in the same vase two pieces of gold, one of which is $\frac{1}{7}$ of an inch, the other above 2 inches, long; each of them has 21 perforations.

The person who endeavoured to save the Treasure had fortunately the presence of mind to stand the silver vase, containing the valuable articles described above, upright in the chest, so that not so much as a bead could fall out, and everything has been preserved uninjured.

Troy and Its Remains, 1875

A stolen treasure

HEINRICH SCHLIEMANN

I now come to three smaller treasures, found at the end of March 1873, at a depth of 30 ft on the east side of the royal house and very close to it, by two of my workmen, one of whom lives at Yeni Shehr, the other at Kalifatli. One of them was found in the owl-headed vase No. 232, which was closed by the pointed foot of another vase; the two other little treasures were found, together with the battle-axe No. 828, close by. But as the statements of the labourers differ as to the particular objects contained in each treasure, I can only describe them here conjointly. The two workmen had stolen and divided the three treasures between themselves, and probably I should never have had any knowledge of it, had it not been for the lucky circumstance that the wife of the workman of Yeni Shehr, who had got his share of the plunder, all the articles Nos. 822-833, besides two more pendants like Nos. 832 and 833, had the boldness to parade one Sunday with the ear-rings and pendants Nos. 822 and 823. This excited the envy of her companions; she was denounced to the Turkish authorities of Koum Kaleh, who put her and her husband in prison; and, having been threatened that her husband would be hanged if they did not give up the jewels, she betrayed the hiding-place, and thus this part of the treasure was at once recovered and is now exhibited in the Imperial Museum of Constantinople. The pair also denounced their accomplice at Kalifatli, but here the authorities came too late, because he had already had his part of the spoil melted down by a goldsmith in Ben Kioi, who, at his desire, had made of it a very large, broad, and heavy necklace, with clumsy flowery ornaments in the Turkish fashion. Thus this part of the treasure is for ever lost to science. I can, therefore, represent here only that part which was taken by the Yeni Shehr thief, because it exists, and everybody can see it in the Constantinople Museum. As both thieves declared separately on oath before the authorities of Koum Kaleh that the owl-vase No. 232, with part of the gold, was found by them immediately to the west of the well, and that the two other treasures were found close by, and indicated the exact spot of the discovery, there can be no doubt as to its accuracy.

Ilios, 1880

A Mycenaean ruler

HEINRICH SCHLIEMANN

Mycenae, 6 December 1876

For the first time since its capture by the Argives in 468 BC, and so for the first time during 2,344 years, the Acropolis of Mycenae had a garrison, whose watch-fires seen by night throughout the whole Plain of Argos carry back the mind to the watch kept for Agamemnon's return from Troy, and the signal which warned Clytemnestra and her paramour of his approach. But this time the object of the occupation by soldiery is of a more peaceful character, for it is merely intended to inspire awe among the country-people, and to prevent them from making clandestine excavations in the tombs, or approaching them while we are working in them. . . .

But of the third body, which lay at the north end of the tomb, the round face, with all its flesh, had been wonderfully preserved under its ponderous golden mask; there was no vestige of hair, but both eyes were perfectly visible, also the mouth, which, owing to the enormous weight that had pressed upon it, was wide open, and showed thirty-two beautiful teeth. From these, all the physicians who came to see the body were led to believe that the man must have died at the early age of thirty-five. The nose was entirely gone. The body having been too long for the space between the two inner walls of the tomb, the head had been pressed in such a way on the breast, that the upper part of the shoulders was nearly in a horizontal line with the vertex of the head. Notwithstanding the large golden breast-plate, so little had been preserved of the breast, that the inner side of the spine was visible in many places. In its squeezed and mutilated state, the body measured only 2 ft 4½ in from the top of the head to the beginning of the loins; the breadth of the shoulders did not exceed 1 ft 1¼ in, and the breadth of the chest 1 ft 3 in; but the large thigh bones could leave no doubt regarding the real proportions of the body. Such had been the pressure of the *débris* and stones, that the body had been reduced to a thickness of 1 in to 1½ in. The colour of the body resembled very much that of an Egyptian mummy. The forehead was ornamented with a plain round leaf of gold and a still larger one was lying on the right eye; I further observed a large and a small gold leaf on the breast below the large golden breast-cover, and a large one just above the right thigh.

The news that the tolerably well preserved body of a man of the mythic heroic age had been found, covered with golden ornaments, spread like wildfire through the Argolid, and people came by thousands from Argos, Nauplia, and the villages to see the wonder. But, nobody being able to give advice how to preserve the body, I sent for a painter to get at least an oil-painting made, for I was afraid that the body would crumble to pieces. Thus I am enabled to give a faithful likeness of the body, as it looked after all the golden ornaments had been removed. But to my great joy, it held out for two days, when a druggist from Argos, Spiridon Nicolaou by name, rendered it hard and solid by pouring on it alcohol, in which he had dissolved gum-sandarac. As there appeared to be no pebbles below it it was thought that it would be possible to lift it on an iron plate; but this was a mistake, because it was soon discovered that there was the usual layer of pebbles below the body, and all of these having been more or less pressed into the soft rock by the enormous weight which had been lying for ages upon them, all attempts made to squeeze in the iron plate below the pebble-stones, so as to be able to lift them together with the body, utterly failed. There remained, therefore, no other alternative than to cut a small trench into the rock all round the body, and make thence a horizontal incision, so as to cut out a slab, two inches thick, to lift it with the pebble-stones and the body, to put it upon a strong plank, to make around the latter a strong box, and to send this to the village of Charvati, whence it will be forwarded to Athens as soon as the Archaeological Society shall have got a suitable locality for the Mycenean antiquities. With the miserable instruments alone available here it was no easy task to detach the large slab horizontally from the rock, but it was still much more difficult to bring it in the wooden box from the deep sepulchre to the surface, and to transport it on men's shoulders for more than a mile to Charvati. But the capital interest which this body of the remote heroic age has for science, and the buoyant hope of preserving it, made all the labour appear light.

Mycenae, 1878

To His Majesty King George of the Hellenes, Athens

I am overwhelmed with joy to inform Your Majesty that I have uncovered the tombs which tradition, as set down in Pausanias, knew as the sepulchres of Agamemnon, Cassandra, Eurymedon and their fellows, all struck down at the banquet by Clytemnestra and her lover Aegisthus. The tombs lay within a double ring of parallel stone slabs, which would only have been erected in honour of the noble persons I have named. Inside the tombs I found a vast mass of treasure consisting of archaic objects made of solid gold. These alone are enough to fill a great museum, which will be the wonder of the world, and which, in centuries to come, will draw to Greece thousands of visitors from every land. Since love of learning alone impels my researches, I naturally make no claim on this treasure, which I am truly happy to hand over intact to Greece. May God grant that this treasure becomes the foundation of a great national prosperity.

Henry Schliemann
Mycenae, 16(28) *November* 1876

His Majesty's Reply

To Doctor Schliemann, Argos

I have the honour to inform you that His Majesty the King has received your despatch, and has graciously instructed me to thank you for your hard work and devotion to learning and to congratulate you on your valuable discoveries. His Majesty hopes that your future endeavours are always crowned with similar happy success.

Secretary to His Majesty the King of the Hellenes
A. Calinskis
Mycenae, 1878

Telegrams translated from the French by V. M. Conrad

1. The Lion Gate as it must have appeared when Schliemann first came to Mycenae. When, after several years of work starting in 1874, he succeeded in bringing to light a whole "Mycenaean culture," he had opened a new chapter of early European history.

2. Herculaneum in the middle of the 18th century. When the first excavators came, they had to dig through a shield of hardened lava up to 65 feet in depth. The city was buried in 79 A.D., in the midst of its bustling life, by an eruption of Vesuvius. Like Pompeii, its twin in disaster, it remains today, more than two hundred years since its discovery, a far from exhausted treasure trove.

Winckelmann in Herculaneum

JOHANN JOACHIM WINCKELMANN

JOHANN JOACHIM WINCKELMANN *(1717-1768) was born in Stendal in Prussian Saxony. His early studies of classical literature gave him a great desire to visit Rome, and in 1754 he was appointed librarian to Cardinal Passionei, adopted the Roman Catholic faith, and settled in Italy. At this time great discoveries were being made at Pompeii and Herculaneum, but the finds were jealously guarded by the excavators, who would not allow observers either on to the site or into the workshops. Winckelmann, with characteristic devious cunning, managed to circumvent this prohibition sufficiently to gather material for several publications.*

In 1768 he went to Vienna, where he was received and honoured by Maria Theresa, but the pecuniary rewards he accepted for his work proved his undoing; on the return journey he was very much too free with his money while staying at an inn at Trieste, and was attacked and murdered by a robber. He was the first archaeologist to study the development of ancient art and to attempt the logical deduction of the history and social background of the ancient world from its surviving artifacts.

A well dug for the prince of Elbeuf, at a small distance from his house, was the first thing that gave occasion to the discovery they are now pursuing. The prince had built this house in order to make his constant residence in it. It lay behind the Franciscan convent, at the extremity of, and upon, a rock of lava near the sea. It afterwards fell into the hands of the house of Falletti of Naples, from whom the present king of Spain purchased it, in order to make a fishing seat of it. The well in question had been sunk near the garden of the barefooted Carmelites. To form it, they were obliged to dig through the lava to the live rock, where the workmen found, under the ashes of mount Vesuvius, three large cloathed female statues. These the Austrian viceroy very justly laid claim to, and, keeping part of them in his hands, ordered them to Rome, where they were repaired. They were then presented to prince

Eugene, who placed them in his gardens at Vienna. On his death, his heiress sold them to the king of Poland for six thousand crowns or florins; which, I cannot positively say. Seven years after my setting out for Italy, they stood in a pavillon of the great royal garden, without the city of Dresden, along with the statues and busts of the palace of Chigi, for which the late Augustus, king of Poland, had given sixty thousand crowns. This collection was added to some ancient monuments, which cardinal Alexander Albani had ceded to the same prince for ten thousand crowns.

On the discovery of these antiquities, orders were given to the prince of Elbeuf, not to dig any further. Thirty years, however, were suffered to elapse, before any more notice was taken of them. At length, the present king of Spain, as soon as by the conquest of Naples he found himself in peaceable possession of it, chose Portico for his spring residence; and, as the well was still in being, ordered the works begun at the bottom of it to be continued, till they reached some buildings. This well still subsists. It runs down perpendicularly through the lava to the middle of the theatre (the first building discovered,) which receives no light but by it. Here an inscription was found containing the name of Herculaneum, which, by giving room to guess what place they had hit upon, determined his majesty to proceed further.

The direction of this work was given to a Spanish engineer, called Roch Joachim Alcunierre, who had followed his majesty to Naples, and is now colonel, and chief of the body of engineers at Naples. This man, who (to use the Italian proverb) knew as much of antiquities as the moon does of lobsters, has been, through this want of capacity, the occasion of many antiquities being lost. A single fact will be sufficient to prove it. The workmen having discovered a large public inscription (to what buildings it belonged, I can't say) in letters of brass two palms high; he ordered these letters to be torn from the wall, without first taking a copy of them, and thrown pell mell into a basket; and then presented them, in that condition, to the king. They were afterwards exposed for many years in the cabinet, where every one was at liberty to put them together as he pleased. Some imagined, they made these two words, IMP. AUG. I shall presently relate how a brazen four-horse chariot was served, by the same engineer's directions.

Don Roche having in time attained a higher rank, the superintendance and conduct of the works in question were committed to a Swiss officer, called Charles Weber, now a major; and it is to his good sense, that we are indebted for all the good steps since taken, to bring to light this treasure of antiquities. The first thing he did was, to make an exact map of all the subterraneous galleries, and the buildings they led to. This map he rendered still more intelligible, by a minute historical account of the whole discovery. The ancient city is to be seen in it as if freed from all the rubbish, with which it is actually incumbered. The inside of the buildings, the most private rooms, and the gardens, as well as the particular spots, where every thing taken out of them was found, appear in this map, just as they would if they were laid quite bare. But nobody is permitted to see those drawings.

The happy issue of the works undertaken at Herculaneum proved a motive for opening the earth in other places; and the doing this soon enabled them to ascertain the situation of the ancient Stabia, and led them, at Pompeii, to the vast remains of an amphitheatre, built on a hill, part of which, however, had been always visible above ground. The diggings in these places proved far less expensive, than the diggings in Herculaneum, as there was no lava to dig through. The subterraneous works at Pompeii are those, which promise most; for there they are not only sure of proceeding step by step in a great city, but have found out the principal street of it, which runs in a strait line. But, notwithstanding all this certainty of their being able to find treasures unknown to our ancestors, the works for that purpose are carried on in a very slow and indolent manner; there being but fifty men, including the Algerine and Tunisian slaves, employed in all these subterraneous places. Great a city as Pompeii is known to have been, I, in my last journey, found but eight men at work on the ruins of it.

To compensate this neglect, the method observed in digging is such, that it is impossible the least spot should escape unnoticed. On both sides of one principal trench, carried on in a right line, the workmen alternately hollow out chambers, fix palms, in length, breadth, and height; removing the rubbish, as they proceed, from every one of these chambers, to the chamber opposite it, that was last hollowed out. This method is taken, not only with a view of lessening the expence, but of supporting the earth over one chamber, with the rubbish taken out of another.

I know, that strangers, particularly travellers, who can take but a cursory view of these works, wish, that all the rubbish was entirely removed, so as to give them an opportunity of seeing, as in the plan of which I have been speaking, the inside of the whole subterraneous city of Herculaneum. They are apt to impeach the taste of the Court, and of those who direct these works. But this is a mere prejudice, which a rational examination of the nature of the spot, and other circumstances, would soon conquer. I must, however, agree with foreigners in regard to the theatre; for it might have been entirely cleared; and it was, certainly, a thing well worth the expence. I am, therefore, very far from being satisfied with their just disencumbering the seats, the form of which could be so easily gathered from the many other ancient theatres still in being; whereas they have left the stage as they found it, though the most essential part of the whole building, and the only one, of which we have no clear and precise ideas. They have, it is true, done something towards giving this satisfaction to the curious and the learned, having cleared the steps leading from the Arena, or Pit, to the stage, so that we may hope to enjoy, one day or another, though under ground, a sight of the whole theatre of Herculaneum.

As to the whole town, I must beseech those who long for a free view of it, to consider, that, the roofs of the houses having given way under the enormous weight of the superincumbent lava, nothing could be seen in that case but the walls. Besides, as those walls which had paintings on them have been cut out, and carried off, that such inestimable pieces might not suffer by the air or rain, no wall, but those of the poorest and meanest houses, would appear entire. Now, I leave any one to judge, how excessively expensive it would be to blow up such a thick and extensive crust of lava, and remove the vast quantity of ashes accumulated under it. And, after all, what would the advantage of it be? That of laying bare a parcel of old ruinous walls, merely to satisfy the ill-judged curiosity of some virtuosi, at the expence of a well built and very populous city. The theatre, indeed, might be entirely laid open at no expence but that of the garden belonging to the barefooted Carmelites, under which it lies.

Those, who have a mind to see the walls of ancient buildings formerly buried in the same manner, may satisfy their curiosity at Pompeii. But few persons, except Englishmen, have resolution enough to go so far on that account. At Pompeii the ground may be dug up, and turned topsy-turvy, without any risk, and at small expence, the land lying over it being of little value. Formerly, indeed, it used to produce the most delicious wine; but that it now produces is so middling, that the country would suffer very little by the entire destruction of its vineyards. I must add, that this country is more subject than any other to those dangerous exhalations called *Musseta* by the inhabitants, which burn up all the productions of the earth. This I had an opportunity of observing on a great number of elms, which, six years before, I had seen in a very thriving way. These exhalations generally precede an eruption, and are first felt in places under ground. Accordingly, a few days before the last eruption, some of the inhabitants dropt down dead on entering their cellars.

It appears by the indolent manner in which these works are conducted, that a fine field of discovery must remain to posterity. As great treasures might perhaps, be discovered at the same expence, by digging at Pozzuoli, Baiae, Cuma, and Misenum, where the Romans had their finest country seats. But the Court is so well satisfied with the discoveries now making, that it has forbid the earth to be dug any where else below a certain depth. Certain it is, that, in the districts I have been mentioning, there are ancient buildings, hitherto little, or not at all, noticed, as appears by what I am going to relate. An English Captain, whose ship lay at anchor two years ago in these parts, discovered under Baiae a spacious and beautiful hall, accessible only by water, in which there still remained very fine ornaments in stucco. It is only since my return from Naples that I heard of this discovery, of which, however, I have seen the drawing. Mr Adams, of Edinburgh in Scotland, gave me a circumstantial account of it. He is a lover of the arts, and intends to visit Greece, and Asia Minor.

A Critical Account of the Situation and Destruction of Herculaneum and Pompeii, 1771

The plaster corpses of Pompeii

AUGUSTUS GOLDSMIDT, ESQ *communicated the following account of the discovery of some skeletons at Pompeii in the spring of the year.*

'Happening to spend last winter in Rome, I made a short excursion during Lent to Naples, being anxious, at the request of several friends, to bring back a particular report of some interesting discoveries of human remains lately made at Pompeii.

'Through the kindness of Signor Vertumni, a Roman artist of some eminence then residing at Naples, I obtained an introduction to the Cavaliere Fiorelli, the government director of the works, who invited me to join a party shortly about to explore the ruins of Pompeii.

'After visiting several of the streets and of the less recently discovered portions of the city, we proceeded to a small museum fitted up under the direction of Signor Fiorelli, and in which he hopes to retain, so far as possible, on the spot the numerous objects of interest daily brought to light in the course of the more extended researches which have been made since the advent of the present government of Italy. In two of the rooms in the museum are deposited the bodies, as nearly as possible in the relative positions in which they were found; and I am much indebted to the kindness and courtesy of the Cavaliere Fiorelli, who afforded me every information on the subject of these discoveries, and also allowed me to inspect the journals which are kept of the progress and result of each day's labour.

'It seems that early in February last the remains of a linen cloth or bag were found in the course of removing the loose soil which now covers the remains of Pompeii, that contained several coins, ornaments, and two iron keys. Close to this a hole was accidentally made by one of the workmen with his pickaxe, and, on investigating this, Signor Fiorelli perceived that there existed a cavity of some extent. He had for some time entertained the idea that there were probably human bodies buried in the ruins of the city, the remains of which might have perished though leaving their impressions in the sandy covering. He therefore caused plaster of Paris in a very liquid state to be poured into the cavity;

this he continued to do, blowing also with considerable force, so as to cause the liquid plaster to permeate the centre cavity.

'As soon as the cavity was filled with plaster, he had the earth round it carefully removed. The ashes in which the bodies were buried must have fallen in a damp state, and hardened gradually by the lapse of time, and as the soft parts of the bodies decayed and shrunk a hollow was formed between the bodies and the crust of soil. This formed the cavity into which the plaster was poured. In the bony parts, the space left void being very small, the coat of plaster is proportionately thin, and many portions of the extremeties and the crania are left exposed.

'So intimately did these ashes penetrate, and so thoroughly has the cast been taken, that the texture of the under garments, drawers, and sort of inner vest with sleeves is distinctly visible. The bodies, it may be noticed, present a tumified appearance in the abdominal region, as if from the action of water.

'In the first room is the figure of a female, apparently about thirty years old, or perhaps more, lying on the right side in a twisted and apparently somewhat contorted position. The left hand is raised, and on the little finger is a ring much corroded, apparently of silver; the head is thrown back, and the hair, which appears to have been very plentiful, is still visible; the folds of the dress are quite distinct; the bones of the feet, which are stretched out, are protruding; the ancles and wrist joints and the extremities of the fingers are most delicately formed, and their slenderness and the great length and better proportions of the thumbs would seem to show that this female was of gentler blood than the two hereafter described.

'In the next room there are two shelves; on the first is the figure of a man lying on his back, with one hand grasping his garment, which he has pulled up to the chest, leaving the whole of the lower portion of the figure exposed, which is of very fine proportions; a curious peculiarity still distinctly traceable is that the hair of the *pubes* is shaved so as to leave it in a semi-circular form, such as may be observed in the statues, and which has, I believe, been generally supposed to be merely a sculptural conventionality. The other hand is extended and strongly clenched, and the limbs in an attitude of rigidity almost amounting to convulsion. These facts, as well as the expression of pain and horror distinctly traceable in the countenance, would seem to show that the unfortunate man died fully conscious of the dreadful fate which awaited him, and against which he vainly struggled. The bones of the feet are exposed.

'On the other slab in the second room lie two female figures, Signor Fiorelli supposes, probably of the family of the man.

'These two are lying with the heads at opposite extremities of the table, so that the lower portion of the one figure is parallel to the other; they are the bodies of a woman apparently from 30 to 40 and a girl of 15 or 16. The woman is lying on the left side, with one arm slightly raised, and the other by her side, apparently in an easier position than the two figures before described, as if she had suffered less.

'The younger is also lying on her left side, the head thus turned in a contrary direction to that of the elder; the face is supported on the left arm, which is placed so as to protect the eyes, and the arm and hand are in an attitude as if holding a cloth or handkerchief over the mouth, apparently protecting herself as much as possible from the falling ashes. The form of this figure is most beautiful, especially the loins and *nates*, which are perfectly modelled; the hand and arm are also very delicate, though both these figures would appear to have been of inferior rank to the first. The tissue of the dress is distinctly visible. I should have mentioned that, in the elder, traces of cloth leglets and the fastenings of a kind of ancle boots are distinctly visible.

'The symmetry of the back and loins of this figure, as well as that of the younger already alluded to, are most remarkable, and, occurring as it does in bodies taken by chance, would seem to go a long way to show that the ancients had actually before them individual specimens of that perfect symmetry which they have handed down to us in those magnificent statues which are still the world's wonder, and that they were not an assemblage of the characteristics of different individuals into one imaginary form.

'These discoveries are in many particulars worthy of the attention of Archaeologists, and reflect much credit on Signor Fiorelli, to whose critical acumen they are due.'

Thanks were returned for these Communications.

Proceedings of the Society of Antiquaries of London, 1863

The discovery of the 'Venus de Milo'

CLAUDE TARRAL

Perhaps the most rewarding age for an archaeologist to live in was the second half of the nineteenth century. Archaeology, regarded as a means of scientific study of the past through its artifacts rather than merely a fruitful source of collectors' pieces, was still in its infancy and offered immense scope to scholar and excavator alike. Their findings created the framework upon which the chronology of the classical world has largely been built, but quite apart from the value of these discoveries as historical evidence, statues were excavated which must rank among the greatest treasures of mankind as pure works of art.

It is exactly forty-four years since chance brought to light the enchanting Venus de Milo, the pearl of the Louvre. Unhappily, this short interval has seen the loss of the leading actors in this magnificent triumph over the passage of time. The young ship's ensign, Dumont d'Urville, the first to be struck by the beauty of this precious statue, and who drew and described it with so much understanding, met a tragic death in a railway accident. Fauvel, the last survivor of the Choiseul expedition, the distinguished scholar Quatrèmere de Quincy, the learned Clarac, Forbin Janson, the Marquis de Rivière, Émeric David, are no longer with us. Marcellus, who had the signal honour of receiving the Venus and transporting it to France, died recently while still in his prime. So we are reduced to drawing almost all our information from the records they have left to posterity. M. Brest, France's consular agent at Melos, who displayed such laudable energy in the acquisition of this masterpiece, is still alive; but he is past eighty, and I fear his memory is no longer very accurate; he believes that both his own superiors and the historians have treated him unjustly; to him our ravishing goddess, far from being a joyful recollection, is a source of great bitterness; if, however, his grievances are well founded, we should pity this venerable old man, and in that case there would still be time to soothe the distress of his last years by a speedy restitution. M. Beulé openly declares that France owes the Venus de Milo to M. Brest; this tribute requires a detailed appraisal. I have before me a very full unpublished report, written two years ago by M. Brest, in which he states that he 'purchased the immortal Venus for France, towards the end of 1819, from a Greek peasant, Theodore Kendrotas, for the sum of 600 piastres plus 18 piastres for packing, a total of 618 piastres, at that time equivalent to the same amount of francs'. M. Brest then had the statue transferred to his house, and retained it, in spite of threats from Prince Mourousi; subsequently the torso was stolen and placed on board a disused ship; M. Brest, assisted by lieutenant Berranger and twelve men from the crew of the schooner *Estafette*, recovered it by main force. It was M. Brest, too, who undertook to secure the leading citizens of the island of Melos against Mourousi's vengeance, and had to pay the fine of 6,000 piastres which the despot imposed on them; only ten years later was M. Brest reimbursed for this outlay, but by then the difference in the exchange rate was very unfavourable to him, and he lost 5,000 francs; this loss, with other sums expended, was never repaid him. M. Brest still declares that in the absence of the Marquis de Rivière, M. Beaurepaire, the chargé d'affaires at Constantinople, contrived to trick him into handing over all the documents and receipts which substantiated his claims. These are indeed serious accusations against the dead; we should accept them only with reservations, for it may be that M. Brest's memory is leading him astray unawares. Here are some grounds for doubting the accuracy of his statements. First, M. Brest has never sought public restitution for these numerous injuries he alleges he suffered. He maintains that he bought the Venus towards the end of 1819; as soon as it was detached and lifted from its niche, he had it removed to his house; however, this last statement is contradicted by Dumont d'Urville; at least four months later (19 April 1820) he saw the upper part of the Venus in a Greek peasant's shed, and found the lower part still in its niche. M. Brest also says that no arms were found, and yet d'Urville saw two arms and a hand holding an apple, which were delivered to Marcellus with the Venus and other fragments. M. Brest mentions only two Hermes figures discovered with the Venus; there were three. Here is enough evidence that M. Brest is mistaken in certain factual details; he may be right in others. It is for the Chancellery of France to examine his claims, and if necessary make him honourable restitution, since it would be shameful to France if ingratitude on such a scale were to taint the possession of a monument of unfading glory.

Here is an abridged account of the discovery of the Venus; it is most unfortunate that the circumstances of that discovery are so poorly documented, for a number of important archaeological points are very puzzling. The first description of the jewel of the Louvre is that of the young d'Urville; it is still the best; though not an archaeologist, his instinctive observation is a model for antiquarians. His remarkable report is little known; it deserves serious study, and as it supports my conjecture, I shall quote the most important passages.

'On April 19 1820,' says d'Urville (*Annales maritimes*, Bajot, 1821, p. 150), 'I went to look over some classical fragments found at Melos shortly before our arrival. About three weeks before we reached the island, a Greek peasant was digging in his field, which lay within the bounds of the site of ancient Melos, when he found some pieces of dressed stone; since these blocks are used by the local people for building their houses and have a certain value, he was impelled to dig deeper, and so came to uncover a kind of niche in which he found a marble statue, two Hermes figures, and some other marble fragments.

'The statue was in two pieces, joined by means of two strong iron pins. The peasant, fearful of losing the fruit of his labours, had the upper part of the statue and the two Hermes figures removed to a shed; the lower part remained in its niche. I examined everything carefully, and the various pieces seemed to me to be of fine style, as far as my poor knowledge of the arts permitted me to judge.

'I measured the two parts of the statue separately, and found the whole to be very nearly 6 feet in height. It was the representation of a nude woman; her left hand was raised, holding an apple, and her right hand supported an intricately folded wrap which fell carelessly from her loins to her feet; but both hands are damaged, and actually detached from the body. The only remaining foot is bare; the ears are pierced, and must have held ear rings. All these attributes would seem sufficiently to fit the Venus of the judgement of Paris; but where, then, are Juno, Minerva and the handsome shepherd? It is true that a foot clad in a buskin and a third hand were found at the same time; however, the name of the island, Melos, is closely akin to the word *melon*, meaning 'apple'. Is it not likely that the chief attribute of the statue indicates this verbal link?

'The two Hermes figures which accompanied it in its niche are undistinguished; one is surmounted by the head of a woman or child and the other has the face of an old man with a long beard. Above the entry to the niche is a marble slab 4½ feet long and 6 to 8 inches broad, carrying an inscription; of this, only the first half has survived weathering; the rest is completely effaced. This loss cannot be evaluated, perhaps we might have gained thereby some light on the history of this island, which by every indication was once most prosperous, but whose fate after the Athenian invasion, that is, for more than twenty-two centuries, is completely unknown to us. We might at least have learnt on what occasion, and by whom, these statues were dedicated. I copied this inscription. The pedestal of one of the Hermes figures must also have carried an inscription, but its letters were too worn for me to decipher. At the time of our journey to Constantinople, the ambassador questioned me about this statue; I gave him my opinion, and I sent M. de Marcellus a copy of the account you have just read. On my return, M. de Rivière informed me that he had purchased the statue for the Museum. I have since learnt that M. de Marcellus reached Melos at the very moment when the statue was awaiting shipment for another destination; but after various difficulties, this friend of the arts finally succeeded in saving this precious relic of antiquity for France.'

In this manner the young naturalist d'Urville personally saw the lower part of the Venus in its niche; he states that the upper part was joined to the lower by two strong iron pins; this would support the belief that the Greek peasant removed them, and that the Venus was entire, and standing upright as M. Brest describes. But other accounts state that the Venus was found in two separate pieces; the clear marks of a spade on the torso bear out this last version. D'Urville is most explicit on the subject of the two hands, the left holding the apple, the right supporting the drapery; he is mistaken in his designation of a Hermes, our little Mercury, which he takes for a woman or child – a fact which shows his lack of classical scholarship; he could not decipher the inscription on its base – which indicates his unfamiliarity with epigrammatic studies. The copy he made of the inscription on the marble slab above the niche has proved very valuable, as I shall show below. It is my belief that Dumont d'Urville played a most important part in acquiring the Venus; M. Brest has no standing in the world of the arts – his opinion could not influence the ambassador at Constantinople; but the enlightened view of d'Urville was a powerful factor in saving this unique monument for France.

Concerning the excavation at Melos, Marcellus has left us some details which seem to be accurate, although they contradict M. Brest.

'Towards the end of February 1820, a Greek named Yorgos was busy digging in his field when he found a kind of oblong niche built in the rock; he managed to clear this little edifice, and also a narrow recess sunk 5 or 6 feet below ground level. Lying there in huddled confusion he found the top part of the statue, which he at once removed to his shed, three Hermes figures, some statue bases and other marble debris; a fortnight later, continuing his investigation, he found the lower part of the same statue and some fragmentary classical sculptures.' Here now is the description of the Venus made on sight by Marcellus. 'The statue was made of two blocks, joined together by an iron pin which has not been recovered; the folds of drapery on the left hip concealed the line where the two pieces met. The whole mass of hair (we must understand by this expression only the chignon) was detached, but quite well preserved and elegant in style. One by one on the bridge of the schooner *Estafette* I displayed the three Hermes figures and the classical fragments, which had all been delivered to me.' In a note Marcellus adds: 'On a marble slab $4\frac{1}{2}$ feet long by 8 inches broad were some words which seemed to have no connection with the statue; this inscription was partially effaced, and was left at Melos.' What extraordinary folly! And yet the intelligent d'Urville had judged it very important and deplored its debasement! Marcellus makes this observation: 'Volumes of dissertations in praise of the Venus have made their appearance; among these works we note the pages of Quatremère de Quincy, Clarac and Saint-Victor, full of taste and scholarship. Some sketches of poses conjecturally restored had been submitted to the King; there had even been an attempt to fit to the statue's shoulders two arms and a hand holding an apple, which I had also brought back; but it was easy to see that these roughly shaped arms could only have belonged to the Venus in a first and crude attempt at restoration, attributed to the eighth-century Christians. It was shown (by whom?) that the statue, loaded with robes, gold necklaces and ear-rings, had represented the Panagia (Holy Virgin) in the little Greek church whose ruins I saw at Melos.' Here are absurdities if you like; diplomacy does not give a man discretion as an amateur archaeologist. I have quoted these sentences to show that Marcellus really did bring to France two fragmentary arms, with a hand holding an apple, the arms and hand exactly described by d'Urville. How could Clarac be unaware of this fact, and write the following: 'It was believed that the left arm was entirely missing; but on visiting Melos to confirm for himself all that concerned the statue, the Marquis de Rivière instituted fresh excavations, and the fragments of an arm and a hand were happily discovered. These, from the quality of the marble and the workmanship, could be supposed to belong to our Venus, and we see from the holes of the pin and the marks of tearing that the arm was fixed to it.' Are this left arm and hand those referred to and brought back by Marcellus? On studying Marcellus and examining the carving of the Venus where the fragment of arm is shaped, one is inclined to tax Clarac with confusion; however, I read in the unpublished report of M. Brest that he was in fact instructed by M. de Rivière to make new excavations at Melos, and that two arms were discovered which M. Brest thought belonged to the Venus. 'The right arm was in three pieces, the fingers of the hand closed on an apple and the left in two pieces, with three fingers closed, and the thumb and the index finger joined, apparently holding something.' M. Brest states that he sent these fragments to Toulon, addressed to M. Bedfort.

In his unpublished report, M. Brest affirms that 'the Venus had no arms; the crumbling of the upper part of the niche could have broken them, and also caused a light grazing on the statue's nose.'

There are a number of divergencies between these historians. M. Brest claims that the Venus had no arms, but d'Urville saw them, and says that the left hand held the apple; Marcellus received the fragmentary hands from M. Brest and brought them back to France. Clarac speaks of a left hand with the apple, M. Brest of a right hand; but, to be honest, M. Brest could very well be wrong here; otherwise it would mean that two fragments of Venus with the apple were dug up at Melos. Today the Louvre has only one piece of the arm and the left hand; I have taken a mould of these, and there is no doubt that they belong to our statue; I believe these two pieces are the same as those seen and described by d'Urville and brought back to France by Marcellus. Clarac only mentions a single arm recovered in the second excavation at Melos; M. Brest says he dug up two. M. de Sartiges, ambassador to Rome, visited Melos some years ago, and he assures me that M. Brest told him of the two arms which he sent to France; M. Gobineau, a most distinguished archaeologist although a skilful diplomat, met M. Brest at Constantinople on returning from a mission to Persia; M. Brest reiterated to him the same statements concerning the two arms. What is certain is that several pieces of the Venus, fragments of a right and left arm and a left hand holding an apple, three Hermes figures, a pedestal with a Greek inscription and part of the statue base passed the threshold of the Louvre; here we must admit a deplorable, inexplicable occurrence: today the Museum no longer possesses either the right hand, the fragment of base, or the pedestal of the Hermes-Mercury, adorned with its priceless Greek inscription. M. de Longpérier has made exhaustive investigations to recover them, even excavating the floors of the cellars, but in vain – these fragments are lost for ever. In the arts, as in politics, prejudice, vanity, scholastic pride and ignorance play a large part. The Greeks and Romans had good reason to make the guardians of their art treasures answerable for failure with their lives. In the reign of Louis Philippe, one man with great influence at the Louvre suggested to the King that he could make him magnificent table-tops from the ancient monuments of Egypt; art, said this scholarly architect, would lose nothing thereby, and the furniture of the Crown would gain a good deal. I have heard a fashionable painter and fine speaker declare that if he were director of the Louvre, he would kick all those ugly Egyptians out of the door. How should we explain the mysterious loss of these fragments of the Venus? It was maintained that they could not have belonged to the original statue, that they were restorations, and therefore merely worthless pieces of marble. Clarac, admittedly, thought the inscription important; but it obstructed his theory that the Venus was the work of Praxiteles. All this tended to expose the fragments to destruction; their loss will be a perpetual stigma on the Louvre authorities, since the worst mutilation of the Venus actually took place within the walls of this sanctuary of the arts!

Forty-three years ago in these precincts, your distinguished permanent secretary, Quatremère de Quincy, came to pay a brilliant tribute to the adorable Venus de Milo; his wise and graceful speech moved his audience profoundly, for then as now the Venus was the topic of conversation in every salon, the preoccupation of every artist. Her dreadful mutilation stirred the imagination of antiquarians; men asked what, before the sacrilege, was the pose of this proud goddess. Every man had his own murmured suggestion. And who better than the author of *Jupiter Olympien* could claim to throw light on so knotty a problem? Quatremère explained with his customary lucid scholarship that the noble figure once represented Venus in victory, grouped with or talking to Paris or Mars, that she was the creation of Praxiteles or his school. But even the great authority of Quatremère failed to convince the world; Clarac opposed the idea of a group propounded by Quatremère; he believed the statue stood alone, but related to other figures which could have been Paris and the two goddesses, to whom in proud disdain, she showed the apple, prize of her victory. The conviction of Clarac was short-lived. The scholar Millingen discovered a Corinthian medallion struck under S. Severus: on it, a half-draped female figure holds a shield in her hands, in which she appears to be admiring her reflection. Using this as a guide, Millingen restored the Venus of Capua, which is so like our famous statue; but he forgot that the base of the Capua statue once bore the two little feet of Cupid: all the same, poor Clarac was seduced by Millingen – the Venus de Milo must also have been admiring her reflection in a shield; farewell apple, farewell his pride, farewell the disdain of the victorious goddess! Emeric David affirmed that the Venus had never formed part of a group, seeing in her a true statue: 'She does not represent Venus, but rather the nymph Melos, that is to say, the personification of the island of Melos.' M. Paillot de Montabert says she is more likely a Muse. Might she not rather be the courtesan and musician, Glycera of Argos, a statue executed by that Herodotus of Olynthus who worked with Praxiteles on the statue of Phryne? Could we not naturally imagine the lyre which she held in her left hand, while the right prepared to play? Who will dare to answer these questions? M. de Montabert says only that our precious Venus 'is no more than a copy which Herodotus of Olynthus would have disowned'. Finally, other scholars of Montabert's calibre suppose the Venus in the act of drawing a bow, dressing her hair, watching her reflection in a mirror, and as a Muse writing history on a great tablet which would automatically conceal her magnificent bust. In conclusion, our distinguished national historian, M. Thiers, believes the Venus to be a Victory blowing a trumpet; he has even shown me the point where the trumpet was attached to her knee; thus even this great connoisseur of the arts commits his little peccadillo . . . (Here the manuscript breaks off)

Revue Archéologique, series IV, vol. VII, 1906

Translated from the French by V. M. Conrad

Max Hirmer

3. The Venus de Milo.

Max Hirmer

4. The Charioteer of Delphi.

The charioteer of Delphi

Tuesday 28 April 1896 must have been a red-letter day in the annals of the great excavation of Delphi. That was the day on which the team working in the ruins of the house of Kounoupis had just broken down a water conduit, crudely fashioned of baked clay, when there appeared the lower part of a bronze statue (inv. 3484), 1·28 metres in height and wearing a tunic which fell in folds 'with the regularity of Ionic column fluting'. Near by they recovered the life-size back leg of a horse, also bronze (inv. 3485). At the same time they took out of the earth an inscribed block bearing a dedication in verse (inv. 3517). A photograph taken at the actual moment of discovery shows the statue and the inscription still half-buried in soil. Two other bronze fragments completed the find: 'a shaft with reins attached' (inv. 3542) and the bent end of a yoke, also with 'reins' attached (inv. 3543).

On the evening of Friday 1 May, the exploration of the house of Kounoupis brought to light 'the upper part of the statue whose feet had been discovered on Tuesday in the same spot' (inv. 3520). Homolle, at first glance, dated it accurately: 'beginning of the fifth century'. Further bronze pieces were extracted: the right forearm (inv. 3540), with fragmentary reins still in its hand; another back leg (inv. 3538) and a horse's tail (inv. 3541).

Discoveries continued to be made in the same place for a few days longer: on Thursday 7 May, it was a horse's foreleg (inv. 3597) and the other end of the yoke (inv. 3598); finally, on Saturday 9 May, a triangular pad (inv. 3618) concluded the series of finds which might be presumed to belong to the same group.

Such were the circumstances in which the Charioteer came to light. They are related above according to the *Journal of excavations* preserved in the archives of the French School. This record, it should be stressed, contains the only reliable account. Written on the spot, day by day, by one of the members of the School who were supervising the dig, it is the sole source for valuable details. These agree with later reports by the excavators, Homolle, Bourguet and Convert. In the face of these expert testimonies, supported by the text of the *Journal*, which was contemporaneous with the discoveries, the recollections of an uneducated workman, sought many years later by a foreign scholar who ignored the authentic records, deserve no credence.

Homolle instantly realised that the find was exceptional. Two telegrams, on 9 and 11 May, alerted the *Académie des Inscriptions.* On 12 May, the Director of the School sent a letter with two photographs to Paris: he transcribed the inscription, identifying it as a dedication by Polyzalos the Deinomenid, and briefly touched on the merits of the statue. On 5 June, he presented an address before the Academy in which we find for the first time a detailed catalogue of the extant fragments of the group, a description of the Charioteer, precise notes on its execution, and an opinion as to its date ('beginning of the second quarter of the fifth century') and style. Finally, as early as the following year, he published in *Monuments et Memoires, Fondation E. Piot,* IV, 1897, pp. 169-208, pl. 15-16, an article entitled '*l'Aurige de Delphes*', which constituted the first scholarly publication on the statue. And so this work, which satisfied every requirement of scientific study of the period, offered the evidence to learned scrutiny barely a year after the discovery.

One does not know which to admire more, the exemplary diligence of the author or his accuracy of judgement. If certain portions of his account, on points of minor importance, are now discounted, all the essential part remains valid. The majority of later commentators have gone astray in just that degree in which they have diverged from Homolle. Undoubtedly modern archaeology is more pedantic than that of a few years ago. It demands minutely detailed descriptions and a great wealth of measurements and calculations. If these modern standards give rise now and then to a certain idle ostentation, yet they are in accord with a very natural feeling, which is the respect for evidence. So it has become necessary, after fifty years of commentaries and controversies, to reissue in a more detailed form the masterly publication of 1897. The work of R. Hampe, in the *Denkmäler* of Brunn-Bruckmann, work in which valuable observations figure side by side with glaring errors, made this new publication still more vital. But the eye which examines is nothing without the spirit which interprets. Homolle, at first glance, both saw accurately and judged exactly. This work could not commence without an open tribute to him. . . .

The Charioteer is an *ephebe* of athletic but slim build: the broad shoulders denote strength, but the delicate extremities, hands and feet, have distinction. The general impression of slightness is accentuated by his dress, which is the long charioteer's tunic, the white *xystis* traditionally worn for racing. It comes down almost to his ankles in long, parallel folds from the belt, which is set very high, above the stomach. This positioning of the waistline, distinctly higher than the hips, emphasises the slimness of the outline. Above the belt, the tunic 'blouses' appreciably, especially at the sides. It shapes to a pointed neckline in front and behind, and ends on the shoulders and arms in a seam which holds a mass of gathers. The combined play of this seaming and of a band which passes under the armpits forms elbow-length sleeves.

The Charioteer stands erect, but without rigidity. His bare feet, set close together, are placed squarely, turned a little outwards, toes slightly curled, giving the body adequate purchase on the unyielding floor of the chariot. By a rotation of the body's axis which becomes more and more pronounced, hips, shoulders, head and the direction of the eyes turn progressively to the right: this controlled movement animates the entire figure. The arms were extended to hold the reins, elbow slightly forward, forearm level: the shoulders are supple and rounded, braced for the motion of the chariot. The right arm, alone preserved below the sleeve, is finely modelled, its long muscles indicated with great subtlety. The long, slim fingers, their nails cut round by an engraving-tool, were closed upon a cylindrical object in addition to the reins: here we can restore the goad (κέντρον) The four reins leading to the two right-hand horses must have been held by the thumb against the stock of the goad, then passing between this and the palm of the hand before falling back vertically to waist height. Three of these reins have been recovered still in place. The left hand must have been similarly positioned, holding the four reins from the two left-hand horses of the quadriga.

The head attracts particular notice. Set on a long, powerful neck, it is modelled within a long oval, with the widest point over the temples. The ears, small and prominent, framed by curls of hair in relief, are the only breaks in this rigorous contour. The hair lies plastered on the skull in short strands, engraved rather than moulded, except on the neck and round the ears, where curls spring out. A few wandering locks sketch side-whiskers on the cheeks. A broad band crosses the forehead and confines the hair at the temples; it is summarily fastened on the neck, where the two ends are merely crossed, without a knot. This band was decorated with inlays which have partially worn away:

between two darker bands, a simple meander pattern, each winding being the frame for a Greek cross. The inlays were in copper (horizontal bands) and silver (meander and Greek cross); the lips were perhaps covered with a thin layer of copper.

The features, despite an evident stylization, are extraordinarily lifelike. The heavy, rounded chin flows without a break into the curve of the jaw. The cheeks are full, yet their delicate planes allow the structure of the cheekbones to be seen. The mouth, with its strong lips, is half open and seems to be drawing breath. The lips are outlined by a slight ridge. A little opening is visible at each corner. The rather narrow nose, with its flat, well-marked bridge, would appear pinched, if the nostrils, emphasised by an engraved line, were not dilated as if inhaling. The eyebrows, in low relief, follow the line from the nose, after a sharp change of direction at its root, then lengthen and fade out towards the temples. Finally, the eyes, long and almond-shaped, are unequally opened, the left a little less than than the right. Between the added eyelashes, cut from bronze wire, the eyeballs have retained their polychrome inlay. The white of the eye is made of white paste, the iris, of a very light chestnut, is rimmed with a black circle and itself forms a narrow border to the black round of the pupil. The harmony of these hard stones is so perfect that the combination seems a single whole: its polish picks up reflections and imparts to the expression a strange intensity. . . .

Erected to commemorate a victory at the Games, the group dedicated by Polyzalos had, above all, to be truthful, but with that higher and more sublime truth which belongs to archaic offerings. It does not represent the winning Charioteer and his chariot: rather, it is identified with the donor, he *is* in a sense the Charioteer, for all time. In addition, he is able, in the dedication, to speak in the first person, within a tradition formula which is not yet emptied of meaning: *Πολυζαλὸς μ' ἀνέθηκεν.* This vital truth of equivalence, in a testimony intended to defy the centuries, imposed the scrupulous reproduction of characteristic features, of functional details, without which the spectator would not have believed in the image. From this springs the careful fidelity both in the anatomical detail of the horses and in the execution of the harness and chariot. From this comes the feeling of presence which the statue creates to this day.

At that period, the consecration of an offering was before everything an act of piety, and the satisfaction of human vanity had as yet intruded only to a minor degree. The Charioteer is the contemporary of

Aeschylus, Pindar and Bacchylides. He belongs to a time of sincere belief; its feeling stamps him. In his slightly stiff bearing, his tinge of lofty reserve, there is something religious, an evocation of the austere nobility of a great chorale. One might say that he was listening to a hymn. He has just bound on the fillet of victory: it is a solemn moment, requiring meditation and devotion. With his skilled, masterful hand – ῥυσίδιφρον χεῖρα πλεξίπποιο φωτός (Pindar, *Isthm.* II, 21) – he has known how to hold back or unleash to good purpose the ardour of his team, and so to gain the favour of Phoebus. He stands there as a good servant both of God and of his prince. The statue is an expression of the man: full of strength and modesty, aware of his achievement, but free from all pride.

More than any other, the severe style in art was fitted to express this attitude. It suited alike the Athenian warriors of Marathon and Salamis and the aristocratic rulers of the Dorian cities, still filled with the greatness of their destiny. In the bronze statue this art finds its supreme expression. The craft of the artist here, by fire and iron, masters an intractable material and bends it to his will. The sculptor, inheriting the swift, continuous advance of generations, still counts it a point of honour to rival nature. But his overriding brain subordinates his creation to an artistic balance. Attracted by subtle indications, the eye may now and then, in the motionless form, catch the trace of a movement. So the work achieves a kind of vibrant stillness, which dazzles.

With admirable conscientiousness, as a craftsman who seeks nothing short of perfection, the sculptor has patiently toiled at his task: he might justly claim to have achieved it. No earthly sensuality is his; no exaltation of the human body as a natural collection of plastic forms. The preoccupation with realism here revealed has no roots in any appreciation of the physical beauty of the world. All is subject to the abstract concept which informs the whole figure, to its very fingertips. It is like a monument where the architect has already calculated every part. Even when it reproduces the model with scrupulous exactitude, one is aware that it has been weighed in the mind and re-ordered.

So abstract a style is hardly conceivable outside Athens. There alone developed, in the archaic period, a new idea of sculpture in which the artist studies the living form as a geometrician, resolving it into formulae, a naturalist, observing in order to understand, and a technician, seeing each difficulty as a challenge. So Attic art possesses a quality of purity, of conscious design, of clarity. This lucid and dedicated art stamps its best sculptures with a slightly cold intellectualism which marks them out almost as a signature: so, at Delphi itself, with the metopes of the Athenian Treasury. The Charioteer is of the same spirit. It is because he exists to be understood that he is examined, peered over and turned to once again. He is not for passive contemplation – the cold look of his stone and enamel eyes forbids it.

Fouilles de Delphes, vol. 4, part 5, 1890

Translated from the French by V. M. Conrad

The discovery of the Hermes of Praxiteles

ERNST CURTIUS

ERNST CURTIUS (*1814–1896*) *was born at Lubeck in Germany. He travelled extensively in Greece and achieved a high reputation as both a historian and an archaeologist, accepting in 1844 the appointment of Extraordinary Professor at the University of Berlin and of Tutor to Prince Frederick William. He is best known, however, for his work at Olympia, where in 1874 he concluded an agreement to excavate the site, which was thereafter entrusted exclusively to German archaeologists. His scholarly and painstaking excavations at Olympia, especially of the Temple of Zeus and the Heraion, brought to light many superb works of Greek sculpture and architecture, but none more deservedly famous than the marble Hermes, thought by many to be an original carving by the fourth-century sculptor Praxiteles.*

A telegram of 8 May eventually brought the most important news. It read: 'Considerable remains of the Heraion 80 metres north of the opisthodom of the temple, 63 feet wide; whereupon one of the oldest and most important buildings within the altis, the length of which Pausanias gives as 63 feet, has been discovered.'

Reports of 8 May give further information on the Temple of Hera. A doric temple with a peristyle and staircase has appeared. A few column drums with twenty grooves, as well as sections of the cella wall 2–3 metres high, still *in situ*; the capitals show ancient forms, the width of the lowest stage is 19·95 metres. How this measurement can be brought into agreement with the incomplete place in Pausanias (V, 16, 1) is still uncertain; the identity of the building has, however, been proved by the finding of a Parian marble statue which Pausanias places in the Temple of Hera. It is a youthful Hermes holding the young Dionysus on his arm, the work of Praxiteles. The statue was discovered in the cella lying on its face where it had fallen, close by the costumed Roman female figure mentioned in Report 17. The arm and the legs beneath the knees of Hermes are missing, as is the upper half of the child; on the other hand, the head of Hermes was found undamaged, and he stands casually supporting himself against a tree trunk which is covered by his discarded cloak; his raised right hand seems once to have held a bunch of grapes. The height of the figure is now 1·80 metres. The composition vividly calls to mind the group of Eirene and Pluto in Munich. A section of the costume which hangs in magnificent folds is formed out of a separate piece of marble; the surface of the whole is superbly preserved. Less important features such as hair and the back are neglected. There are traces of red paint on lips and hair. As a result of this important find everything is being done to excavate as much as possible of the Temple of Hera before the end of this season.

Archaeologische Zeitung, vol. 35, part 1, 1877

Translated from the German by C. M. Kaine

Max Hirmer

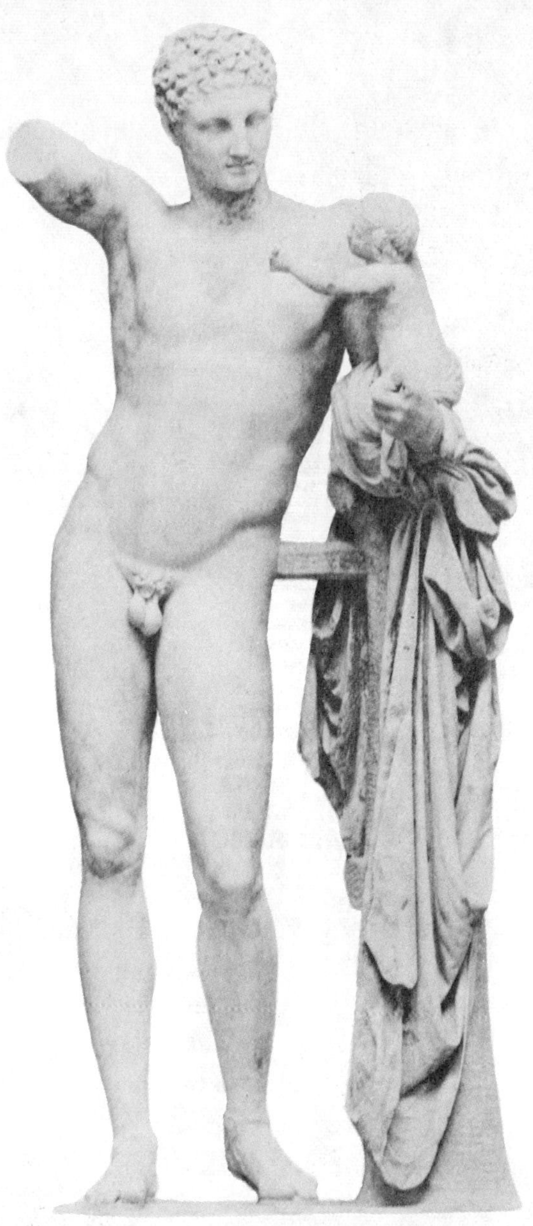

5. The Hermes of Praxiteles.

American School of Oriental Studies

6. The reconstructed Stoa of Attalus in Athens, with the Acropolis in the background. In 1953 Homer A. Thompson set to work on this most prodigious and expensive (2 million dollars) of reconstructions, faithful to the original in the smallest detail, using the original materials.

The rebuilding of the Stoa

PAUL MACKENDRICK

PAUL MACKENDRICK *is an American, and was educated at Harvard University and Balliol College, Oxford. He was formerly Professor of Classics at the University of Wisconsin, and now holds the post of Professor in charge of classical studies at the American Academy in Rome.*

The Attalids were not content to adorn only their own city. Attalus II (159–138) had been educated in Athens, and in gratitude he built on the east side of the Athenian Agora the stoa that bears his name. Attalus' brother, Eumenes II (197–159), had already set the example by building a stoa on the south slope of the Athenian Acropolis, between the theater of Dionysus and the spot where later the Odeum of Herodes Atticus was to stand. Both served practical purposes: promenade, shopping center, grandstand – the Panathenaic procession passed the Stoa of Attalus on its way to the Parthenon. The Middle Stoa, at right angles to the Stoa of Attalus, half promenade, half market, like the Stoa of Philip V at Delos (to be described later) was probably the gift of Attalus' brother-in-law and fellow-student in Athens, King Ariarthes V of Cappadocia (162–130). What the excavators call South Stoa II belongs to the same period. It served, with the Middle and East Stoas, to separate off a smaller area from the main square. But it was not a commercial agora: the excavators found no shops, booths, stalls, weights, or measures in it.

The Stoa of Attalus has been completely rebuilt, and now houses the Agora Museum, storerooms, and offices. A description of the Agora excavations as a whole is best postponed to the chapter on the Greek world under Roman sway, since the Agora reached its peak of development under Augustus, but this is the place to describe the Stoa and its reconstruction.

Its dimensions (382 feet long, 64 feet broad) and plan (two-storied double colonnade, with twenty-one shops behind on each floor) had been known since Greek excavations of 1859–1862. It was then that the discovery of epistyle fragments bearing King Attalus' name put the identification of the building beyond doubt. Much of the remains had been shielded by the so-called 'Valerian Wall' which was built right through the ruins of the building after its woodwork had been burned in the Herulian sack of AD 267. Under the north end were found several Mycenean chamber tombs, and a room in use in the fifth and fourth centuries was part of a law court, an inference from some jurors' ballots found in it. These are bronze disks with an axle through the middle, pierced for conviction, solid for acquittal. If the juror held the disk by the axle between thumb and forefinger, he could drop his ballot into the urn without anyone's knowing how he had voted. These ballots had apparently fallen by accident at the time the room was abandoned. A gutter-block that had settled out of position proved to conceal a well that yielded sixty-five five-gallon containers of sherds datable 520-480 BC, obviously from a retail potter's shop, since many of the vases were of the same type or even by the same hand. The Hellenistic shops served a variety of purposes; several have been restored for museum exhibits, with shelving modeled on the ancient, whose position was revealed by cuttings in the walls. One shop yielded surgical instruments. At the north end the oldest visible arch in the history of Greek architecture masks the end of a barrel-vault supporting the stairs.

The story of the reconstruction of the Stoa provides one of the most interesting examples in the history of archaeology of scientific inference at work. The guiding spirit was Homer A. Thompson, Director of the Agora Excavations, acutely and ingeniously assisted by John Travlos, the Agora architect. From surviving ancient blocks they knew the materials needed: blue Hymettus marble for the steps, gray Piraeus limestone for the walls, white Pentelic marble for the façade, columns, and interior trim, clay from the claypits of Attica for the roof tiles. Materials from the same places was used when the reconstruction began in 1953. The drums for the columns were delivered from the quarry roughly squared; the corners were then chamfered, and with careful hand work, by sixty marble-workers, using toothed and straight-edged chisels little changed since antiquity, the marble began slowly to assume cylindrical shape. The restorers knew from surviving capitals that the outer columns were Doric on the ground floor, double Ionic above, with a balustrade for safety closing the intercolumniations. Only the outer row of columns was fluted, since fluting depends for its effect on being struck by the sun. The inner row was Ionic on the ground floor, palmleaf above, the latter capital being one much favored by Pergamene architects. The columns of the bottom outer row, since each consisted of three drums, were best fluted *in situ*, the bottom drum being unfluted to avoid damage from foot traffic. Teams of four men worked seventy-six man-days to flute the first column, at a cost of $300. (The Erechtheum building-accounts show that in 407-406 teams of five to seven men worked 350 man-days per column, at 350 drachmas per man, but those were taller columns, fully fluted, and of harder stone.) The original floors had been a rough mosaic of marble chips (*lithostroton*); the reconstruction uses the same material, which, polished, is called *terrazzo*. The ancient beams were restored for protection against fire, in reinforced concrete, revetted with laminated wood (imported, but so must the wood have been to deforested Attica in Hellenistic times). The position and size of the beams were determined from sockets in the ancient stone work. Reinforced concrete piers were inserted in the heart of the ancient walls, but enough ancient blocks were bonded with the modern to show the evidence on which the reconstruction was based.

In September 1956, the finished Stoa was dedicated by the Patriarch of Athens and All Greece in the presence of King Paul and Queen Frederica, and 1,500 invited guests, for all of whom the building successfully discharged its original function of keeping crowds of people cool on a hot day. Again as in Attalus' time it serves as a screen between market and city. Since it sits low, it does not compete with the buildings on the Acropolis or the Hephaistaion, and, as the loving hand-work weathers, it serves better and better to allow modern visitors a unique opportunity to appreciate the scale and spatial effect of a splendid piece of Hellenistic civic architecture. And ten shops thrown together on the ground floor house the Agora Museum, whose displayed finds, from Neolithic to Turkish, span 5,000 years of Athenian history. In the lower portico, statues and inscriptions are set up near where they were found, showing to advantage in a raking light. In the basement and upper story a large bulk of material (over 68,000 inventoried items, plus over 94,000 coins, in June, 1961), unsuitable for public display, is made accessible to scholars, and a model of the Agora enables visitors (47,000 the first year, 150,000 the second, the numbers growing annually) to orient themselves from a point of vantage. Thus a phil-hellenic gesture of a Hellenistic philanthropist from the east has been repeated in our time by philanthropists from the west: the new world redressing the balance of the old.

The Greek Stones Speak, 1962

The London Mithraeum

RUPERT LEO SCOTT BRUCE-MITFORD

Rupert Leo Scott Bruce-Mitford (*1914–*) *was born in London and educated at Christ's Hospital and Hertford College, Oxford. From 1950 to 1954 he held the post of Secretary to the Society of Antiquaries, and since 1954 he has been Keeper of British and Medieval Antiquities at the British Museum.*

The last investigation to be covered by this necessarily brief survey involves a return to the centre of the city.

In topographical terms the site enclosed by the wall consists of twin hills, Cornhill on the east, the hill of St Paul's on the west. These hills are separated by a small shallow valley, that of a stream which since early times has been called Walbrook – a name now preserved by the small street linking the modern Bank area with Cannon Street.

When in 1952 news of impending building developments on the large bombed site on the west side of Walbrook Street made an examination of the area desirable, an east-to-west cutting was undertaken (in broken lengths because of modern obstructions), the purpose of which was to obtain a section across the valley. Since almost the whole site was covered with bomb-rubble to a depth of some feet, the choice of position was, in fact, restricted to a narrow lane through the débris at a point approximately midway along the length of Walbrook Street.

The excavation proved to be one of considerable difficulty because of subterranean water. Most of the trenches were permanently flooded at a depth of about 4 feet below the cellar-floors, and water was present in increasing quantity as the floors of the cuttings were lowered. In spite of this and other handicaps, however, a fairly complete picture of this part of the valley was obtained. The natural profile was established as that of a broad shallow hollow, the western lip of which lay near Sise Lane, while the eastern lip was just to the east of Walbrook Street. The stream in its original 'Roman' form flowed approximately down the middle of this hollow and was thus some distance to the west of the assumed line referred to above. The full width of the channel unfortunately was not seen, but was not more than 12–14 feet; the stream itself was shallow, with a bottom 32–35 feet below modern street level. . . .

This picture is perhaps somewhat different from that which has usually been assumed for the Roman Walbrook, which, as it approaches the Thames, now becomes a squalid brook flowing through an 'undeveloped' area of scattered wooden buildings, more permanent houses and other buildings appearing on the fringes. It was only at a comparatively late date that buildings began to appear in the hollow itself. The first of these to the north, near Bucklersbury, was represented only by a tiny fragment of wall with associated mosaic pavement, presumably (but not necessarily) part of a house the remainder of which had been completely destroyed by later activities on the site. The second was the Walbrook temple of Mithras.

The first indications of this building presented themselves at an early stage in the most easterly cutting. By good fortune they appeared immediately under the cellar floor. As the section was deepened successive floors were uncovered. The latest of these (that is, the first to be encountered), was continuous over the whole surface; at a lower level earlier floors were associated with a sleeper wall aligned with the jamb of the apse and carrying spaced-out concrete 'pads' or 'settings' for columns. On the limited view given by the cutting, therefore, it was possible to decide that the building had originally been of basilican type – that is, a columned hall with at least one apsidal end – which in course of time had been remodelled internally by the removal of the columns and by the raising and re-laying of the floor to convert it into a single compartment. . . .

The Mithraeum was made up of two parts: the rectangular temple proper, about 60 feet by 25 feet, its main axis set east-to-west; and attached to its eastern end a narthex or vestibule, which came to light only at a later stage in the investigation. The body of the building was divided longitudinally by its colonnades into nave and side-aisles. In its original form the interior reflected basic Mithraic practice: the floor of the nave, which was the setting for the ritual, was sunken; those of the aisles, on which the worshippers gathered, were raised; and the number of columns, seven on each side, symbolised the seven grades into which the devotees of the cult were divided. At the western end, the floor of the semicircular sanctuary was raised high above that of the nave; on it would have stood the chief sculpture, Mithras Tauroctonus, the god slaying the sacred bull from whose blood sprang all earthly life. The front of the apse was broken by a slightly raised central portion, probably part of an arrangement involving the use of columns or other supports for a beam to take a curtain, behind which the group would have been concealed, except at the appropriate times in the ritual. Wooden steps provided access from the nave to the sanctuary, and one or more altars would have been set up before it, as well as probably elsewhere in the body of the nave.

At the eastern end the entrance opened from the narthex: the stone door-sill, though badly worn, was well preserved, with the iron collars for the door-pivots still in place in their sockets. Here, too, wooden steps provided for access to the floor of the nave. The narthex floor, which was presumably at Roman street level, was nearly 2½ feet higher; but little is known of the narthex, most of which probably lies under the modern Walbrook: the part that remains has yet to be examined.

A feature of the exterior of the building was the massive external buttresses at the west end. The semicircular buttresses flanking the apse must have given an impression of a triple apse in their complete state: they and a large square buttress on the crest of the apse were added while the building was being erected and clearly reflect the unstable character of the site, with the Roman Walbrook only a few feet away to the west.

The temple in its original form appears to have been built towards the end of the second century AD: a more exact date must depend upon a detailed examination of the evidence now being attempted. In time, however, the building underwent extensive modification. No doubt reflecting the waterlogged condition of the surrounding area, the floor-level of the nave was gradually raised during the third century, and the earlier changes were accompanied by corresponding alterations in the level of the aisles. As an accompaniment to these changes there had been drastic remodelling of the superstructure: the colonnades were removed and finally a uniform floor converted the interior into the single chamber mentioned above.

But before this process was completed trouble, or the threat of it, had overtaken the temple and led to the burial of at any rate some of the most important sacred images. In one hole near the north-east corner of the nave had been placed the heads of Mithras and Minerva; in another near by, with a stone laver, a gigantic marble hand clasping the pommel of a dagger, a small figure of Mercury, and the head of Serapis. All the signs were that here was another instance of the conflict between

Mithraism and Christianity which led the Mithraists to bury their cult-objects and destroy their temples when in the early fourth century Christianity achieved the ascendancy. Yet the Walbrook temple itself does not appear to have suffered a fate parallel to that of the images; at least two floors sealed the pits containing the marbles, to indicate that the building went on in use; and there was no sign of destruction which could be said to be deliberate. . . .

The group of marbles as a whole is without parallel in Britain: all are of foreign workmanship. The Serapis particularly is in almost perfect condition; but Mithras, with the upturned eyes which show that it was derived from a bull-slaying, stands apart from the others in its sensitive rendering. The larger-than-life-size hand presents its own problem; if indeed it was derived from yet another sacrifice-group, the complete work must have been so large than its accommodation in the temple would have been difficult. The many questions raised by these and many other finds, must, however, be left for discussion in another place. Here it must suffice to say that the presence of these and other deities is in accordance with the all-embracing character of the Mithraic cult, which tended to assimilate to itself classical cults with similar or related attributes: such a one was the Graeco-Egyptian god of the underworld, Serapis.

And, secondly, the Walbrook Mithraeum exemplifies the second of the two main aspects of Mithraism. Mithras, god of strength and of the manly virtues, drew his followers largely from the Roman soldiery: his temples are numerous in the military areas of the Empire. But Mithras was also the god of upright dealing and as such a favourite of the merchant community. Mithraea are therefore common in the ports; and the London temple reflects the wealth and the contacts of the city's prosperous commercial class, with its comparatively rare architectural treatment and its wealth of works of art of the highest quality and refinement, contrasting with the often crude but vigorous elements in the military shrines.

Recent Archaeological Excavations in Britain, 1956

Traces of the Etruscans

GEORGE DENNIS

GEORGE DENNIS (*1814–1898*) *made his career in the diplomatic service, holding successive consular posts in Benghazi, Crete, Sicily and Smyrna. During his service in the Mediterranean area, his deep interest in archaeology led to the organization of expeditions to Cyrenaica and Asia Minor, and in 1842 and 1847 to journeys of exploration in Etruria. Largely as a result of his publication on the Etruscans, a model of detail and accuracy for its time, public interest in this civilization revived and a whole new branch of archaeological studies and researches came into being.*

In former chapters I have spoken of the ancient city of Vetulonia, and of various sites that have been assigned to it; and have shown that all of them are far from satisfactory. In the course of my wanderings through the Tuscan Maremma in the spring of 1844, I had the fortune to fall in with a site, which, in my opinion, has stronger claims to be considered that of Vetulonia than any of those to which that city has hitherto been referred.

Vague rumours had reached my ear of Etruscan antiquities having been discovered near Magliano, a village between the Osa and the Albegna, and about eight miles inland; but I imagined it was nothing beyond the excavation of tombs, so commonly made at this season throughout Etruria. I resolved, however, to visit this place on my way from Orbetello to Saturnia. For a few miles I retraced my steps towards Telamone, then, turning to the right, crossed the Albegua some miles higher up, at a ferry called Barca del Grassi; from this spot there was no carriage-road to Magliano, and my vehicle toiled the intervening five miles through tracks sodden with the rain.

Magliano is a squalid, innless village of three hundred souls, at the foot of a mediaeval castle in picturesque ruin. On making enquiries here I was referred to an engineer, Signor Tommaso Pasquinelli, then forming a road from Magliano to the Saline at the mouth of the Albegna. I found this gentleman at a convent in the village, amid a circle of venerable monks, whose beards far outshone the refectory table-cloth in whiteness. I was delighted to learn that it was he who had made the rumoured discovery in this neighbourhood, and that it was not of tombs merely, but of a city of great size. The mode in which this was brought to light was singular enough. Nothing was visible above ground – not a fragment of ruin to indicate prior habitation; so that it was only by extraordinary means he was made aware that here a city had stood. The ground through which his road had to run being for the most part low and swampy, and the higher land being a soft friable tufo, he was at a loss for the materials he wanted, till he chanced to uncover some large blocks, buried beneath the surface, which he recognised as the foundations of an ancient wall. These he found to continue in an unbroken line, which he followed out, breaking up the blocks as he unearthed them, till he had traced out the periphery of a city.

With the genuine politeness of Tuscany, that 'rare land of courtesy', as Coleridge terms it, he proposed at once to accompany me to the site. It was the first opportunity he had had of doing the honours of his city, for though the discovery had been made in May 1842, and he had communicated the fact to his friends, the intelligence had not spread, save in vague distorted rumours, and no antiquary had visited the spot. News always travels on foot in Italy, and generally falls dead lame on the road. I had heard from the antiquaries of Florence that something, no one knew what, had been found hereabouts. One thought it was tombs; another had heard it was gold *roba*; another was in utter ignorance of this site, but had heard of a city having been discovered on Monte Catini, to the west of Volterra.

The city lay between Magliano and the sea, about six and a quarter miles from the shore, on a low table-land, just where the ground begins to rise above the marshy plains of the coast. In length, according to Signor Pasquinelli, it was somewhat less than a mile and a half, and scarcely a mile in breadth; but taking into account its quadrilateral form, it must have had a circuit of at least four miles and a half. On the south-east it was bounded by the streamlet Patrignone, whose banks rise in cliffs of no great height; but on every other side the table-land sinks in a gentle slope to the plain. At the south-western extremity, near a house called La Doganella, the only habitation on the site, was found a smaller and inner circuit of wall; and this, being also the highest part of the table-land, was thus marked out as the site of the Arx.

Though scarcely a vestige remained of the walls, and no ruins rose above the surface, I had not much difficulty in recognising the site as Etruscan. The soil was thickly strewn with broken pottery, that infallible and ineffaceable indicator of bygone habitation; and here it was of that character found on purely Etruscan sites, without any admixture of marbles, or fragments of verd-antique, porphyry, and other valuable stones, which mark the former seats of Roman luxury. Though the walls, or rather their foundations, had been almost entirely destroyed since the first discovery, a few blocks remained yet entire, and established the Etruscan character of the city. From these little or nothing could be ascertained as to the style of masonry; but the blocks themselves were indicative of an Etruscan origin – some being of *macigno*, resembling those of Populonia in their size and rude shaping; others of tufo, or of the soft local rock, like that of Corneto, agreeing in size and form with the usual blocks of this material found on Etruscan sites. Some of the former had been found nine or ten feet in length. But the blocks were not generally of large dimensions, though always without cement. On the spot, where a portion of the walls had been uncovered, at the verge of a hollow, a sewer opening in them was disclosed.

Within the walls a road or street had been traced by the foundations of the houses on either hand. Many things had been dug up, but no statues, or marble columns, as on Roman sites – chiefly articles of bronze or pottery. I myself saw a piece of bronze drawn from the soil, many feet below the surface, which proved to be a packing-needle, ten inches in length, with eye and point uninjured! It must have served some worthy Etruscan, either in preparing for his travels, perhaps to the Fanum Voltumnae, the parliament of Lucumones, perhaps for the *grand tour*, such as Herodotus made, which is pretty nearly the *grand tour* still; or, it may be, in shipping his goods to foreign lands from the neighbouring port of Telamon. This venerable needle is now in my possession.

While it is to be lamented that to future travellers scarcely a trace of this city will be visible, it must be remembered, that but for the peculiar exigencies of the engineer, which led to the destruction of its walls, we should have remained in ignorance of its existence. Other accidents might have led to the uncovering of a portion of the wall; but it is difficult to conceive that any other cause could have brought about the excavation of the entire circuit, and the consequent determination of the precise limits of the city. So that in spite of the wholesale macadamisation, the world is greatly indebted to the gentleman who made the discovery.

Cities and Cemeteries of Etruria, 3rd edition, vol. II, 1883

The Bull of Minos

ARTHUR EVANS

SIR ARTHUR EVANS (*1851–1941*) *was born at Nash Mills, Hertfordshire, educated at Harrow, at Brasenose College of which he became a Fellow, and at Gottingen University. After visiting the Balkans in 1875 he became deeply interested in the archaeology of the region, but his attention was diverted to Crete by a study of engraved gems known to have been found on the island. In 1899 after prolonged negotiation he bought the site of Knossos, and his excavations there revealed a brilliant and sophisticated people antedating even the recently-discovered Mycenaean civilization, to whom he gave the name of Minoans. His large private fortune and all the resources of his extensive scholarship were subsequently devoted to the examination and publication of his findings at Knossos, and to the repair and restoration of the palace. Little is known of the religious practices of the Minoans but their art frequently depicts one of its most spectacular and dangerous rituals.*

The remains of these 'Taureador Frescoes' – as they may be fittingly called – belong to several panels. Although the figures in these are three or four times larger than those of the miniature panels – 32 cm (*c.* 12¾ in) as against 10–8 cm (*c.* 4–3⅛ in) – the panels have this in common, that they were comparatively low. The height of that restored in Fig 144 is 72·8 centimetres, including the decorative framing. This height, approximating to 80 cm, corresponds with that conjecturally assigned to the 'Miniature Frescoes'. It also agrees with that already arrived at for the painted friezes of the 'House of the Frescoes'. In these cases the fresco bands seem to have run immediately under beams forming the continuation of those of the lintels and would have been superposed on low dadoes about 1 metre high. In the case of the 'Partridge Frieze' of the Caravanserai Pavilion, however, there is clear evidence that the painted band ran above the level of the lintel beams and, from the artistic point of view, was consequently somewhat 'skied'. In the present case we may suppose that the 'Taureador' panels were set above dadoes of the full height of somewhat over 2 metres, and this seems best in keeping with the decorative methods in vogue within the Palace at the time of the L.M. I restoration, though a lower position, like those of the 'House of the Frescoes', might have suited the designs better.

It is certainly difficult to place these 'Taureador Frescoes' later than the First Late Minoan Period. The delicate delineation of some and the fine enamelled surface, especially in the case of the white paint themselves, point to an age when the art of wall-painting had reached its highest level. On the other hand certain accessory details, such as the imitation *intarsia* work on variegated stones that decorates the borders, betray a certain sympathy with a style of border fashionable in the last age of the Palace (L.M. II).

The designs were originally distributed in several panels and in the case of one of these it was possible to restore the whole composition. Here, besides the male performer of the usual ruddy hue who is turning a back-somersault above the bull, are two female taureadors, distinguished not only by their white skin but by their more ornamental attire. Their loin-cloth and girdle is identical with that of the man but of more variegated hue: his is plain yellow, theirs are decorated with black stripes and bars. They wear bands round their wrists and double necklaces – one of them beaded – and, in the case of some of the figures, blue and red ribbons round their brows. But perhaps their most distinctive feature is the symmetrical arrangement of short curls over their foreheads and temples, already noticed in the case of the female 'cow-boy' of the Vapheio cup. . . . Their foot-gear consists of short gaiters or stockings and pointed mocassin-like shoes.

In the design seen in Fig 144 the girl acrobat seizes the horns of a coursing bull at full gallop, one of which seems to run under her left arm-pit. The object of her grip, clearly shown in the enlarged reproduction of this section in Fig 145, seems to be to gain a purchase for a backward somersault over the animal's back, such as is being performed by the boy. The second female performer behind stretches out both her hands as if about to catch the flying figure or at least to steady him when he comes to earth the right way up. The stationing of this figure handy for such an art raises some curious questions as to the arrangements within the arena.

Apart from this, certain features in the design have provoked the scepticism of experts acquainted with modern 'Rodeo' performances. A veteran in 'Steer-wrestling', consulted by Professor Baldwin Brown, was of opinion that anyone who had anything to do with that sport would pronounce the endeavour to seize the bull's horns as a start for a somersault as quite impossible 'for there is no chance of a human person being able to obtain a balance when the bull is charging full against him'. The bull, as he further remarked, has three times the strength of a steer, and when running 'raises his head sideways and gores anyone in front of him'.

'That a somersault was performed over the back of a charging bull seems evident and does not seem to present much difficulty, but surely if the bull were at full gallop the athlete would not alight on its back, but on the ground well behind it?'

All that can be said is that the performance as featured by the Minoan artist seems to be of a kind pronounced impossible by modern champions of the sport. The fresco design shown in Fig 144 does not, as we shall see, stand alone, and the successive acts that it seems to imply find at least partial confirmation in a clay seal-impression and in the bronze group, where the acrobatic feat is illustrated by the diagrammatic figure. . . .

These highly sensational episodes are primarily exhibitions of acrobatic skill. In this respect, as already noted, they differ from the parallel performances of the Minoan cow-boys, the aim of which was rather the catching of wild or half-wild animals. That girls actually took part in this more practical side of the sport, as occasionally in the 'Wild West' of America today, has been shown from a scene on a Vapheio Cup, but the elegance and ornaments of the female acrobats shown in the 'Taureador Frescoes' belong to a different sphere. The ribbons and beaded necklaces are quite out of place in rock-set glens or woodland glades. To the Palace circus they are more appropriate. The animals themselves were no doubt carefully trained. Like the bulls of the Spanish arenas they may often have been of established pedigree and reared in special herds or *ganaderias*. It is clear that in all these scenes the attention of the Minoan artist is largely centred on the animal itself, which is rendered of disproportionate size, as befitting what was to them evidently quite as much as the lion, the King of Beasts. . . .

The idea of the performance as here conceived by the modeller of this bronze group seems to have been essentially the same as that of the fresco painter who executed the original of Fig 44. This design, indeed, fits on to the whole series of gem types such as those illustrated above, and involving three separate actions – the seizure of the horns, the landing over the head, and the final somersault behind, where timely assistance is rendered by an attendant figure.

The first part of this acrobatic cycle, as thus logically conceived, has rightly been shown to transcend the power and skill of mortal man. . . .

That the painted reliefs of bull-grappling scenes such as those that remained in part at least in position above the Northern Entrance Passage at a time when the Greek settlement was already in existence may have left their impress on later traditions of the Minotaur and of the captive boys and girls is itself, as already suggested, by no means improbable. But there is no reason to go farther than this and to suppose that the acrobatic figures of either sex engaged in these dangerous feats actually represent captives, trained like the Roman gladiators to 'make sport' for the Minoan holidays. Still farther are we away from any comparison with the primitive and more ferocious custom, illustrated by the monuments of prehistoric Egypt, in which prisoners of war were exposed to wild bulls.

The youthful participants in these performances – like those of the boxing and wrestling bouts, that can hardly be separated from the same general category – have certainly no servile appearance. They are, as we have seen, elegantly tired, and, specially in the hand-to-hand contests to be described below, often of noble mien. In these champions of either sex we must rather recognise the flower of the Minoan race, executing, in many cases under a direct religious sanction, feats of bravery and skill in which the whole population took a passionate delight.

The lithe sinewy forms of those engaged in the sports of the Minoan arena, with their violent muscular action and conventionally constricted waists, were as much the theme of the contemporary artists as were the more symmetrical shapes of her *ephebi* to those of classical Greece. In both cases it was the glorification of athletic excellence, manifesting itself in feats of which the Gods themselves were witnesses. So, too, the participation of women in the Minoan bull-grappling scenes can by no means be regarded as a symptom of bondage or of a perverse tyrant's whim. It was rather, as we have seen, the natural outcome of the religious organisation in which the female ministers of the Goddess took the foremost place in her service. At Sparta, where the Minoan religious tradition seems to have had a considerable hold, girl athletes continued to take part in the public games.

The Palace of Minos, vol. III, 1930

Reconstruction work at Knossos

ARTHUR EVANS

The preservation of the 'Domestic Quarter' – greatly due to the comparative protection against earthquake shocks afforded by the cutting on three sides into the Neolithic strata of the 'Tell' – had more the aspect of a miracle than anything that excavation might reasonably have been supposed to bring to light. The 'Grand Staircase', especially – of which three flights were unearthed in their entirety and sufficient evidences of two more – now once more restored to such a condition as to fulfil its original functions after an interval of over three and a half millennia – still stands forth as a monument of constructive skill.

In the whole exploration of the Palace site the most surprising development was that which occurred on emerging south from the Corridor of the Bays that flanked the Royal Magazines where the 'Medallion Pithoi' were stored. The pavement that was followed out, resting on the Neolithic clay, seemed to represent the level above and below which it was hopeless to expect further remains in this direction. The hot season had begun and the work of excavation had in fact begun to grow rather weary when, on opening out here a blocked doorway, a landing came to light, beyond which further clearance showed an ascending and descending flight of gypsum steps – afterwards discovered to belong to the second and third flight of a magnificent stone staircase. . . .

Something has been already said of the peculiar difficulties and even dangers encountered in making our way down the lower flights and through the corridors and halls of the ground floor beyond. It was certainly a fortunate circumstance that amongst the workmen then employed were two from the Laurion Mines, and under their guidance we were able, with the constant use of mine props, to tunnel down the lower flights and along the vaults beyond. It was then realised that though the massive wooden framework that played so great a part in the structural features of the last Middle Minoan period, including substantial posts and cross-beams as well as the wooden columns and capitals, was reduced to a carbonised condition – more by chemical action than by fire – the fabric for the most part was still held in position, in places even as far as the level of the second story.

This was the result of the intrusion into the spaces below of fallen materials, mostly, no doubt, sun-dried bricks from the uppermost stories of this part of the building. But the full explanation of the phenomena was not supplied till later, when the 'Caravanserai' on the opposite side of the gorge to the south of the Palace was excavated. It was there found that the springs on that side, which were largely impregnated with gypsum, combining with the native clay and in this case too with crude bricks fallen from above had formed a concretion as hard as cement and which could only be penetrated with sharp steel picks at the cost of considerable time and labour. It is clear that the same result as that naturally produced by the springs from the Gypsàdes hill beyond acting on the clay materials had, in the case of the covered spaces of the lower floors and flights of stairs, been owing to the dissolved effect of rain-water on the debris of the gypsum blocks, pavements, and dado slabs of the uppermost stories. The deleterious effect of rain on the gypsum elements of the Palace is rapid in its action and the progress of disintegration had made itself very perceptible in exposed parts of the building since the first days of the Excavations. The extent to which the gypsum is liable to be thus dissolved depends, it is true, on the individual consistency of the stone. Some of the earlier Palace slabs are of specially fine quality, with waving translucent veins and laminations pale brown and amber tinted, and such seem to have still an almost unlimited power of resisting the elements. But exposed surfaces as a rule are gradually reduced to a rough mass of crystals, and in some cases one is almost tempted to compare the effect of a drop of water on a lump of loaf sugar.

One inevitable conclusion from this disintegrating process was that in order to save any part of such remains it was necessary that they should be covered over. But the excavation of the staircase and the halls it served brought with it still more urgent needs. The hewing away of the clay concretions and the extraction of the various rubble and earthy materials in the intervening spaces left a void between the upper and lower spaces that threatened the collapse of the whole. The carbonised posts and beams and shafts, although their form and measurements could be often observed, splintered up when exposed and of course, could afford no support. The recourse to mine props and miscellaneous timbering to hold up the superincumbent mass was at most temporary and at times so insufficient that some dangerous falls occurred.

New Era in Reconstitution due to Use of Ferro-concrete

To relax our efforts meant that the remains of the upper stories would have crashed down on those below, and the result would have been an indistinguishable heap of ruins. The only alternative was to endeavour to re-support the upper structures in some permanent manner. In the early days of the Excavation the Architect, Mr Christian Doll, who manfully grappled with this Atlantean task, had perforce largely to rely on iron girders brought from England at great expense, and these were partly masked with cement. The shafts of the columns were replaced by stone blocks concealed by a stucco coating and the capitals were actually cut out. Even then wood, which it was hard to obtain properly seasoned, was allowed to play a part in these reconstructions. The cypress trunks and beams that had supported solid masses of masonry in the old work were of course no longer obtainable so we had to learn that even the pinewood of Tyrol, imported through Trieste, which in the chalets of its own country might have resisted the elements for generations – could be reduced to rottenness and powder in a few years by the violent extremes of the Cretan climate.

But with the increasing use of ferro-concrete – the material of which was reinforced by thick iron wires – for constructive work of all kinds, a new era of reconstitution and conservation opened on the Palace site. It has already been shown how in the west wing of the building the new method made it possible much more efficaciously and cheaply to replace upper floors with the old elements at the same time set on their proper level, while columns, capitals, and other features, even those involving elaborate details, had no longer to be hewn and carved from the actual stone, but could be 'cast' wholesale in wooden moulds, which the native carpenters were skilful in turning out. The carbonised beams and posts were at the same time restored by the same methods in the new cement material, while, by flooding it over a temporary boarding, supported by posts below, it was possible to lay out considerable areas of the pavement and at the same time permanently to protect from the weather the gypsum slabs and blocks and other perishable features of the basement rooms and magazines. The whole framework of the building on this side was so well compacted together by this new material that it successfully resisted the severe earthquake of 26 June 1926.

The Palace of Minos, vol. III, 1930

Ventris deciphers the Cretan script

WILLIAM TAYLOUR

MICHAEL GEORGE FRANCIS VENTRIS *(1922–1956) was born at Wheathampstead and became an architect by profession. From his earliest years he had been deeply interested in languages and in problems of decipherment, and during the war became expert at breaking codes. The method used by the military was largely based on statistical analysis, and it occurred to Ventris that this method could equally effectively be applied to the Linear B tablets, where the problems of translating an unknown language written in an unknown script had hitherto proved insuperable. Finding that he needed the assistance of an expert philologist, he approached Professor J. Chadwick, who was so impressed that he agreed readily to co-operate. When their results were published they were so conclusive that very little opposition was possible, but Ventris did not live to see this triumph of his method, for he was killed in a traffic accident at the age of thirty-four.*

Civilisation by definition in ancient history means a literate society. Indeed the very complexity of civilised society requires a discipline of records to function at all. The Mycenaean civilisation was no exception to this rule, though earlier excavations had provided little evidence of the fact. Some knowledge of writing was inferred from curious signs painted on a certain number of Mycenaean stirrup-jars found at Mycenae, Tiryns, Orchomenos, and Thebes; but not until the excavations, begun at Pylos in 1939, produced hundreds of clay tablets inscribed with a similar script was it realised that the knowledge of writing may have been general and widespread in Mycenaean Greece. These clay tablets were not unique. They had already been found in Crete at Knossos as early as 1900 by Sir Arthur Evans, who from the first recognised their importance. Knossos has produced the largest number of such records, between 3,000 and 4,000, though many of them are fragmentary; but they have also been found elsewhere in that island in the palaces of Phaistos, Hagia Triada, and Mallia. Pylos has the next largest number, just over 1,200, and each year's excavation on that site produces its annual increment. Mycenae so far has accounted for little more than seventy; and the greater number of these come from houses outside the Citadel.

It seems indeed strange that the dynamic centre and inspiration of the civilisation, which we call Mycenaean, should have produced so small a number. The explanation seems to be twofold: the perishability of the substance and perhaps the inability of the earlier excavators to recognise these rather undistinguished lumps of clay for what they were. The latter explanation is a fairly common one given by modern archaeologists, but I do not think that all tablets could have escaped the keen eye of Schliemann who prided himself upon the care with which he collected and preserved what, even to him, were the most insignificant objects. It is true that tablets are not easy to recognise. The so-called Linear B tablets – the only kind found in the Greek mainland – are oblong pieces of clay about three inches in length. Some are much larger and almost square; others are long, narrow, and tapering, like a palm-leaf. In the dust and dirt of excavation tablets could be taken for fragments of coarse pottery, except that one surface to the discerning eye would display incised markings. But unlike pottery they are not baked in a kiln, which would have rendered them indestructible. They were shaped out of ordinary clay, inscribed with a record when the clay was still soft, and then put out in the sun to dry. So long as they were stored in a dry place they were likely to survive, but once subjected to the effects of water they quickly dissolved into a shapeless mass. (This unfortunate fate befell some tablets stored by Sir Arthur Evans in a shed with a leaking roof!) It is largely due to the violent destruction of a site that tablets have survived at all. The fierce fires burnt them to the hardness of pottery; even so, some of them are rather friable.

At Pylos the majority of tablets were concentrated in one area and in the course of excavation it became clear that these represented the palace archives. They were stored near the entrance to the palace in a small room with low benches that supported free-standing shelving, or so it could be inferred from careful observation of the burnt debris filling the room. It could also be deduced that the tablets were kept in wicker baskets, as an impression of the wickerwork was preserved on several pieces of burnt clay found adhering to 'labelling' tablets, that is, tablets stating in an abbreviated form the subject of the contents. Another type of storage seems to have been wooden boxes. Within the Citadel of Mycenae no archives have been found. A few tablets, eight in all, were recovered in 1960 in further excavations of Mycenaean houses within the Citadel and near the Grave Circle, but they were very fragmentary. The circumstances of their findings suggest that they were but a remnant of a large hoard which was all but annihilated by the devastating fire that destroyed the buildings in which they were housed. The surviving tablets were found embedded in conglomerate masses of molten stone, brick, and clay fused to the consistency and hardness of concrete. Spattered about in this rock-like, calcined debris were specks and fragments of a reddish brown substance, which could have been potsherds or bits of disintegrated tablets. If the latter, it would seem that the tablets in this case were stored in stone cupboards or containers. The very evident marks of the fire that destroyed the palace on the crown of the Citadel show that here too the conflagration was of equal intensity and violence to the one farther down the slope of the hill. In this manner any archives that may have existed within the palace would have been obliterated or have left so little trace as to have eluded the vigilance of the excavators.

These records in clay from Greece and Crete, and a few from Cyprus, are practically the only written documents that have survived from the Aegean world of the second millennium. It may well be that other media for writing were used, substances such as wood, leather, parchment, palm leaves, or papyrus, none of which would survive under normal conditions. The conversion of the papyrus plant into a very adequate writing material was a specialised industry of Egypt and there is plenty of evidence of trade relations between the Aegean and that country. Writing in clay was the system adopted in Babylonia and neighbouring kingdoms – there the tablets were oven-baked – and an implement with a wedge-shaped end was used to reproduce the cuneiform script (*cuneus*=a wedge). But the Aegean scribe preferred a stylus or pointed tool and it may be that the more important documents were written on other materials more adapted to such an instrument. The tablets, on the other hand, which could be cheaply and easily produced on the spot, would serve for day-to-day business records, and that is in fact what they are.

How do we know this? So much was deduced by Sir Arthur Evans from pictorial signs on the Knossos tablets recognisable as horses, chariots, weapons, etc., but it was not until recent times, 1952 to be exact, that the many attempts at deciphering the script met with success. This was largely due to the genius, brilliance, and application of a young architect, Michael Ventris, assisted at a critical stage of his work by the Cambridge philologist, John Chadwick. To understand this colossal achievement one must appreciate that Ventris was attempting a far more difficult task than the problem that faced Champollion in solving the riddle of Egyptian hieroglyphics or Grotefend and Rawlinson in the decipherment of cuneiform. These early pioneers had bilingual or trilingual texts to help them and at least they knew the linguistic group to which the language belonged. Ancient Egyptian, though much modified, lived on in the Coptic tongue; Assyrian and Babylonian were related, it became clear, to ancient Hebrew and Semitic languages in general. But Ventris was faced with one script alone and without a clue as to what language it might stand for.

Many of course had preceded Ventris in the unrewarding quest. Sir Arthur Evans himself was a pioneer and laid the foundations for future research. He was able to demonstrate the different stages in the development of the script. First, the hieroglyphic signs that are mainly found on Cretan gems and seal-stones belonging to the first half of the second millennium; a few tablets with hieroglyphs are also known. Secondly, a cursive and simplified version of these signs, which Sir Arthur termed Linear A; this was inscribed on tablets (said to be oven-baked), vases, stone, and on bronze. Finally, a later and more advanced script, closely related to Linear A, which he called Linear B. No exact dates can be given for the periods in which these scripts were in vogue, but it can be said that Linear A overlaps the hieroglyphic script and may have started as early as the eighteenth century. It seems to have gone out of use in the early part of the fifteenth century. Linear B, which is almost exclusively recorded on tablets, begins before or just after 1400 BC. The latest tablets can be dated to around 1200 BC. Linear B is the only form of the script known on the Greek mainland.

In his study of the material, Evans had established certain basic points: that the tablets were lists or accounts, that a numerical system was clearly recognisable, that some of the signs were ideograms (pictures of the objects designated), and that the other signs were most likely syllabic. This list he assumed because he had noted that groups of signs were separated from other groups by vertical strokes; hence each group probably represented a word of so many syllables. Beyond these general conclusions Evans was not prepared to commit himself. Many of his less cautious and immediate followers – and distinguished scholars among them – were to rely too much on guess-work, choosing a language that might be shown to have some affinity with the script and trying to make the two fit. Method was lacking in nearly all these schemes. Without a detailed analysis of the inscriptions there was little chance of success. One of the few who adopted a methodical approach was the American, Dr Alice E. Kober. She was able to demonstrate by her analysis of the Linear B signs that it was an inflected language, that is, one in which words have varying suffixes added to denote gender, plural, etc. (as in Latin). For instance, she noted that the totalling formula for men and a certain class of animals differed from that used for women and another class of animals and this suggested a distinction in gender. But her greatest contribution to the decipherment was her demonstration that certain words made up of two, three or more syllabic signs could have two variants by adding a different sign or by changing their terminal sign into another sign. (An example in English would be: wo-man; woman's; wo-men). Such variations are referred to in linguistic circles as 'Kober's triplets'! Professor Emmett L. Bennett, Jr was also one of the few to use a methodical approach. Apart from elucidating the system of weights and measures used in the script, his most important contribution was the ordering and classification of the whole Linear B signary. The division of the signs into two classes, ideographic and syllabic, was clarified and from a detailed study of variants in the orthography (bad handwriting is nothing new) he was able to narrow down the number of syllabic signs to just short of ninety.

There was one valuable, but deceptive, clue to attacking the problem of decipherment. A related script is found in Cyprus and is referred to as Cypro-Minoan. Only a few tablets have been found there, of which the oldest is said to date from the early fifteenth century and has affinities with Linear A. Two features about these tablets call for special comment. A blunted stylus was used and the tablets were baked in fire. The technique is therefore different from the tablets we have been discussing and is more closely linked to that of the civilisations to the East. This is not surprising in view of the geographical position of Cyprus. Yet another script, the Classical Cypriot script, was in use on the island from the sixth to the third or second century BC and is obviously related to Linear B. In most, if not all, cases Greek was written in it; hence decipherment was possible. Seven of the signs are similar to or can be equated with Linear B and the phonetic values of the Cypriot Syllabary are known. The signs represent either a vowel or a consonant plus vowel. As this is a syllabic and not an alphabetic script, difficulties occur in words where two or more consonants follow one another or where a word ends in a consonant. Using this syllabic script, '*pastor*' would be spelt *pa-so-to-re*.

The final vowel of *-re* would not be pronounced, neither would the *o* of *-so*; such would be regarded as 'dead' vowels. But the choice of the syllabic sign *-so* (from the five syllabic signs beginning with *s*: *-sa*, *-se*, *-si*, *-so*, *-su*) is governed by, and must conform to, the vowel of the syllabic sign following, in this case, the *o* of *-to*. So for '*prison*' the spelling could be *pi-ri-so-ne* (the final 'dead' vowel is always *e*). Yet a further complication in the Cypriot Syllabary is that *n* before a consonant is not written. Thus '*contralto*' would appear as *co-ta-ra-lo-to*. It must be clear from these examples that the Syllabary would be a very clumsy method of writing English. It is even more so for Greek. The word *anthropos* 'man' has to be written *a-to-ro-po-se*. Now a very large number of Greek words end in *s* and, as the Cypriot syllabic sign *-se* is identical with one of the Linear B signs, it could easily be demonstrated whether Linear B was a likely candidate for Greek or not. It was found that the *-se* sign very rarely occurred as a terminal sign in the Linear B script. The natural conclusion therefore was that the language was not Greek.

The preliminary, basic, and essential work carried out by Kober and Bennett was invaluable to Ventris who now brought an added dimension to tackle the problem of decipherment, a knowledge of cryptography. In theory any code can be broken provided there is enough coded material to work on. A detailed analysis of the material should reveal certain recurring features and underlying patterns. We have already commented on those that had been noted by Dr Kober. Ventris was able to add to the number of pregnant observations. On the basis of the material available, considerably augmented by the publication in 1951 of Bennett's transcription of the tablets found at Pylos in 1939, he prepared statistical tables showing the over-all frequency of each sign. He was able to deduce – and here he had the collaboration of Bennett and the Greek scholar Ktistopoulos – that three of these signs were probably vowels from the fact that they occurred predominantly at the beginning of sign groups. A suffix was provisionally identified as the conjunction 'and', used like *-que* in Latin. Other inflexional variations of words identifiable as nouns were noted and, as some of these occurred with the ideogram of man and woman, it could be seen that in such cases the inflexion was often one of gender rather than case.

The relative accumulated data were arranged by him in tabular form, in what he called the 'grid'. The grid was constantly being revised and rearranged. In one of its latest forms it consisted in the main of fifteen rows of consonants and five columns of vowels; as none of the values of the consonants or vowels was known, these were simply given numbers. Within these seventy-five spaces were arranged the most frequently recurring Linear B syllabic signs (fifty-one out of a possible total of ninety) on the basis of statistical data that had been assembled about them. If the system was sound and the data correctly diagnosed, signs in the same column should share the same vowel and signs in the same row should start with the same consonant. Therefore, if the phonetic values of but a few syllabic signs could be established, the values of the others would automatically follow from the grid.

We have already mentioned that seven of the signs from the Cypriot syllabary can be equated with Linear B signs; it was permissible therefore to experiment with the Cypriot phonetic value of these signs. This Ventris did. Furthermore, he had concluded from the constantly recurring position of certain groups of signs in the tablets that these sign-groups represented the names of places. Working on these two suppositions he made tests with ancient place-names. For the Knossos tablets the choice was naturally made from Cretan names that were known in Classical times or mentioned by Homer – Knossos itself, Amnisos (a harbour town near by), and Tulissos; and they could be recognised in the following syllabic spellings: *ko-no-so*, *a-mi-ni-so*, *tu-ri-so*. These identifications were certainly valid on the Cypriot spelling convention, double consonants (*km*, *mn*) being split into syllables. The *ri* instead of *li* in *tu-ri-so* (Tulissos) was not a difficulty. Ventris had already recognised that *r* and *l* were interchangeable, as they are in several languages, including Ancient Egyptian. One marked difference from the Cypriot is that the final *s* is not written. Similarly *l*, *m*, *n*, *r*, *s* are omitted at the end of a word or when preceding another consonant, and there are other spelling rules imposed by the decipherment that do not correspond with the Cypriot conventions.

If the results of these tests were promising, they still did not provide any clue as to the language concealed in the script. Ventris's own opinion was that the language was Etruscan and to the very last he tried conclusions in that direction. It was only as 'a frivolous digression' (his own words) that in the final stages of the decipherment he experimented with Greek. To his surprise, with Greek many of the tablets made sense. Admittedly as many more remained incomprehensible, but if the language was indeed Greek, it would of necessity be a very archaic form of the tongue that was recorded in the Linear B script a full 500 years before Homer – and Homer's Greek is itself archaic. If the language was Greek, one would expect to find many of these Homeric archaisms foreshadowed in the Linear B texts and the fact that this was so contributed very largely to the favourable reception accorded by the majority of scholars to Ventris's revolutionary pronouncement. One has only to recall the contention and controversy that arose over the success claimed for the decipherment of cuneiform and Egyptian hieroglyphics to marvel at the comparative acquiescence and applause with which this far more spectacular and controversial achievement was received. Oppostion to the claim there naturally was, but before it could become articulate a remarkable and dramatic piece of new evidence supervened.

About the same time that Ventris was reaching his solution of the Linear B problem, a tablet was being unearthed at Pylos that went far to confirm the correctness of his system. It was one of about 400 that were discovered during the 1952 excavations. Early in the following year they were being cleaned and studied in Athens by Professor Blegen, their finder. He tried out Ventris's syllabary on several of them, and on this one with striking results. It was a tablet with an inventory of tripods and various kinds of vases, some with four handles, some with three, and one with none; the different ideogram used in every case made this clear. But each ideogram was preceded by a description and, although the meaning of every word in the description was not self-evident, some could be given the following phonetic values – and no other – according to the Ventris syllabary: *ti-ri-po*, *qe-to-ro-we*, *ti-ri-o-we*. The *ti-ri-po* word only appears with the tripod sign. Following the spelling convention previously demonstrated, it is clearly the Greek word *tripos*, a tripod. O-we, which occurs in the three other words given above, means 'eared'; the word 'ear' is regularly used in Greek for the handle of a pot. It is found above in combination with *quetro* (Greek *tetra*, Latin *quattuor*), *tri* (as in *tripos*), and *an*, the Greek negative prefix, i.e. no handles. That the above-given words should only occur with the ideograms to which they refer was beyond the possibility of coincidence. The basic soundness of the decipherment of Linear B as an archaic form of Greek was thereby established and the publication of this tablet in 1953 served to convince many who up till then were only partly converted. But it did not convince all and to this day there is a small minority of scholars who will not accept the decipherment. Nevertheless, their most distinguished protagonist, Professor Beattie, fully appreciates the awkward implications of the tripod tablet and that it must in some manner be explained away. He has therefore been driven to the desperate expedient of suggesting that

Ventris had foreknowledge of this tablet before he arrived at his final solution. Such a suggestion is not only unworthy but completely without foundation.

How is one to explain the opposition, however diminished, to the idea of Linear B being Greek? The objections concern admitted difficulties in translation. Many words still do not make sense and, on account of the great variety of possible alternative readings in certain cases, one cannot always be sure of the Greek form of these doubtful words. . . . It is argued that no scribe could make himself intelligible to another with such an elastic script. For instance, the sign for *ka* may represent as many as seventy different syllables: *ka*, *ga*, *kha*, *kai*, *kas*, *kan*, etc. This is so, but it is not true of all the syllabic signs; and signs are not read in isolation but in combination as words. Certain combinations occur again and again. A pictogram is often there to supplement a hesitant memory. But there are many cases in our own language where we have a choice between variant readings. A word like 'invalid' is capable of two meanings and two different pronunciations. . . . Like the Mycenaean scribe we may hesitate for a moment before making a choice; it is familiarity and the context that ultimately decide.

If it is generally accepted today – at least by the greater number of distinguished Greek scholars – that the language of Linear B is Greek, it has to be admitted that the written material so far available is limited in quantity and quality. What is the quality thereof? Inventories for the most part and catalogues: inventories of stores, livestock, and agricultural produce; catalogues of men, women, and children. And of the latter category a great part of the text is taken up with proper names and the occupations of the individuals concerned. At least 65 per cent of the sign groups are proper names. . . . About 200 or so are almost certainly place-names, although quite a number of these cannot be identified geographically. Some 3,500 tablets have been studied and these have yielded a total vocabulary of 630 words, of which about 40 per cent can be read with a fair degree of certainty. The number of texts that contain sentences of any length is limited and consequently our knowledge of grammar and syntax is equally so. These are the 'chariot', 'land tenure', and 'furniture' tablets. It is necessary to emphasise these limitations in order to retain a due sense of proportion. The decipherment of Linear B has enlarged our view of Mycenaean civilisation considerably but we cannot always be certain how much of the picture is in focus.

The Mycenaeans, 1964

Part Three

THE BOOK OF THE PYRAMIDS

The tourist and the monuments

AUGUSTE MARIETTE

AUGUSTE FERDINAND FRANCOIS MARIETTE (*1821–1881*) *was born at Boulogne. He first went to Egypt in 1850 entrusted with a mission to seek out and buy for the national collection any suitable manuscripts in the Coptic, Syriac, Arabic, and Ethiopic languages, but he shortly abandoned this intention in favour of active exploration and excavation of the ancient monuments. After discovering the Serapeum where the sacred bulls of Apis were buried, he spent the next four years digging and despatching his finds to the Louvre, of which he was appointed assistant curator on his return. In 1858 he was made conservator of Egyptian monuments, and moved with his family to Cairo. Among the many sites he explored in detail were Memphis and the Saqqara pyramids, Meydum, Abydos and the Thebes necropolis, Karnak, Medinet Habu and Deir el-Bahari, and the temple which had long been hidden by drifts of sand between the paws of the Sphinx. His immeasurable contributions to archaeology were honoured by the Egyptians with the successive titles of Bey and Pasha.*

There is no need to enlarge upon the importance of the monuments that cover the banks of the Nile. They are the witnesses of Egypt's former greatness, and, so to speak, the patents of her ancient nobility. They represent in the eyes of strangers the tattered pages of the archives of one of the most glorious nations in the world.

But the higher the esteem in which we hold Egypt's monuments, the more it behoves us to preserve them with care. On their preservation partly depends the progress of those interesting studies which have for their object the history of ancient Egypt. Moreover, they are worthy of being preserved, not only for the sake of all such among us as appreciate them, but also for the sake of future Egyptologists. Five hundred years hence Egypt should still be able to show to the scholars who shall visit her the same monuments that we are now describing. The amount of information already obtained from the deciphering of hieroglyphs, though this science is still in its infancy, is already immense. What will it be when several generations of savants shall have studied those admirable ruins, of which one may truly say that the more they are known, the more they repay the labour bestowed upon them?

We therefore earnestly beg again and again all travellers in Upper Egypt to abstain from the childish practice of writing their names on the monuments. Let anyone, for instance, visit Tih's tomb, at Saḳḳá-rah, and he will rest satisfied that this tomb has actually suffered more damage by the hand of tourists during the last ten years than it had during the whole of the previous six thousand years of its existence. Sethi I's beautiful tomb at Bab-el-Molouk is almost entirely disfigured, and it is all we can do to prevent the evil from increasing. M. Ampère, who visited Egypt in 1844 has, perhaps, overstepped the mark in the following lines extracted from his journal; yet we will transcribe them to show to what opprobrium those travellers expose themselves who thoughtlessly engrave their names on the monuments: 'The first thing that strikes one on approaching the monument (Pompey's Pillar) is the number of names traced in gigantic characters by travellers, who have thus impertinently engraved a record of their obscurity on the time-honoured column. Nothing can be more silly than this mania, borrowed from the Greeks, which disfigures the monuments when it does not altogether destroy them. In many places, hours of patient toil have been expended in carving on the granite the large letters which dishonour it. How can anyone give himself so much trouble to let the world know that an individual, perfectly unknown, has visited a monument, and that this unknown individual has mutilated it?' We recommend the perusal of the above lines to the young American traveller who, in 1870, visited all the ruins in Upper Egypt with a pot of *tar* in one hand and a brush in the other, leaving on all the temples the indelible and truly disgraceful record of his passage.

We have no advice to give to those travellers who wish to purchase antiquities and to take them home as souvenirs of their visit to Egypt. They will find more than one excellent factory at Luxor.

But to travellers who wish really to turn their journey to some account, we would recommend the search after papyri. In fact, there is nothing in the way of monuments more precious than a papyrus. One knows fairly well what may be expected from a temple or from a tomb; but with the papyrus one is in the dark. In fact, such a papyrus might be discovered as would prove of more importance than an entire temple; and certain it is that if ever one of those discoveries that bring about a revolution in science should be made in Egyptology, the world will be indebted for it to a papyrus.

As all excavations are interdicted in Egypt and no permissive firman has ever been given, one might imagine that opportunities of purchasing papyri can never present themselves. Such, however, is not the case. All travellers in Upper Egypt must have seen fellahs working in those parts of the ruins where the crude-brick walls are crumbling into powder. What they are seeking is the dust which comes from the crumbling bricks, and which they use for manure. Now and then, however, a piece of good luck awaits them, and it is not an uncommon occurrence for a papyrus to be found in this manure. Nor must it be forgotten that, in spite of all prohibitions, clandestine searches are made, particularly at Thebes, and in this way also, among many other monuments, papyri may be discovered. It is for the traveller to make inquiries and to examine into the matter, not at Thebes only, but at all the stations where the *dahabeah* stops. The fine collection of Mr Harris, at Alexandria, was formed in no other manner; and it was by mere accident that Madame d'Orbiney purchased the papyrus, now in the British Museum, which has rendered her name famous. In the present state of Egyptology, no greater service can be rendered to science than in securing any papyrus which accidentally falls into the hands of the fellahs, and which, sooner or later, must be entirely lost, if not thus preserved from destruction.

Monuments of Upper Egypt, 1877

Excavations in Egypt

JOHANN LUDWIG BURCKHARDT

JOHANN LUDWIG BURCKHARDT (*1784–1817*) *was born in Lausanne and received his education in Germany. He travelled to England with letters of introduction to the President of the Royal Society who was also the founder of the African Association. After three years' study in London and Cambridge he was instructed by the Association to go to Syria to study the Arabic language and customs in preparation for a journey of exploration to the regions south of the Sahara. This he did, and in 1812 he arrived in Cairo but, unable to find a suitable caravan for his intended destination, travelled instead up the Nile, eastward from Shendi to Suakin, thence to Mecca and Modena, through Suez and back to Cairo, arriving in 1815. He remained there for two years, and died without ever carrying out the Sahara expedition.*

You will be pleased to hear that the colossal head from Thebes has at last, after many difficulties, safely arrived at Alexandria. Mr Belzoni, who offered himself to undertake this commission, has executed it with great spirit, intelligence, and perseverance. The head is waiting now at Alexandria for a proper conveyance to Malta. Mr Salt and myself have borne the expenses jointly, and the trouble of the undertaking has devolved upon Mr Belzoni, whose name I wish to be mentioned, if ever ours shall on this occasion, because he was actuated by public spirit fully as much as ourselves. The Committee need not be under any apprehension, that this transaction has caused my name to become of public notoriety in Egypt; which would certainly have been the case, if it had been known that I have had any thing to do with it. The Kahirines ascribe it entirely to Mr Salt and Mr Belzoni, who, they say, send it to England to have it taken to pieces, in order to find the invaluable jewel which it contains. The residence of the French Savans in Egypt has not taught them to form better notions, and the same kind of belief which caused the Shikh of Tedmor to resist my carrying off a small mutilated bust, found near the portico at Palmyra, still operates in every part of Egypt.

The peasants of Gourne reported to me, that the French had in vain endeavoured to carry off this head; and that they had even cut a hole in the lower part of the bust, to blow off part of the stone, and render it thus more transportable. I am ignorant for what reason they relinquished that scheme, but it is somewhat curious to find that in the drawing which they have given of that head, in their great work, they have represented it as it would probably have been, after the lower part should have been destroyed.

The discoveries of Mr Belzoni in Upper Egypt, are too interesting not to deserve notice here. He has half cleared the temple of Ebsambal in Nubia, of the sands that obstructed it. The frontispiece of the temple, which has thus been discovered, is full of hieroglyphics; of the four colossi which stand before it, the face of one only (which I have mentioned in my journal), remains perfect; one of the three others has been reduced by mutilation to a mere lump of rock.

Behind Gourne he has discovered a new tomb of the kings, about one mile distant from the most western 'insulated tomb', as the French laid it down in their map. He says it is beautiful, and larger than any of the others, with a sarcophagus in it. All the paintings are done upon a white stucco, adhering loosely to the wall, and thus easily to be removed.

By digging at Gourne, in the plain between the Memnonium, and Medinet Habou, in a western direction from the two sitting colossi, about half a mile distant from them, he found a mutilated colossal head of granite, of much larger dimensions than the one he carried off, or any other at Thebes, being from ten to twelve feet across the front.

You remember the small pond, within the enclosure of the interior part of the temple of Karnak, towards the side of Luxor, which encircles on three sides an elevated ground. A row of Andro-sphynxes, or whatever they may be called, stand there, which the French had dug up, and of which Mr William Banks carried off last year the two best. In digging farther on in the line in which these statues stood, Mr Belzoni has discovered eighteen others, of similar shape, but of much superior workmanship, all in beautiful preservation; he has brought down six of them to Mr Salt, who had furnished him with money for the express purpose of procuring antiquities; besides the commission to carry off the head. By the side of these figures he has found another statue, of a hard, large grained sand stone: it is a whole length naked figure, sitting upon a chair, with a ram's head upon the knees; the face and body entire; with plaited hair falling down to the shoulders. This is one of the finest, I should say the finest Egyptian statue I have seen; the expression of the face is exquisite, and I believe it to be a portrait. From the beautiful preservation of all these figures, which is so rare in Egypt, Mr Belzoni argues, that the Egyptians used this place to hide their idols, when the Persians came to destroy them, and he hopes, in going up a second time to Thebes, to find at the same place other treasures. He has likewise found at Karnak, the four sided monument, with figures in high relief on three sides of it, of which the French talk so highly in their work, and of which they have given a drawing. But it was in quite a different place from that indicated by them, for Mr Belzoni found it under ground far to the east of the adytum of Karnak. This, with a dozen of Sphynxes, he has been obliged to leave on the shore of the river near Karnark, the boat being already over loaded. The head alone weighs, I believe, from twelve to fifteen tons.

Mr Belzoni, who is as enterprising as he is intelligent, high-minded, and disinterested; further informs us, that he has dug up the colossus, indicated by the French upon their map of Karnak, as laying on the N.W. side of the abovementioned pond, under the name of 'Colosse renversé.' He has turned it up, and finds it to be a torso without head, or feet, about thirty feet in length, of beautiful workmanship; he says that he has seen nothing in Egypt, not even excepting our head, that can be compared to it, as it is a true imitation of nature, not done in the usual hard style, but according to the best rules of art.

If Mr Belzoni had had a flat bottomed boat at his command, he is confident that he should have been able to float down one of the small obelisks of Philæ, about twenty five feet in length. He handles masses of this kind with as much facility as others handle pebbles, and the Egyptians who see him a giant in figure, for he is six feet and a half high, believe him to be a sorcerer. Manual labour is so very cheap in Upper Egypt, that a little money goes a great way: the hire for a Fellah per day, is about four-pence; although upwards of one hundred Fellahs were occupied for many days with our head, and that we paid one hundred pounds for the boat only, and made a present to Mr Belzoni, small indeed, but as much as our circumstances permitted, the total expense incurred by us, as far as Alexandria, does not amount to more than three hundred pounds, and Mr Belzoni's whole expedition, to about four hundred and fifty pounds. The Pasha of Egypt is luckily not yet aware of the value of these statues; if he was, he would probably imitate Wely Pasha of the Morea, and ask for passage money, for he extends his extortions over every article of Egyptian produce, and condescends even to farm out the trade of camel and sheep's dung. Mr Belzoni, who is known in England as a hydraulic engineer, and is married to an English woman, who has accompanied him to Egypt, entered last year the service of the Pasha, as a mechanic, but not being able to contend with the intrigues of a Turkish court, and too honourable to participate in them, he was dismissed as unfit for his business, and five months of pay still remain due to him. So much for the Pasha's encouragement of European artists. They are enticed into his service by his emissaries in the Mediterranean, but are soon left to bewail their credulity.

You will find in the notes accompanying my translation of Macrizi, the account of some other very interesting discoveries, in the Eastern mountains of Upper Egypt; and last month, the old and so often visited pyramid of Djize was so well rummaged, that much curious new matter has come to light. Mr Caviglia, an Italian, and Mr Kabitch, a German, settled here, formed the project of exploring the well in the great pyramid. In the course of the operation they have discovered that a continuation of the descending passage leads to a chamber under the centre of the pyramid, and they find that no other well descends into the passage.

I have been led to believe from various circumstances, that this new discovered continuation of the entrance passage was opened in the time of the Khalif who opened the pyramid, and that it has been choaked up ever since. If I am to believe Sherif Edrys, the author of a history of the Pyramids, a book, I believe, unknown in Europe, and which I have lately purchased here, the interior of the pyramid is full of passages and rooms, and several sarcophagi are yet to be discovered. This author wrote in the twelfth century, and himself minutely examined the pyramid.

Travels in Nubia, 1819

A visit to Thebes

DOMINIQUE VIVANT DENON

DOMINIQUE VIVANT, BARON DENON (*1745–1825*), *was born at Châlon-sur-Saone and studied law at Paris. He was a highly versatile man of many talents, and soon turned to arts and letters, writing a successful comedy at the age of twenty-two, after which he took up drawing and painting. He rose to favour in court circles and carried out several commissions, both diplomatic and artistic, for Louis XV. When the Revolution broke out he was on a mission to Naples but he immediately returned to France, where he managed to survive in spite of his aristocratic connection under the protection and patronage of the famous painter David. Napoleon, whose universal mind neglected no possible detail which could lead to the aggrandisement of France, invited Denon to join the group of scholars who followed the army to Egypt to study antiquities, and he made meticulous notes and drawings of all he saw, often conducting his observations with the utmost coolness in the middle of a major battle. He was later appointed Director General of Museums, and followed several other campaigns in the same way.*

About noon we arrived at the territory of Thebes; and at the distance of three-quarters of a league from the Nile, we saw the ruins of a large temple, which have never been noticed by travellers, and which may give an idea of the immensity of that city, since, if we suppose that this was the farthest edifice on the eastern side, it is more than two leagues and a half distant from Medinet-Abu, where we observed the most western temple. It was now the third time of my passing Thebes; but, as if fate had willed that I should invariably be in haste, I could take but a hasty view of what so strongly interested me; I therefore confined myself to endeavour to account for what I saw, and to a few notes relating to what I might delineate on my return, provided I should then be more fortunate. I wished to ascertain whether at Thebes the arts had had different epochs and a chronology. If a palace once existed in Egypt, the ruins of it must be sought at Thebes, since this had been the metropolitan city; and if there were in reality epochs in the arts, the result of the first attempts must also be sought for in this capital, because luxury and magnificence have departed progressively from this point of simplicity, since they proceed only in company of opulence and superfluity. At length we arrived at Karnac, a village built on a small part of the site of a single temple, the circumference of which, as has been somewhere said, would require half an hour to perform its circumition. Herodotus, by whom it was not visited, has, notwithstanding, given a correct idea of its grandeur and magnificence. Diodorus and Strabo, who only examined it in its ruinous state, seem to have given the description of its present conditions; and all the travellers by whom they have been copied, have mistaken a great extent of masses for the proportions of beauty, and, having suffered themselves rather to be taken by surprise than to be delighted on an inspection of the largest ruins in the universe, have not dared to prefer the temple of Apollinopolis at Etfu, that of Tintyra, and the simple portico at Esneh, to the ruins in question. The temples of Karnac and Luxor were probably built in the time of Sesostris, when the flourishing state of Egypt gave birth to the arts, and when these arts were perhaps first displayed to an admiring world. The vanity of erecting colossi, was the first consideration of opulence; and it was not then known, that a perfection in the arts bestows on their productions a grandeur independent of their relative proportions: as, at first, it is not ascertained, that the small rotunda of Vicensa is a finer edifice than St Peter's at Rome; and that the school of surgery in Paris is, in point of style, as grand as the pantheon of the French capital; or that a cameo may be preferable to a colossal statue. It is therefore the sumptuousness alone of the Egyptians which must be observed at Karnac, where not only quarries, but mountains are heaped together, and sculptured into massive proportions, the units of which are feebly executed, and the parts aukward in appearance; and these masses are overspread with uncouth bas-reliefs, and tasteless hieroglyphics, as barbarous as the sculpture itself. The only objects there which are sublime, both with regard to their dimensions, and the skill of their workmanship, are the obelisks, and a few remains of the outer gates, the style of which is truly admirable. If in the other parts of this edifice the Egyptians appear to us to be giants, in the last mentioned production they are genii. Hence I am convinced, that these sublime embellishments were posteriorly added to the colossal monuments. It cannot however be denied, that the plan of the temple is noble and grand. But the art of contriving beautiful plans, has, in architecture, invariably preceded that of the fine execution of the respective parts, and has survived for several centuries the corruption of the latter, as is proved at once by a comparison of the monuments of Thebes with those of Esneh and Tintyra, as well as by the edifices of the reign of Dioclesian, when compared with those of the golden age of Augustus.

To the descriptions of this great edifice of Karnac, which are already known, I must observe, that it was but a temple, and could be nothing else. All that exists at present belongs to a very small sanctuary, and had been disposed in this way to inspire a due degree of veneration, and to form a kind of tabernacle. While examining the whole mass of these ruins, the imagination is fatigued with the mere thought of describing them. The portico of this temple alone contains an hundred columns; the smallest are seven feet and an half in diameter, and the largest eleven. The space occupied by its circumvallation contained lakes and mountains; while avenues of sphinxes reached even to the very gates. In short, to form a competent idea of so much magnificence, it is necessary that the reader should fancy what is before him to be a dream, for even the spectator cannot believe his eyes. But with respect to the present state of this edifice, it is necessary at the same time to observe, that a great part of the effect is lost by its very degraded condition. The sphinxes have been wantonly thrown down; but barbarism, wearied with destroying, has spared a few of them; and on examining these, it is easy to perceive that some of them had a woman's head, others that of a lion, a ram, or a bull. The avenue which leads from Karnac to Luxor was of the last mentioned description; and this space, which is nearly half a league in extent, contains a constant succession of these figures scattered to the right and left, together with fragments of stone walls, of small columns, and of statues. The position being in the centre of the city, the part which was the most advantageously situated, there is reason to suppose that the palace of the kings or great people was erected on that site. But though several traces render this probable, the fact is not proved by any extraordinary magnificence.

Luxor, the finest village in these environs, is also built on the site of the ruins of a temple, not so large as that of Karnac, but in a better state of preservation, time not having yet destroyed the masses, nor have they fallen by their own pressure. The most colossal parts consist of fourteen columns of ten feet in diameter, and of two statues in granite, at the outer gate, buried up to the middle of the arms, and having in front of them the two largest and best preserved obelisks in the whole country. It is, without doubt, flattering to the pomp of Thebes, that the richest and most powerful republic in the world should not possess means sufficient, not to hew out, or merely to transport these two monuments, which are no more than a fragment of one of the numerous edifices of that astonishing city.

One peculiarity belonging to the temple of Luxor, is, that a quay, provided with a demibastion, secured the eastern part, which was near the river, from the damages which might have been occasioned by the inundations.

This means of defence, which since its origin has been repaired and augmented by brick-work, proves that the river has not changed its bed; and its state of preservation also proves, that the Nile has never been banked by other quays, since no traces of similar constructions are to be met with in other parts of the city.

The entrance of the village of Luxor exhibits a striking mixture of beggary and magnificence, and impresses me with an awful idea of the gradation of ages in Egypt. It appears to me to be the most picturesque group, and the most striking representation of the history of the times: never were my eyes and my imagination so forcibly struck as by the sight of this monument. I often came to meditate on this spot, to enjoy the past and the present, to compare the successive generations of inhabitants by their respective works, which were before my eyes, and to store in mind volumes of materials for future meditations. One day the sheik of the village accosted me whilst sitting down on these ruins, and asked me if it was the French or the English who had erected the monuments; and this question put an end to my reflections.

There are two obelisks of rose-coloured granite, which are still seventy feet above the ground, and to judge by the depth to which the figures seem to be covered, we may suppose about thirty feet more to be concealed from the eye, making in all one hundred feet for the height of these monuments. Their preservation is perfect, the hieroglyphics with which they are covered are cut deep, and in relief at the bottom, and shew the bold hand of a master. What an admirable sharpness must the gravers possess, that could touch such hard materials! what time required for the labour! what machines to drag such enormous blocks out of the quarries, to transport them hither, and to set them erect! There are also two colossi of the same material, but they are worn and decayed; yet the parts that remain shew that they had been completed in the most perfect manner. We may here remark, that the custom of piercing the ears was known to the ancient Egyptians, as these statues still bear the impression of auricular perforations. Two large masses which form the gate are covered with sculpture, representing battles between chariots arranged in lines, drawn by two horses, and containing a single champion.

Nothing can possibly be more grand than the gate just mentioned, nor nothing more simple than the small number of objects of which this entrance is composed. No city whatever makes so proud a display at its approach as this wretched village, the population of which consists of two or three thousand souls, who have taken up their abodes on the roofs and beneath the galleries of the temple, which has nevertheless the semblance of being in a state of desolation.

During the time I was occupied in taking a plan, our cavalry was engaged with a small party of straggling Mamelukes, two of whom were killed, and the others escaped by swimming across the river, leaving behind them their arms, horses, and accoutrements.

Travels in Upper and Lower Egypt, 1802

7. Baron Vivant Denon, shown here preparing to draw the ruins of Hierakonopolis. While Napoleon set out in 1798 to conquer the new Egypt with the sword, an artist in his entourage captured the old Egypt with his sketch pad and pencil.

8. The "second" pyramid of Giza. For a long time nobody knew whether all the pyramids of Egypt were really royal mausoleums. Especially that of King Chefren seemed to be nothing more than a massive hill of stone—until Belzoni, a former circus athlete, discovered the entrance shown here.

The opening of a pyramid

GIOVANNI BATTISTA BELZONI

GIOVANNI BATTISTA BELZONI (1778–1823) was born in Padua and began his remarkable career as a strong man in a circus. In this capacity he travelled extensively, and in 1815 another aspect of this versatile character became evident when he went to Egypt to offer to the government a hydraulic irrigation machine of his own invention. His offer was not accepted, but his engineering talents were called on when, through the influence of the British consul, he was commissioned to go to Thebes and arrange the transportation for the British Museum of the head of Ramesses II known as the Colossus of Memnon. This he achieved so successfully that he decided to continue his work on Egyptian antiquities, which he did with immense energy and enthusiasm. He explored Edfu, Elephantine and Philae, cleared the sand from the temple at Abu Simbel, excavated extensively at Karnak, discovered the tomb of Seti I which contained a magnificent sarcophagus now to be seen in the Soane Museum, London, and was the first to penetrate the second pyramid at Giza. In 1819 he returned to England to supervise an exhibition of his finds, and in 1823 he was commissioned to undertake a journey to Timbuktoo, but died on the way.

Before my departure for Thebes I visited the pyramids in company with two other persons from Europe. On our arrival at these monuments they went into the first pyramid, while I took a turn round the second. I seated myself in the shade of one of those stones on the east side, which form the part of the temple that stood before the pyramid in that direction. My eyes were fixed on that enormous mass, which for so many ages has baffled the conjectures of ancient and modern writers. Herodotus himself was deceived by the Egyptian priests, when told there were no chambers in it. The sight of the wonderful work before me astonished me as much as the total obscurity in which we are of its origin, its interior, and its construction. In an intelligent age like the present one of the greatest wonders of the world stood before us, without our knowing even whether it had any cavity in the interior, or if it were only one solid mass. The various attempts which have been made by numerous travellers to find an entrance into this pyramid, and particularly by the great body of French savans, were examples so weighty, that it seemed little short of madness, to think of renewing the enterprise. Indeed, the late researches made by Mr Salt himself, and by Captain Cabilia, during four months, round these pyramids, were apparently sufficient to deter any one. A short time before this period the few Franks who resided in Egypt had some idea of obtaining permission from Mahomed Ali, and by the help of a subscription, which was to be made at the various Courts in Europe to the amount of at least £20,000, were to force their way into the centre of this pyramid by explosions, or any other means that could be suggested. Mr Drouetti was to have had the superintendence of this work. Indeed it had created some difference among themselves who was to have had the direction of the whole concern. Was not this enough to show the difficulties I had to encounter, and to make me laugh at myself, if any thought of such an attempt should cross my mind? Besides, there was another obstacle to overcome. I had to consider, that in consequence of what I had the good fortune to do in Upper Egypt, and under the circumstances above mentioned, it was not likely that I should obtain permission to make such an attempt: for if it could be supposed, that there was any possibility of penetrating into the pyramid, the operation would certainly be given to people of higher influence than myself.

With all these thoughts in my mind I arose, and by a natural impulsion took my walk toward the south side of the pyramid. I examined every part, and almost every stone. I continued to do so on the west – at last I came round to the north. Here the appearance of things became to my eye somewhat different from that at any of the other sides. The constant observations enabled me to see what other travellers did not: indeed, I think this ought to be considered as a standing proof, that in many cases practice goes farther than theory. Other travellers had been also in various places where I had been, and came often to the same spot where I was, but perhaps did not make the observations I did. I certainly must beg leave to say, that I often observed travellers, who, confident of their own knowledge, let slip opportunities of ascertaining whether they were correct in their notions; and if an observation was made to them by any one, who had not the good fortune of having received a classical education, they scorned to listen to it, or replied with a smile, if not a laugh of disapprobation, without investigating whether the observation were just or not. I had often the satisfaction of seeing such travellers mortified by the proof of being wrong in their conjecture. I do not mean to say, that a man, who has had a classical education, should think himself under a disadvantage in regard to knowing such things, compared with him who has not; but, that a man, who thinks himself well informed on a subject, often does not examine it with such precision as another, who is less confident in himself.

I observed on the north side of the pyramid three marks, which encouraged me to attempt searching there for the entrance into it. Still it is to be remarked, that the principal signs I discovered there were not deduced solely from the knowledge I had acquired among the tombs of the Egyptians at Thebes; for any traveller will acknowledge, that the pyramids have little in common with the tombs, either in their exterior appearance, or in any shape whatever: – they are two different things, – one is formed by a vast accumulation of large blocks of stones: – the other is entirely hewed out of the solid rock. My principal guide, I must own, was the calculation I made from the first pyramid, and such was my assurance on this point, that I then almost resolved to make the attempt. I had been at the pyramids various times before, but never with any intention of examining into the practicability of finding the entrance into them, which was deemed almost impossible. The case was now different – I saw then what I had not seen before – I observed, that just under the centre of the face of the pyramid the accumulation of materials, which had fallen from the coating of it, was higher than the entrance could be expected to be, if compared with the height of the entrance into the first pyramid, measuring from the basis. I could not conceive how the discovery of the entrance into the second pyramid could be considered as a matter to be despaired of, when no one had ever seen the spot, where it must naturally be presumed to exist, if there were any entrance at all. I farther observed, that the materials which had fallen exactly in the centre of the front were not so compact as those on the sides; and hence concluded, that the stones on that spot, had been removed after the falling of the coating. Consequently I perceived the probability of there being an entrance into the pyramid at that spot. Encouraged by these observations, I rejoined my companions in the first pyramid. We visited the great sphinx, and returned to Cairo the same evening.

I resolved to make a closer examination the next day, which I did accordingly, without communicating my intention to any one, as it would have excited great enquiry among the Franks at Cairo, and in all probability I should not have obtained permission to proceed in my design. The next day's examination encouraged me in the attempt. I was confident, that, if my purpose had been known to certain persons, who had influence at the court of the Bashaw, I should never succeed in obtaining permission. On the following day therefore I crossed the Nile to Embabe, as the Cacheff who commanded the province which includes the pyramids resided there. I introduced myself to him, and acquainted him with my intention to excavate the pyramids, if it met his approbation. His answer was, as I expected, that I must apply to the Bashaw, or to the Kakia Bey, for a firman, without which it was not in his power to grant me permission to excavate at the harrans, or pyramids. I asked him, whether he had any other objection, provided I obtained the firman from the Bashaw; he replied, 'none whatever'. I then went to the citadel, and as the Bashaw was not in Cairo, I presented myself to the Kakia Bey, who knew me from the time I was at Soubra, and who, on my request for permission to excavate at the pyramids, had no other objection, than that of not being certain, whether round the harrans there were any ploughed grounds, on which he could not grant permission to dig. He sent a message to the above Cacheff at Embabe, who assured him, that round the harrans there was no cultivated land, but that on the contrary it was solid rock.

With such an assurance I obtained a firman to the Cacheff, to furnish me with men to work at the pyramids. My undertaking was of no small importance: it consisted of an attempt to penetrate into one of the great pyramids of Egypt, one of the wonders of the world. I was confident, that a failure in such an attempt would have drawn on me the laughter of all the world for my presumption in undertaking such a task: but at the same time I considered, that I might be excused, since without attempting we should never accomplish any thing. However, I thought it best to keep my expedition as secret as possible; and I communicated it only to Mr Walmas, a worthy Levantine merchant of Cairo, and partner in the house of Briggs. It is not to be understood, that I intended to conceal the attempt I wished to make on the pyramids, for the effects of my work would plainly show themselves; but being near the capital, where many Europeans resided, I could not prevent myself from being interrupted during my operations; and as I knew too well how far the influence and intrigues of my opponents could be carried, I was not certain, that the permission I had procured might not have been countermanded, so as to put an end to all my proceedings.

Accordingly having provided myself with a small tent, and some provision, that I might not be under the necessity of repairing to Cairo, I set off for the pyramids.

My sudden departure from Cairo was supposed to be an expedition to the mountain of Mokatam, for a few days, as I had given out. At the pyramids I found the Arabs willing to work, and immediately set about the operation.

My purse was but light, for very little remained of what I received as a present from Mr Burckhardt, and the consul; and though it had been a little strengthened by the two statues I lately disposed of to the Count de Forbin, who had paid me one-third of the money on account, my whole stock did not amount to two hundred pounds, and if I did not succeed in penetrating the pyramid before this was exhausted, I should have been at a stand, before the accomplishment of my undertaking, and perhaps prepared the way for others stronger than myself in purse.

Two points principally excited my attention: the first was on the north side of the pyramid, and the second on the east. There is on the latter side part of a portico of the temple which stood before the pyramid, and which has a causeway descending straight towards the great sphinx. I thought, that by opening the ground between the portico and the pyramid I should necessarily come to the foundation of the temple, which in fact I did. I set eighty Arabs to work, forty on the above spot, and forty in the centre of the north side of the pyramid where I observed the earth not so solid as on the east and west. The Arabs were paid daily one piastre each, which is sixpence English money. I had also several boys and girls to carry away the earth, to whom I gave only twenty paras, or three pence, a day. I contrived to gain their good will by trifles I gave as presents, and by pointing out to them the advantage they would gain, if we succeeded in penetrating into the pyramid, as many visitors would come to see it, and they would get bakshis from them. Nothing has so much influence on the mind of an Arab as reasoning with him about his own interest, and showing him the right way to benefit himself. Any thing else he seems not to understand. I must confess, at the same time, that I found this mode of proceeding quite as efficacious in Europe.

The works on each side continued for several days without the smallest appearance of any thing. On the north side of the pyramid, the materials which were to be removed, consisting of what had fallen from the coating, notwithstanding the appearance of having been removed at a later period than the first, were so closely cemented together, that the men could scarcely proceed. The only instrument they had to work with was a kind of hatchet or spade, which being rather thin, and only fit to cut the soft ground, could not stand much work among stones and mortar, which latter I suppose, as it fell from the pyramid, had been moistened by the dew, and gradually formed itself almost into one mass with the stones.

On the east side of the pyramid, we found the lower part of a large temple connected with the portico, and reaching within fifty feet of the basis of the pyramid. Its exterior walls were formed of enormous blocks of stone, as may now be seen. Some of the blocks in the porticoes are twenty-four feet high. The interior part of this temple was built with calcareous stones of various sizes, but many finely cut at the angles, and is probably much older than the exterior wall, which bears the appearance of as great antiquity as the pyramids. In order to find the basis of the pyramid on this side, and to ascertain whether there were any communication between it and the temple, I had to cut through all the material, there accumulated, which rose above forty feet from the basis, and consisted of large blocks of stone and mortar, from the coating, as on the north side. At last we reached the basis, and I perceived a flat pavement cut out of the solid rock. I caused all that was before me to be cut in a right line from the basis of the pyramid to the temple, and traced the pavement quite to the back of it, so that there was evidently a spacious pavement from the temple to the pyramid; and I do not hesitate to declare my opinion, that the same pavement goes all round the pyramid. It appeared to me, that the sphinx, the temple, and the pyramid, were all three erected at the same time, as they all appear to be in one line, and of equal antiquity. On the north side the work advanced towards the basis; a great number of large stones had been removed, and a great part of the face of the pyramid was uncovered, but still there was no appearance of any entrance, or the smallest mark to indicate that there ever had been one.

The Arabs had great confidence in the hopes I had excited among them, that if any entrance into the pyramid were found, I would give great bakshis, in addition to the advantage they would derive from other strangers. But after many vain expectations, and much hard labour in removing huge masses of stone, and cutting the mortar, which was so hard that their hatchets were nearly all broken, they began to flag in their prospect of finding any thing, and I was about to become an object of ridicule for making the attempt to penetrate a place, which appeared to them, as well as to more civilised people, a mass of solid stone. However, as long as I paid them they continued their work, though with much less zeal. My hopes did not forsake me, in spite of all the difficulties I saw, and the little appearance of making the discovery of an entrance into the pyramid. Still I observed, as we went on with our work, that the stones on that spot were not so consolidated as those on the sides of them, and this circumstance made me determine to proceed, till I should be persuaded that I was wrong in my conjecture. At last, on the 18th of February, after sixteen days of fruitless labour, one of the Arabian workmen perceived a small chink between two stones of the pyramid. At this he was greatly rejoiced, thinking we had found the entrance so eagerly sought for. I perceived the aperture was small, but I thrust a long palm-stick into it upwards of two yards. Encouraged by this circumstance, the Arabs resumed their vigour on the work, and great hopes were entertained among them. Thus it served my purpose, as the work now went on briskly. I was aware, that the entrance to the pyramid could not be between two stones in this manner; but I was in hopes, that the aperture would furnish some clew by which the right entrance would be discovered. Proceeding farther, I perceived, that one of the stones, apparently fixed in the pyramid, was in fact loose. I had it removed the same day, and found an opening leading to the interior. This sort of rough entrance was not more than three feet wide, and was choked up with smaller stones and sand, which being removed, it proved to be much wider within. A second and third day were employed in clearing this place; but the farther we advanced, the more materials we found. On the fourth day I observed, that sand and stones were falling from the upper part of this cavity, which surprised me not a little. At last I found, that there was a passage from the outside of the pyramid by a higher aperture, which apparently was thought to have had no communication with any cavity. When all the rubbish was taken out, and the place cleared, I continued the work in the lower part beneath our feet; and in two days more we came to an opening inward. Having made it wide enough, I took a candle in my hand, and, looking in, perceived a spacious cavity, of which I could not form any conjecture. Having caused the entrance to be cleared of the sand and stones, I found a tolerably spacious place, bending its course towards the centre. It is evidently a forced passage, executed by some powerful hand, and appears intended to find a way to the centre of the pyramid. Some of the stones, which are of an enormous size, are cut through, some have been taken out, and others are on the point of falling from their old places for want of support. Incredible must have been the labour in making such a cavity, and it is evident, that it was continued farther on towards the centre; but the upper part had fallen in, and filled up the cavity to such a degree, that it was impossible for us to proceed any farther than a hundred feet. Half this distance from the entrance is another cavity, which descends forty feet, in an irregular manner, but still turns towards the centre, which no doubt was the point intended by the persons who made the excavation. To introduce many men to work in this place was dangerous, for several of the stones above our heads were on the point of falling; some were suspended only by their corners, which stuck between other stones, and with the least touch would have fallen, and crushed any one that happened to be under them. I set a few men to work, but was soon convinced of the impossibility of advancing any farther in that excavation. In one of the passages below, one of the men narrowly escaped being crushed to pieces. A large block of stone, no less than six feet long and four wide, fell from the top, while the man was digging under it; but fortunately it rested on two other stones, one on each side of him, higher than himself, as he was sitting at his work. The man was so incarcerated, that we had some difficulty in getting him out; yet, happily, he received no other injury than a slight bruise on his back. The falling of this stone moved many others in this passage: indeed, they were so situated, that I thought it prudent to retreat out of the pyramid, or we might have reason to repent when too late; for the danger was not only from what might fall upon us, but also from what might fall in our way, close up the passage, and thus bury us alive. My expectation in this passage was not great, as I perceived from the beginning it could not be the true entrance into the pyramid, though I had strong hopes that it would lead to some clew for the discovery of the real entrance; but, alas! it gave me none, and I remained as ignorant of it as I was before I began.

Having spent so many days at the pyramids without being discovered by any of the people at Cairo, I did not expect, that my retreat could be concealed much longer, as there were constantly Franks from Cairo making a Sunday's excursion to the pyramids, or travellers, who, of course, made it a point to see these wonders on their first arrival at the metropolis. In fact, the very day I was to have quitted this work, I perceived, in the afternoon, some people on the top of the first pyramid. I had no doubt they were Europeans, as the Arabs or Turks never go up, unless to accompany somebody, to gain money. They saw part of my men at work at the second pyramid, and concluded that none but Europeans could be conducting such an operation. They fired a pistol as a signal, and I returned another. They then descended the angle which led towards us; and on their arrival proved to be Monsieur L'Abbé de Forbin, who had accompanied his cousin, the celebrated Count, into Egypt, but did not proceed higher. With them were the father superior of the convent of Terra Santa. Mr Costa, an engineer, and Mr Gaspard, vice-consul of France, by whom I was introduced to the Abbé. They all entered into the newly discovered passage; but it gave the Abbé less pleasure than a cup of coffee, which he honoured me by accepting in my humble tent. Naturally, after such a visit, all the Franks in Cairo knew what I was doing; and not a day passed without my having some visitors.

I was determined to proceed still farther with my researches, the recent disappointment making me rather more obstinate than I was before. I had given a day's rest to the Arabs, which I dedicated to a closer inspection of the pyramid. It often happens, that a man is so much ingulfed in the pursuit of his views, as to be in danger of losing himself, if he do not quickly find the means either of an honourable retreat, or of attaining the accomplishment of his intended purpose. Such was my case. The success of my discovery of the false passage was considered as a failure. I cared little what was thought of it, but I was provoked at having been deceived by those marks, which led me to the forced passage, with the loss of so much time and labour. However, I did not despair. I strictly noticed the situation of the entrance into the first pyramid, and plainly saw, that it was not in the centre of the pyramid. I observed that the passage ran in a straight line from the outside of the pyramid to the east side of the king's chamber; and this chamber being nearly in the centre of the pyramid, the entrance consequently must be as far from the middle of the face as the distance from the centre of the chamber to the east side of it.

Having made this clear and simple observation, I found, that, if there were any chamber at all in the second pyramid, the entrance or passage could not be on the spot where I had excavated, which was in the centre, but calculating by the passage in the first pyramid, the entrance into the second would be near thirty feet to the east.

Satisfied with this calculation, I repaired to the second pyramid to examine the mass of rubbish. There I was not a little astonished when I perceived the same marks, which I had seen on the other spot in the centre, about thirty feet distant from where I stood. This gave me no little delight, and hope returned to cherish my pyramidical brains. I observed in this spot also, that the stones and mortar were not so compact as on the east side, which mark had given me so much encouragement to proceed in the first attempt; but what increased my hopes was an observation I made on the exterior of the front where the forced passage is. I observed the stones had been removed several feet from the surface of the pyramid, which I ascertained by drawing a line with the coating above to the basis below, and found the concavity was inclined to be deeper towards the spot where I intended to make my new attempt. Any traveller, who shall hereafter visit the pyramids, may plainly perceive this concavity above the true entrance. Such has been the effect of two different hints; first my old guide from Thebes, I mean the spots where the stony matter is not so compact as the surrounding mass; and, secondly, the concavity of the pyramid over the place where the entrance might have been expected to be found, according to the distance of the entrance into the first pyramid from its centre.

I immediately summoned the Arabs to work the next day. They were pleased at my recommencing the task, not in hopes of finding the entrance into the pyramid, but for the continuation of the pay they of course were to receive. As to expectation that the entrance might be found, they had none; and I often heard them utter, in a low voice, the word '*magnoon*', in plain English, madman. I pointed out to the Arabs the spot where they had to dig, and such was my measurement, that I was right within two feet, in a straight direction, as to the entrance into the first passage . . . and I have the pleasure of reckoning this day as fortunate, being that on which I discovered the entrance into the great tomb of Psammethis at Thebes. The Arabs began their work, and the rubbish proved to be as hard as that of the first excavation, with this addition, that we found larger blocks of stone in our way, which had belonged to the pyramid, besides the falling of the coating. The stones increased in size as we went on.

A few days after the visit of the Abbé de Forbin I was surprised by the appearance of another European traveller. It was the Chevalier Frediani, who, on his return from the second cataract of the Nile, came to visit the great pyramids. I had known him at Thebes on his ascending the Nile, and was much pleased to see him, as I thought he might be an impartial spectator of the event of my operations, which in fact he was. He greatly approved of my undertaking, but after being two days with me was ready to take his departure. I suppose he had as much expectation, that I should open the pyramid, as the Arabs who named me the *magnoon*. It happened, that on the very day he was to set off for Cairo, I perceived in the excavation a large block of granite, inclining downward at the same angle as the passage into the first pyramid, and pointing towards the centre. I requested the Chevalier to stay till the morrow, thinking perhaps he might have the pleasure of being one of the first who saw the entrance into the pyramid. He consented, and I was pleased to have a countryman of my own to be a witness of what passed on this important occasion. The discovery of the first granite stone occurred on the 28th of February, and on the 1st of March we uncovered three large blocks of granite, two on each side, and one on the top, all in an inclined direction towards the centre. My expectation and hope increased, as to all appearance, this must prove to be the object of my search. I was not mistaken, for on the next day, the 2nd of March, at noon, we came at last to the right entrance into the pyramid. The Arabs, whose expectation had also increased at the appearance of the three stones, were delighted at having found something new to show to the visitors, and get bakshis from them. Having cleared the front of the three stones, the entrance proved to be a passage four feet high, three feet six inches wide, formed of large blocks of granite, which descended towards the centre for a hundred and four feet five inches at an angle of twenty-six degrees. Nearly all this passage was filled up with large stones, which had fallen from the upper part, and as the passage is inclined downwards, they slid on till some larger than the rest stopped the way.

I had much ado to have all the stones drawn out of the passage, which was filled up to the entrance of the chamber. It took the remainder of this day and part of the next to clear it, and at last we reached a portcullis. At first sight it appeared to be a fixed block of stone, which stared me in the face, and said *ne plus ultra*, putting an end to all my projects as I thought; for it made a close joint with the groove at each side, and on the top it seemed as firm as those which formed the passage itself. On a close inspection however I perceived, that, at the bottom, it was raised about eight inches from the lower part of the groove, which is cut beneath to receive it; and I found, by this circumstance, that the large block before me was no more than a portcullis of granite, one foot three inches thick.

Having observed a small aperture at the upper part of the portcullis, I thrust a long piece of barley straw into it, and it entered upwards of three feet, which convinced me, that there was a vacuum ready to receive the portcullis. The raising of it was a work of no small consideration. The passage is only four feet high, and three feet six inches wide. When two men are in it abreast of each other they cannot move, and it required several men to raise a piece of granite not less than six feet high, five feet wide, and one foot three inches thick. The levers could not be very long, otherwise there was not space in the four feet height to work with them; and if they were short, I could not employ men enough to raise the portcullis. The only method to be taken was, to raise it a little at a time; and by putting some stones in the grooves on each side, to support the portcullis while changing the fulcrum of the levers, it was raised high enough for a man to pass. An Arab then entered with a candle, and returned saying, that the place within was very fine. I continued to raise the portcullis, and at last made the entrance large enough to squeeze myself in; and after thirty days exertion I had the pleasure of finding myself in the way to the central chamber of one of the two great pyramids of Egypt, which have long been the admiration of beholders. The Chevalier Frediani followed me, and after passing under the portcullis we entered a passage not higher or wider than the first. It is twenty-two feet seven inches long, and the works including the portcullis occupy six feet eleven inches in all. Where the granite work finishes at the end of this passage, there is a perpendicular shaft of fifteen feet, and at each side of the passage, an excavation in the solid rock, one of which, on the right as you enter, runs thirty feet in an upward direction, approaching the end of the lower part of the forced passage. . . . Before us we had a long passage running in a horizontal direction towards the centre. We descended the shaft by means of a rope. At the bottom of it I perceived another passage running downward at the same angle of 26° as that above, and toward the north. As my first object was the centre of the pyramid, I advanced that way, and ascended an inclined passage, which brought me to a horizontal one, that led toward the centre. I observed, that after we entered within the portcullis, the passages were all cut out of the solid rock. The passage leading toward the centre is five feet eleven inches high, and three feet six inches wide.

As we advanced farther on we found the sides of this passage covered with arborizations of nitre; some projecting in ropes, some not unlike the skin of a white lamb, and others so long as to resemble an endive-leaf. I reached the door at the centre of a large chamber. I walked slowly two or three paces, and then stood still to contemplate the place where I was. Whatever it might be, I certainly considered myself in the centre of that pyramid, which from time immemorial had been the subject of the obscure conjectures of many hundred travellers, both ancient and modern. My torch, formed of a few wax candles, gave but a faint light; I could, however, clearly distinguish the principal objects. I naturally turned my eyes to the west end of the chamber, looking for the sarcophagus, which I strongly expected to see in the same situation as that in the first pyramid; but I was disappointed when I saw nothing there. The chamber has a painted ceiling; and many of the stones had been removed from their places, evidently by some one in search of treasure. On my advancing toward the west end, I was agreeably surprised to find, that there was a sarcophagus buried on a level with the floor.

By this time the Chevalier Frediani had entered also; and we took a general survey of the chamber, which I found to be forty-six feet three inches long, sixteen feet three inches wide, and twenty-three feet six inches high. It is cut out of the solid rock from the floor to the roof, which is composed of large blocks of calcareous stone, meeting in the centre, and forming a roof of the same slope as the pyramid itself. The sarcophagus is eight feet long, three feet six inches wide, and two feet three inches deep in the inside. It is surrounded by large blocks of granite, apparently to prevent its removal, which could not be effected without great labour. The lid had been broken at the side, so that the sarcophagus was half open. It is of the finest granite; but, like the other in the first pyramid, there is not one hieroglyphic on it.

Looking at the inside, I perceived a great quantity of earth and stones, but did not observe the bones among the rubbish till the next day, as my attention was principally bent in search of some inscription that would throw light on the subject of this pyramid. We examined every part of the walls, and observed many scrawls executed with charcoal, but in unknown characters, and nearly imperceptible. They rubbed off into dust at the slightest touch; and on the wall at the west end of the chamber I perceived an inscription in Arabic . . . and the various interpretations given of it compel me to explain some points, which will perhaps lead to a satisfactory explanation. It appears to me, that all the difficulty lies in the last letters of the inscription, which are supposed to be obscure. This indeed is the fact; but I must say, that these letters were so blotted on the wall, that they were scarcely visible. The transcriber was a Copt, whom I had brought from Cairo for the purpose, as I would not trust to my own pen; and not being satisfied of his protestations of accuracy, though it was copied under my own eyes, I invited many other persons, who were considered as the best skilled in the Arabic language of any in Cairo, and requested them to compare the copy with the original on the wall. They found it perfectly correct, except the concluding word, which indeed appeared obscure; but if it be considered how much that word resembles the right one, we shall find a correct sense, and the whole inscription made out.

Translation of the Inscription by Mr Salame

'The Master Mohammed Ahmed, lapicide, has opened them; and the Master Othman attended this (*opening*); and the King Alij Mohammed at first (*from the beginning*) to the closing up.'

I must add, that the circumstance of the pyramid having been again closed up agrees with what I have said of my finding it so.

On several parts of the wall the nitre had formed many beautiful arborations like those in the passage, but much larger and stronger. Some were six inches long, resembling in shape a large endive leaf, as I mentioned before. Under one of the blocks that had been removed, I found something like the thick part of a hatchet, but so rusty, that it had lost its shape. At the north and south sides are two holes, which run in an horizontal direction, like those that are seen in the first pyramid, but higher up.

Returning out of this chamber we reached the passage below. At the bottom of the perpendicular shaft were so many stones as nearly to choke up its entrance, and after removing these we found the passage running to the north, at the same inclination as above, an angle of 26°.... This passage is forty-eight feet six inches in length, when it joins an horizontal passage of fifty-five feet still running north. Half-way up this passage on the right is a recess eleven feet long and six feet deep. On the left, opposite to it, is another passage, running twenty-two feet with a descent of 26° towards the west. Before we proceeded any farther toward the north, we descended this passage, and entered a chamber thirty-two feet long, nine feet nine inches wide, and eight feet six inches high. This chamber contains many small blocks of stone, some not more than two feet in length. It has a pointed roof like that before mentioned, though it is cut out of the solid rock; for it is to be understood, as I before observed, that, after we entered through the portcullis, all the passages, and the large chamber, as high as the roof, are cut out of the solid rock of calcareous stone. On the walls and roof of this chamber are several unknown inscriptions, as there are in the upper chamber. They are perhaps Coptic. Reascending into the horizontal passage, at the end of it we found grooves for a portcullis like the former; but the stone of granite which served for this purpose had been taken down, and is to be seen under the rubbish and stones near the place. Passing the portcullis we entered into a passage, which ascended in a direction parallel with that above. . . . This passage runs up forty-seven feet six inches. Here we found a large block of stone, placed there from the upper part; and by calculation I found, that this passage ran out of the pyramid at its basis, as, from the upper part of this square block, I could perceive other stones, which filled up the passage to the entrance, so that this pyramid has two entrances to it. Half-way up the horizontal passage, which leads into the large chamber, is some mason's work; but I believe it to be only the filling up of a natural cavity in the rock.

Having made all my observations, we came out of the pyramid with no small degree of satisfaction; and I was highly gratified with the result of my labour, of very little more than a month, the expense of which did not amount in all to £150, though I had accomplished a task, which was supposed would have required several thousands.

The Chevalier Frediani went to Cairo the same day, and the news of the opening of the pyramid soon brought the Franks to visit its interior. As I had no fear that the Arabian women would break the pyramid, I left the entrance open (*pro bono publico*); and in that place where the perpendicular descent, just inside the portcullis, is, I made a stone step for the accommodation of visitors, leaving half of the passage to enter into the lower chamber.

Narrative of Operations and Recent Researches in Egypt and Nubia, 1820

A cache of mummies at Thebes

GIOVANNI BATTISTA BELZONI

A traveller is generally satisfied when he has seen the large hall, the gallery, the staircase, and as far as he can conveniently go: besides, he is taken up with the strange works he observes cut in various places, and painted on each side of the walls; so that when he comes to a narrow and difficult passage, or to have to descend to the bottom of a well or cavity, he declines taking such trouble, naturally supposing that he cannot see in these abysses any thing so magnificent as what he sees above, and consequently deeming it useless to proceed any farther. Of some of these tombs many persons could not withstand the suffocating air, which often causes fainting. A vast quantity of dust rises, so fine that it enters into the throat and nostrils and chokes the nose and mouth to such a degree, that it requires great power of lungs to resist it and the strong effluvia of the mummies. This is not all; the entry or passage where the bodies are is roughly cut in the rocks, and the falling of the sand from the upper part of ceiling of the passage causes it to be nearly filled up. In some places there is not more than a vacancy of a foot left, which you must contrive to pass through in a creeping posture like a snail, on pointed and keen stones, that cut like glass. After getting through these passages, some of them two or three hundred yards long, you generally find a more commodious place, perhaps high enough to sit. But what a place of rest! surrounded by bodies, by heaps of mummies in all directions; which, previous to my being accustomed to the sight, impressed me with horror. The blackness of the wall, the faint light given by the candles or torches for want of air, the different objects that surrounded me, seeming to converse with each other, and the Arabs with the candles or torches in their hands, naked and covered with dust, themselves resembling living mummies, absolutely formed a scene that cannot be described. In such a situation I found myself several times, and often returned exhausted and fainting, till at last I became inured to it, and indifferent to what I suffered, except from the dust, which never failed to choke my throat and nose; and though, fortunately, I am destitute of the sense of smelling, I could taste that the mummies were rather unpleasant to swallow. After the exertion of entering into such a place, through a passage of fifty, a hundred, three hundred, or perhaps six hundred yards, nearly overcome, I sought a resting-place, found one, and contrived to sit; but when my weight bore on the body of an Egyptian, it crushed it like a band-box. I naturally had recourse to my hands to sustain my weight, but they found no better support; so that I sunk altogether among the broken mummies, with a crash of bones, rags, and wooden cases, which raised such a dust as kept me motionless for a quarter of an hour, waiting till it subsided again. I could not remove from the place, however, without increasing it, and every step I took I crushed a mummy in some part or other. Once I was conducted from such a place to another resembling it, through a passage of about twenty feet in length, and no wider than that a body could be forced through. It was choked with mummies, and I could not pass without putting my face in contact with that of some decayed Egyptian; but as the passage inclined downwards, my own weight helped me on; however, I could not avoid being covered with bones, legs, arms, and heads rolling from above. Thus I proceeded from one cave to another, all full of mummies piled up in various ways, some standing, some lying, and some on their heads. The purpose of my researches was to rob the Egyptians of their papyri; of which I found a few hidden in their breasts, under their arms, in the space above the knees, or on the legs, and covered by the numerous folds of cloth, that envelop the mummy. The people of Gournou, who make a trade of antiquities of this sort, are very jealous of strangers, and keep them as secret as possible, deceiving travellers by pretending, that they have arrived at the end of the pits, when they are scarcely at the entrance. I could never prevail on them to conduct me into these places till this my second voyage, when I succeeded in obtaining admission into any cave where mummies were to be seen.

My permanent residence in Thebes was the cause of my success. The Arabs saw that I paid particular attention to the situation of the entrance into the tombs, and that they could not avoid being seen by me when they were at work digging in search of a new tomb, though they are very cautious when any stranger is in Gournou not to let it be known where they go to open the earth; and as travellers generally remain in that place a few days only, they used to leave off digging during that time. If any traveller be curious enough to ask to examine the interior of a tomb, they are ready to show him one immediately, and conduct him to some of the old tombs, where he sees nothing but the grottoes in which mummies formerly had been deposited, or where there are but few, and these already plundered; so that he can form but a poor idea of the real tombs, where the remains were originally placed.

The people of Gournou live in the entrance of such caves as have already been opened, and, by making partitions with earthen walls, they form habitations, for themselves, as well as for their cows, camels, buffaloes, sheep, goats, dogs, and etc.

Narrative of Operations and Recent Researches in Egypt and Nubia, 1820

The Temple of Abu Simbel

JOHANN LUDWIG BURCKHARDT

The rock-cut temple built at Abu Simbel by Ramesses II was drifted over with sand for many centuries, and when Burckhardt made his journey through Nubia only the heads of the Ramesside colossi showed above the surface. It was left to that most energetic of Egyptologists, Belzoni, to clear the sand and explore the temple, which inevitably became a focus of attraction for serious scholars and for adventurous Victorian travellers like Mrs Amelia Edwards, who accompanied a later expedition to Abu Simbel. Its emergence from the sand had endured for only a small part of its long history when it was threatened with a more permanent and more destructive inundation; it was calculated that when the new High Dam at Aswan was finished, the water level would rise to flood the temple and the porous sandstone sculptures would be completely destroyed. An appeal was launched by Unesco in the hope of raising enough money to have the entire structure lifted above water level, but funds for so costly an undertaking were not forthcoming, and, in order to save the temples, it is planned to cut them into 30-ton blocks and remove them for rebuilding beyond the reach of the Nile.

Having, as I supposed, seen all the antiquities of Ebsambal, I was about to ascend the sandy side of the mountain by the same way I had descended; when having luckily turned more to the southward, I fell in with what is yet visible of four immense colossal statues cut out of rock, at a distance of about two hundred yards from the temple; they stand in a deep recess, excavated in the mountain; but it is greatly to be regretted, that they are now almost entirely buried beneath the sands, which are blown down here in torrents. The entire head, and part of the breast and arms of one of the statues are yet above the surface; of the one next to it scarcely any part is visible, the head being broken off, and the body covered with sand to above the shoulders; of the other two, the bonnets only appear. It is difficult to determine whether these statues are in a sitting or standing posture; their backs adhere to a portion of rock, which projects from the main body, and which may represent a part of a chair, or may be merely a column for support. They do not front the river, like those of the temple just described, but are turned with their faces due north, towards the more fertile climes of Egypt, so that the line on which they stand, forms an angle with the course of the stream. The head which is above the surface has a most expressive, youthful, countenance, approaching nearer to the Grecian model of beauty, than that of any ancient Egyptian figure I have seen; indeed, were it not for a thin oblong beard, it might well pass for a head of Pallas. This statue wears the high bonnet usually called the corn-measure, in the front of which is a projection bearing the figure of a nilometer; covered with hieroglyphics, deeply cut in the sandstone, and well executed; the statue measures seven yards across the shoulders, and cannot, therefore, if in an upright posture, be less than from sixty-five to seventy feet in height; the ear is one yard and four inches in length. On the wall of the rock, in the centre of the four statues, is the figure of the hawk-headed Osiris, surmounted by a globe; beneath which, I suspect, could the sand be cleared away, a vast temple would be discovered, to the entrance of which the above colossal figures probably serve as ornaments, in the same manner as the six belonging to the neighbouring temple of Isis. I am also led to conjecture, from the presence of the hawk-headed figure, that this was a temple dedicated to Osiris. The levelled face of the rock behind the colossal figures is covered with hieroglyphic characters; over which is a row of upwards of twenty sitting figures, cut out of the rock like the others, but so much defaced, that I could not make out distinctly, from below, what they were meant for; they are about six feet in height. Judging from the features of the colossal statue visible above the sand, I should pronounce these works to belong to the finest period of Egyptian sculpture; but, on the other hand, the hieroglyphics on the face of the rock are of very indifferent execution, and seem to be of the same age as those in the temple at Derr. A few paces to the south of the four colossal statues, is a recess hewn out of the rock, with steps leading up to it from the river; its walls are covered with hieroglyphic inscriptions, and representations of Isis; and the hawk-headed Osiris.

The temple of Ebsambal serves as a place of refuge to the inhabitants of Ballyane, and the neighbouring Arabs, against a Moggrebyn tribe of Bedouins, who regularly every year, make incursions into these parts. They belong to the tribes which are settled between the Great Oasis and Siout. When they set out, they repair first to Argo, where they commence their predatory course, plundering all the villages on the western bank of the river; they next visit Mahass, Sukkot, Batn el Hadjar, Wady Halfa, the villages opposite Derr, and lastly Dakke; near the latter place, they ascend the mountain, and return through the desert towards Siout. The party usually consists of about one hundred and fifty horsemen, and as many camel-riders; no one dares oppose them in Nubia; on the contrary, the governors pay them a visit, when they arrive opposite to Derr, and make them some presents. The incursions of this tribe are one of the principal reasons why the greater part of the western bank of the Nile is deserted. Whenever they advance towards Ballyane, its inhabitants retreat with their cattle to the temple of Ebsambal. The Moggrebyns, last year attempted to force this place of refuge, but failed, after losing several men.

Travels in Nubia, 1819

Coffee at Abu Simbel

AMELIA EDWARDS

At this juncture, seeing that the men's time hung heavy on their hands, our Painter conceived the idea of setting them to clean the face of the northernmost Colossus, still disfigured by the plaster left on it when the great cast was taken by Mr Hay more than half a century before. This happy thought was promptly carried into effect. A scaffolding of spars and oars was at once improvised, and the men delighted as children at play, were soon swarming all over the huge head, just as the carvers may have swarmed over it in the days when Rameses was king.

All they had to do was to remove any small lumps that might yet adhere to the surface, and then tint the white patches with coffee. This they did with bits of sponge tied to the ends of sticks: but Reis Hassan, as a mark of dignity, had one of the Painter's old brushes, of which he was immensely proud.

It took them three afternoons to complete the job: and we were all sorry when it came to an end. To see Reis Hassan artistically touching up a gigantic nose almost as long as himself: Riskalli and the cook-boy staggering to and fro with relays of coffee, brewed 'thick and slab' for the purpose; Salame perched cross-legged, like some complacent imp, on the towering rim of the great pschent overhead; the rest chattering and skipping about the scaffolding like monkeys, was, I will venture to say, a sight more comic than has ever been seen at Abou Simbel before or since.

Rameses' appetite for coffee was prodigious. He consumed I know not how many gallons a day. Our cook stood aghast at the demand made upon his stores. Never before had he been called upon to provide for a guest whose mouth measured three feet and a half in width.

Still, the result justified the expenditure. The coffee proved a capital match for the sandstone; and though it was not possible wholly to restore the uniformity of the original surface, we at least succeeded in obliterating those ghastly splotches, which for so many years have marred this beautiful face as with the unsightliness of leprosy.

A Thousand Miles up the Nile, 1889

Appeal by Mr Vittorino Veronese

DIRECTOR-GENERAL OF UNESCO

Work has begun on the great Aswan dam. Within five years, the Middle Valley of the Nile will be turned into a vast lake. Wondrous structures, ranking among the most magnificent on earth, are in danger of disappearing beneath the waters. The dam will bring fertility to huge stretches of desert: but the opening up of new fields to the tractors, the provision of new sources of power to future factories, threatens to exact a terrible price.

True, when the welfare of suffering human beings is at stake, then, if need be, images of granite and prophyry must be sacrificed unhesitatingly. But no one forced to make such a choice could contemplate without anguish the necessity for making it.

It is not easy to choose between a heritage of the past and the present well-being of a people, living in need in the shadow of one of history's most splendid legacies: it is not easy to choose between temples and crops. I would be sorry for any man called on to make that choice who could do so without a feeling of despair: I would be sorry for any man who, whatever decision he might reach, could bear the responsibility for that decision without a feeling of remorse.

It is not surprising, therefore, that the governments of the United Arab Republic and Sudan have called on an international body, on Unesco, to try to save the threatened monuments. These monuments, the loss of which may be tragically near, do not belong solely to the countries who hold them in trust. The whole world has the right to see them endure. They are part of a common heritage which comprises Socrates' message and the Ajanta frescoes, the walls of Uxmal and Beethoven's symphonies. Treasures of universal value are entitled to universal protection. When a thing of beauty, whose loveliness increases rather than diminishes by being shared, is lost, then all men alike are the losers.

Moreover, it is not merely a question of preserving something which may otherwise be lost; it is a question of bringing to light as yet undiscovered wealth for the benefit of all. In return for the help the world gives them, the governments of Cairo and Khartoom will open the whole of their countries to archaeological excavation and will allow half of whatever works of art may be unearthed by science or by hazard to go to foreign museums. They will even agree to the transport, stone by stone, of certain monuments of Nubia.

A new era of magnificent enrichment is thus opened in the field of Egyptology. Instead of a world deprived of a part of its wonders, mankind may hope for the revelation of hitherto unknown marvels.

So noble a cause deserves a no less generous response. It is, therefore, with every confidence that I invite governments, institutions, public or private foundations and men of goodwill everywhere to contribute to the success of a task without parallel in history. Services, equipment and money are all needed. There are innumerable ways in which all can help. It is fitting that from a land which throughout the centuries has been the scene – or the stake in – so many covetous disputes should spring a convincing proof of international solidarity.

'Egypt is a gift of the Nile'; for countless students this was the first Greek phrase which they learnt to translate. May the peoples of the world unite to ensure that the Nile in becoming a greater source of fertility and power does not bury beneath its waters marvels which we of today have inherited from generations long since vanished.

Unesco Courier, 1960

Translated from the French

P. A. Clayton

9. The Great Temple of Abu Simbel, some thirty years after its discovery. The structure, with the four enormous seated effigies of Ramses II the Great, is one of the most remarkable monuments of mankind. When it became evident that the erection of the Aswan Dam would lead to the total submergence of the temple under the waters of the Nile, UNESCO succeeded in uniting more than twenty nations in a vast rescue operation.

E. Brugsch, 1881

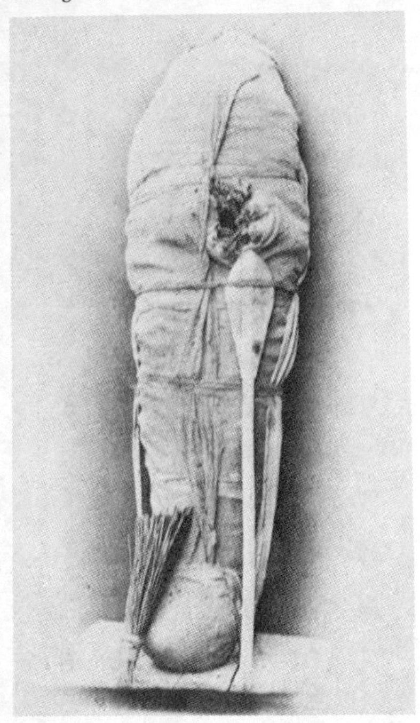

10. The mummy of Tuthmoses III as it was found at Deir-el-Bahri.

11. The mummy of Tuthmoses III after unwrapping.

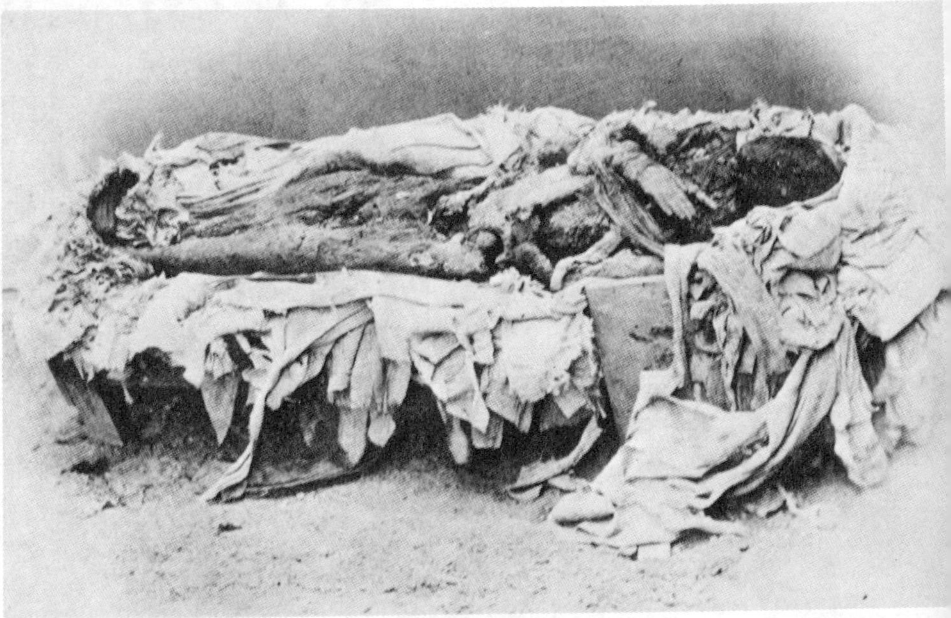

E. Brugsch

A hoard of royal mummies

GASTON MASPERO

GASTON CAMILLE CHARLES MASPERO (*1846–1916*) *was born in Paris. In his second year at the École Normale he met the great Egyptologist Mariette, who was in Paris supervising the Egyptian section of the Great Exhibition, and, with his advice and encouragement, concentrated his studies upon archaeology. In due course he became teacher of Egyptian language and archaeology at the École des Hautes Études, and by 1874 he held the Chair of Champollion at the Collège de France. In 1880 he went to Egypt at the head of a team of excavators, and was shortly offered the post of Director General of excavations and antiquities of Egypt, which, apart from three years in Paris from 1886 to 1889, he held until his retirement. He was responsible for extensive work in rehousing and cataloguing the collections, and made many important finds.*

For some several years past it had been realised that the Arabs of Gurna had found one or two royal tombs whose whereabouts they refused to divulge. In the spring of 1876 an English general named Campbell had shown me the hieratic ritual papyrus of the high-priest Pinotem, bought in Thebes for £400. In 1877 M. de Saulcy sent me on behalf of one of his friends in Syria, photographs of a long papyrus belonging to Queen Notmit, mother of Herihor, the end of which is now in the Louvre and the beginning in England. M. Mariette had also negotiated at Suez the purchase of two other papyri written in the name of a Queen Tiuhathor Henttaui. About the same time funerary statuettes of King Pinotem appeared on the market, some of fine workmanship and the others coarse. Briefly the fact that a discovery had been made became so certain that as early as 1878 I could definitely state concerning a tablet belonging to Rogers Bey that 'it came from a tomb close to the, as yet, unlocated tombs of the Herihor family'. . . .

To find the site of these royal tombs was therefore, if not the main, at least one of the principal objects of a trip which I made to Upper Egypt during March and April 1881. My intention was not to carry out any sondages or to settle down to excavations in the Theban necropolis; the problem was far more difficult. It was necessary to extract from the fellahin the secret which they had so zealously guarded until now. I had learnt only one thing: the principal dealers in antiquities were a certain Abd-er-Rassoul Ahmed, of Sheik Abd-el-Gurna, and a certain Mustapha Aga Ayad, vice-consul of England and Belgium at Luxor. To harass the latter was not so easy: protected as he was by diplomatic immunity he could escape the proceedings of the Directorate of Excavations. On April 4 I sent an order for the arrest of Abd-er-Rassoul Ahmed to the chief of police at Luxor, and I telegraphed to His Excellency Daud Pasha, Mudir (Governor) of Qena, as well as to the Ministry of Public Works requesting permission to open an immediate enquiry against his person. Questioned on board ship first by M. Emile Brugsch, and then by M. de Rochemonteix who kindly gave me the assistance of his experience, he denied everything that I charged him with, the discovery of the tomb, the sale of papyri and funerary statuettes and breaking up coffins contrary to the almost unanimous assertions of European travellers. I accepted his offer to have his house searched, less in the hope of finding any incriminating objects than to give him the chance of changing his mind and coming to an arrangement with us. Mildness, threats, nothing succeeded, and, on April 6, the warrant arrived to open the official enquiry, so I sent Abd-er-Rassoul Ahmed and his brother Hussein Ahmed to Qena, where the Mudir was demanding their appearance to stand trial.

The investigation was soundly pursued but on the whole gained nothing. The questions and arguments put by the magistrates of the Mudiria (province) in our delegate's presence, the inspector of Dendera, Aly-Effendi Habib, were notable for the number of testimonies evoked favourable to the accused. The foremost citizens and mayors of Gurna swore several times on oath that Abd-er-Rassoul Ahmed was one of the most upright and unselfish men of the district, and that he was incapable of diverting the most insignificant antiquity let alone robbing a royal tomb. The only interesting detail which came to light during the investigation was the insistance with which Abd-er-Rassoul Ahmed asserted that he was the servant of Mustapha Aga, the English vice-consul at Luxor, and that he lived in that person's house. He thought that in making out he was in the vice-consul's service he benefited from diplomatic privileges and came under Belgian or British protection. Mustapha Aga had encouraged both him and his associates in this error; he had persuaded them that in hiding behind him they would be safe henceforth from the local administrative agents, and by this simple trick he had managed to concentrate all the antiquities trade in the Theban plain into his hands.

Abd-er-Rassoul Ahmed was meanwhile provisionally released upon the surety of two of his friends, Ahmed Serour and Ismail Sayid Nagib, and returned home with a spotless certificate of honour conferred upon him by the foremost citizens of Gurna. But his arrest and the two months' imprisonment, together with the severity with which His Excellency Daud Pasha had conducted the enquiry, had clearly shown him that Mustapha Aga was unable to protect even his most faithful agents; it was also known that I intended to reopen the investigation when I returned to Thebes during the winter and that the Mudiria would also make further investigations. Several vague denunciations reached the Museum, and we learnt several new pieces of information from abroad, but the best news of all was of squabbles starting between Abd-er-Rassoul and his four brothers: some thought the danger finally over and the Museum authorities beaten, others thought it might be more prudent to come to terms with the Museum and divulge the secret. After a month of discussions and quarrels, the eldest of the brothers, Mohammed Ahmed Abd-er-Rassoul, suddenly decided to speak. He went secretly to Qena and told the Mudir that he knew the whereabouts of the site which had been vainly sought for several years; the tomb contained not one or two mummies but about forty, and the majority of the coffins had the small serpent on the front, like those seen on the head-dresses of pharaohs. His Excellency Daud Pasha immediately referred this to the Minister of the Interior, who conveyed the despatch to His Excellency the Khedive. His Highness, to whom I had spoken concerning the affair upon my return from Upper Egypt, recognised without any difficulty the importance of this unexpected denunciation and decided to send a member of the museum staff to Thebes. I had just returned to Europe but I had left M. Emile Brugsch, my assistant curator, the necessary powers to act for me in my stead. Having received the order to proceed, he left for Thebes on Saturday, 1st July, accompanied by a trustworthy friend and Ahmed Effendi Kamal, the Museum secretary-interpreter. A surprise awaited him at Qena: Daud Pasha had seized several precious objects at the house of the Abd-er-Rassoul brothers including three papyri of Queen Makere, Queen Isiemkheb and the princess Nesikhonsu. It was a promising beginning. To ensure the happy outcome of this delicate operation that was just beginning, His Excellency had placed his *wekil* at the service of our agents and also several employees of the Mudir. . . .

On Wednesday, the 6th, Messrs Emile Brugsch and Ahmed Effendi Kamal were led by Mohammed Ahmed Abd-er-Rassoul directly to the place where the funeral vault was located. The Egyptian engineer who had excavated it so long ago had laid his plans in a most skilful manner; never was a hiding place more cleverly concealed. The line of hills which separates the Biban-el-Moluk [Valley of the Kings] from the Theban plain here forms a series of natural circular clefts between the Assassif and the Valley of the Queens, of which the best known is that where the temple of Deir el-Bahari was built. In the rock face which separates Deir el-Bahari from the next cleft just behind the hill of Sheikh Abd-el-Gurna, about sixty metres above the level of the cultivated ground, a shaft eleven and a half metres deep and about two metres in diameter had been dug. At the bottom of the shaft, on the west side was the entrance to a passage 1·4 metres wide and 80 cm high. After running for 7·40 metres it turned suddenly northwards and continued for another 60 metres, the measurements never remaining constant: in places the passage was two metres wide and in others not more than 1·30 metres; near the middle five or six roughly cut steps showed a marked change of level, and on the right hand side an unfinished niche indicated that another change in direction of the passage had at one time been considered. Finally it opened out into an irregular, oblong chamber about eight metres long.

The first object which had presented itself to M. Emile Brugsch's gaze when he reached the bottom of the shaft was a white and yellow coffin inscribed with the name Nesikhonsu. It was in the passage about sixty centimetres from the entrance; a little farther on was a coffin of XVII dynasty style, then the Queen Tiuhathor Henttaui, then Seti I. Beside the coffins and scattered on the ground were wooden funerary statuettes, canopic jars, bronze libation vases, and, at the back in the corner angle made by the passage as it turned northward was the funeral tent of Queen Isiemkheb bent and crumpled like a valueless object, which a priest in a hurry to get out had thrown carelessly into a corner. The entire length of the main passage was similarly obstructed and disordered: it was necessary to advance on all fours not knowing where one was putting hands and feet. The coffins and the mummies rapidly glimpsed by the light of the candle bore historic names, Amenhetep I, Tuthmoses II, in the niche near the steps, Ahmose I and his son Siamun, Sequenre, Queen Ahotpe, Ahmose, Nefertari and others. The chamber at the end was the height of confusion but it was possible to see at first glance that the style of the XXth dynasty predominated. Mohammed Ahmed Abd-er-Rassoul's report which had at first seemed exaggerated hardly expressed the truth: where I had expected to find one or two minor kings, the Arabs had dug up a vault full of Pharaohs. And what Pharaohs! Probably the most famous in the history of Egypt, Tuthmoses III and Seti I, Ahmose the Liberator and Ramesses II the Conqueror. M. Emile Brugsch thought that he must be dreaming coming upon such an assemblage so suddenly. Like him I still ask myself if it is true and if I am dreaming when I see and touch the bodies of all these people when we never thought to know more than their names.

Two hours were sufficient for the preliminary examination, then the work of getting the coffins out began. Three hundred Arabs were quickly assembled by the Mudir's officials and put to work. The Museum's boat, hastily summoned, had not yet arrived; but one of its pilots, Reis Mohammed, who was perfectly trustworthy, was present. He descended to the bottom of the shaft and supervised the removal of its contents. Messrs Emile Brugsch and Ahmed Effendi Kamal received the objects and sorted them out as best they could on the ground without relaxing their vigilance for a moment, then the objects were carried to the bottom of the hill and laid side by side. Forty-eight hours of hard work got everything out of the cache; but the task was by no means finished. It was still necessary for the convoy to cross the Theban plain to the river's edge near Luxor. Several of the coffins, lifted only with the greatest difficulty by a dozen or sixteen men, took seven to eight hours to make the journey to the river, and it can easily be imagined what such a journey was like in the dust and heat of July.

At last, on the evening of the eleventh, all the mummies and coffins were at Luxor, carefully wrapped in matting and canvas. Three days later the Museum's steamer arrived and no sooner was it loaded than it set sail back to Bulaq with its cargo of kings. A strange thing happened! From Luxor to Quft on both banks of the Nile the wailing fellahin women with dishevelled hair followed the boat and the men fired off their guns, just as they do at funerals. Mohammed Abd-er-Rassoul was rewarded with five hundred pounds sterling, and I thought it best to appoint him reis of excavations at Thebes: if he serves the Museum with the same skill which he had used for so many years against it, we may hope for some magnificent discoveries.

Institut Égyptien Bulletin, series 2, no. 2, 1881

Translated from the French by P. A. Clayton

A false interpretation of the hieroglyphs

ATHANASIUS KIRCHER

ATHANASIUS KIRCHER *(1601–1680) was born at Geisa near Fulda. He entered the Jesuit college of Fulda and in 1618 became a novice of that order. He rose to the position of professor of philosophy, mathematics, and oriental languages at Wurzburg, but in 1631 the upheavals of the Thirty Years War drove him to remove himself to Avignon. In 1635 Cardinal Barberini secured him a position in Rome teaching mathematics at the Collegio Romano, and after eight years in this post he resigned in order to devote himself entirely to the study of antiquities. He was not a scholar of great original genius, and his work, which includes an entirely incorrect solution to the Egyptian hieroglyphics, is valuable only for its historical interest as a demonstration of the errors of earlier archaeologists. The following passage is from his explanatory introduction; there would be no point in including his entirely imaginary hieroglyphic grammar and vocabulary.*

PREFATORY LETTER

To the judicious and benevolent reader

If ever I realised the truth of that Hebrew saying, 'He who increases knowledge increases sorrow', it was surely in the revival of the study of this language hitherto unknown in Europe, in which there are as many pictures as letters, as many riddles as sounds, in short as many mazes to be escaped from as mountains to be climbed. The story clearly illustrates the difficulties which one encounters in undertaking arduous and unfamiliar tasks and opening up untrodden paths without a guide, and the dangers inherent in the investigation of the mysteries of a language which no one has previously studied. However, perseverance has triumphed over the difficulties of this abstruse subject, a consuming interest in the problem has lightened the endless work involved, and the burning desire implanted in me by nature to promote and restore studies neglected by reason of their difficulty has overcome all tribulations. Toil soon issued in rest, dislike was transformed into delight, and the fears which I had entertained as to the difficulties of getting to the root of the problem and solving it were turned into joy.

Knowing that I am to be judged by you, I ought not to fear the criticism of others, nor seek to defend my work. I am conscious, however, of having fallen upon times in which the noblest things are those most exposed to censure, the most serious topics are the most ridiculed and the most honourable enterprises are viewed with the deepest suspicion. Moreover, the minds of many people are such that they are not disposed to believe anything new and strange and outside their experience unless it is proved by convincing evidence and the testimony of reliable men, and unless its practical value is apparent. So, in order to increase confidence in my work and gain greater authority for it, I have thought it worth while briefly and clearly to explain how it came to be written and how the Autograph first came into my hands, adding at the same time an example showing how useful the work will be. In this way I trust I may the more easily escape the absurd but shameful charge of forgery, which the fertile imagination of certain ill-disposed persons might devise.

It happened like this. Urged on by his love of philosophy and antiquity, the honourable D. Petrus à Valle, knight and patrician of Rome, travelled like a second Apollonius through Greece, Palestine, Persia, India, Arabia and almost the whole eastern world, and came finally to Egypt, the fruitful source of all learning, intending to explore for himself the wonders of which he had read. Among the memorable things which he diligently investigated, he came upon this Copto-Arabic vocabulary or word-list, hidden away among men whose ignorant minds were incapable of appreciating it. He examined it carefully, and found that it would be invaluable for reviving the ancient language of Egypt, which had almost perished with age. He therefore purchased it for a considerable sum, and after a long and dangerous journey brought it joyfully to Rome, treating it with the greatest care, in order that he might make it available to the world at large, to the use and profit of many. To provide convincing proof of this account, it is well to add the authentic testimony of a passage at the beginning of the Autograph:

'At the end of the year of grace 1615 I was in the city of Cairo, most famous of the cities of Egypt at that time, diligently investigating the neglected monuments of antiquity, and there I found this book, hidden away among men whose ignorant minds were incapable of appreciating it. After a long and difficult journey I finally brought it to Rome, in order that with its unique assistance the ancient language of Egypt, which had almost died out among the Egyptians themselves, might eventually live again and shed much light on sacred and secular literature. May posterity be pleased to accept my contribution to this enterprise, and the duty which I owe to the Eternal City and to my country, the fount of good learning. Farewell.'

Meanwhile D. Nicolaus Fabricius, royal senator at the court of Aix, that distinguished ornament of letters, had been fully informed of this treasure recently brought from Egypt, and left no stone unturned to publish it as soon as possible in a Latin translation. A suitable person to undertake this task was sought abroad, especially in France where the study of foreign languages and of letters in general flourished exceedingly. At length I, who had adopted France as my country when I left Germany on account of the Swedish disturbances there, was prevailed upon to undertake the work, though I was by no means equal to it, at the instigation of my friends and above all at the urgent request of my dear friend Fabricius. When word of these endeavours reached the ears of His Eminence Cardinal Barberini, he too devoted himself to the cause with no less enthusiasm. He wished me to come to Rome with all speed to carry out this work there and to revive the study of hieroglyphics. I reached Rome, not without some danger, began the work entrusted to me, and with God's help brought it to the desired conclusion within two years. The book was finished, then, and ready for the press, but it was held up by a journey to Sicily and Malta which I had undertaken, and by the lack of apparatus necessary to print the characters, and was delayed again and again. Because of these hindrances the work was at a standstill for several years, and the author's intention to publish it all but vanished. Indeed, it seemed not unlikely that the treasure rescued with such great effort from the moths and bookworms should return to its former chaos. While I was pondering these things, the Holy Roman Emperor, well knowing the reasons for this delay, of his great and natural munificence most generously provided funds sufficient to procure types of all the oriental languages and other things necessary to complete the work. I mention this in order that the reader may appreciate the incomparable virtues of this indomitable emperor, who was not so overwhelmed by the barbarity of war and wave after wave of invasion as to devote himself to Mars to the exclusion of Pallas Athene. More might be said here of this invincible emperor's great wisdom, of his enthusiasm for all the arts and his almost incredible kindness. However, I intend to consider these things elsewhere, and, since they could not be told here with sufficient brevity, I have contained myself for the present. Types were therefore acquired, thanks to the emperor's generosity, and the work so long awaited went to press and at last saw the light of day.

You will see that it is in three parts. The first section is concerned with grammar, the second with vocabulary, and the third contains a list of words arranged in alphabetical order. You will scarcely believe the pains we have taken to make an accurate translation of the names of things. Indeed we should have collapsed but for the assistance of two Copts and others, especially of Abraham Ecchell, a scholar in many branches of learning, including oriental languages, who helped us in all sorts of ways, notably by their careful collation of everything with the Autograph.

Moreover, we have taken care in our translation to render everything into Latin word for word. In the interests of integrity and also of clarity, we have shunned conjecture and marked with an asterisk those places where the translation is in doubt because damp has made the original illegible. To guard against serious error in the translation of other ambiguous and equivocal words, we have looked these up – and the extent of this task you may imagine – in the manuscripts of the Holy Scriptures at the Vatican. God willing, we have attained by our unremitting labours the degree of accuracy in translation necessary for the revival of the study of hieroglyphics and the restoration of this neglected discipline.

I trust that this will suffice to ward off the attacks of those who may gnaw at our work with envious teeth. This book has been promoted and eagerly awaited by the general public and by people of quality; indeed, the most eminent men of our time in the republic of letters, not only in Europe but also in Asia and Africa, have given it their approval and looked forward to its completion, as we could abundantly demonstrate from the letters which we have received from Jews, Greeks, Arabs, Armenians, Syrians, Ethiopians and Persians, from Constantinople, Aleppo, Damascus, Alexandria, Cairo, Ephesus, Tunis and other places. However, we leave it to Oedipus to bear out what we have said. For, if the goodness of God prolongs his life, Oedipus will declare how much we have achieved in reviving this language. Unless I am much mistaken, students of these abstruse subjects in future times will admit that the monumental labours of Oedipus could never have been brought to fruition without the help of this language, and we trust that we shall win some thanks from a grateful posterity when in due course it reaps the full harvest of our work. What we have done is to produce a Silenus, rough and uncultured at his first appearing, but who in his own time will, we have no doubt, shine forth and light up dark places. These are the facts of which, O Reader, we thought it would be well to inform you. And so Farewell, and be good enough to further my work by letting me know if you discover anything which may help Oedipus.

Lingua Aegyptiaica, 1643

Translated from the Latin by H. Powell

How the Rosetta Stone came to the British Museum

TOMKYNS HILGROVE TURNER

Sir Tomkyns Hilgrove Turner *(1766?–1843) was a professional soldier all his life and achieved considerable distinction both in his military career and as an antiquarian. From 1793 onwards he was continuously engaged in campaigns in the Low Countries and France, and in 1801 he went with his regiment to Egypt, where he fought in the battles of Aboukir Bay and Alexandria. After the capitulation of this city, one of the articles of the surrender terms required the French to hand over many of the antiquities their scientific commission had collected, and it was Turner who negotiated the actual transfer of these objects, and insisted that the collection should include the most important find brought to light by the French – the Rosetta Stone. Turner wrote an account of these transactions for the Society of Antiquaries, on whose premises the stone was displayed before its removal to the British Museum, where it has subsequently remained.*

Read 8 June, 1810

Argyle Street, 30 May, 1810

Sir,
The Rosetta Stone having excited much attention in the learned world, and in this Society in particular, I request to offer them, through you, some account of the manner it came into the possession of the British army, and by what means it was brought to this country, presuming it may not be unacceptable to them.

By the sixteenth article of the capitulation of Alexandria, the siege of which city terminated the labours of the British army in Egypt, all the curiosities, natural and artificial, collected by the French Institute and others, were to be delivered up to the captors. This was refused on the part of the French General to be fulfilled, by saying they were all private property. Many letters passed; at length, on consideration that the care in preserving the insects and animals had made the property in some degree private, it was relinquished by Lord Hutchinson; but the artificial, which consisted of antiquities and Arabian manuscripts, among the former of which was the Rosetta Stone, was insisted upon by the noble General with his usual zeal for science. Upon which I had several conferences with the French General Menou, who at length gave way, saying, that the Rosetta Stone was his private property; but, as he was forced, he must comply as well as the other proprietors. I accordingly received from the under secretary of the Institute, Le Pere, the secretary Fourier being ill, a paper, containing a list of the antiquities, with the names of the claimants of each piece of sculpture: the stone is there described of black granite, with three inscriptions, belonging to General Menou. From the French sçavans I learnt, that the Rosetta Stone was found among the ruins of Fort St Julien, when repaired by the French, and put in a state of defence: it stands near the mouth of the Nile, on the Rosetta branch, where are, in all probability, the pieces broken off. I was also informed, that there was a stone similar at Menouf, obliterated, or nearly so, by the earthen jugs being placed on it, as it stood near the water; and that there was a fragment of one, used and placed in the walls of the French fortifications of Alexandria. The Stone was carefully brought to General Menou's house in Alexandria, covered with soft cotton cloth, and a double matting, where I first saw it. The General had selected this precious relick of antiquity for himself. When it was understood by the French army that we were to possess the antiquities, the covering of the stone was torn off, and it was thrown upon its face, and the excellent wooden cases of the rest were broken off; for they had taken infinite pains, in the first instance, to secure and preserve from any injury all the antiquities. I made several remonstrances, but the chief difficulty I had was on account of this stone, and the great sarcophagus, which at one time was positively refused to be given up by the Capitan Pasha, who had obtained it by having possession of the ship it had been put on board of by the French. I procured, however, a centry on the beach from Mon. Le Roy, prefect maritime, who, as well as the General, behaved with great civility; the reverse I experienced from some others.

When I mentioned the manner the stone had been treated to Lord Hutchinson, he gave me a detachment of artillerymen, and an artillery-engine, called, from its powers, a devil cart, with which that evening I went to General Menou's house, and carried off the stone, without any injury, but with some difficulty, from the narrow streets, to my house, amid the sarcasms of numbers of French officers and men; being ably assisted by an intelligent serjeant of artillery, who commanded the party, all of whom enjoyed great satisfaction in their employment: they were the first British soldiers who entered Alexandria. During the time the Stone remained at my house, some gentlemen attached to the corps of sçavans requested to have a cast, which I readily granted, provided the Stone should receive no injury; which cast they took to Paris, leaving the Stone well cleared from the printing ink, which it had been covered with to take off several copies to send to France, when it was first discovered.

Having seen the other remains of ancient Egyptian sculpture sent on board the Admiral, Sir Richard Bickerton's ship, the *Madras*, who kindly gave every possible assistance, I embarked with the Rosetta Stone, determined to share its fate, on board the *Egyptienne* frigate, taken in the harbour of Alexandria, and arrived at Portsmouth in February 1802. When the ship came round to Deptford, it was put in a boat and landed at the Custom-House; and Lord Buckinghamshire, the then Secretary of State, acceded to my request, and permitted it to remain for some time at the apartments of the Society of Antiquaries, previous to its deposit in the British Museum, where I trust it will long remain, a most valuable relick of antiquity, the feeble but only yet discovered link of the Egyptian to the known languages, a proud trophy of the arms of Britain (I could almost say *spolia opima*), not plundered from defenceless inhabitants, but honourably acquired by the fortune of war.

I have the honour to be, Sir,
Your most obedient, and most humble servant,
H. TURNER, Major General.

NICHOLAS CARLISLE, ESQ.,
Secretary to the Society of Antiquaries, &c., &c.

Archaeologia, vol xvi, 1812

Champollion deciphers the hieroglyphs

Jean Francois Champollion *(1790–1832) was born at Figeac and early showed signs of an amazing aptitude for languages which was fostered and encouraged by his self-effacing elder brother. When he was sixteen years old he read a paper to the Academy at Grenoble which astonished the scholars who heard it and, at an age when most pupils were still seeking admission, he was made a teacher. His work was often interrupted by the political disturbances of the age, but in 1821 he was able to bring out the paper which proved to be the definitive solution to the Egyptian hieroglyphs. His ideas were in direct contradiction to those propounded by most scholars of his day, and met with bitter opposition, but his work successfully withstood all tests and acceptance could not long be denied. In 1831 a Chair was specially created for him at the Collège de France in recognition of his achievement.*

Letter to M. Dacier concerning the alphabet of the phonetic hieroglyphs

Sir,

It is to your generous patronage that I owe the indulgent attention which the *Académie Royale des Inscriptions et Belles-Lettres* has been pleased to accord to my work on the Egyptian scripts, in allowing me to submit to it my two reports on the *hieratic*, or priestly, script and the *demotic*, or popular one; after this flattering trial, I may as last venture to hope that I have successfully shown that these two types of writing are neither of them composed of alphabetic letters, as had been so widely supposed, but consist of *ideograms*, like the hieroglyphs themselves, that is, expressing the *concepts* rather than the *sounds* of a language; and to believe that after ten years of dedicated study I have reached that point where I can put together an almost complete survey of the general structure of these two forms of writing, the origin, nature, form and number of their signs, the rules for their combination by means of those symbols which fulfil purely logical and grammatical functions, thus laying the first foundations for what might be termed the *grammar* and *dictionary* of these two scripts, which are found on the majority of monuments, and the interpretation of which will throw so much light on the general history of Egypt. With regard to the *demotic* script in particular, there is enough of the precious Rosetta inscription to identify the whole; scholastic criticism is indebted first to the talents of your illustrious colleague, M. Silvestre de Sacy, and successively to the late M. Akerblad and Dr Young, for the first accurate ideas drawn from this monument, and it is from this same inscription that I have deduced the series of demotic symbols which, taking on syllabic-alphabetic values, were used in *ideographic* texts to express the proper names of persons from outside Egypt. It is by this means also that the name of the Ptolemies was discovered, both in this same inscription and in a papyrus manuscript recently brought from Egypt.

Accordingly, it only remains, in completing my study of the three types of Egyptian writing, for me to produce my account of the pure *hieroglyphs*. I dare to hope that my latest efforts will also have a favourable reception from your famous society, whose goodwill has been so valuable an encouragement to me.

However, in the present condition of Egyptian studies, when relics abound on every side, collected by kings as much as by connoisseurs, and when, too, with regard to these relics, the world's scholars eagerly devote themselves to laborious researches and strive for an intimate understanding of those written memorials which must serve to explain the rest, I do not think I should delay in offering to these scholars, under your honoured auspices, a short but vital list of new discoveries, which belong properly to my account on the *hieroglyphic* script, and which will undoubtedly spare them the pains I took in establishing them, and perhaps also some grave misconceptions about the various periods of the history of Egyptian culture and government in general: for we are dealing with the series of *hieroglyphs* which, making an exception to the general nature of the signs of this script, were given the property of expressing word *sounds*, and served for the inscription on Egyptian national monuments of the *titles, names* and *surnames of the Greek or Roman rulers* who successively governed the country. Many truths concerning the history of this famous country must spring from this new result of my researches, to which I was led quite naturally.

The interpretation of the *demotic* text on the Rosetta inscription, by means of the accompanying Greek text, had made me realise that the Egyptians used a certain number of *demotic* characters, which assumed the property of expressing sounds, to introduce into their ideographic writings *proper names* and *words foreign to the Egyptian language*. We see at once the indispensable need for such a practice in an ideographic system of writing. The Chinese, who also use an ideographic script, have an exactly similar provision, created for the same reason.

The Rosetta monument shows us the application of this auxiliary method of writing, which I have termed *phonetic*, that is, expressing the sounds, in the proper names of the kings *Alexander* and *Ptolemy*, the queens *Arsinoe* and *Berenice*, in the proper names of six other persons, *Aetes*, *Pyrrha*, *Philinus*, *Areia*, *Diogenes* and *Irene*, and in the Greek words *ΞΥΝΤΑΞΙΣ* and *ΟΥΗΝΝ*. . . .

The hieroglyphic text of the Rosetta inscription, which would have lent itself so felicitously to this study, owing to its cracks, yielded only the name *Ptolemy*.

The obelisk found on the island of Philae and recently brought to London also contains the hieroglyphic name of a Ptolemy, written in the same symbols as on the Rosetta inscription and similarly enclosed in a cartouche, and this is followed by a second cartouche, which must contain the proper name of a woman, a Ptolemaic queen, since this cartouche ends with the feminine hieroglyphic signs which also follow the hieroglyphic proper names of every Egyptian goddess without exception. The obelisk was, as it were, *tied* to a pedestal bearing a Greek inscription which is a supplication from the priests of Isis at Philae to the king, Ptolemy, his sister Cleopatra and his wife Cleopatra. If this obelisk and its hieroglyphic inscription resulted from the plea of the priests, who actually mention the consecration of a similar monument, the cartouche with the female name could only be that of a Cleopatra. This name, and that of Ptolemy, which have certain like letters in Greek, had to serve for a comparative study of the hieroglyphic symbols which composed the two; and if identical signs in these two names stood for *the same sounds* in both cartouches, they would have to be *entirely phonetic* in character.

A preliminary comparison had also made me realise that these same two names, written phonetically in the demotic script, contained a number of identical characters. The resemblance between the three Egyptian scripts in their general principles caused me to look for the same phenomenon and the same correspondences when the same names were given *in hieroglyphs*: this was soon confirmed by simple comparison of the hieroglyphic cartouche containing the name Ptolemy and that on the Philae obelisk which I believed, according to the Greek text, must contain the name Cleopatra.

The first sign in the name *Cleopatra*, which resembles a kind of *quadrant*, and which would represent the *K*, should have been absent from the name Ptolemy. It was.

The second sign, a *lion couchant*, which would give the *Λ*, is exactly similar to the fourth sign in the name Ptolemy, also an *Λ* (*Πτολ*).

The third sign in the name Cleopatra is a *feather* or *leaf*, standing for the short vowel *E*; we also see two similar *leaves* at the end of the name Ptolemy, which, from their position, can only have the value of the diphthong *AI*, in *AIOΣ*.

The fourth character in the cartouche for the hieroglyphic Cleopatra, the representation of a kind of *flower with a bent stem*, would stand for the *O* in the Greek name of this queen. It is in fact the third character in the name Ptolemy (*Πτο*).

The fifth sign in the name Cleopatra, which appears as a parallelogram and must represent the *Π*, is equally the first sign in the hieroglyphic name Ptolemy.

The sixth sign, standing for the vowel *A* of *ΚΛΕΟΠΑΤΡΑ*, is a *hawk*, and does not occur in the name Ptolemy, nor should it.

The seventh character is an *open hand*, representing the *T*; but this hand does not occur in the word Ptolemy, where the second letter, the *T*, is expressed by a *segment of a circle*, which, none the less, is also a *T*; for we shall see below why these two hieroglyphs have the same sound.

The eighth sign of *ΚΛΕΟΠΑΤΡΑ*, which is a frontal *mouth*, and which would be the *P*, does not occur in the cartouche of Ptolemy, nor should it.

Finally, the ninth and last sign in the queen's name, which must be the vowel *A*, is in fact the *hawk* which we have already seen representing this vowel in the third syllable of the same name. This proper name ends in the two hieroglyphic symbols for the feminine gender: that of Ptolemy ends in another sign, which consists of a bent shaft, equivalent to the Greek *Σ*, as we shall see below.

The combined signs from the two cartouches, analysed phonetically, thus already yielded us twelve signs, corresponding to eleven consonants, vowels or diphthongs in the Greek alphabet, *A*, *AI*, *E*, *K*, *Λ*, *M*, *O*, *Π*, *P*, *Σ*, *T*.

The phonetic value of these twelve signs, already very probable, becomes indisputable if, applying these values to other cartouches or small enclosed panels containing proper names and taken from Egyptian hieroglyphic monuments, we are enabled to read them effortlessly and systematically, producing the proper names of rulers foreign to the Egyptian language. . . .

You, sir, will doubtless share all my astonishment when the same alphabet of phonetic hieroglyphs, applied to a host of other cartouches carved on the same piece of work, will give you titles, names and even surnames of Roman emperors, spoken in *Greek* and written with these same phonetic hieroglyphs.

We read here, in fact:

The imperial title *Αυτοκρατωρ*, occupying a whole cartouche to itself, or else followed by other *still persisting* ideographic titles, transcribed *AOTOKPTP*, *AOTKPTOP*, *AOTAKPTP* and even *AOTOKΛTΛ*, the *Λ* being used as a bastard substitute (pardon the expression) for the *P*.

The cartouches containing this title are almost always next to, or connected with, a second cartouche containing, as we shall shortly see, the *proper names* of emperors. But occasionally we also find this word in absolutely isolated cartouches. . . .

But it remains, sir, for us to survey briefly the nature of the phonetic system governing the writing of these names, to form an accurate estimate of the character of the signs used, and to investigate the reasons for adopting the image of one or another object to represent a particular consonant or vowel more than another. . . .

I am in no doubt, sir, that if we could definitely determine the object represented or expressed by all the other phonetic hieroglyphs comprised in our alphabet, it would be a relatively easy matter for me to show, in the Egyptian-Coptic lexicons, that the names of these same objects begin with the consonant or vowels which their image represents in the phonetic hieroglyph system.

This method, followed in the composition of the Egyptian phonetic alphabet, gives us an idea to what point we could, if we wished, continue multiplying the number of phonetic hieroglyphs without sacrificing the clarity of their expression. But everything seems to indicate that our alphabet, by and large, contains them. We are, in fact, justified in drawing this conclusion, since this alphabet is the result of a series of phonetic proper names carved on Egyptian monuments during a period of about *five centuries* in various parts of the country.

It is easy to see that the vowels of the hieroglyphic alphabet are used indiscriminately one for another. On this point we can do no more than establish the following general rules:

1. The hawk, the ibis and three other kinds of bird are consistently used for *A*;

2. The leaf or feather can stand for both the short vowels *Ă* and *Ĕ*, sometimes even *Ŏ*.

3. The twin leaves or feathers can equally well represent the vowels *I* and *H*, or the diphthongs *IA* and *AI*.

All I have just said on the origin, formation and anomalies of the *phonetic hieroglyph* alphabet applies almost entirely to the *demotic phonetic* alphabet. . . .

These two systems of phonetic writing were as intimately connected as the *hieratic ideographic* system was with the *popular ideographic*, which was no more than its descendant, and the *pure hieroglyphs*, which were its source. The demotic letters are generally, in fact, as I have said, the same as the *hieratic* signs for hieroglyphs which are themselves phonetic. You, sir, will have no difficulty in recognising the truth of this assertion, if you trouble to consult the comparative Table of hieratic signs classified beside the corresponding hieroglyph, the Table which I presented before the *Académie des Belles-Lettres* more than a year ago. So there is basically no other difference between the *hieroglyphic* and *demotic* alphabets but the actual form of the signs, their values and even the reasons for those values being identical. Finally I would add that since these popular phonetic symbols were merely unchanged hieratic characters, there cannot, of necessity, have been more than *two* phonetic writing systems in Egypt;

1. the *phonetic hieroglyph* script, used on public monuments;
2. the *hieratic-demotic* script, used for Greek proper names in the middle text of the Rosetta inscription and the demotic papyrus in the royal library . . . , and which we shall perhaps see one day used to transcribe the name of some Greek or Roman ruler in the rolls of papyrus written in the hieratic script.

Phonetic writing, then, was in use among every class of the Egyptian nation, and they employed it for a long time as a necessary adjunct to the three ideographic methods. When, as a result of their conversion to Christianity, the Egyptian people received the alphabetic Greek script from the apostles, and then had to write all the words of their maternal tongue with this new alphabet, adoption of which cut them off for ever from the religion, history and institutions of their ancestors, all monuments being, by this act, 'silenced' for these neophytes and their descendants, yet these Egyptians still retained some trace of their ancient phonetic method; and we see in fact that in the oldest Coptic texts, in the Theban dialect, most of the short vowels are completely omitted, and that often, like the hieroglyphic names of Roman emperors, they consist of no more than strings of consonants interspersed at long intervals by a few vowels, almost always long. This resemblance seemed to me worth noting. The Greek and Latin writers have left us no formal remarks on the Egyptian phonetic script; it is very difficult to deduce even the existence of this system, forcing the sense of certain passages where something of the kind would seem to be vaguely hinted at. So we must abandon the attempt to study through historical tradition the period when the phonetic scripts were introduced into the ancient Egyptian picture-writing.

But the facts speak well enough for themselves to enable us to say with fair certainty that the employment of an auxiliary script in Egypt to represent the sounds and articulations of certain words preceded Greek and Roman domination, although it seems most natural to attribute the introduction of the semi-alphabetic Egyptian script to the influence of these two European nations, which had long been using a true alphabet.

Here I base my opinion on the two following considerations, which, sir, may seem to you a solid enough weight to tip the scales.

1. If the Egyptians had invented their phonetic script in imitation of the Greek or Roman alphabets, they would naturally have established a number of phonetic signs equal to the known elements of the Greek or Latin alphabet. But there is nothing of the kind; and the incontestable proof that the Egyptian phonetic writing arose for a totally different purpose from that of expressing the sounds of proper names of Greek or Roman rulers is found in the Egyptian transcription of these very names, which are mostly corrupted to the point of being unrecognisable; firstly by the suppression or confusion of most of the vowels, secondly by the persistent use of the consonants *T* for *Δ*, *K* for *Γ*, *Π* for *Φ*; and lastly by the accidental use of *Λ* for *P* and *P* for *Λ*.

2. I am positive that the same signs in *phonetic hieroglyphs* used to represent the sounds of Greek and Roman proper names were also used in ideographic texts carved long before the Greeks reached Egypt, and that they already had, in certain contexts, the same value representing sounds or articulations as in the cartouches carved under the Greeks and Romans. The development of this valuable and decisive point is connected with my work on the pure hieroglyphs. I could not set out the proof in this letter without plunging into extraordinarily prolonged complications.

Thus, sir, I believe that *phonetic* writing existed in Egypt at a far distant time; that it was first a necessary part of the ideographic script; and that it was then used also, after Cambyses, as we have it, to transcribe (crudely, it is true) in ideographic texts the proper names of peoples, countries, cities, rulers and individual foreigners who had to be commemorated in historic texts or monumental inscriptions.

I dare say more: it would be possible to recover, in this ancient Egyptian phonetic script, imperfect though it may be in itself, if not the source, at least the model on which the alphabets of the western Asiatic nations were framed, above all those of Egypt's immediate neighbours. If you note in fact, sir:

1. that each letter of the alphabets which we term Hebrew, Chaldean and Syriac bears a distinguishing name, very ancient appellations, since they were almost all transmitted by the Phoenicians to the Greeks when the latter took over the alphabet;

2. that the *first consonant or vowel of these names* is also, in these alphabets, the *vowel or consonant to be read*,

you will see, with me, in the creation of these alphabets, a perfect analogy with the creation of the phonetic alphabet in Egypt: and if alphabets of this type are, as everything indicates, primitively formed from signs representing ideas or objects, it is evident that we must recognise the nation who invented this method of written expression in those who particularly used an ideographic script; I mean, in sum, that Europe, which received from ancient Egypt the elements of the arts and sciences, is yet further in her debt for the inestimable benefit of alphabetic writing.

However, I have only tried here to indicate briefly the many important consequences of this discovery, and it arose naturally from my main subject, the *alphabet of the phonetic hieroglyphs*, the general structure of which, together with some applications, I proposed to expound at the same time. The latter produced results which have already met with a favourable response from the illustrious members of the *Académie*, whose scholastic studies have given Europe the first principles of solid learning, and continue to offer her the most valuable of examples. My attempts may perhaps add something to the record of definite achievements by which they have enriched the history of ancient peoples; that of the Egyptians, whose just fame still echoes round the world; and it is certainly no little achievement today that we can take with assurance the first step in the study of their written memorials, and thence gather some precise notion of their leading institutions, to which antiquity itself gave a name for wisdom which nothing has yet overthrown. As for the remarkable monuments erected by the Egyptians, we can at last read, in the cartouches which adorn them, their fixed chronology from Cambyses and the times of their foundation or their successive accretions under the various dynasties which ruled Egypt; the majority of these monuments bear simultaneously the names of pharaohs and of Greeks and Romans, the former, characterised by their small number of signs, perpetually resisting every attempt to apply to them successfully the *alphabet* I have just discovered. Such, sir, I hope, will be the value of this work, which I am flattered to produce under your honoured auspices; the enlightened public will not refuse me its admiration or its support, since I have obtained those of the venerable Nestor of scholarship and French literature, whose devoted studies honour and adorn them, and who, with a hand at once protective and encouraging, is ever pleased to support and guide, in the hard course which he has so gloriously covered, so many young imitators who have later wholly justified his enthusiastic patronage. Happy to rejoice in my turn, I would not, however, venture to make a reply but for my deep gratitude, and my respectful affection; permit me, I beg you, sir, to repeat publicly all my assurances of that affection.

Paris, 22 September 1822 J. F. CHAMPOLLION the younger

Lettre à M. Dacier Relative à l'alphabet des Hiéroglyphes Phonétiques, 1822
Translated from the French by V. M. Conrad

A fantastic interpretation of the Great Pyramid

CHARLES PIAZZI SMYTH

CHARLES PIAZZI SMYTH (*1819-1900*) *was born in Naples, and his second name was chosen in honour of the famous Sicilian astronomer. He justified this choice by making astronomy his career, obtaining first a post as assistant in the Royal Observatory at the Cape of Good Hope, and then the appointment of Astronomer-Royal of Scotland. As long as he confined himself to astronomy and the related fields of meteorology and spectroscopy he produced results of great value and originality, but in middle life he developed an interest in pyramidology, and made a journey to Egypt to survey and measure the Great Pyramid, being firmly convinced that these measurements held invaluable revelations about the past and future of the human race. Among his curious delusions was the notion that the design of the pyramid had been divinely revealed to 'its creator Melchisedec', that it heralded the beginning of the millennium in 1882 – a prophesy he had the misfortune to live to see disproved – and that the measurements, properly interpreted, would produce a cryptographic solution to the problem of squaring the circle. His actual interpretations are too lengthy and too fantastic to come within the scope of this book, so a part of his explanatory introduction has been selected.*

The Pyramids of Egypt have very safely, because according to the collected opinions of the leading antiquaries of all nations, been allowed to be the most ancient existing remains of the most ancient form and fashion of the architecture of that most anciently inhabited land they are found in. They constitute, exhibit, and illustrate, therefore, the nearest approach amongst the intellectual works of man to his doing immediately after the days of the Biblical Dispersion of mankind; and are, in fact, the only *contemporary* proofs that can now be claimed or referred to, for what went on in those exceedingly early times before the birth of written history.

The number of these most remarkable monuments may amount to thirty-seven, or possibly thirty-eight; but that exact number is of little importance, for after the first seven or eight of the largest of them have been passed in review, built, too, as they are, with admirable skill in hewn stone, and appearing on that distant horizon like colossal crystals of mountain size, – the others fail so rapidly in height, breadth, quality of material and lasting power, as to have crumbled into rounded, ruinous masses, and in some of the later cases to be hardly distinguishable from moderate-sized hillocks.

They are, or were, all of them square-based Pyramids, with four triangular sloping flanks for sides, meeting towards the top in a point, over the centre of the base. They are, moreover, nearly solid constructions, whether built of stone or sun-dried brick; and are all situated on the Western, Lybian and more desert side of the Nile, occupying positions there, at intervals, along a line nearly seventy miles in length. This line begins near the Southern point of the Delta land of Lower, that is Northern Egypt, within view, but across the river, of the modern city of Cairo, and extending thence Southward or towards Upper Egypt. But never reaching it; for there all the architecture is of the adorned Temple kind, and is of a much later date in Egyptian history, though still of far greater antiquity than any of the Classic remains of Greece or Rome.

If, too, we should proceed, at this mere preliminary stage of our prospective and exclusive enquiry, to declare, that as to the Pyramids of Egypt in *general*, they were built to serve as lasting sepulchres for the great Egyptian dead, both Pharaohs and their relatives, we shall be supported by all the Egyptological science of modern times. And yet there is one amongst them which refuses to yield to this mode of explanation; and unfortunately it is the greatest, the best built, the best preserved of them all; one that for ages has acquired the name *par excellence* of the Great Pyramid, is spoken of more frequently than any other for and by itself alone, has attracted more frequent historic notice from travellers and writers of all times and all ages; has been considered also almost, if not absolutely quite, the earliest of this very early description of monument raised by man; and was held to be both the greatest and oldest of the seven wonders of the world in the days of the Greeks; while it is now the only one of them all which is still in existence on the surface of the earth.

Locally, this Pyramid is known as that of Jeezeh, Geezeh, or Ghizeh, because, standing on a low, flat-topped hill of that modern Arabic name, in the African desert position already described; where it has, however, several companions of later date and smaller size. Yet they are quite sufficient to discriminate all the travellers who visit them into two sharply divided classes; those who, with the world in general, are enthusiastic about 'the Pyramids' (*i.e.* in the plural) 'of Egypt', with anything else thoroughly Egyptian also; and, on the other side, those who confine their admiration and their interest to the one Great Pyramid, on account of what is there of anti-Egyptian character. For there have been, however it came about, such persons in all ages; though the idea has only begun to bear intellectual fruit in recent years, and has received at last a justification worthy of all Biblical scholars and Christian believers to occupy themselves with enquiring into.

This new idea which solves with a hitherto unknown certainty the chief standing mystery of the civilised world through all the ages, the said world owes to the late Mr John Taylor of London, in a book published in AD 1859, and entitled *The Great Pyramid; why was it built? and who built it?* He had not visited the Pyramid himself, but had been for thirty years previously collecting and comparing all the published accounts, and specially all the better-certified mensurations (for some were certainly poor indeed) of those who had been there; and while so engaged, and quite spontaneously (as he described to me by letter), the new theory opened out before him.

Though mainly a rigid induction from tangible facts of scientific bearing and character, Mr Taylor's result was undoubtedly assisted by means of the mental and spiritual point of view from whence he commenced his researches; and which is, in the main, simply this:

That whereas other writers have generally esteemed that a certain grand but unknown existency, whom they all allow, in their historical enquiries, did direct the building of the one Great Pyramid (and to whom the Egyptians in their early traditions and for ages afterwards gave an immortal and even abominable character) must, therefore, have been very bad indeed – so that the world at large, from that time to this, has ever been fond of treading on and insulting that dead lion whom they really knew nothing of – he, Mr John Taylor, seeing in every characteristic mention of them in the *Bible*, how religiously bad the idol-inventing Egyptians themselves were, was led to conclude that the unknown leader and Architect whom they hated, and could never sufficiently abuse, might perhaps have been pre-eminently *good*; or was, at all events, of a *purer religious faith* than that of the Mizraite sons of Ham.

Then, remembering, with *mutatis mutandis* what Christ himself says respecting the suspicion to be attached, when all the *world* speaks well of any one, Mr Taylor followed up this idea by what the Old Testament does record touching the most vital and distinguishing part of the Israelitish religion; and which is therein described, some centuries after the building of the Great Pyramid, as notoriously an 'abomination to the Egyptians'; and combining this with certain unmistakable and undisputed, by any one, historical facts, he successfully deduced sound and Christian reasons for believing that the director of the building, and perhaps his immediate assistants who controlled the myriads of *native* builders at the Great Pyramid, were by no means Egyptians, but strangers of the *chosen* race, sons of Shem, and in the line of, though preceding Abraham; so early, indeed, as to be closer to Noah than to Abraham. Men, at all events, who had been enabled by Divine favour to appreciate the appointed idea, as to the absolute necessity of a sacrifice and atonement for the sins of man by the blood and free-offering of a Divine Mediator, as in the most earnest and Evangelical form of Christianity.

This very crucial idea of our present faith was nevertheless of an antiquity coeval with the contest between Cain and Abel, and had descended through the Flood to certain predestined families of mankind; but yet was an idea which no one of Egyptian born would ever contemplate with a moment's patience. For every ancient Egyptian, from first to last, and every Pharaoh of them more especially, just as with the Ninevites and Babylonians generally, was an unmitigated Cainite in thought, act, and feeling to the very backbone; confident of, and professing nothing so much, or so constantly, as his own perfect righteousness and absolute freedom by his own innate purity, and by his own invariable, complete, and unswerving rectitude throughout his whole life from every kind of sin, large or small, against God or man.

On this general ground it was that Mr Taylor took his stand; and, after disobeying the world's long-formed public opinion of too passively obedient accord with profane Egyptian tradition, and after thereby also setting at naught some of the most time-honoured prejudices of modern Egyptological scholars, so far as to give a full, fair and impartial examination to the whole case from the beginning, announced that he had discovered in some of the arrangements and measures of the Great Pyramid – when duly corrected for injuries and dilapidations of intervening time – certain scientific results, which speak of neither Egyptian nor Babylonian, and much less of Greek or Roman learning, but of something much more than, as well as quite different from, any ordinary human ways of those several contemporary times.

For, besides coming forth *suddenly* in the primeval history of its own remote day, without any preliminary period of childhood, or known ages of evolution and preparation – the actual facts of the Great Pyramid, in the shape of builded proofs of an exact numerical knowledge of the grander cosmical phenomena of both earth and heavens – not only rise above, and far above, the extremely limited and almost infantine knowledge of science humanly attained to by any of the Gentile nations of 4,000, 3,000, 2,000, nay only 300 years ago; but they are also, in whatever of the great physical secrets of nature they chiefly apply to, essentially above the best knowledge of philosophers in our own time as well.

This is indeed a startling assertion to be put forth about an ancient stone monument. Never ventured, too, by any one, let it be duly borne in mind, for the 'Pyramids of Egypt' in the plural; but only for the one great and strange Pyramid *in* Egypt; and which, though standing *there*, is yet not at all *of*, or *according to*, native ideas, whether in science or religion, as they were graven in the hieroglyphics of Egypt, and as she herself has described them in her own history. Yet the assertion admits of the completest and most positive refutation, if at all as untrue for the Great Pyramid as it undoubtedly is for any other ancient building whatever. For the exact science of the present day, compared with that of only a hundred years ago, is a marvel of development; and is capable of giving out no uncertain sound, both in asserting itself, and stating not only the fact, but the order and time of the invention of all the practical means humanly necessary to the minutest steps of each separate discovery yet made.

Much more then can this modern science of the mathematical kind speak with positiveness, when comparing its own presently extended knowledge against the little that was known to man, by his own efforts and by his then school methods, in those early epochs before accurate and numerical physical science had begun, or could have been begun, to be seriously cultivated at all. That is, in the truly primeval day when men were few on the earth, and yet the Great Pyramid was built, finished, sealed up, and left as we see it now, modern dilapidations only excepted, in the midst of an unbelieving world, to guard its own secret through the ages, and serve at last its intended purpose, whatever that was to be, in the latter days of mankind.

Let us proceed, then, to examine all well known Great Pyramid facts by the light of modern science, so far as that can be brought to bear; keeping our eyes duly open all the time to the necessity of guarding, on one side against accidental coincidences in favour of this theory of the Great Pyramid; and on the other, to the possibility of any intentional features really detected there being common to any of the other Pyramids as well.

Before the many difficulties of such an enquiry, and the practical skill required, I should myself have been very loath to pronounce any positive conclusions on reading alone any number of so-called book authorities. But having actually visited the Pyramid field in Egypt; encamped there in 1864 and 1865 for several months, making daily use of a variety of scientific measuring apparatus; and since then having spent more than twenty years in working out, and fighting for, every step of the enquiry, I do humbly trust that, by the grace of God, I may not only have arrived at many true results, but may be able to show that the steps of the work and the progress of the proof are much easier than might have been anticipated to all who are in heart inclined to follow, and desire to make securely their own.

Our Inheritance in the Great Pyramid, 1890

The underwater tomb

WILLIAM FLINDERS PETRIE

Sir William Matthew Flinders Petrie (*1853–1942*) *was born at Charlton and took an early interest in antiquities. He began with a study of Stonehenge, and published a book on the subject in 1880, which was also the year of his first expedition to Egypt. He was largely responsible for the establishment of the Egyptian chronology in the form in which it is used today; and as founder of the British School of Archaeology in Egypt, under whose auspices the site of Memphis was discovered and excavated, he ensured the continuity of scientific study of Egyptian antiquities. The sites of his surveys and explorations included the temple of Tanis, the Greek city of Naucratis, the Delta towns, the Fayum, Meydum and the Pyramids of Giza.*

When considering the places favourable for future excavations I had named Hawara and Illahun, amongst other sites, to M. Grébaut; and he proposed to me that I should work in the Fayum province in general. The exploration of the pyramids of this district was my main object, as their arrangement, their date, and their builders were quite unknown. Hawara was not a convenient place to work at, as the village was two miles from the pyramid, and a canal lay between; I therefore determined to form a camp of workmen to live on the spot, as at Daphnae. For this purpose I needed to recruit a party from a little distance, and began my work therefore at the ancient Arsinoe or Crocodilopolis, close to Medinet el Fayum. Here I cleared the pylon of the temple, of which a few disturbed blocks remain, and found a second mention of Amenemhat II beside that already known; but his work had all been altered and rebuilt, probably by Ramessu II. Four or five different levels of buildings, and reconstruction could be traced, and the depth of rubbish over the approach to the temple in the shallowest part of the mounds was twenty-four feet. Within the great enclosure of mud-brick wall, the site of the temple could be traced by following the bed of sand, on which the foundations had been laid; but scarcely a single stone was left. One re-used block had a figure of a king of the nineteenth dynasty, probably Ramessu II; and this leads us to date as late as

Ptolemy II the temple which we can trace here. He doubtless built a large temple, as the place received much attention in his time, and was dedicated to his sister-wife Arsinoe: she was specially worshipped along with the great gods, as we know from the stele of Pithom. The only early objects found here were flint knives in the soil of the temple; these belong to the twelfth dynasty, as we know from later discoveries.

A short work of a few days at Biahmu resolved the questions about the so-called pyramids there. So soon as we began to turn over the soil we found chips of sandstone colossi; the second day the gigantic nose of a colossus was found, as a broad as a man's body; then pieces of carved thrones, and a fragment of inscription of Amenemhat III. It was evident that the two great piles of stone had been the pedestals of colossal seated monolithic statues, carved in hard quartzite sandstone and brilliantly polished. These statues faced northward, and around each was a courtyard wall with sloping outer face, and red granite gateway in the north front. The total height of the colossi was about sixty feet from the ground. The limestone pedestal rose twenty-one feet, then the sandstone colossus had a base of four feet, on which the figure, seated on its throne, rose to a height of thirty-five feet more. Thus the whole statue and part of its pedestal would be visible above the enclosing courtyard wall, and it would appear from a distance as if it were placed on a truncated pyramid. The description of Herodotos, therefore, is fully accounted for; and it shows that he actually saw the figures, though from a distance, as any person who visited them closely would not have described them in such a manner.

Having by this time formed and organised a good body of workmen, I moved over to Hawara, with as many men as I wanted; and the only difficulty was to restrain the numbers who wished to work. The pyramid had never been entered in modern times, and its arrangement was wholly unknown; explorers had fruitlessly destroyed much of the brickwork on the north side but yet the entrance was undiscovered. In Roman times the stone casing had been removed, and as the body of the structure was of mud bricks, it had crumbled away somewhat: each side was therefore encumbered with chips and mud. After vainly searching the ground on the north side for any entrance, I then cleared the middle of the east side, but yet no trace of any door could be found. As it was evident then that the plan was entirely different to that of any known pyramid, and it would be a hopeless task to clear all the ground around it, I therefore settled to tunnel to the midst. This work was very troublesome as the large bricks were laid in sand, and rather widely spaced; hence as soon as any were removed, the sand was liable to pour out of the joints, and to loosen all the surrounding parts. The removal of each brick was therefore done as quietly as possible, and I had to go in three times a day and insert more roofing boards, a matter which needed far more skill and care than a native workman would use. After many weeks' work (for there was only room for one man), I found that we were halfway through, but all in brick. On one side of the tunnel, however, I saw signs of a built wall, and guessing that it had stood around the pit made for the chamber during the building, I examined the rock-floor, and found that it sloped down slightly, away from the wall. We turned then to the west, and tunnelling onwards, we reached the great roofing beams of the chamber in a few days. No masons of the district, however, could cut through them, and I had to leave the work till the next season. Then, after a further search on all the four sides for the entrance, the masons attacked the sloping stone roof, and in two or three weeks' time a hole beneath them was reported; anxiously I watched them enlarge it until I could squeeze through, and then I entered the chamber above the sepulchre; at one side I saw a lower hole, and going down I found a broken way into the sandstone sepulchre, but too narrow for my shoulders. After sounding the water inside it, a boy was put down with a rope-ladder; and at last, on looking through the hole, I could see by the light of his candle the two sarcophagi, standing rifled and empty. In a day or two we cleared away the rubbish from the original entrance passage to the chamber, and so went out into the passages, which turned and wandered up and down. These were so nearly choked with mud, that in many parts the only way along them was by lying flat, and sliding along the mud, pushed by fingers and toes. In this way, sliding, crawling, and wading, I reached as near to the outer mouth of the passage as possible; and then by measuring back to the chamber, the position of the mouth on the outside of the pyramid was pretty nearly found. But so deep was it under the rubbish, and so much encumbered with large blocks of stone, that it took about a fortnight to reach it from the outside.

The pyramid had been elaborately arranged so as to deceive and weary the spoiler, and it had apparently occupied a great amount of labour to force an entrance. The mouth was on the ground level, on the south side, a quarter of the length from the south-west corner. The original explorers descended a passage with steps to a chamber, from which apparently there was no exit. The roof consisted of a sliding trap-door, however, and breaking through this another chamber was reached at a higher level. Then a passage opened to the east, closed with a wooden door, and leading to another chamber with a trap-door roof. But in front of the explorer was a passage carefully plugged up solid with stone; this they thought would lead to the prize, and so all the stones were mined through, only to lead to nothing. From the second trap-door chamber a passage led northward to the third chamber. From that a passage led west to a chamber with two wells, which seemed as if they led to the tomb, but both were false. This chamber also was almost filled with masonry, which all concealed nothing, but had given plenty of occupation to the spoilers who removed it in vain. A filled-up trench in the floor of the chamber really led to the sepulchre; but arriving there no door was to be found, as the entrance had been by the roof, an enormous block of which had been let down into place to close the chamber. So at last the way had been forced by breaking away a hole in the edge of the glassy-hard sandstone roofing block, and thus reaching the chamber and its sarcophagi. By a little widening of the spoilers' hole I succeeded in getting through it into the chamber. The water was up to the middle of my body, and so exploration was difficult; but the floor was covered with rubbish and chips which might contain parts of the funereal vessels, and therefore needed searching. The rubbish in the sarcophagi I cleared out myself; and then I set some lads to gather up the scraps from the floor on the flat blade of a hoe (as it was out of arms' reach under water), and after searching them they threw them into the sarcophagi. Thus we anxiously worked on for any inscribed fragments; my anxiety being for the cartouche of the king, the boys' anxiety for the big bakhshish promised, at *per* hieroglyph found, extra value given for cartouches. The system worked, for in the first day I got the coveted prize, a piece of an alabaster vessel with the name of Amenemhat III, proving finally to whom the pyramid belonged; and other parts of inscribed vessels were found. Still there was a puzzle as to the second sarcophagus, which had been built up between the great central one and the chamber side. On clearing in the chamber which led to the sepulchre, however, they found a beautiful altar of offerings in alabaster, covered with figures of the offerings all named, over a hundred in all, and dedicated for the king's daughter, Neferu-ptah; near it were parts of several bowls in the form of half a trussed duck, also bearing her name: so doubtless the second interment was hers; and she must have died during her father's life, and before the closing of the pyramid. Of the actual bodies I found a few scraps of charred bones, besides bits of charcoal and grains of burnt diorite in the sarcophagi; also a beard of lazuli for inlaying was found in the chamber. The wooden inner coffins, inlaid with hard stone carving, had therefore been burnt. The chamber itself is a marvellous work; nearly the whole height of it is carved out of a single block of hard quartzite sandstone, forming a huge tank, in which the sarcophagus was placed. In the inside it is twenty-two feet long and nearly eight feet wide, while the sides are about three feet thick. The surface is polished, and the corners so sharply cut that I mistook it for masonry, until I searched in vain for the joints. Of course it was above water level originally; but all this region had been saturated by a high level canal of Arab times. Afterwards I had all the earth removed from the pyramid passages as far as practicable, but nothing further was found there. No trace of inscription exists on either the walls or sarcophagi; and but for the funereal furniture, even the very name would not have been recovered.

Ten Years' Digging in Egypt, 1892

The discovery of the Amarna tablets

ERNEST BUDGE

Sir Ernest Alfred Wallis Budge (*1857-1934*) *was born in Cornwall and educated at Christ's College, Cambridge, where he became Assyrian and Hebrew Scholar. He entered the service of the British Museum in 1883 and ultimately became Keeper of Egyptian and Assyrian antiquities; in 1920 he was knighted for his services to archaeology. He made many expeditions to the eastern Mediterranean region, and besides conducting excavations he obtained for the British Museum a large number of antiquities, papyri and manuscripts, in the Greek, Coptic, Arabic, Syriac and Ethiopic languages. His most significant acquisition, however, was a collection of documents written at the end of the XVIII dynasty, known as the Amarna tablets.*

In the course of the day a man arrived from Hajjî Kandîl, bringing with him some half-dozen of the clay tablets which had been found accidentally by a woman at Tall al-'Amârnah, and he asked me to look at them, and to tell him if they were *kadim*, i.e. 'old' or *jadid*, i.e. 'new' – that is to say, whether they were genuine or forgeries. The woman who found them thought they were bits of 'old clay', and useless, and sold the whole 'find' of over 300 tablets to a neighbour for 10 piastres (*2s.*)! The purchaser took them into the village of Hajjî Kandîl, and they changed hands for £E10. But those who bought them knew nothing about what they were buying, and when they had bought them they sent a man to Cairo with a few of them to show the dealers, both native and European. Some of the European dealers thought they were 'old' and some thought they were 'new', and they agreed together to declare the tablets forgeries so that they might buy them at their own price as 'specimens of modern imitations'. The dealers in Upper Egypt believed them to be genuine, and refused to sell, and, having heard that I had some knowledge of cuneiform, they sent to me the man mentioned above, and asked me to say whether they were forgeries or not; and they offered to pay me for my information. When I examined the tablets I found that the matter was not as simple as it looked. In shape and form, and colour and material, the tablets were unlike any I had ever seen in London or Paris, and the writing on all of them was of a most unusual character and puzzled me for hours. By degrees I came to the conclusion that the tablets were certainly not forgeries, and that they were neither royal annals nor historical inscriptions in the ordinary sense of the word, nor business or commercial documents. Whilst I was examining the half-dozen tablets brought to me, a second man from Hajjî Kandîl arrived with seventy-six more of the tablets, some of them quite large. On the largest and best written of the second lot of tablets I was able to make out the words 'A-na Ni-ib-mu-a-ri-ya', i.e. 'To Nibmuariya', and on another the words '(A)-na Ni-im-mu-ri-ya shar mâtu Mi-is-ri', i.e. 'to Nimmuriya, king of the land of Egypt'. These two tablets were certainly letters addressed to a king of Egypt called 'Nib-muariya' or 'Nimmuriya'. On another tablet I made out clearly the opening words 'A-na Ni-ip-khu-ur-ri-ri-ya shar mâtu (Misri)', i.e. 'To Nibkhurririya, king of the land of (Egypt') and there was no doubt that this tablet was a letter addressed to another king of Egypt. The opening words of nearly all the tablets proved to be letters or despatches, and I felt certain that the tablets were both genuine and of very great importance.

Up to the moment when I arrived at that conclusion neither of the men from Hajjî Kandîl had offered the tablets to me for purchase, and I suspected that they were simply waiting for my decision as to their genuineness to take them away and ask a very high price for them, a price beyond anything I had the power to give. Therefore, before telling the dealers my opinion about the tablets, I arranged with them to make no charge for my examination of them, and to be allowed to take possession of the eighty-two tablets forthwith. They asked me to fix the price which I was prepared to pay for the tablets, and I did so, and though they had to wait a whole year for their money they made no attempt to demand more than the sum which they agreed with me to accept.

I then tried to make arrangements with the men from Hajjî Kandîl to get the remainder of the tablets from Tall al-'Amârnah into my possession, but they told me that they belonged to dealers who were in treaty with an agent of the Berlin Museum in Cairo. Among the tablets was a very large one, about 20 inches long and broad in proportion. We now know that it contained a list of the dowry of a Mesopotamian princess who was going to marry a king of Egypt. The man who was taking this to Cairo hid it between his inner garments, and covered himself with his great cloak. As he stepped up into the railway coach this tablet slipped from his clothes and fell on the bed of the railway, and broke in pieces. Many natives in the train and on the platform witnessed the accident and talked freely about it, and thus the news of the discovery of the tablets reached the ears of the Director of Antiquities. He at once telegraphed to the Mudir of Asyût, and ordered him to arrest and put in prison everyone who was found to be in possession of tablets, and, as we have seen, he himself set out for Upper Egypt to seize all the tablets he could find. Meanwhile, a gentleman in Cairo who had obtained four of the smaller tablets and paid £E100 for them, showed them to an English professor, who promptly wrote an article upon them, and published it in an English newspaper. He postdated the tablets by nearly 900 years, and entirely misunderstood the nature of their contents. The only effect of his article was to increase the importance of the tablets in the eyes of the dealers, and, in consequence, to raise their prices, and make the acquisition of the rest of the 'find' more difficult for everyone.

By Nile and Tigris, vol. I, 1920

Thames and Hudson Archives

12. The sarcophagus of Sekhem Khet, found inside the buried pyramid of Saqqara. It was empty!

Ashmolean Museum, Oxf

13. Carter and his colleagues at the doorway of Tutankhamen's tomb.

Tutankhamen

HOWARD CARTER

HOWARD CARTER *(1873-1939) was born in Swaffham, Norfolk, and educated privately. At the age of seventeen he entered the service of the Egyptian Exploration Fund, and Flinders Petrie was among those who supervised his training in archaeological techniques. He took part in several excavations under the auspices of the Fund until 1899 when he was appointed Inspector General of the Antiquities department of the Egyptian government. From 1902 onwards he supervised Davis' excavations in the Valley of the Kings, which brought to light the tombs of Tuthmoses IV and Queen Hatshepsut. After this he was engaged to take charge of an excavation under the patronage of Lord Carnarvon, and in 1922 he discovered the tomb of the XVIII dynasty pharaoh Tutankhamen, which was the first and only intact royal burial to be discovered in the Valley of the Kings.*

It was on February 3 (1924) that we first had a clear view of this sepulchral masterpiece, ranking as it does among the finest specimens of its kind the world possesses. It has a rich entablature consisting of a cavetto-cornice, taurus moulding and frieze of inscription. But the outstanding features of the sarcophagus are the guardian goddesses Isis, Nephthys, Neith and Selkit, carved in high relief on each of the four corners, so placed that their full spread wings and outstretched arms encircle it with their protective embrace. Round the base is a dado or protective symbols *Ded* and *Thet*. The corners of the casket rested upon alabaster slabs. Between the last shrine and the sarcophagus there were no objects, save for a *Ded*-symbol placed on the south side for 'Strength' and possibly 'Protection' of the owner.

As our light fell on the noble quartzite monument, it illuminated, in repeated detail, that last solemn appeal to gods and men, and made us feel that, in the young king's case, a dignity had been added even to death. With the profound silence that reigned the emotion deepened, the past and present seemed to meet – time to stand and wait, and one asked oneself, was it not yesterday that, with pomp and ceremony, they had laid the young king in that casket? – so fresh, so seemingly recent, were those touching claims on our pity that, the more we gazed on them, the more the illusion gathered strength. It made one wish that his journey through those grim tunnels of the Underworld might be unperturbed until he attained complete felicity! – as those four goddesses, sculptured in high relief at the corners, seemed to plead as they shielded their charge. For in them had we not a perfect Egyptian elegy in stone?

The lid made of rose granite tinted to match the quartzite sarcophagus, was cracked in the middle and firmly embedded in the rebated top edges. The cracks had been carefully cemented and painted over to match the rest, in such a way as to leave no doubt that it had not been tampered with. Undoubtedly the original intention must have been to provide a quartzite lid in keeping with the sarcophagus itself; it would therefore appear that some accident had occurred. It may be that the intended lid was not ready in time for the burial of the king, and that this crudely made granite slab was substituted in its place.

The crack greatly complicated our final effort, the raising of this lid, for had it been intact the operation would have been far easier. The difficulty, however, was overcome by passing angle irons along and closely fitting the sides of the slab, which permitted it to be raised by differential pulleys as one piece. . . .

Many strange scenes must have happened in the Valley of the Tombs of the Kings since it became the royal burial ground of the Theban New Empire, but one may be pardoned for thinking that the present scene was not the least interesting or dramatic. For ourselves it was the one supreme and culminating moment – a moment looked forward to ever since it became evident that the chambers discovered, in November 1922, must be the tomb of Tut-ankh-Amen, and not a cache of his furniture as had been claimed. None of us but felt the solemnity of the occasion, none of us but was affected by the prospect of what we were about to see – the burial custom of a king of ancient Egypt of thirty-three centuries ago. How would the king be found? Such were the anticipatory speculations running in our minds during the silence maintained.

The tackle for raising the lid was in position. I gave the word. Amid intense silence the huge slab, broken in two, weighing over a ton and a quarter, rose from its bed. The light shone into the sarcophagus. A sight met our eyes that at first puzzled us. It was a little disappointing. The contents were completely covered by fine linen shrouds. The lid being suspended in mid-air, we rolled back those covering shrouds, one by one, and as the last was removed a gasp of wonderment escaped our lips, so gorgeous was the sight that met our eyes: a golden effigy of the young boy king, of most magnificent workmanship, filled the whole of the interior of the sarcophagus. This was the lid of a wonderful anthropoid coffin, some seven feet in length, resting upon a low bier in the form of a lion, and no doubt the outermost coffin of a series of coffins, nested one within the other, enclosing the mortal remains of the king. Enclasping the body of this magnificent monument are two winged goddesses: Isis and Neith, wrought in rich gold-work upon gesso, as brilliant as the day the coffin was made. To it an additional charm was added, by the fact that, while this decoration was rendered in fine low bas-relief, the head and hands of the king were in the round, in massive gold of the finest sculpture, surpassing anything we could have imagined. The hands, crossed over the breast, held the royal emblems – the Crook and the Flail – encrusted with deep blue faience. The face and features were wonderfully wrought in sheet-gold. The eyes were of aragonite and obsidian, the eyebrows and eyelids inlaid with lapis lazuli glass. There was a touch of realism, for while the rest of this anthropoid coffin, covered with feathered ornament, was of brilliant gold, that of the bare face and hands seemed different, the gold of the flesh being of different alloy, thus conveying an impression of the greyness of death. Upon the forehead of this recumbent figure of the young boy king were two emblems delicately worked in brilliant inlay – the Cobra and the Vulture – symbols of Upper and Lower Egypt, but perhaps the most touching by its human simplicity was the tiny wreath of flowers around these symbols, as it pleased us to think, the last farewell offering of the widowed girl queen to her husband, the youthful representative of the 'Two Kingdoms'.

Among all that real splendour, that royal magnificence – everywhere the glint of gold – there was nothing so beautiful as those few withered flowers still retaining their tinge of colour. They told us what a short period three thousand three hundred years really was – but Yesterday and the Morrow. In fact, that little touch of nature made that ancient and our modern civilisation kin.

Thus from stairway, steep descending passage, Antechamber and Burial Chamber, from those golden shrines and from that noble sarcophagus, our eyes were now turned to its contents – a gold-encased coffin, in form a recumbent figure of the young king, symbolising Osiris or, it would seem, by its fearless gaze, man's ancient trust in immortality. Many and disturbing were our emotions awakened by that Osiride form. Most of them were voiceless. But, in that silence, to listen – you could almost hear the ghostly footsteps of the departing mourners.

Our lights were lowered, once more we mounted those sixteen steps, once more we beheld the blue vault of the heavens, where the Sun is Lord, but our inner thoughts still lingered over the splendour of that vanished Pharaoh, with his last appeal upon his coffin written upon our minds: 'Oh Mother Nût! spread thy wings over me as the Imperishable Stars.'

The Tomb of Tut-ankh-Amen, vol. II, 1927

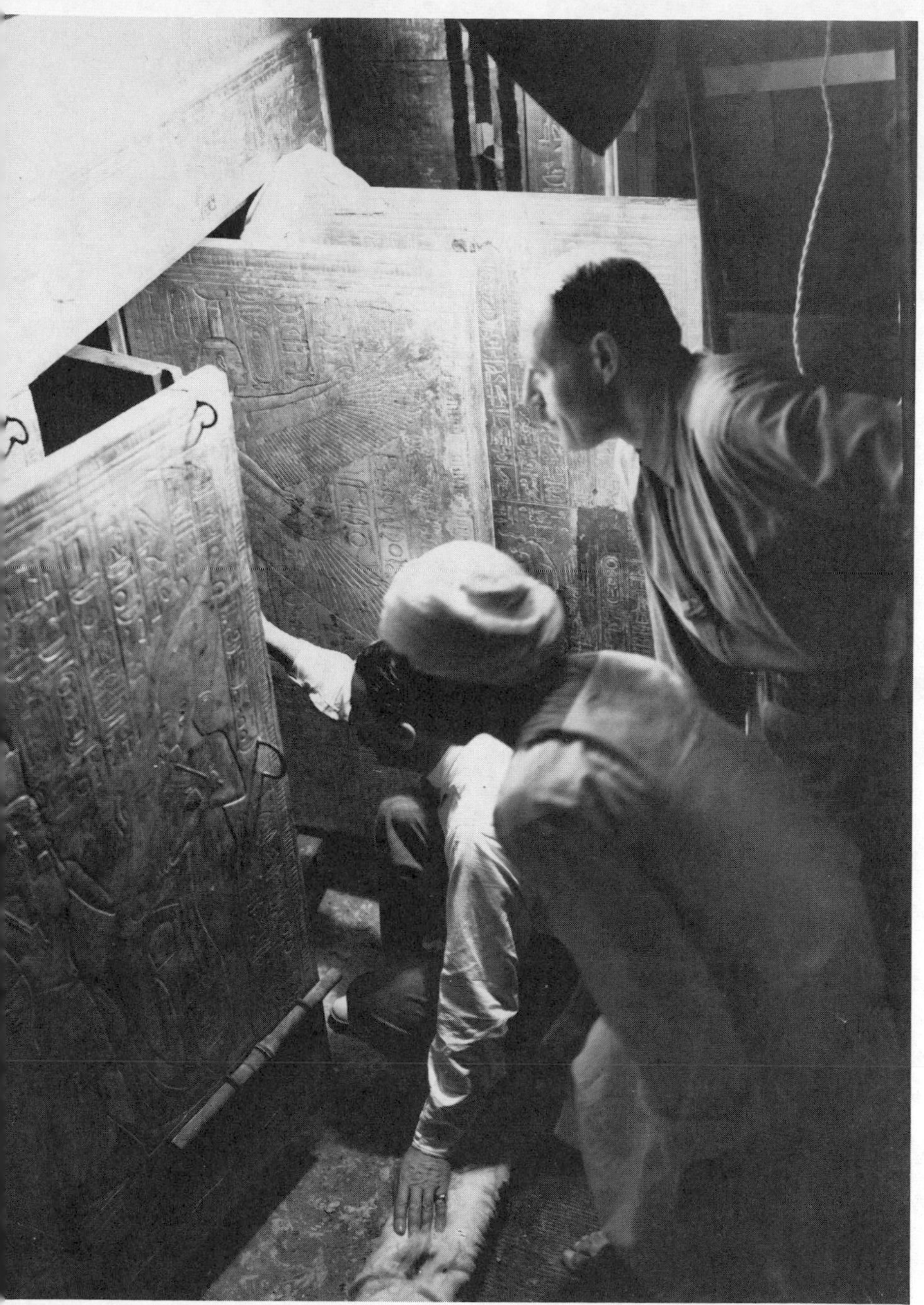

hmolean Museum, Oxford

14. Opening the doors of the shrine which contained the golden coffins of Tutankhamen.

The golden coffin

HOWARD CARTER

Thus our season had begun. The Valley, awakened from its summer sleep for the last two days by bawling workmen and screaming boys, was at peace again, and quiet will possess it until the winter migrants and their followers invade its golden silence.

The Antechamber freed of its beautiful furniture, the Burial Chamber denuded of its golden shrines, leaves the now open stone sarcophagus in the centre with its coffins within alone retaining their secret.

The task before us now was to raise the lid of the first outermost coffin, as it rested in the sarcophagus.

This great gilded wooden coffin, 7 feet 4 inches in length, anthropoid in shape, wearing the *Khat* head-dress, with face and hands in heavier sheet-gold, is of *Rishi* type – a term applied when the main decoration consists of a feather design, a fashion common to coffins of the preceding Intermediate and Seventeenth Dynasty Theban periods. During the New Empire, in the case of burials of high officials and commoners, the style of decoration of coffins completely changes at the beginning of the Eighteenth Dynasty; but in the case of the royal coffin, as we now see, the older fashion still survived, with only very slight modification, such as the addition of figures of certain tutelary goddesses. This is a complete inversion of the usual order of things – fashion generally changing more rapidly with the upper than with the lower stations in life. May not this connote some religious idea in connexion with a king? There may be tradition behind it. The goddess Isis once protected the dead body of Osiris by taking him within her wings, thus she protects this new Osiris as represented by the effigy.

After careful study of the coffin it was decided that the original silver handles – two on each side – manifestly made for the purpose, were sufficiently well preserved still to support the weight of the lid, and could be used without danger in raising it. The lid was fixed to the shell by means of ten solid silver tongues, fitted into corresponding sockets in the thickness of the shell (four on each side, one at the head-, and one at the foot-end) where they were held in place by substantial gold-headed silver pins. Could we remove the silver pins by which the lid was fixed to the shell of the coffin without disturbing the coffin in the sarcophagus? As the coffin filled up nearly the whole of the interior of the sarcophagus, leaving only the smallest space, especially at the head- and foot-ends, it was by no means easy to extract the pins. By careful manipulation, however, it was found possible to withdraw them, with the exception of the pin at the head-end where there was only space enough enough to pull it half out. It had therefore to be filed through before the inner half could be withdrawn.

The next step was to place in position the hoisting tackle necessary for lifting the lid. This tackle consisted of two sets of three sheaf pulley-blocks provided with automatic brakes, fixed to an overhead scaffold, the pulleys being slung so as to come immediately above the centre of the lid opposite each pair of handles. The tackle was attached to the handles of the lid of the coffin by means of slings, and thus a correct centralization of its weight was assured, otherwise there would have been a danger of the lid bumping against the sides of the sarcophagus the moment it became free and pendent.

It was a moment as anxious as exciting. The lid came up fairly readily, revealing a second magnificent anthropoid coffin, covered with a thin gossamer linen sheet, darkened and much decayed. Upon this linen shroud were lying floral garlands, composed of olive and willow leaves, petals of the blue lotus and cornflowers, whilst a small wreath of similar kind had been placed, also over the shroud, on the emblems of the forehead. Underneath this covering, in places, glimpses could be obtained of rich multi-coloured glass decoration encrusted upon the fine gold-work of the coffin.

Some time was spent in the previous summer working out the methods to be followed in this undertaking, and in providing the necessary appliances, thus it was completed in one morning when otherwise it would have occupied several days at least. The tomb was closed, everything being left undisturbed to await Mr Harry Burton's photographic records.

Thus far our progress had been fairly satisfactory, but we now became conscious of a rather ominous feature. The second coffin, which, so far as visible through the linen covering, had every appearance of being a wonderful piece of workmanship, showed distinct signs of the effect of some form of dampness and, here and there, tendency for its beautiful inlay to fall away. This was, I must admit, disconcerting, suggesting as it did the existence of former humidity of some kind within the nest of coffins. Should this prove the case, the preservation of the royal mummy would be less satisfactory than we had hoped.

On October 15 Mr Burton arrived, and on the 17th, early in the morning, he successfully completed the photographic records of the shroud and floral garlands that covered the second coffin, as it rested, within the shell of the first, in the sarcophagus.

These records complete, we had now to consider how best to deal with the second coffin, as well as the shell of the first. Manifestly, our difficulties were increased on account of the depth of the sarcophagus, and it was evident that the outer shell and the second coffin, neither of which was in a condition to bear much handling, must be raised together. This was eventually accomplished by means of pulleys as before, attachment being attained by means of steel pins passed through the tongue-sockets of the first outermost shell. In this way hoisting was possible with minimum of handling.

In spite of the great weight of the coffins – far heavier than at first seemed possible – they were successfully raised to just above the level of the top of the sarcophagus, when wooden planks were passed under them. In the confined space, and with the restricted head-room available, the task proved one of no little difficulty. It was much increased by the necessity of avoiding damage to the fragile gesso-gilt surfaces of the outermost coffin.

Further records having been taken, I was then able to remove the chaplet and garlands, and roll back the covering shroud. It was one more exciting moment. We could now gaze, with admiring eyes, upon the finest example of the ancient coffin-maker's art ever yet seen – Osiride, again in form, but most delicate in conception, and very beautiful in line. As it now lay in the outer shell which rested upon the modern improvised trestles, it presented a wonderful picture of Majesty lying in State.

The chaplet and garlands placed upon the shroud in memory of 'the wreaths given to Osiris on his triumphant exit from the Judgment-hall of Heliopolis', which, as Dr Gardiner remarks, reminds us of the 'crown of righteousness' (2 Tim. iv. 8), were but illustration of Pliny's description of ancient Egyptian wreaths. When the care and precision with which these are fashioned is recognised, there is strong reason for the belief that this particular occupation with the ancient Egyptians, as in later days, must have been a specialised trade.

This second coffin, 6 feet 8 inches in length, sumptuously inlaid on thick gold-foil with cut and engraved opaque glass, simulating red jasper, lapis lazuli and turquoise respectively, is similar in form and design to the first. It symbolises Osiris, it is *Rishi* in ornament, but it differs in certain detail. In this case the king wears the *Nemes* headdress, and in place of the protective figures of Isis and Nephthys, the body is embraced with the wings of the vulture Nekhebet and of the serpent Buto. The arresting feature is the delicacy and superiority of the conception, which confer upon it at once the position of a masterpiece.

We were now faced by a complicated problem, not unlike the one we had to solve two seasons before when the covering shrines were dismantled. It was again a case of the unexpected happening. Conclusions drawn from former evidence or example are not to be trusted. For some unknown reason the reverse too often proves to be the case. On seeing that there were handles on the outer coffin for lowering or raising it, we were led to expect similar metal handles on the second coffin. There was none, and their absence placed us in a dilemma. The second coffin proved exceedingly heavy; its decorated surface very fragile; it fitted the outer shell so closely that it was not possible to pass one's little finger between the two. Its lid was fixed, as in the case of the outer coffin, with gold-headed silver pins which, as the coffin lay in the outer shell, could not be extracted. It was evident that it would have to be lifted in its entirety from the outer shell before anything further could be done. Thus the problem which confronted us was to discover a method of doing this with the minimum risk of damage to its delicate inlay, that had already suffered from some kind of humidity, the origin of which was then unknown.

It may be, under the strain of such operations as these, that one is too conscious of the risk of irreparable damage to the rare and beautiful object one desires to preserve intact. Much in the early days of Egyptian archaeological research had undoubtedly been lost to us by too eager or careless handling, more still from want of necessary appliances at the right moment; but against ill-luck, even when every possible precaution has been taken, no man is secure. Everything may seem to be going well until suddenly, in the crisis of the process, you hear a crack – little pieces of surface ornament fall. Your nerves are at an almost painful tension. What is happening? All available room in the narrow space is crowded by your men. What action is needed to avert a catastrophe? There is, too, another danger. As the lid is being raised, the excitement of seeing some new and beautiful object may attract the workmen's attention; for a moment their duty is forgotten, and irreparable damage in consequence may be done.

Such are often the anxious impressions uppermost in the archaeologist's memory when his friends enquire what his emotions in these thrilling moments may have been. Only those who have had to handle heavy yet fragile antiquities in circumstances of similar difficulty, can realise how exacting and nerve-racking the strain and responsibility may become. Moreover, in the case before us, we could not be sure that the wood of the coffin was sufficiently well preserved to bear its own weight. However, after long consultations, and having studied the problem for nearly two days, we devised a plan. To remove the second coffin from the shell of the first, some points of attachment were necessary. There were, it will be remembered, no handles, so it was judged best to make use of the metal pins which fastened down the lid.

Inspection showed, however, that although the space between the shell of the outer coffin and the second coffin was insufficient to enable us to withdraw these pins entirely, they could still be pulled out about a quarter of an inch, so as to permit stout copper wire attachments to be fixed to them and to the overhead scaffold. This we did successfully. Strong metal eyelets were then screwed into the thickness of the top edge of the shell of the outer coffin so as to enable it to be lowered from the second coffin by means of ropes working on the pulleys.

On the following day, after these preparations, we were able to proceed with the next stage. It proved to be one of the most important moments in the dismantling of the tomb. The process adopted was the reverse of that which might at first appear to be the natural order of things. We lowered the outer shell from the second coffin, instead of lifting the second coffin out of the first. The reason for this was that the head-room was insufficient, and the weight being stationary, there would be less risk of undue stress upon those ancient silver pins. The operations proved successful. The shell of the outer coffin was lowered once more into the sarcophagus, leaving for a moment, the second coffin suspended in mid-air by means of the ten stout wire attachments A wooden tray sufficiently large to span the opening of the sarcophagus was then passed under it, and thus the second coffin strongly supported, stood before us free and accessible. The wire attachments having been severed, the overhead gear removed, Mr Burton made his records, and we were able to turn our energies to the raising of its lid.

The entire inlaid surface was indeed, as already mentioned, in a very fragile condition, and any handling, so far as possible, had to be avoided. In order therefore to lift the lid without causing injury, metal eyelets, to serve as handles, were screwed into it at four points where there would be no danger of permanent disfigurement. To these eyelets our hoisting tackle was fixed, the gold-headed silver nails were extracted and the lid was slowly raised. There was at first some slight tendency for the lid to stick, but gradually it rose from its bed and, when high enough to clear the contents of the coffin, it was lowered on to a wooden tray placed at the side to receive it. This revealed a third coffin which, like its predecessors, was Osiride in form, but the main details of the workmanship were hidden by a close-fitting reddish-coloured linen shroud. The burnished gold face was bare; placed over the neck and breast was an elaborate bead and floral collarette, sewn upon a backing of papyrus, and tucked immediately above the *Nemes* headdress was a linen napkin.

Mr Burton at once made his photographic records. I then removed the floral collarette and linen coverings. An astounding fact was disclosed. This third coffin, 6 feet $1\frac{3}{4}$ of an inch in length, was made of solid gold! The mystery of the enormous weight, which hitherto had puzzled us, was now clear. It explained also why the weight had diminished so slightly after the first coffin, and the lid of the second coffin, had been removed. Its weight was still as much as eight strong men could lift.

The face of this gold coffin was again that of the king, but the features though conventional, by symbolising Osiris, were even more youthful than those on the other coffins. In actual design it reverted to that of the outermost coffin, inasmuch as it was *Rishi*, and had engraved upon it figures of Isis and Nephthys, but auxiliary to this design were winged figures of Nekhebet and Buto. These latter protective figures, emblematic of Upper and Lower Egypt, were the prominent feature, for they are superimposed in gorgeous and massive cloisonné work over the richly engraved ornament of the coffin – their inlay being natural semi-precious stones. In addition to this decoration, over the conventional collarette of 'the Hawk' – again in auxiliary cloisonné work – was a double detachable necklace of large disk-shaped beads of red and yellow gold and blue faience, which enhanced the richness of the whole effect. But the ultimate details of the ornamentation were hidden by a black lustrous coating due to liquid unguents that had evidently been profusely poured over the coffin. As a result this unparalleled monument was not only disfigured – as it afterwards proved, only temporarily – but was stuck fast to the interior of the second coffin, the consolidated liquid filling up the space between the second and third coffins almost to the level of the lid of the third.

These consecration unguents, which had obviously been used in great quantity, were doubtless the cause of the disintegration observed when dealing with the outer coffins which, as they were in a practically hermetically sealed quartzite sarcophagus, cannot have been affected by outside influences. As a further result it may be mentioned that the covering shroud and floral collarette mingled with blue faience beads had suffered, and although these at first appeared to be in good condition, they proved so brittle that the material broke the very instant it was touched.

We raised the third coffin contained in the shell of the second, which now rested on the top of the sarcophagus, and moved them into the Antechamber where they were more accessible, both for examination and manipulation. It was then that the wonder and magnitude of our last discovery more completely dawned upon us. This unique and wonderful monument – a coffin over 6 feet in length, of the finest art, wrought in solid gold of 2½ to 3½ millimetres in thickness – represented an enormous mass of pure bullion.

How great must have been the wealth buried with those ancient Pharaohs! What riches that valley must have once concealed! Of the twenty-seven monarchs buried there, Tut-ankh-Amen was probably of the least importance. How great must have been the temptation to the greed and rapacity of the audacious contemporary tomb robbers! What stronger incentive can be imagined than those vast treasures of gold! The plundering of royal tombs, recorded in the reign of Rameses IX, becomes easily intelligible when the incentive to these crimes is measured by this gold coffin of Tut-ankh-Amen. It must have represented fabulous wealth to the stone-cutters, artisans, water-carriers and peasants – to contemporary workers generally, such as the men implicated in the tomb robberies. These plunderings occurred in the reigns of the latter Ramessides (1200-1000 BC) and are recorded in legal documents now known as the Abbott, Amherst, Turin, and Mayer papyri, discovered in Thebes about the beginning of last century. Probably the thieves, who made their practically ineffectual raid on Tut-ankh-Amen's tomb, were aware of the mass of bullion covering the remains of the young Pharaoh under its protective shrines, sarcophagus and nested coffins. . . .

The external ornaments and inlaid gold trappings having been removed, the king's mummy lay bare with its simple outer coverings and gold mask. It occupied the whole of the interior of the gold coffin, measuring in total length 6 feet 1 inch.

The outer wrappings consisted of one large linen sheet, held in position by three longitudinal (one down the centre and one at each side) and four transverse bands of the same material, corresponding in position to the flexible inlaid gold trappings already mentioned. These linen bands had evidently been fastened to the linen covering by some such adhesive as Herodotus has described. They were doubled, and varied from $2\frac{3}{4}$ to $3\frac{1}{2}$ inches in width. The central longitudinal band, beginning in the middle of the abdomen (in reality thorax), was passed under the lower layer of each of the three transverse bands, over the feet, under the soles, and doubled back below the second layer of transverse bands. At each side of the feet the linen wrappings had been rubbed, the result probably of friction against the sides of the metal coffin during transport to the tomb. The mummy lay at a slight angle, suggesting that it had been subjected to some shock when lowered into the sarcophagus. There was also similar evidence to imply that the unguents had been poured over the mummy and coffin before they were lowered into the sarcophagus – the liquid being at different levels on the two sides, suggesting the tilting of the coffin.

In consequence of the fragile and carbonised condition of the linen swathing, the whole of the exposed surface was painted over with melted paraffin wax of such a temperature that when congealed it formed a thin coating on the surface, with minimum penetration of the decayed wrappings beneath. When the wax had cooled, Dr Derry made a longitudinal incision down the centre of the outer binding to the depth penetrated by the wax, thus enabling the consolidated layer to be removed in large pieces. Nor did our troubles end here. The very voluminous under-wrappings were found to be in even worse condition of carbonisation and decay. We had hoped, by removing a thin outer layer of bandage from the mummy, to free it at the points of adhesion to the coffin so that it might be removed, but in this we were again disappointed. It was found that the linen beneath the mummy and the body itself had been so saturated by the unguents which formed a pitch-like mass at the bottom of the coffin and held it embedded so firmly, that it was impossible to raise it except at risk of great damage. Even after the greater part of the bandages had been carefully removed, the consolidated material had to be chiselled away from beneath the limbs and trunk before it was possible to raise the king's remains.

The bandages that actually enveloped the head were in a better state of preservation than those on the rest of the body, inasmuch as they had not been saturated by the unguents, and consequently had only suffered from indirect oxidation. This was also the case to a large extent with the wrappings on the feet.

The general system of bandaging so far as could be discovered was of normal character; it comprised a series of bandages, sheets and pads of linen, where the latter were required to complete the anthropoid form, the whole showing evidence of considerable care. The linen was evidently of a very fine cambric-like nature. The numerous objects found upon the mummy were enclosed in alternate layers of the voluminous wrappings, and literally covered the king from head to foot; some of the larger objects were caught up in many different layers of bindings which were wound crosswise and transversely.

Although the actual examination had necessarily to be carried out beginning from the feet upwards, for the sake of clarity, in the following description, I will describe it from the head downwards, enumerating each object and point of interest in proper sequence.

Upon the top of the head was a large pad of conic form, composed of wads of linen, wrapped in the manner of a modern surgical head-bandage, and in shape suggestive of the *Atef* crown of Osiris, without such accessories as the horns and feathers. The purpose of this pad is obscure; from its shape it might be thought to be a crown, but, on the other hand, it could well be merely a tall pad to support and fill the empty space within the hollow of the *Nemes* headdress of the gold mask, especially in view of the fact that the mask is an integral part of the external equipment of the mummy, making it coincide with the effigies upon the coffins.

Beneath this crown-like pad, lying on the back of the mask, was a small amuletic *Urs* pillow, or head-rest, made of iron, which, according to the 166th Chapter of the 'Book of the Dead', has the following significance: 'Rise up from non-existence, O prostrate one . . . overthrowest thou thy enemies, triumphest thou over what they do against thee.' Such amulets are usually made of haematite, but in this case pure iron has taken the place of that ore, a fact that gives us a very important milestone in the development and growth of the history of civilisation....

Next to the pad and encircling the top of the head, was a double tie (the Arabic *aqal*), not unlike that of the Bedouin headdress, made of fibre tightly bound with cord and having loops at the ends to which were doubtless attached tapes for tying at the back of the head. Its use is unknown, its like or parallel never before having been found. It suggests a relief to the head from the pressure of a crown.

The removal of a few layers of wrappings revealed a magnificent diadem completely encircling the king's head – an object of extreme beauty and of simple fillet type. In design it comprises a richly ornamented gold ribbon of contiguous circles of carnelian, having minute gold bosses affixed to their centres, with, at the back, a floral and disk-shaped bow, from which hang two ribbon-like gold appendages similarly decorated. On both sides of the fillet are appendages of a like but broader kind, and having a massive pendent uraeus attached to their front margins. The insignia of northern and southern sovereignty of this diadem, I should here mention, were found lower down, separate, and on the right and left thighs respectively and as the king lay within the sarcophagus, east and west – his head towards the west – the uraeus of Buto being on the left side, and the vulture of Nekhebet on the right, the insignia took their correct geographical position, as did also those emblems on the coffins. Both of these golden emblems of royalty have grooved fastenings on the back, into which fit corresponding T-shaped tongues upon the diadem. They are thus movable and could be fitted on to whatever crown the king might have worn.

The golden Nekhebet with obsidian eyes is a remarkable example of fine metal-work. The shape of the head, occiput covered with wrinkles, and at the back of the neck a partial collar of short stiff feathers, make it quite clear that the bird, representing the Upper Egyptian goddess, was *Vultur auricularis*, Daud. – the sociable vulture. This particular species is today plentiful in Nubia, but uncommon in the middle and southern provinces of Egypt, but seldom if ever seen in Lower Egypt.

This diadem must have had a very early origin, inasmuch as it seems to have derived its name *Seshnen* and form from the circlet-ribbon worn on the head by men and women of all classes, as far back as the Old Kingdom, some 1,500 years before the New Empire. . . .

More than often when this type of diadem is depicted upon the monuments, the king is represented wearing it around a wig in conjunction with, and surmounted by, the *Atef* crown of Osiris.

Around the forehead, underneath a few more layers of linen, was a broad temple-band of burnished gold terminating behind and above the ears. At its extremities are slots through which linen tapes were passed and tied in a bow at the back of the head. This band held in place over the brow and temples, a fine cambric-like linen *Khat* headdress, unfortunately reduced by decay to such an irreparable condition that it was only recognisable from a portion of the kind of pigtail at the back, common to this headdress. Sewn to this *Khat* headdress were the royal insignia, being a second set found upon the king. The uraeus, with body and tail in flexible sections of gold-work threaded together, and bordered with minute beads, was passed over the axis of the crown of the head as far back as the *lambda*, whilst the Nekhebet vulture (in this case with open wings, and with characteristics identical with those already described) covered the top of the head-dress, its body being parallel with the uraeus. In order that the soft linen of this head-dress should take its conventional shape, pads of linen had been placed under it and above the temples.

Beneath the *Khat* headdress were further layers of bandaging that covered a skull-cap of fine linen fabric, fitting tightly over the shaven head of the king, and embroidered with an elaborate device of uraei in minute gold and faience beads. The cap was kept in place by a gold temple-band similar to that just described. Each uraeus of the device bears in its centre the *Aten* cartouche of the Sun. The fabric of the cap was unfortunately much carbonised and decayed, but the bead-work had suffered far less, the device being practically perfect, since it adhered to the head of the king. To have attempted to remove this exquisite piece of work would have been disastrous, so it was treated with a thin coating of wax and left as it was found.

The removal of the final wrappings that protected the face of the king needed the utmost care, as owing to the carbonised state of the head there was always the risk of injury to the very fragile features. We realised the peculiar importance and responsibility attached to our task. At the touch of a sable brush the last few fragments of decayed fabric fell away, revealing a serene and placid countenance, that of a young man. The face was refined and cultured, the features well formed, especially the clearly marked lips, and I think I may here record, without wishing to encroach on the province of Drs Derry and Saleh Bey Hamdi, the first and most striking impression to all present – namely, the remarkable structural resemblance to his father-in-law, Akh-en-Aten – an affinity that has been visible on the monuments.

The Tomb of Tut-ankh-Amen, vol. II, 1927

The buried pyramid

ZAKARIA GONEIM

ZAKARIA GONEIM *was born in Egypt. He took his diploma in Egyptology from the University of Giza in 1934 under the supervision of Newberry, Junker and Vikentiev. In 1937 he was appointed to the Antiquities Service, and began his career at Saqqara. In 1939 he was made Inspector of Antiquities at Aswan and Edfu, and in 1943, Conservator of the Theban necropolis. He carried out this work so successfully that in 1946 he was promoted to the post of Inspector-in-Chief of Upper Egypt, and in 1951 he was placed in sole charge of the antiquities of Saqqara. It was here that he made his remarkable discovery of a new pyramid enclosure. Unfortunately his work was interrupted by political and economic considerations in 1956, and he died in most unfortunate circumstances in 1959.*

During the last few days of September 1951, Hofni and I went around the vast site looking for a suitable place to begin our work. Our attention was drawn to an outcropping of rubble masonry just appearing above the surface on the western border of the terrace. So we began to dig at this point. To our delight, on the first day a massive wall of rubble-coursed masonry appeared. We dug down to the bottom of the wall which was about 27 feet deep, and found that it was built on the rock strata and had a thickness of over 60 feet. It was built in three parts, like a sandwich. The middle of the sandwich was an upright course about 11 feet thick, faced on each side with another course about 41 feet thick, the outer sides of which sloped inward at an angle of 72 degrees. Architects call this type of construction a 'battered' wall.

This discovery reassured me that my original conception was correct, and during the following two months we continued to make further excavations at points along the length of this massive wall. I increased my gang of workmen to fifty. Under Hofni Ibrahim's direction, the 'Decauville' railway was laid down to carry the excavated sand and rock from the site to a suitable dumping-place. The terrace lies in the south-east corner of the great depression, which is situated to the south-west of Djoser's enclosure. I chose as my dumping-ground an area to the west of the west border of the terrace, having first examined the place by digging other trial pits to make sure that it was only rock strata and did not conceal tombs or monuments. The 'Decauville' is a light, narrow-gauge railway, which can be rapidly laid down and equally rapidly removed to a new site when required. Steel tip-trucks run along it, and the rumble of these, mingled with the songs and rhythmic chanting of the workmen, is a sound with which all Egyptian archaeologists are familiar. It is music to the excavator's heart!

The wall was built of large uniform blocks of local grey limestone, and the upper part appeared to have been quarried in antiquity. When I had defined this wall I searched for the corners, and eventually established the limits. I found that it was built around a rectangular enclosure, which had a north–south axis of about 1,700 feet and an east–west axis of about 600 feet.

The enormous thickness of this wall – 66 feet – and the fact that it was not faced with fine limestone, as was Djoser's circuit wall, puzzled me at first. Then I realised that it was really a foundation platform on which the upper wall had originally been built. The lie of the land showed why this was. Djoser's pyramid complex stands on a commanding site on the very edge of the plateau, overlooking the valley; but the king for whom the newly discovered enclosure was built did not have this advantage. His monument had to be built in a depression, and in order to overcome this his architect had first built this massive stone platform of local limestone, which would not perhaps be visible to the eye, and on top of this he had built the *real* enclosure wall, of similar type to that of Djoser, projecting bastions and probably dummy gates, all of which would be visible from afar. Most of this 'curtain' wall had disappeared; the fine limestone of which it was built had been too great a temptation to subsequent builders. The kings of Ancient Egypt frequently plundered their ancestors' monuments, and this wall had fallen a victim like the rest. Nevertheless, I had no doubt that the uppermost wall had been completed, because we came across several fragments of it in the extreme northern limit of the enclosure, with panelled bastions and 'curtains' having the same measurements as those of Djoser's wall. This, incidentally, is one of the reasons why I believe that the king who built this enclosure was later than Djoser, since, if the latter king's monument had not already existed, the builders of this other structure would have raised it nearer to the edge of the plateau, not only because of the more advantageous position, but because they would have been nearer the western bank of the Nile, at which the facing stones would have to be unloaded. For although the cores of the pyramids were built of local limestone, the fine-grained stone needed for the facing-blocks was quarried from the hills on the eastern bank of the Nile.

Further excavations in the northern area of the rectangular terrace revealed several rubble walls, running parallel with one another in an east–west direction, and joined together with small cross-walls, also of rubble; the whole strikingly resembling some of the embankments and fillings in Djoser's step pyramid enclosure. It took us about two months to excavate and examine this bewildering complex of cross-walls, for it was difficult to know where to begin digging in this vast enclosure. I must emphasise at this point the immensity of the place. It was not like excavating a simple tomb in a small circumscribed spot, but comparable to digging out an area several times the size of Trafalgar Square in London. Dozens of times I went with Hofni Ibrahim to re-examine Djoser's enclosure, particularly at its northern end, in the hope of finding clues to the lay-out of the newly discovered enclosure. We found the same complex of walls in several places, but chiefly in the northern end.

The reason for the existence of these cross-walls was as follows. When the builders of that remote period wished to raise the level of an area, they first built cross-walls, dividing the area into compartments which they afterwards filled in with stone. Also it is very important to remember that the buildings in Djoser's enclosure were not real buildings intended for human habitation, but dummies. They were practically solid, and these walls were used in the construction of such dummy structures.

Let me put it this way. If one is excavating, say, a house or a temple, one can tell which were walls and which were spaces between the walls for chambers. But in this case the spaces left within the structures were so small that the whole construction looked as if it was one solid mass. Most of these buildings were, in fact, symbolic, and designed to represent certain elements in the king's palace at Memphis which were deemed necessary for his habitation in the after-life and to assert his rights of sovereignty.

The difficulty of establishing the lay-out of such buildings when they have been reduced to foundation-level can be imagined, and this was why I returned frequently to the enclosure of Djoser, which has been systematically excavated, to see if I could gain information which would enable me to interpret the lay-out of the new structure. The resemblances were striking, and I became increasingly convinced that this was indeed the enclosure of a step pyramid, though at the time few others believed me.

In work of this kind the archaeologist sometimes runs into blind-alleys – both literally and figuratively – and one such distraction occurred while we were digging in this area. We noticed that most of the fragments used in the fillings were chips of soft clay, called in Arabic *tafl*, which are usually found in the debris from subterranean galleries. This led us to suspect that there might be subterranean galleries underneath, perhaps leading to tombs, the more so since similar complexes of walls are found over such galleries in the northern part of Djoser's enclosure. So we searched for the entrance, and I remember my two chief workmen and I spent a long time conjecturing where it might be. The other workmen joined enthusiastically in the search, and, as usually happens on such occasions, each had his own special theory. Cries would go up 'The entrance is here! . . . No, it is here!' and so on, and every day brought new conjectures. It was very difficult to see one's way out of this maze, particularly as visitors and other archaeologists came to see us, and after viewing the site, expressed the opinion that the enclosure had never been completed and that we would find nothing.

The search for a tomb having proved vain, I decided at last to shift the whole work a few yards farther north. It was at Christmas 1951 that I told *Reis* Hofni to move the Decauville railway to the north. Imagine our joy when, on New Year's Day, 1952, we suddenly found a flight of steps leading to an enormous cross-wall, which ran from east to west across the enclosure. This wall was quite different from those I had discovered earlier. It was faced with fine white limestone and built with bastions and curtains, just like those of Djoser's enclosure wall. Also it was similarly panelled. For some reason it had never been completed and had been embedded in a mass of dry masonry composed of rubble cross-walls built at intervals over and against its bastions and curtains, the gaps being filled up with debris. Owing to this, the wall was found intact to the length of 138 feet at the very stage when its construction was broken off, probably because of an alteration in the architect's design. As it gradually revealed itself in all its beauty, exactly as the workmen had left it nearly five thousand years ago, I realised that here was a find of major importance. . . .

The New Year seemed full of hope for us all. Hofni, his brother, and the rest of the workmen were as delighted as I was. In the past they had worked on some great excavations, and it was a point of honour for them that at every site on which they worked something important should be found. Naturally, such expectations are not always realised, and when they are there is great rejoicing. Such experiences then become part of their life-history, which they tell to their children.

Perhaps some readers will wonder why such a fuss should be made of a mere stone wall. But this was no ordinary wall. It is very rare in Egypt to find such a structure untouched by time, and as we cleared more and more of its length, we found incontestable evidence that the White Wall, as we named it, must have been buried very shortly after its construction. We were looking at something which no human eye had seen for nearly fifty centuries.

This evidence consisted of marks and drawings in red paint left on the white limestone surface by the ancient builders. For instance, on some of the stone blocks were quarry marks, painted on the stones before they left the quarries on the opposite side of the Nile. Those on the White Wall were mere symbols of which the meaning is lost, but we know from other examples found in the later pyramids that some of these marks indicated the names of the gangs or crews who cut the stone. These crews are believed to have consisted of some eight hundred to a thousand men. For instance, here are the names of some of the crews who quarried stone for the Pyramids of Cheops and Mycerinus:

The Crew, Cheops excites love.

The crew, the White Crown of Khnmw-Khufu (Cheops) is powerful.

Other marks have been translated as follows:

This side up

To be taken away

For the royal tomb (per nwb).

These roughly drawn signs and inscriptions bring one very near to the ancient builders. On the White Wall, for example, we found the actual levelling-lines, made by stretching a cord dipped in red paint across the surface and 'flipping' it, just as a modern mason does to this day. These were evidently made to ensure that workmen should lay the stones at the same level along the entire length of the wall. Even though this was perhaps only the second or third attempt at building monumental walls in stone masonry, the builders had evidently acquired great skill.

Then we found something which brought the remote past very near to us; a rare human touch on a royal Egyptian monument. Here and there the workmen had been beguiling a leisure moment by drawing on the wall, in red ochre or lamp-black, pictures of men, animals, and boats. There was a figure of a Lybian man in a long robe and tall head-dress, carrying a bow. The Lybians, nomads living in the West Desert, were of course foreigners to the Egyptians whose dress was quite dissimilar. Then there were unmistakable drawings of lions. At that time lions and other beasts of prey were still found in the deserts of Egypt, and the men must have seen them many times roaming the desert fringes. Other drawings showed boats, some with sails and some without, and barges similar to those which were used by the Ancient Egyptians to bring blocks of limestone from the east to the north-east bank of the Nile.

I must repeat at this point that no evidence had so far been uncovered to indicate that I had found a pyramid. I had found an enclosure which bore certain resemblances to that of King Djoser, and a magnificent cross-wall which was so like that of that king's enclosure wall as to leave no doubt that it must have been built at a period very close to that of Djoser. But that was all. Apart from the White Wall, visitors to the site in those early months of 1952 found little to impress them: only the bare plateau, of sand and rock, pitted with a few holes, from one of which the Decauville ran to the rubbish-dump. 'Where's the pyramid?' my professional colleagues would ask jocularly, and I had no answer; only an inner faith that somewhere beneath that vast expanse of sand I would eventually find what I was looking for. But when I thought of my modest and rapidly dwindling allowance I became anxious, for if the money was spent on fruitless digging, it might be difficult to obtain more. The site of each trial pit would have to be chosen with great care, and night after night, when I returned to my house after the day's work, I would study the plan of the area, consult the works of other archaeologists who had worked on pyramids, form and reject theories, and talk far into the night with my chief workmen, Hofni and Hussein.

At this stage I would like to refer my readers to the plan of the pyramid enclosure. . . . They will notice that north of the point where the White Wall joins the north–south walls of the enclosure there is a curious change of alignment. We discovered this shortly after the wall was revealed, and it puzzled me for some time. In fact, there were two features which gave me cause for thought. First, there was the fact that, from the White Wall onwards, in a northerly direction, the east–west walls of the enclosure did not follow the same line as before, but were inset to a depth of about 6 feet, forming an angle. This indicated either another monument attached to the first on the northern side, or else *an extension of the original monument*. Later I found that this latter supposition was correct.

The second strange feature was that this northern extension, beyond the White Wall, was raised above the level of the southern part of the enclosure, forming a kind of raised platform. Why was this done? Only further excavations will provide a final answer.

In the meantime, in an endeavour to find an answer to the puzzle, I began to excavate the whole breadth of the enclosure from west to east, following the line of the White Wall. We first encountered large blocks of fine limestone so arranged as to form a flight of steps built at the western end of the massive wall, and designed to facilitate its exploitation as a quarry.

The wall itself proved to be comprised of a thick, regularly built inner core of local limestone, faced outside with dressed white limestone. The whole outer face of the wall was panelled and constructed with bastions and curtains (panels). The whole magnificent structure presented exactly the same design as Djoser's enclosure wall. The panels had the same breadth and depth. The bastions and 'curtains' had the same measurements, with equal spaces in the larger bastions for carving imitation closed double gates, as in Djoser's wall. I was delighted, because it was now quite clear that I had found an enclosure built on lines similar to that of Djoser.

Throughout the rest of the 1952 season, from January to March, we continued to work on this wall, and excavated 150 feet of its length, only stopping when we found that at its eastern end, nearest to the necropolis, it had been damaged by quarrying.

However, we noticed two essential differences in the structural disposition of the stones. The dimensions of the stones here were much larger than those of Djoser's enclosure; in the new wall, the height of the course is 50–52 centimetres, while in the lower parts of Djoser's wall it is only 24–26 centimetres. On the other hand, the fine limestone was employed much more thriftily in the casing.

These two factors are extremely important in the dating of the monument. It is certain that already in Djoser's reign there had been a tendency to increase the size of the stone blocks, as the builders ultimately came to learn that an increase in size meant an economy in the work of cutting out the stones, and lent more strength and a greater degree of cohesion to walls. Therefore the size of the stones and the way in which they were used in this new wall suggest a date *later* than Djoser, although still Third Dynasty. The economy of the casing also suggests a more rational, hence more developed method of construction. But the wall had been abandoned during construction, and the northern limit of the enclosure had been moved 600 feet farther north. That it was abandoned during construction is proved by the fact that the sixth and uppermost course had not been faced and had been left rough. In addition, several partition walls of coarse limestone leaned directly against the panelled façade, and the surface of the wall had not been smoothed, but bore the numerous quarry marks and mason's lines which I have already described.

Throughout this time my workmen and I still kept a look-out for signs of subterranean galleries such as exist beneath the northern part of Djoser's enclosure, and one day we found something which raised our hopes. It was a hole made by one of the ancient tomb-robbers. . . . To the archaeologist such holes can be a cause of both hope and despair. Hope, because they indicate that, thousands of years ago, some enterprising rascal had known or suspected that there was a tomb near by; despair, lest he should have found and plundered it!

In this case hope triumphed. We went down the hole and followed the robber's tunnel for a distance of 62 feet. It plunged down into the rock and described a wide semicircle. We had to proceed carefully for fear of falling rock or a total collapse of the tunnel, but when Hofni and I reached the end and found only the rock, we were delighted and relieved. On this occasion the robber had drawn a blank and given up in disgust. But had he perhaps succeeded elsewhere? The answer to that question still lay in the future.

The period from January to the beginning of April 1952 was spent in clearing the White Wall down to its base, and along its length to the point where quarrying had damaged much of the structure. During this time the lay-out of the enclosure had become somewhat clearer to me. When I am excavating a site I always try to identify myself with the ancient builders, to get inside their minds in order to understand *why* their monument assumed its present shape. They often changed their plans during construction, and by observation and reflection, and by drawing on one's knowledge of other monuments, it is sometimes possible to estimate where and why such changes have occurred, and to make an intelligent guess at what may lie under the sand. . . .

For instance, I became fairly certain that the White Wall had originally formed the northern limit of the enclosure, but that for some reason not yet explained the builders decided to extend it to the north at a higher level. Also, that since this was clearly an enclosure, it must have had a central edifice, which should be near the geometrical centre of the *original* enclosure. It could be objected that the builders might have abandoned the enclosure before beginning the central edifice, whatever it was – pyramid or *mastaba*; but this was unlikely, since we know from other structures that the building of the various component parts went on at one and the same time. But there was no sign of any such central edifice, not even an outcropping of masonry such as had guided me to the enclosure wall.

Early in April I surveyed the original enclosure with a theodolite in order to determine its exact geometrical centre. I explained to Hofni my idea, and he showed an enthusiastic interest. He had not worked before on pyramids of this very early date, though he had played an important part in the excavation of the famous Pyramid of King Senusret II (Dyn. XII) at el-Lahun. In fact it was Hofni Ibrahim who found one of the most beautiful objects ever discovered in an Egyptian pyramid. Over thirty years ago he was working for Sir Flinders Petrie in the tomb of Princess Sit-Hathor-Iunet, daughter of Senusret II, when, during the clearing of a recess in the corner of the tomb, he found a rare specimen of the royal *uræus* or sacred snake, in gold, with a head of lapis-lazuli, eyes of garnet, and hood ornamented with carnelian, turquoise and lazuli. This royal symbol, signifying dominion over Lower Egypt, was worn by the Pharaohs in their crowns. Embedded in mud, it was overlooked by the tomb-robbers when they rifled the tomb, and had remained untouched for four thousand years until Hofni found it. He once told me that he often visits the Cairo Museum just to admire the *uræus* in it glass case, and to recall that day, thirty-six years ago, when he first held it in his hands. It is memories such as this which lend glory to the lives of these men, and inspire them with hope whenever they tackle a new site. So it was with considerable excitement that my workmen began the next phase of the excavation, which was to try to locate the central edifice, if it existed.

In all work of this kind luck and judgment both play their part, and on this occasion we were lucky. I had established the spot where the central building should lie, but when I gave instructions for the sinking of the first trial pit I had no idea whether we should strike the edge of the structure or some point within it. Judge my satisfaction when on January 29th, 1952, Hofni came to me excitedly and said that they had found masonry. By good fortune we had located the actual southern edge of the hidden structure, from which point it would not be difficult to follow it along to its corners, and define the limits of the whole edifice.

It proved to be composed of a series of independent walls leaning one on the other and inclining inwards at an angle of about 75 degrees, and *the stone courses were at right angles to the slope of the walls.* Readers who have carefully followed Chapter One, in which I described the construction of step pyramids, will realise that this was a valuable clue to the age of the structure. For in the few surviving examples of step pyramids we know, the accretion walls are built in this manner, whereas in later pyramids built subsequent to the time of Snofru the courses were laid horizontally. I immediately went to Monsieur Lauer, the architect of the Antiquities Department who has worked for many years on Djoser's step pyramid. (He is responsible for restoration and consolidation of monuments.) I found him as usual at work near this pyramid, and together we made our way to the terrace where Hofni, Hussein, and the other workmen were clearing the newly discovered walls. When he had seen and examined them he said to me: 'I have no doubt whatsoever that this forms part of a step pyramid.'

Even so, there were still many who doubted us, and unfortunately we had now come to the end of the 1952 season, and I knew it would be some time before these doubts could be finally resolved, as I was sure they would be. Excavations closed down in May 1952 and were not resumed until November 1953. Work had reached a critical point, and I felt I needed time to study the finds and decide carefully on my next course of action. It was also necessary to obtain an additional grant in order that the work could continue.

In November 1953 I reassembled my workmen, and once again the loaded trucks began to rumble along the Decauville as we laboured to uncover more of this mysterious building. I first concentrated my attention on finding its limits. First we extended the pit and assured ourselves that the structure continued on both the east and west sides. Then I gave orders to shift the work some distance to the west on the same line, at a point where I judged the corner of the building might be. We found that the southern side was covered up with soft clay resulting from the cutting of subterranean galleries, so this almost imperceptible evidence showed where the artificial fillings ended and the debris resulting from later quarrying of the pyramid began. When we dug below the desert surface, it was clear where this intentional covering material ended. Not long after this work was begun I was engaged at another point in the enclosure when Hussein Ibrahim, the brother of Hofni, came running towards me with outstretched arms and crying: '*Mabruk elnasia!*' which means 'Congratulations! We have found the corner!'

I went back with him and found to my joy that they had struck the corner of a pyramid, for this I was now more convinced it was. It could hardly have been a *mastaba*, partly because of its size, but chiefly because no *mastabas* are known to exist with 'accretion walls' and inclined courses. These are typical of pyramid construction.

Every archaeological site has its own characteristics, and one has to work for a very long time to find them and to recognise what happened in ancient times. Because of the immense surface covered by the enclosure, I adopted the method of finding first the main points; otherwise I would have had to expend much time and money on fruitless labour before being able to understand the lay-out.

For example, having uncovered this first corner it was easy for us to find the other three. From the photographs it will be seen that this was a stepped structure, but that only one step remains. The masonry is of good quality, but the limestone blocks are relatively small, as in Djoser's pyramid. The builders had not yet reached the stage when they built with huge megalithic blocks. The whole structure is 400 feet square; the base thus presented is larger than that of Djoser's pyramid. In its unfinished state it has a maximum height of about 23 feet, but I believe that it might have been built originally to double this height and that it has been reduced by quarrying in later times. No traces of an outer casing were found, and it may be assumed that only the core of the pyramid was begun and that it was never finished.

This is a square layer-structure consisting of probably fourteen skins of masonry which diminished in height from the centre outwards and leaned on a central nucleus at an angle varying between 71 and 75 degrees, with the beds of the courses at right angles to the facing lines. The 'accretion faces' were left in the rough. Assuming that each pair of these skins of masonry was designed to form one step, as is the case in Djoser's pyramid, we may infer that the new pyramid was intended to have seven steps in place of Djoser's six.

Had this pyramid been finished, it would probably have stood to a height of about 230 feet, i.e. 30 feet higher than Djoser's. It stands directly on the rock, and was built of local, coarse grey limestone. The blocks are roughly squared and are set in a mortar composed of soft clay (*tafl*) obtained from the tunnelling of underground passages, mixed with limestone chips. The stones were generally laid in alternate courses of 'headers and stretchers' in imitation of mud-bricks. The courses are level and parallel, and the bedding joints are much wider than the rising joints. A fragment of a boundary *stela* bearing the name of Djoser was found re-used in the masonry, a further indication that the new pyramid must have been built at a later date than Djoser's.

The Buried Pyramid, 1956

Part Four

THE BOOK OF THE TOWERS

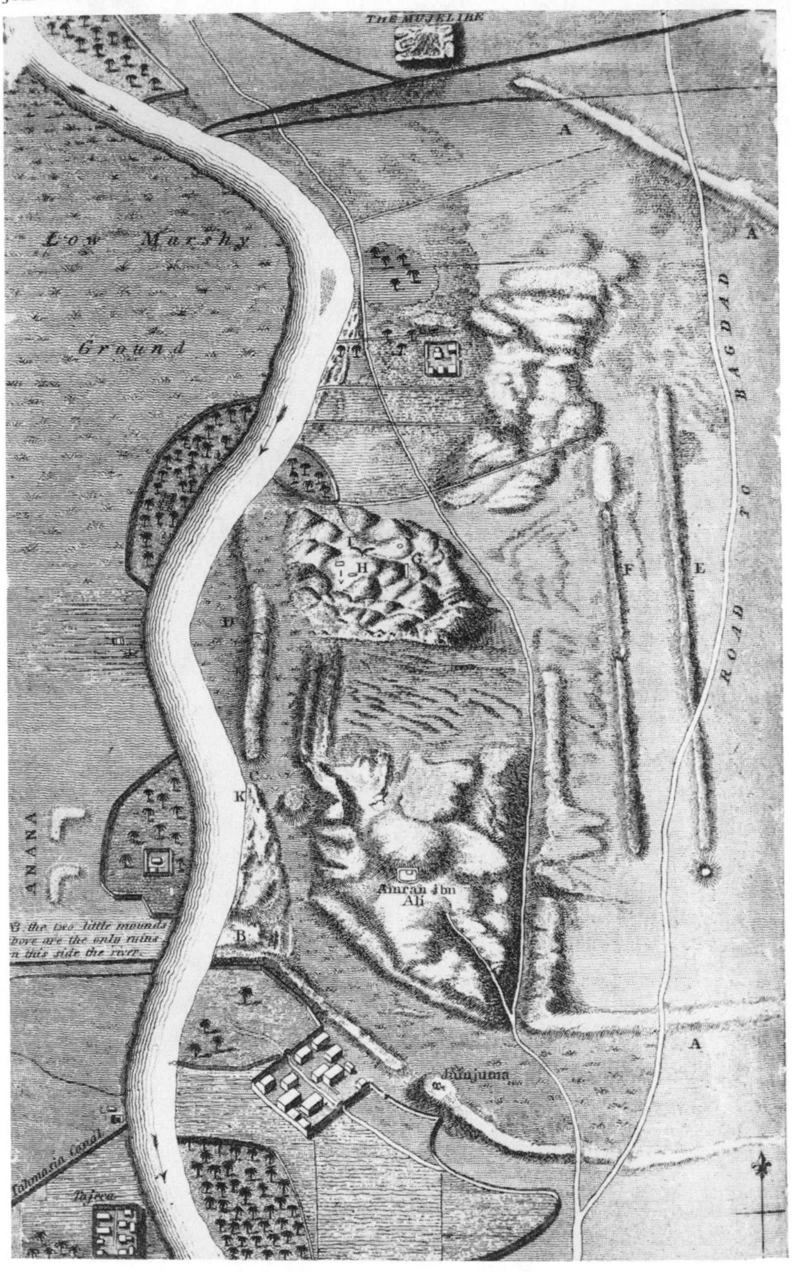

15. One of the oldest of "modern" maps: a sketch of the ruins of Babylon, made in 1811 by the great explorer and linguistic genius Claudius Rich.

A second solution to the cuneiform script

HENRY RAWLINSON

Sir Henry Creswicke Rawlinson (1810–1895) was born at Chadlington in Oxfordshire. In 1827 he went to India as an officer cadet of the East India Company, and after six years he was transferred to Persia with several other officers to reorganise the troops of the Shah. At this time cuneiform writing was known in fairly substantial quantities but only the German Grotefend had found any clue to its decipherment and Rawlinson, who did not know of Grotefend's work, became deeply interested in the problem. With considerable danger and difficulty he scaled the rock of Behistun and transcribed part of the inscription, but international political friction made it necessary for him to leave the country before he finished the work. In 1840 he became political agent for Kandahar and requested to be sent to Turkish Arabia; he settled in Baghdad and continued his researches into the problem of the inscription. It was at this time that he transcribed, deciphered and interpreted the remainder of the Behistun inscription. During two years' leave in England he placed his valuable collection of antiquities in the charge of the British Museum, who gave him a grant to continue the excavations begun by Sir Austen Layard which he carried on until his retirement in 1855. He was awarded the K.C.B. for his work, and during the remainder of his life, which was largely spent in London, he continued to be active in cuneiform scholarship and in international affairs.

'On my arrival at Baghdad during the present year I deferred the completion of my translations, and of the Memoir by which I designed to establish and explain to them, until I obtained books from England which might enable me to study with more care the peculiarities of Sanskrit grammar; and in the mean time I busied myself with comparative geography. It was at this period that I received through the Vice-President of the Royal Asiatic Society, a letter from Professor Lassen, containing a précis of his last improved system of interpretation, and the Bonn alphabet I recognised at once to be infinitely superior to any other that had previously fallen under my observation. The Professor's views indeed coincided in all essential points with my own, and since I have been enabled, with the help of Sanskrit and Zend affinities, to analyse nearly every word of the Cuneiform inscriptions hitherto copied in Persia, and thus to verify the alphabetical power of almost every Cuneiform character, I have found the more reason to admire the skill of Professor Lassen, who with such very limited materials as were alone with his disposal in Europe, has still arrived at results so remarkably correct. The close approximation of my own alphabet to that adopted by Professor Lassen, will be apparent on a reference to the comparative table, and although in point of fact, the Professor's labours have been of no farther assistance to me than in adding one new character to my alphabet, and in confirming opinions which were sometimes conjectural, and which generally require verification, yet as the improvements which his system of interpretation makes upon the alphabet employed by M. Burnouf appear to have preceded not only the announcement, but the adoption of my own views, I cannot pretend to contest with him the priority of alphabetical discovery. Whilst employed in writing the present Memoir, I have had further opportunities of examining the Persepolitan inscriptions of Mr Rich, and the Persian inscription of Xerxes which is found at Ván; and I have also, in the pages of the *Journal Asiatique*, been introduced to a better knowledge of the Pehlevi, by Dr Müller, and I have obtained some acquaintance with Professor Lassen's translations, from the perusal of one of the critical notices of M. Jacquet.

'Having thus briefly described the progress of my Cuneiform studies during the last four years, and having explained the means by which I have been enabled to complete my alphabet, I have now to make a few particular remarks on the translations. This branch of the study although depending upon, and necessarily following the correct determination of the characters, is of course the only really valuable part of the enquiry. It is in fact the harvest springing from the previous cultivation of a rugged soil, and as far as I am aware, it has been hitherto but poorly reaped.

'The translations of Professor Grotefend and of Saint Martin are altogether erroneous and merit no attention whatever. The memoir of M. Burnouf on the inscriptions of Hamadán is confined to the illustration of twenty short lines of writing, containing an invocation to Ormand, a few proper names, and a bare enumeration of royal titles. Some of the grammatical peculiarities are, it is true, from their identity with similar formations in Zend, correctly developed; but the nature of the inscriptions has necessarily rendered the labours of the Paris secretary, ample and erudite as they are, deficient in historical interest; and the faulty condition of his alphabet has, moreover, led him into several important errors of translation. His incidental examination of the geographical names contained in one of Niebuhr's Persepolitan inscriptions constitutes by far the most interesting portion of his researches; yet in a list which exhibits the titles of twenty-four of the most celebrated nations of ancient Asia, he has correctly deciphered ten only of the names.

'Of Professor Lassen's translations I have no means of judging, except from the specimen which he has sent me of his system of interpretation applied to Niebuhr's Geographical inscription, and from M. Jacquet's critique on the same subject. The highly improved condition of the Bonn alphabet has rendered the Professor's identification of the geographical names at Persepolis far superior in correctness to that of M. Burnouf, but still he is not, I think, without error in his reading and appropriation of these names, and that he has also in many cases misunderstood both the etymology of the words and the grammatical structure of the language, will be apparent from the appendix to the present Memoir, where I have compared the Professor's translation of Niebuhr's inscription with my own.

'In the present case, then, I do put forth a claim to originality, as having been the first to present to the world a literal and, as I believe, a correct grammatical translation of nearly two hundred lines of Cuneiform writing, a memorial of the time of Darius Hystaspes, the greater part of which is in so perfect a state as to afford ample and certain grounds for a minute orthographical and etymological analysis, and the purport of which to the historian must, I think, be of fully equal interest with the peculiarities of its language to the philologist. I do not affect at the same time to consider my translations as unimpeachable; those who expect in the present paper to see the Cuneiform Inscriptions rendered and explained with as much certainty and clearness as the ancient tablets of Greece and Rome will be lamentably disappointed. It must be remembered that the Persian of the ante-Alexandrian ages has long ceased to be a living language; that its interpretation depends on the collateral aid of the Sanskrit, the Zend, and the corrupted dialects which in the forests and mountains of Persia have survived the wreck of the old tongue; and that in a few instances, where these cognate and derivative languages have failed to perpetuate the ancient roots, or where my limited acquaintance with the different dialects may have failed to discover the connexion, I have then been obliged to assign an arbitrary meaning, obtained by comparative propriety of application in a very limited field of research. I feel, therefore, that in a few cases my translations will be subject to doubt, and that as materials of analysis continue to be accumulated and more experienced Orientalists prosecute the study, it may be found necessary to alter or modify some of the significations that I have assigned; but at the same time I do not, and cannot, doubt, but that I have accurately determined the general application of every paragraph, and that I have been thus enabled to exhibit a correct historical outline, possessing the weight of royal and contemporaneous recital, of many great events which preceded the rise and marked the career of one of the most celebrated of the early sovereigns of Persia.'

When I wrote the foregoing introduction in the year 1839, it was my intention to have merely published the text of the Behistun Inscriptions, with a running commentary illustrative of such points of philology, history, and geography, as appeared particularly to deserve attention, and I confidently expected that the Memoir in this humble form would be ready for the press before the expiration of the year. As I proceeded however with my task the labour grew insensibly on my hands. The examination of a language, so venerable from its age, and so interesting from its close affinity to the Vedic Sanskrit, seemed to demand more care than could be bestowed on it in a mere series of critical notes; while the historical and geographical questions that started up in rapid succession at each progressive stage of the enquiry, threatened to bury the text under a load of commentary, and to obscure, or perhaps entirely efface, the force and perspicuity of the argument. I set to work, accordingly, in the autumn of 1839 to recast the Memoir, arranging the material under different heads, and devoting a separate chapter to the treatment of each particular subject. This distribution was of the greatest assistance to me. The progress of the work was necessarily slow, but it was constant and uniform; and I might have still hoped to publish the Memoir in its amended form in the spring of 1840, had not circumstances, over which I had no control, and which I could neither have desired nor foreseen, arrested my enquiries in mid-career and superseded for a long period the possibility of their resumption.

It is not my intention to dwell with any minuteness on the interruption which I thus sustained. Let it suffice to say that my services were called into activity by the Government, that I was suddenly transferred from the lettered seclusion of Baghdad to fill a responsible and laborious office in Afghanistan, and that I continued in that situation during the entire period of our eventful occupation of the country. Those who have experienced a difficulty of combining a sustained application to literary matters with the ordinary distractions of business, will I believe admit that in the emergent condition of the public service in Afghanistan, calling for undivided attention and untiring care, I had no alternative but the abandonment of antiquarian research. To have continued my labours on the inscriptions during the few hours of leisure that I could legitimately command would have produced no result; to have devoted any considerable portion of my time to the enquiry, would have been incompatible with my duty to the Government.

But years rolled on, and in December, 1843, I found myself again at Baghdad. The interest in the inscriptions with which my original researches had inspired me, had never flagged; it was sharpened perhaps by the accidents that had so long operated to delay its gratification; and I thus hastened with eager satisfaction to profit by the first interval of relaxation that I had enjoyed for many years to resume the thread of the enquiry. Mr Westergaard, well known for his contributions to Sanskrit literature, who had been travelling in Persia during the year 1843, for the express purpose of collecting Palaeographic and antiquarian materials, supplied me at this period in the most liberal manner with several new inscriptions which he had copied at Persepolis. The inscription on the portal close to the great staircase, which had escaped all former visitors, was of much value; equally so were the corrections of Niebuhr's inscriptions H and I, and the restoration of all the minor tablets upon the platform; but the gem of his collection, the most important record in fact of the class which exists in Persia, with the exception of the tablets of Behistun, I found to be the long inscription at Nakhsh-i-Rustam engraved on the rock-hewn sepulchre of Darius. This inscription was no less remarkable for its extent and interest than for the correctness of its delineation. I could not but observe indeed that Mr Westergaard's copy, defective as it necessarily was, both from the abrasion of the rock and from the difficulty of tracing letters through a telescope at so great an elevation, still indicated, in its superiority over all the specimens of Niebuhr, Le Brun, Porter, and Rich, the immense advantage which a transcriber acquainted with the character and language enjoys over one who can only depend for the fidelity of his copy on the imitative accuracy of an artist.

I have derived the greatest assistance in my recent labours from Mr Westergaard's inscriptions, as well as from the Median copy of the inscription at Nakhsh-i-Rustam, with which soon after my arrival at Baghdad I was most kindly furnished by M. Dittel, a Russian Orientalist, who was Mr Westergaard's coadjutor at Persepolis; and I trust that both these gentlemen will permit me to express in a public form, the obligations which I thus owe to them.

It is probable that with these extended materials at my command, and with the improved acquaintance with the language which such material supplied, I should have thought it advisable under any circumstances to undertake a third revision of the Memoir that I was writing; but such a course was rendered absolutely necessary by the fortunate result of a visit which I was enabled again to make to the rock of Behistun in the autumn of last year, and in which I succeeded in copying the whole of the Persian writing at that place, and a very considerable portion also of the Median and Babylonian transcripts. I will not speak of the difficulties or dangers of the enterprise. They are such as any person with ordinary nerves may successfully encounter; but they are such, at the same time, as have alone prevented the inscriptions from being long ago presented to the public by some of the numerous travellers who have wistfully contemplated them at a distance.

On returning to Baghdad from my tour in Southern Kurdistan, public avocations and indifferent health again prevented me for some time from continuing my labours. The same causes have operated, with more or less effect, in impeding their prosecution during the spring and summer, and if I had not been fortunately able to avail myself of the ready hand of Lieutenant Jones, an accomplished officer of the Indian Navy, who has delineated the sculptures of Behistun and contributed in a great measure to the execution of the text, I might have been altogether frustrated in my hope of early publication. I may observe, at the same time, that in February of the present year, I took the precaution of forwarding to the Royal Asiatic Society, a literal translation of every portion of the Persian writing at Behistun, and of thus placing beyond the power of dispute the claim of the Society at that date to the results which are published in the following Memoir.

I now proceed to notice the contemporaneous march of discovery upon the Continent during the interval which had elapsed since the publication of the Bonn and Paris Memoirs of 1836. Professor Lassen,

I believe, established a Journal at Bonn in the year 1838, devoted exclusively to the elaboration of Palaeography and Eastern literature, and in that journal, I have been given to understand several pages on the Cuneiform Inscriptions have from time to time appeared. One of these papers, containing a translation of the inscription of Artaxerxes Ochus, was explained to me (for unfortunately I am ignorant of German) by Dr Aloys Sprenger, at Calcutta, in 1843; but of the contents of the others I have no cognizance whatever. I am indebted to Mr Westergaard for the information that Professor Grotefend undertook in 1839 to call in question the discoveries of Professor Lassen, and to place in opposition to them the infallible claims of the antiquated alphabet of 1815, a proceeding which was justly regarded by the German literati as little better than fatuity.

Professor Grotefend may take up the high position of primitive, though imperfect discovery; but Professor Lassen may contest with him even in the numerical identification of alphabetical powers; while in all the essentials of interpretation the old has no pretention whatever to be brought into comparison with the modern system. I also learn from the same source that other Orientalists with whose labours I am very imperfectly acquainted have been engaged in the enquiry. To Dr Beer of Leipsic, it appears, is conceded in Germany the discovery of the two characters [cuneiform] *h*, and [cuneiform] *y*, and the lamented M. Jacquet is said to have appropriated to his own researches the determination of the letter [cuneiform] *ch* and [cuneiform] *jh*. The only identifications in the present Memoir that I presume to be essentially different from those which are universally received at present upon the Continent, are [cuneiform] and [cuneiform] *m'*, but the attribution of the power *sh*, instead of *s*, to the character [cuneiform], and of *tř* (with a dormant rather than an articulated liquid) to the character [cuneiform], are modifications of some consequence, and two new letters [cuneiform] and [cuneiform] will also be remarked, which I respectively represent by *ñ'* and *ñ*. To those who are interested in tracing the exact progress of alphabetical announcement, the tabular statement which heads Chapter III, on the Persian Cuneiform alphabet, will afford full and satisfactory information. For the mere purpose of reading the inscriptions the phonetic powers which are given in the right-hand column of the Table will be an ample and sufficient guide.

It remains that I should pay another tribute to Professor Lassen's acumen and research. It appears that Mr Westergaard on his return to Europe at the commencement of 1844, placed his Persian inscriptions in the hands of Professor Lassen, and that these new materials were justly deemed of sufficient consequence to demand an elaborate and immediate analysis. Professor Lassen accordingly devoted an early number of his Journal to the subject, and he took occasion at the same time to collect all the other inscriptions of the class and to publish the whole series together, in an amended text, and with revised translations. This is I believe the last work that has appeared upon the subject, and as might have been expected, it anticipates in some degree the novelty of the present Memoir. I have received a copy of the pamphlet whilst I have been writing the following pages, and I have found it of the greatest convenience, as a manual of reference. The marginal notes, indeed, that I have added to the present text, will show the care with which I have consulted it; but at the same time, I am bound to say that my translations, already completed when the book arrived, were, if not independent of assistance, at any rate beyond the reach of alteration, and I have further to regret that an ignorance of German has deprived me of that aid on questionable points of grammar, which, if I had been able to follow the Professor's arguments, I could not have failed to derive from the matured opinions of so eminent and correct a scholar.

I have only further to observe, that although the present Memoir, in consequence of the great augmentation of material, has been re-written during the present year, it is, as far as the original materials extended, and in all essential points of grammatical and etymological construction, absolutely identical with that which I had brought into a forward state of preparation for the press in the year 1839. If the translations can be amended (and imperfectly acquainted as I am with the niceties of Zend and Sanskrit grammar, I submit them with diffidence and deference to the public,) they must be indebted for their improvement to a critical examination of the text; for the materials available for analysis or verification, are not, I believe, entirely exhausted; and unless excavations should be undertaken on a great scale either at Susa, Persepolis, or Pasargadae, we must rest content with the sorrowful convictions that we have here, comprised in a few pages, all that remains of the ancient Persian languages and all that contemporary native evidence records of the glories of the Achaemenides.

The Persian Cuneiform Inscriptions at Behistun, 1846

Was Babylon here?

CLAUDIUS JAMES RICH

CLAUDIUS JAMES RICH *(1787–1820) was born at Dijon in Burgundy, but grew up in Bristol. He was always interested in languages and began to study Arabic at the age of nine. It was probably this skill which led the East India Company to post him to Egypt when he became a cadet in 1803, but on his way to his first appointment he was shipwrecked and after spending some time in Malta, then in Italy, he was directed to Constantinople and Smyrna. He travelled widely in Asia Minor and then moved on to Egypt. His knowledge of the Arab language and customs was so thorough that he was able to disguise himself as a Mameluke and journey undetected throughout Egypt, Syria and Palestine, even succeeding in entering the Great Mosque at Damascus. In 1807 he was appointed to Bombay but the Company shortly decided that his unique abilities could best be used in Asia Minor and posted him to Baghdad, where he proved a most able and respected administrator. His work did not occupy him so fully that he had no time for further studies; he made a journey to the ruins of Babylon in 1811, and in 1820 he planned a much more extensive expedition through Kurdistan, Nineveh, Shiraz, Persepolis and down the Tigris to Baghdad. There was, however, an outbreak of cholera at Shiraz and when Rich stopped to give what assistance he could he caught the disease himself and died. His books, manuscripts and many valuable antiquities were bought by the British Museum.*

Those who have investigated the antiquities of Babylon have laid much stress on the authority of Diodorus, probably adverting more to the quantity than the quality of the information he supplies. He never was on the spot: he lived in an age when, as he himself tells us, its area was ploughed over: he has therefore recourse to Ctesias; and it must be owned that the want of discrimination in the ancients, and the credulity of Diodorus himself, were never more strongly exemplified than in his choice of a writer who confounds the Euphrates with the Tigris, and tells us that Semiramis erected a monument to her husband, which from the dimensions he specifies must have been of superior elevation to Mount Vesuvius, and nearly equal to Mount Hecla. If these are not 'fairy tales', I certainly know not to what the term can be applied. When an author can in so many instances be closely convicted of ignorance and exaggeration, we are certainly not justified in altering what is already before our eyes, to suit it to his description. We have only the very questionable authority of Ctesias for the second palace, and the wonderful tunnel under the river; but even he does not say whether the Tower of Belus stood on the east or west side. Herodotus, who will ever appear to greater advantage the more he is examined and understood, is the only historian who visited Babylon in person; and he is in every respect the best authority for its state in his time. The circumference he assigns to it has been generally deemed exaggerated; but after all we cannot prove it to be so. He says nothing to determine the situation of the Palace (for he speaks but of one) and Temple; he has no mention of east or west, or of proximity to the river. It is true, it has been attempted to establish from him, that the Temple was exactly in the centre of one of the halves into which the city was divided by the river: which, by the way, if clearly made out, would not agree with Major Rennel's position of it on the river's banks: but the error appears to have arisen from translating μέσος, *centre*. . . . Strabo, as might be expected, contains much fewer particulars than Herodotus; and the other Grecian and Roman historians still less: they are consequently of little use in a topographical enquiry. It appears, therefore, that none of the ancients say whether the Tower of Belus was on the east or the west of the Euphrates; that its position in the centre of the city, or even of one of its divisions, is by no means clearly made out; and that while the description of the best ancient author involves no difficulties, the only particulars which embarrass us are supported by the sole testimony of the worst. . . .

I therefore repeat my belief, formed from the inspection of the ruins about Hilla, that they are of one character, and must be received altogether as a part of Babylon, or wholly rejected without reserve. And I must here state what seems to me to be the best evidence for their antiquity, independent of their appearance, dimensions, and correspondence with the descriptions of the ancients – The burnt bricks of which the ruins are principally composed, and which have inscriptions on them in the cuneiform character, only found in Babylon and Persepolis, are all invariably placed in a similar manner, viz. with their faces or written sides downwards. This argues some design in placing them, though what that might have been it is now impossible to say. It, however, proves sufficiently that the buildings must have been erected when the bricks were made, and the very ancient and peculiar form of characters on them in use. When these bricks are found in more modern constructions, as in Baghdad and Hilla, they are of course placed indifferently, without regard to the writing on them. In the greatest depth in the excavations at the Kassr, at the subterraneous passage or canal, I have myself found small pieces of baked clay covered with cuneiform writing, and sometimes with figures indisputably Babylonian: these shall be described when I come to speak of the Babylonian antiques. Had the ruins been more recent than is here presumed, these inscriptions would not have been found in this order and manner, and we should in all probability have found others in the character of language then in use. Thus, had the town been Mahometan or Christian, we might reasonably expect to meet with fragments of Coufic or Stranghelo. There is another equally remarkable circumstance in these ruins, and which is almost conclusive with respect to their antiquity. In the very heart of the mound called the Kassr, and also in the ruins on the bank of the river, which have been crumbled and shivered by the action of the water, I saw earthen urns filled with ashes, with some small fragments of bones in them; and in the northern face of the Mujelibè I discovered a gallery filled with skeletons inclosed in wooden coffins. Of the high antiquity of the sepulchral urns no one will for an instant doubt; and that of the skeletons is sufficiently ascertained, both from the mode of burial, which has never been practised in this country since the introduction of Islam, and still more by a curious brass ornament which I found in one of the coffins. These discoveries are of the most interesting nature; and though it is certainly difficult to reconcile them with any theory of these ruins, yet in themselves they sufficiently establish their antiquity. The two separate modes of burial too are highly worthy of attention. There is, I believe, no reason to suppose that the Babylonians buried their dead; the old Persians we know never did. It is not impossible that the difference may indicate the several usages of the Babylonians and Greeks, and that the urns may contain the ashes of the soldiers of Alexander and of his successors. . . .

It now remains for me to notice the most interesting and remarkable of all the Babylonian remains, viz. the Birs Nemroud. – If any building may be supposed to have left considerable traces, it is certainly the Pyramid or Tower of Belus; which by its form, dimensions, and the solidity of its construction, was well calculated to resist the ravages of time; and, if human force had not been employed, would in all probability have remained to the present day, in nearly as perfect a state as the pyramids of Egypt. Even under the dilapidation which we know it to have undergone at a very early period, we might reasonably look for traces of it after every other vestige of Babylon had vanished from the face of the earth. When, therefore, we see within a short distance from the spot fixed on, both by geographers and antiquarians, and the tradition of the country, to be the site of ancient Babylon, a stupendous pile, which appears to have been built in receding stages, which bears the most indisputable traces both of the violence of man and the lapse of ages, and yet continues to tower over the desert, the wonder of successive generations, – it is impossible that their perfect correspondence with all the accounts of the Tower of Belus should not strike the most careless observer, and induce him to attempt clearing away the difficulties which have been suggested by Major Rennel against its reception within the limits of Babylon. I am of opinion that this ruin is of a nature to fix of itself the locality of Babylon, even to the exclusion of those on the eastern side of the river: and if the ancients had actually assigned a position to the Tower irreconcileable with the Birs, it would be more reasonable to suppose that some error had crept into their accounts, than to reject this most remarkable of all the ruins. But there is no necessity for either supposition. From the view of the ancient historians, I have taken in the foregoing part of this Memoir, it will appear that none of them has positively fixed the spot where the Tower of Belus stood; and if we receive the dimensions of Babylon assigned by the best of the ancient historians – himself an eye-witness – both the Birs and the eastern ruins will fairly come within its limits. Against receiving his testimony we have only our own notions of probability. We have reduced the dimensions merely because they do not accord with our ideas of the size of a city: but we know Babylon to have been rather an inclosed district than a city; and there can of course be no hesitation in abandoning less accurate evidence, and receiving the statement of Herodotus, if there be any traces on the spot to justify it.

The whole height of the Birs Nemroud above the plain to the summit of the brick wall is two hundred and thirty-five feet (235). The brick wall itself which stands on the edge of the summit, and was undoubtedly the face of another stage, is thirty-seven (37) feet high. In the side of the pile a little below the summit is very clearly to be seen part of another brick wall, precisely resembling the fragment which crowns the summit, but which still encases and supports its part of the mound. This is clearly indicative of another stage of greater extent. The masonry is infinitely superior to any thing of the kind I have ever seen; and leaving out of the question any conjecture relative to the original destination of this ruin, the impression made by a sight of it is, that it was a solid pile, composed in the interior of unburnt brick, and perhaps earth or rubbish; that it was constructed in receding stages, and faced with fine burnt bricks, having inscriptions on them, laid in a very thin layer of lime cement; and that it was reduced by violence to its present ruinous condition. The upper stories have been forcibly broken down, and fire has been employed as an instrument of destruction, though it is not easy to say precisely how or why. The facing of fine bricks has partly been removed, and partly covered by the falling down of the mass which it supported and kept together. I speak with the greater confidence of the different stages of this pile, from my own observations having been recently confirmed and extended by an intelligent traveller, who is of opinion that the traces of *four* stages are clearly discernible. As I believe it is his intention to lay the account of his travels before the world, I am unwilling to forestall any of his observations; but I must not omit to notice a remarkable result arising out of them. The Tower of Belus was a stadium in height; therefore, if we suppose the eight towers or stages which composed the Pyramid of Belus to have been of equal height, according to Major Rennel's idea, which is preferable to that of the Count de Caylus (see *Mem. de l'Academie*, vol. xxxi), we ought to find traces of them in the fragment which remains, whose elevation is 235 feet; and this is precisely the number which Mr Buckingham believes he has discovered. This result is the more worthy of attention, as it did not occur to Mr B himself.

The Birs Nemroud is apparently the Tower of Belus of Benjamin of Tudela, who says it was destroyed by fire from heaven – a curious remark, as it proves he must have observed the vitrified masses on the summit. M. Beauchamp speaks of it under the appellation of Brouss: he never visited it himself; indeed the undertaking is not always practicable without a strong escort. The excellent Niebuhr, whose intelligence, industry, and accuracy cannot be too often praised, suspects the Birs to have been the Tower of Belus. He gives a very good account of it even from the hasty view which circumstance would allow of his taking. 'Au sud ouest de Hellè à 1¼ mille, et par conséquent à l'ouest de l'Euphrate, on trouve encore d'autres restes de l'ancienne Babylone: ici il y a toute une colline de ces belles pierres de murailles dont j'ai parlé; et au dessus il y a une tour qui à ce qui parait est intérieurement aussi toute remplie de ces pierres de murailles cuites; mais les pierres de dehors (qui sait combien de pieds d'épaisseur) sont perdues par le tems dans cette épaisse muraille, ou plutôt dans ces grands tas de pierres: il y a ici et là de petits trous qui percent d'un coté jusqu'à l'autre, sans doute pour y donner un libre passage à l'air, et pour empêcher au dedans l'humidité, qui auroit pu nuire au batiment.' (*Voyage*, vol. ii, p. 235.) In this description the Birs may be recognised, even through the obscurity of a job translation.

After this, I was certainly surprised to find that Major Rennel not only excludes it from the limits of Babylon, but even doubts the mound being artificial. So indisputably evident is the fact of the whole mass being from top to bottom artificial, that I should as soon have thought of writing a dissertation to prove that the Pyramids are the work of human hands, as of dwelling on this point. Indeed, were there anything equivocal in the appearance of the mound itself, the principles of physical geography utterly forbid the supposition of there being an isolated hill of natural formation in ground formed by the depositions of a river; and therefore, if any traveller fancied he saw a natural hill at Musseil, or any other place in that direction, he was most unquestionably mistaken.

The same reasons prove that there could never have been bitumen springs in Babylon. (See *Geog.* of Herod., p. 369.) Diodorus, indeed, does not say, as Major Rennel supposes, that bitumen was found in Babylon, – but in Babylonia, which is a very different thing.

The Birs Nemroud is in all likelihood at present pretty near in the state in which Alexander saw it; if we give any credit to the report that ten thousand men could only remove the rubbish, preparatory to repairing it, in two months. If, indeed, it required one half of that number to disencumber it, the state of dilapidation must have been complete. The immense masses of vitrified brick which are seen on the top of the mount appear to have marked its summit since the time of its destruction. The rubbish about its base was probably in much greater quantities, the weather having dissipated much of it in the course of so many revolving ages; and, possibly, portions of the exterior facing of fine brick may have disappeared at different periods.

In the foregoing observations I have endeavoured to show that the ruins of Babylon in their present state may be perfectly reconciled with the best descriptions of the Grecian writers, without doing violence to either. I feel persuaded that the more the subject is investigated the stronger will the conformity be found; but it is one in which the spirit of system would be peculiarly misplaced: and I am so far from being bigoted to my own opinions, that should I in the course of my researches happen to discover particulars which may reasonably appear to militate against them, I will be the first to lay them before the public.

Bagdad, July 1817.

P.S. Since writing the above I have received an extract from the Supplement to the fifth edition of the *Encyclopaedia Britannica*, containing a summary of my former accounts of Babylon, with the author's own ideas on the subject. It is peculiarly gratifying to me to find that my opinions have the confirmation of such a writer.

Second Memoir on Babylon, 1818

The walls of Babylon

ROBERT KOLDEWEY

ROBERT KOLDEWEY (*1855–1925*) *studied architecture, archaeology and ancient history at Berlin, Munich and Vienna. His first archaeological investigation was on the Acropolis of Assos, after which he was commissioned by the German Archaeological Institute to excavate in Lesbos, and in 1887 the British Museum sent him to Iraq. For the next ten years he alternated between teaching at Gorlitz and excavating in the Mediterranean region. In 1897 the Deutsche Orient-Gesellschaft, wishing to acquire new finds of cuneiform tablets, commissioned him to survey for promising sites in Mesopotamia, and he reported favourably on Babylon. In 1899 he began to excavate, and remained there for the next eighteen years, only leaving during World War I when the British advance was on the point of cutting off his last retreat to safety. His expedition was perhaps the most scientific and certainly one of the best equipped of its time, being the first to instal a light railway for moving debris, and to employ over 200 men, and it is largely owing to his work that the legendary Babylon of the Bible became known and investigated as a historical and geographical fact.*

In the time of Nebuchadnezzar the traveller who approached the capital of Babylonia from the north would find himself where the Nil Canal flows today, face to face with the colossal wall that surrounded mighty Babylon. Part of this wall still exists and is recognisable at the present time in the guise of a low earthen ridge about 4 to 5 kilometres in length. Up to the present we have only excavated a small part, so that it is only possible to give a detailed description of the most noteworthy features of these fortifications, that were rendered so famous by Greek authors.

There was a massive wall of crude brick 7 metres thick, in front of which, at an interval of about 12 metres, stood another wall of burnt brick 7·8 metres thick, with the strong wall of the fosse at its foot, also of burnt brick and 3·3 metres thick. The fosse must have been in front of this, but so far we have not searched closely for it, and therefore the counterscarp has not yet been found.

Astride on the mud wall were towers 8·37 metres (about 24 bricks) wide, that projected beyond the wall on both its faces. Measured from centre to centre these towers were 52·5 metres apart. Thus there was a tower at intervals of about 100 ells, for the Babylonian ell measured roughly half a metre.

Owing to the unfinished state of the excavations it is not yet possible to say how the towers on the outer wall were constructed. The space between the two walls was filled in with rubble, at least to the height at which the ruins are preserved and presumably to the crown of the outer wall. Thus on the top of the wall there was a road that afforded space for a team of four horses abreast, and even for two such teams to pass each other. Upon this crown of the wall the upper compartments of the towers faced each other like small houses.

This broad roadway on the summit of the wall, which was of world-renown owing to the descriptions of it given by classical writers, was of the greatest importance for the protection of the great city. It rendered possible the rapid shifting of defensive forces at any time to that part of the wall which was specially pressed by attack. The line of defence was very long; the north-east front, which can still be measured, is 4,400 metres long, and on the south-east the ruined wall can be traced without excavations for a length of 2 kilometres. These two flanks of the wall certainly extended as far as the Euphrates as it flowed from north to south. With the Euphrates they enclosed that part of Babylon of which the ruins exist at the present time, but according to Herodotus and others they were supplemented on the other side of the Euphrates by two other walls, so that the town site consisted of a quadrangle through which the Euphrates flowed diagonally. Of the western walls nothing is now to be seen. Whether the traces of a line of wall to the south near the village of Sindjar will prove to have formed part of them has yet to be ascertained.

The excavations carried on up to the present time have yielded no surrounding walls beyond this fortification. The circuit extended for about 18 kilometres. Instead of this, Herodotus gives about 86 kilometres and Ctesias about 65 kilometres. There must be some error underlying this discrepancy. The 65 kilometres of Ctesias approximate so closely to four times the correct measurement that it may well be suspected that he mistook the figures representing the whole circumference for the measure of one side of the square. We shall later turn more in detail from the testimony of the ancient writers to the evidence of the ruins themselves. Generally speaking, the measurements given are not in accordance with those actually preserved, while the general description, on the contrary, is usually accurate. Herodotus describes the wall of Babylon as built of burnt brick. To an observer from without it would no doubt appear as such, as only the top of the inner mud wall could be seen from outside. The escarp of the fosse was formed of the square bricks that are so extraordinarily numerous in Babylon, that measure 33 centimetres and bear the usual stamp of Nebuchadnezzar. Those of the brick wall are somewhat smaller (32 centimetres) and unstamped. These smaller unstamped bricks are common previous to the time of Nebuchadnezzar, but nevertheless they may very well date from the early years of his reign, as we shall see farther on. To what period the mud-brick wall may be assigned we do not yet know; it is certainly older. It apparently possessed an escarp, of which there are some scanty remains within the great brick wall. It appears to have been cut through on the outside by the latter.

Up to the present we have found about 15 of the towers on the mud wall only. They are the so-called Cavalier towers, and project both at the front and the back, thus placed astride on the wall. They were, of course, higher than the walls, but we can get no clue from the ruins as to the height of walls or towers, as only the lower parts remain. The towers are 3·36 metres wide and are placed 44 metres apart. Thus on the entire front there were about 90, and on the whole circumference – provided the town formed a square – there must have been 360 towers. How many there were on the outer wall we do not know. Ctesias gives the number as 250. No gateway has yet been found, which is not surprising, considering the limited extent of the excavations.

During the Parthian period these lines of fortification can have been no longer in a condition to afford protection. On the town side of the mud wall there are Parthian sarcophagi, inserted in holes dug in the wall itself.

While the foundations of the brick wall are below the present water-level, the mud wall stands on an artificial embankment. As a general rule mud walls were not provided with deep foundations. The mortar employed for the mud wall was clay, and for the brick wall bitumen was used. The same method of construction can be recognised in other parts of the city, where it is better preserved and can be more satisfactorily studied.

At the northern end of our line of wall, which enclosed the mound of ruins, called 'Babil', with a hook-like curve, the inner wall also was built of brick. This appears, at least, from the two deep trenches left by plunderers which occur here, but it must be inferred pending excavation. The digging for the valuable bricks which occurred in recent times has left deep traces in the otherwise smooth surface of the ground which we do not find in the attempted demolitions of more ancient times.

For this reason, with the exception of the portion near Babil there is nothing to be seen of the burnt-brick wall without excavating, while the mud wall, which has merely suffered from the ravages of time, has left behind a clearly marked line of ruins of some height. The town wall of Seleucia on the Tigris, likewise a mud wall, stands out similarly above its mounds of debris to a considerable height. It cannot therefore be said that a burnt-brick wall of 480 stadia, the gigantic dimensions recorded by Herodotus, must necessarily have left considerable and unmistakeable traces, and it is not this consideration that leads us to doubt the existence of an encircling wall of such dimensions, which has been accepted as an established fact since Oppert's excavations in Babylon. Neither does the immense size of itself demand dismissal as fantastic. The great wall of China, 11 metres high and 7·5 metres broad, with its length of 2,450 kilometres, is just 29 times as long as that of Herodotus. There are other overwhelming considerations which we shall investigate later. In any case the city, even in circumference, was the greatest of any in the ancient East, Nineveh itself not excepted, which in other respects rivalled Babylon. But the period in which the fame of Babylon's vast size spread over the world was the time of Herodotus, and then Nineveh had already ceased to exist.

A comparison with modern cities can scarcely be made without further consideration. It must always be remembered than an ancient city was primarily a fortress of which the inhabited part was surrounded and protected by the encircling girdle of the walls. Our great modern cities are of an entirely different character, they are inhabited spaces, open on all sides. A reasonable comparison can, therefore, only be made between Babylon and other walled cities, and when compared with them Babylon takes the first place, both for ancient and modern times, as regards the extent of its enclosed and inhabited area.

Nebuchadnezzar frequently mentions this great work in his inscriptions. The most important passage occurs in his great *Steinplatten* inscription, col. 7 1. 22–55: 'That no assault should reach Imgur-Bel, the wall of Babylon; I did, what no earlier king had done, for 4,000 ells of land on the side of Babylon, at a distance so that it (the assault) did not come nigh, I caused a mighty wall to be built on the east side of Babylon. I dug out its moat, and I built a scarp with bitumen and bricks. Its broad gateways I set within it and fixed in them double doors of cedar wood overlaid with copper. In order that the enemy who devised (?) evil should not press on the flanks of Babylon, I surrounded it with mighty floods, as is the land with the wave-tossed sea. Its coming was like the coming of the great sea, the salt water. In order that no breach should be made in it, I piled up an earthen embankment by it, and encompassed it with quay walls of burnt brick. The bulwark I fortified cunningly and made the city of Babylon into a fortress' (cf. H. Winckler, *Keilinschriftliche Bibliothek*, vol. iii, 2, p. 23). It can hardly be expected that we can yet reach absolute certainty as to the meaning of all the details here given. That can best be afforded by a complete excavation, which is urgently to be desired.

The Excavations at Babylon, 1914

A curious sculpture

ROBERT KOLDEWEY

At the north-east corner before our excavations began there was a great basalt figure of a lion trampling on a man who lay beneath him with his right hand on the flank of the animal, and the left on his muzzle. This latter has been chopped away by superstitious hands, and he is marked all over by the stones and flint balls that have been, and are still, flung at him; for he is regarded as the much-feared 'Djin'. On one side the Arabs have dug out a deep hole in his flanks, which is now filled in with cement. The reason of this is as follows. A European once came here, and enquired about the lion, which he had probably read of in the books of earlier travellers. The Arabs showed it to him, and after looking at it attentively, he chose from among the small holes in the basalt the right one, into which he thrust a key and turned it, whereupon his hand was immediately filled with gold pieces. Having accomplished his practical joke the traveller went his way, unable as he was to speak Arabic. The worthy Arabs, however, in order to render the treasure available, hammered this hole in the lion, which must have caused them immense labour, for the stone is extremely hard. The figure is not completely carved, and is still little more than blocked out. It therefore looks more ancient than it really is, for it can scarcely be earlier than the time of Nebuchadnezzar. People are divided as to its meaning. Some see in it Daniel in the lions' den, and others Babylonia above defeated Egypt. But a concrete past is throughout this period never represented otherwise than in reliefs, and, on the other hand, it is foreign to Babylonian art to take as a basis the representation of an abstract idea.

The Excavations at Babylon, 1914

Problems at the excavation of Nineveh

PAUL EMILE BOTTA

PAUL EMILE BOTTA (*1805–1870*) *was the son of a prominent Italian politician and historian. In 1826 he sailed on a voyage round the world which took him three years, and on his return he travelled extensively in the eastern Mediterranean region, including an expedition to Sennaar as physician to the Arab leader Mehemet Ali. He then entered the diplomatic service and in 1836 was posted to Tripoli where he remained for the next twenty years. It was during this stay that he made his expedition to the mounds of Kouyunjik and Khorsabad, the site of Nineveh, and began the excavations which were later continued by Layard. His work as both a diplomat and an antiquarian received recognition in 1845 when he was created a member of the Légion d'Honneur.*

I told you, Sir, that the wall turned northward at its extremity, and there formed a sort of recess; this measures about one metre and a half in depth, and is occupied by a symbolical half-length statue, representing the fore part of a bull, human headed, projecting from the wall. Although the legs are very natural and admirably sculptured, the upper portion is not only much decayed, but it appears entirely conventional. Scales, regularly striated, seem to indicate wings; the beard is formally plaited, and the fetlock is delineated by a broad band of horizontal furrows. The head is fallen and in bad condition, yet there can be no doubt that the face was human. This statue must have been about 5 metres high, and was carved out of one single block of gypsum.

Wall xxxiii, constituting the recess, displays another symbolical figure, viz. a winged personage with the head of a bird. The beak, though rather long, appertains to a bird of prey; the hair is stiffly plaited, and the head surmounted by a kind of tuft descending to the shoulders. The neck is encircled by a collar or carcanet, the arms and wrists are adorned with bracelets; the right hand is elevated, and the left certainly holds a basket similar to those carried by the winged figures of passage No. II. This personage is clad in a short tunic, and a fringed girdle of increased width at its extremity, hangs between his legs. In evidence of the profusion of sculptures decorating this monument, I must remark that the small surface of wall between the bull and this winged figure is likewise ornamented with bas-reliefs.

The construction of this edifice is invariably the same; always large and small gypsum slabs set upright against the earth of the mound. I cannot believe such walls have ever supported a stone roof, and this is one reason for my suspecting it was of wood. Nevertheless, I have acquired no certain knowledge on this subject; the charcoal, very abundant in some places, is not seen in others where, however, the walls offer an equally calcined appearance. I therefore remain undecided. I shall merely observe that the dimensions of the bull are so enormous, it is impossible to suppose it could have been conveyed to its place through narrow passages excavated in the mound. Perhaps it was stationed outside one of the portals. In this case, the wall must have formed the exterior part of this monument, and, consequently, the state of preservation in which both the sculptures and stone itself are found is fully explained. It would not have suffered by the falling in of the burning roof. But the time has not yet come for entering upon these discussions; when everything is disinterred we may probably understand all that at present seems doubtful. By making enquiries I have endeavoured, but in vain, to learn whether this village had not anciently some other name of more Chaldean sound than Khorsabad, or Khestéabad (for so it is still written); there is no local tradition on the subject, and even the inhabitants themselves were ignorant of the archaeological treasures lying buried under their feet, and which chance enable me to discover; my researches shall continue, notwithstanding. With regard to the future direction of the works, I have, Sir, the satisfaction of informing you that, in all probability, I shall encounter no further obstacles. His Excellency the Minister of the Interior having kindly assisted my labours, I am able to act more freely, and have succeeded in persuading the Chief of the village to vacate his house, which barred our passage; he will take up his abode in the plain, and the rest of the people will follow him; the entire mound will thus be left at my disposal, and nothing shall escape my scrutiny. I am, however, compelled to stop the excavations for some time; the air of Khorsabad is particularly unhealthy, as I not only myself experienced, but likewise all those who accompanied me. Already, I have frequently been obliged to change the workmen; and their head, who served me with intelligence, is now dangerously ill. For this reason I cannot return to Khorsabad before the heats are over, and were the works to proceed at this moment, such is the condition of the sculptures, they would be lost before I could go and draw them; I have therefore suspended my labours for a short period, and reinterred those parts which I had not time to copy. As for the others, I regret to say they will soon fall to atoms. Being no longer supported, the walls yield to the swelling of the ground, the action of the sun reduces the surface to powder, and even now a considerable portion has disappeared. This is truly grievous, but I can devise no remedy, unless the whole, as I draw it, should be again filled up, and thus preserved for future investigation; this is my present purpose, since, everything considered, it will always be possible to make a fresh clearing, whilst, by leaving the walls uncovered, in three months not a vestige of them would remain.

Letters on the Discoveries at Nineveh, 1850

Excavations at Nimrud

AUSTEN HENRY LAYARD

SIR AUSTEN HENRY LAYARD (*1817-1894*) *was born in Paris and was educated in Italy, France, Switzerland and England. His father was a Civil Servant and there is no doubt that his cosmopolitan upbringing contributed to his love of travel and the fine arts. He began his professional career in the office of a London solicitor, but after six years he left with the intention of travelling overland to Ceylon where he planned to follow his father into the Civil Service. When he reached the Near East, however, he gave up any idea of continuing his journey, and for some years engaged in unofficial diplomatic missions, during the course of which he became familiar with the ruins of Nimrud, Nineveh and Babylon. After securing official assistance and encouragement for his expedition he undertook the excavation of the mound of Nineveh, and shortly after this, of Babylon, acquiring the greater part of the magnificent collection of Assyrian sculptures now in the British Museum.*

I was again amongst the ruins by the end of October. The winter season was fast approaching, and it was necessary to build a proper house for the shelter of myself and servants. I marked out a plan on the ground, in the village of Nimroud, and in a few days our habitations were complete. My workmen formed the walls of mud bricks dried in the sun, and roofed the rooms with beams and branches of trees. A thick coat of mud was laid over the whole, to exclude rain. Two rooms for my own accommodation were divided by an Iwan, or open apartment, the whole being surrounded by a wall. In a second court-yard were huts for my Cawass, Arab guests, and servants, and stables for my horses. Ibrahim Agha displayed his ingenuity by making equidistant loopholes, of a most warlike appearance, in the outer walls; which I immediately ordered to be filled up, to avoid any suspicion of being the constructor of forts and castles, with the intention of making a permanent Frank settlement in the country. We did not neglect precautions, however, in case of an attack from the Bedouins, of whom Ibrahim Agha was in constant dread. Unfortunately, the only shower of rain, that I saw during the remainder of my residence in Assyria, fell before my walls were covered in, and so saturated the bricks that they did not dry again before the following spring. The consequence was, that the only verdure, on which my eyes were permitted to feast before my return to Europe, was furnished by my own property – the walls in the interior of the rooms being continually clothed with a crop of grass.

On the mound itself, and immediately above the great winged lions first discovered, were built a house for my Nestorian workmen and their families, and a hut, to which any small objects discovered among the ruins could at once be removed for safety. I divided my Arabs into three parties, according to the branches of the tribe to which they belonged. About forty tents were pitched on different parts of the mound, at the entrance to the principal trenches. Forty more were placed round my dwelling, and the rest on the bank of the river, where the sculptures were deposited previous to their embarkation on the rafts. The men were all armed. I thus provided for the defence of my establishment.

Mr Hormuzd Rassam lived with me; and to him I confided the payment of the wages, and the accounts. He soon obtained an extraordinary influence amongst the Arabs, and his fame spread through the desert.

The workmen were divided into bands. In each set were generally eight or ten Arabs, who carried away the earth in baskets; and two, or four, Nestorian diggers, according to the nature of the soil and rubbish which had to be excavated. They were overlooked by a superintendent, whose duty it was to keep them to their work, and to give me notice when the diggers approached any slab, or exposed any small object to view, that I might myself assist in its uncovering or removal. I scattered a few Arabs of a hostile tribe amongst the rest, and by that means I was always made acquainted with what was going on, could easily learn if there were plots brewing, and could detect those who might attempt to appropriate any relics discovered during the excavations. The smallness of the sum placed at my disposal, compelled me to follow the same plan in the excavations that I had hitherto adopted, – digging trenches along the walls of the chambers, and exposing the whole of the slabs, without removing the earth from the centre. Thus, few chambers were fully explored; and many small objects of great interest may have been left undiscovered. As I was directed to bury the buildings with earth after they had been examined, I filled up the trenches, to avoid unnecessary expense, with the rubbish taken from those subsequently opened, having first copied the inscriptions, and drawn the sculptures.

The excavations were recommenced, on a large scale by the 1st of November. My working parties were distributed over the mound – in the ruins of the N.W. and S.W. palaces; near the gigantic bulls in the centre; and in the south-east corner, where no traces of buildings had as yet been discovered.

It will be remembered that the greater number of slabs forming the southern side of the large hall in the N.W. palace had fallen with their faces to the ground. I was, in the first place, anxious to raise these bas-reliefs, and to pack them for transport to Busrah. To accomplish this, it was necessary to remove a large accumulation of earth and rubbish – to empty, indeed, nearly the whole chamber, for the fallen slabs extended almost half-way across it. The sculptures on nine slabs were found to be in admirable preservation, although broken by the fall. The slabs were divided, as those already described, into two compartments, by inscriptions which were precisely similar.

The sculptures were of the highest interest. They represented the wars of the king, and his victories over foreign nations. The upper bas-reliefs, on the first two slabs, formed one subject – the king, with his warriors, in battle under the walls of a hostile castle. He stood, gorgeously attired, in a chariot drawn by three horses richly caparisoned, and was discharging an arrow either against those who defended the walls; or against a warrior, who, already wounded, was falling from his chariot. An attendant protected the person of the king with a shield, and a charioteer held the reins, and urged on the horses. Above the king was the emblem of the supreme Deity, represented as at Persepolis by a winged figure within a circle, wearing a horned cap resembling that of the human-headed lions. Like the king, he was shooting an arrow, the head of which was in the form of a trident.

Behind the king were three chariots; the first drawn by three horses – one of which was rearing and another falling – and occupied by a wounded warrior demanding quarter of his pursuers. In the others were two warriors, one discharging an arrow, the other guiding the horses, which were at full speed. In each Assyrian chariot was a standard – the devices which were enclosed in a circle ornamented with tassels and streamers, being an archer, with the horned cap but without wings, standing on a bull; and the two bulls, back to back. At the bottom of the first bas-relief were wavy lines, to indicate water or a river, and trees were scattered over both. Assyrian footmen, fighting or slaying the enemy, were introduced in several places; and three headless bodies above the principal figures in the second bas-relief represented the dead in the background.

On the upper part of the two slabs following the battle-scene was the triumphal return after victory. In front of the procession were warriors throwing the heads of the slain at the feet of the conquerors. Two musicians, playing on stringed instruments, preceded the charioteers, who were represented unarmed, and bearing their standards; above them was an eagle with a human head in its talons. The king came next in his chariot, carrying in one hand his bow, and in the other two arrows – the attitude in which he is so frequently represented on Assyrian monuments, and probably denoting triumph over his enemies. Above the horses was the presiding divinity; also holding a bow. The attendant, who in war bore the shield, was now replaced by an eunuch, raising the open parasol – the Eastern emblem of royalty. The horses were led by grooms, although the charioteer still held the reins. Behind the king's chariot was a horseman leading a second horse, gaily caparisoned.

After the procession, was the castle and pavilion of the victorious king, – the former represented by a circle, divided into four equal compartments, and surrounded by towers and battlements. In each compartment were figures evidently engaged in preparing the feast: one was slaying a sheep; another appeared to be baking bread; and others stood before bowls and utensils placed on tables. The pavilion was supported by three columns; one surmounted by a fir-cone, – the emblem so frequently seen in the Assyrian sculptures; the others by figures of the ibex or mountain goat. It was probably of silk or woollen stuff, richly ornamented and edged with a fringe of fir-cones and tulip-shaped ornaments. Beneath the canopy was a groom cleaning one horse; whilst others, picketed by their halters, were feeding at a trough. An eunuch stood at the entrance of the tent, to receive four prisoners, who, with their hands bound behind, were brought to him by an Assyrian warrior. Above this group were two singular lion-headed figures, one holding a whip or thong in the right hand, and grasping his under jaw with the left, the other raising his hands. They were clothed in tunics, descending to the knees, and skins falling from the head, over the shoulders, to the ankles, and were accompanied by a man raising a stick.

The four following bas-reliefs recorded a battle, in which were represented the king, two warriors with their standards, and an eunuch in chariots, and four warriors, amongst whom was also an eunuch, on horses. The enemy were on foot, and discharged their arrows against the pursuers. Eagles hovered above the victors, and were feeding on the slain. The winged divinity in the circle was again seen above the king.

These bas-reliefs in many respects illustrate the manners and civilisation of the Assyrians. We here find the eunuch commanding in war and engaging with the enemy in combat, as we have before seen him ministering to the king during religious ceremonies, or waiting upon him as his arms-bearer during peace. That eunuchs rose to the highest rank among the Assyrians, and were even generals over their armies, we learn from Scripture, where the Rabaris, or chief of the eunuchs, is mentioned as one of the three principal officers of Sennacherib, and as one of the princes of Nebuchadnezzar. They appear, indeed, to have held the same important posts, and to have exercised the same influence in the Assyrian court, as they have enjoyed in Turkey and Persia, where they have frequently attained to the post of vizir or prime minister.

The horses of the archers were led by mounted warriors, wearing circular skull caps, probably of iron. Horsemen are frequently mentioned in the Bible as forming an important part of the Assyrian armies. Ezekiel (xxiii, 6.) describes 'the Assyrians clothed in blue, captains and rulers, all of them desirable young men, horsemen riding upon horses'; and Holofernes had no less than 12,000 archers on horseback. The rider is seated on the naked back of the horse, which is only adorned with a cloth when led behind the chariot of the king, probably for his use in case of accident to the chariot.

The horses represented in the sculptures appear to be of noble breed. Assyria, and particularly that part of the empire which was watered by the Tigris and Euphrates, was celebrated at the earliest period for its horses, as the same plains are to this day for the noblest races of Arabia. The Jews probably obtained horses for their cavalry from this country; and horses were offered to them by the general of the Assyrian king, as an acceptable present. On Egyptian monuments horses from Mesopotamia are continually mentioned amongst the spoil or tribute. The horse of the Assyrian bas-reliefs was evidently drawn from the finest model. The head is small and well shaped, the nostrils large and high, the neck arched, the body long, and the legs slender and sinewy. The prophet exclaims of the horses of the Chaldaeans, 'They are swifter than the leopards, and more fierce than the evening wolves'; and the magnificent description of the war-horse in the book of Job is familiar to every reader. At a later period the plains of Babylonia furnished horses to the Persians, both for the private use of the king and for his troops. The rich pasture-grounds of Mesopotamia must have always afforded them ample sustenance, whilst those vast plains, exposed to the heats of summer and cold of winter, inured them to hardship and fatigue.

Nineveh and its Remains, 1867

Courtesy, Trustees of the British Museum

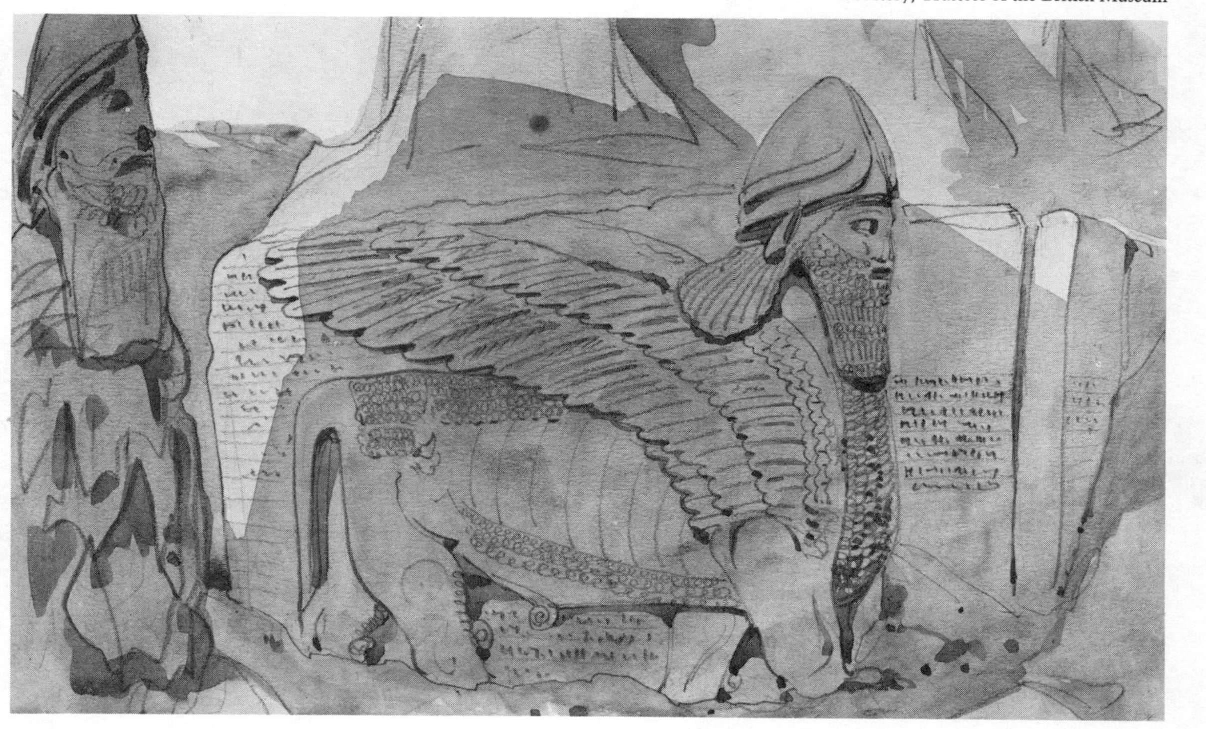

16. A winged bull with a human head comes to light during the Nimrud excavations, and with it the first news of the high culture of ancient Assyria.

17. A. H. Layard, the great excavator of Nineveh, at work; drawn in 1850 by a visitor to the site.

Discoveries and alarms

AUSTEN HENRY LAYARD

On the morning following these discoveries, I had ridden to the encampment of Sheikh Abd-ur rahman, and was returning to the mound, when I saw two Arabs of his tribe coming towards me and urging their mares to the top of their speed. On reaching me they stopped. 'Hasten, O Bey', exclaimed one of them – 'hasten to the diggers, for they have found Nimrod himself. Wallah! it is wonderful but it is true! we have seen him with our eyes. There is no God but God'; and both joining in this pious exclamation, they galloped off, without further words, in the direction of their tents.

On reaching the ruins I descended into the newly opened trench, and found the workmen, who had already seen me, as I approached, standing near a heap of baskets and cloaks. Whilst Awad advanced and asked for a present to celebrate the occasion, the Arabs withdrew the screen they had hastily constructed, and disclosed an enormous human head sculptured in full out of the alabaster of the country. They had uncovered the upper part of a figure, the remainder of which was still buried in the earth. I saw at once that the head must belong to a winged lion or bull, similar to those of Khorsabad and Persepolis. It was in admirable preservation. The expression was calm, yet majestic, and the outline of the features showed a freedom and knowledge of art, scarcely to be looked for in works of so remote a period. The cap had three horns, and, unlike that of the human-headed bulls hitherto found in Assyria, was rounded and without ornament at the top.

I was not surprised that the Arabs had been amazed and terrified at this apparition. It required no stretch of imagination to conjure up the most strange fancies. This gigantic head, blanched with age, thus rising from the bowels of the earth, might well have belonged to one of those fearful beings which are described in the traditions of the country as appearing to mortals, slowly ascending from the regions below. One of the workmen, on catching the first glimpse of the monster, had thrown down his basket and had run off towards Mosul as fast as his legs could carry him. I learnt this with regret, as I anticipated the consequences.

Whilst I was superintending the removal of the earth, which still clung to the sculpture, and giving directions for the continuation of the work, the noise of horsemen was heard, and presently Abd-ur rahman, followed by half his tribe, appeared on the edge of the trench. As soon as the two Arabs I had met had reached their tents, and published the wonders they had seen, every one mounted his mare and rode to the mound to satisfy himself of the truth of these inconceivable reports. When they beheld the head they all cried together, 'There is no God but God, and Mohammed is his Prophet!' It was some time before the Sheikh could be prevailed upon to descend into the pit, and convince himself that the image he saw was of stone. 'This is not the work of men's hands,' exclaimed he, 'but of those infidel giants of whom the Prophet, peace be with him! has said, that they were higher than the tallest date tree; this is one of the idols which Noah, peace be with him! cursed before the flood.' In this opinion, the result of a careful examination, all the bystanders concurred.

I now ordered a trench to be dug due south from the head, in the expectation of finding a corresponding figure, and before night-fall reached the object of my search about twelve feet distant. Engaging two or three men to sleep near the sculptures, I returned to the village, and celebrated the day's discovery by a slaughter of sheep, of which all the Arabs near partook. As some wandering musicians chanced to be at Selamiyah, I sent for them, and dances were kept up during the greater part of the night. On the following morning Arabs from the other side of the Tigris, and the inhabitants of the surrounding villages, congregated on the mound. Even the women could not repress their curiosity, and came in crowds, with their children, from afar. My Cawass was stationed during the day in the trench, into which I would not allow the multitude to descend.

As I had expected, the report of the discovery of the gigantic head, carried by the terrified Arab to Mosul, had thrown the town into commotion. He had scarcely checked his speed before reaching the bridge. Entering breathless into the bazaars, he announced to every one he met that Nimrod had appeared. The news soon got to the ears of the Cadi, who called the Mufti and the Ulema together, to consult upon this unexpected occurrence. Their deliberations, ended in a procession to the Governor, and a formal protest, on the part of the Mussulmans of the town, against proceedings so directly contrary to the laws of the Koran. The Cadi had no distinct idea whether the very bones of the mighty hunter had been uncovered, or only his image; nor did Ismail

Pasha very clearly remember whether Nimrod was a true-believing prophet, or an infidel. I consequently received a somewhat unintelligible message from his Excellency, to the effect that the remains should be treated with respect, and be by no means further disturbed; that he wished the excavations to be stopped at once, and desired to confer with me on the subject.

I rode to Mosul at once and called upon him accordingly. I had some difficulty in making him understand the nature of my discovery. At last he was persuaded that I had only discovered part of an ancient figure in stone, and that neither the remains of Nimrod nor of any other personage mentioned in the Koran had been disturbed. However, as he requested me to discontinue my operations until the excitement in the town had somewhat subsided, I returned to Nimroud and dismissed the workmen, retaining only two men to dig leisurely along the walls without giving cause for further interference. I ascertained by the end of March the existence of a second pair of winged-human-headed lions, differing from those previously discovered in form, the human shape being continued to the waist, and being furnished with human arms, as well as with the legs of the lion. In one hand each figure carried a goat or stag, and in the other, which hung down by the side, a branch with three flowers. They formed a northern entrance into the hall or chamber, of which the human-headed lions previously described formed the western portal. I completely uncovered the latter, and found them to be entire. They were about twelve feet high and twelve feet long. The body and limbs were admirably portrayed; the muscles and bones, although strongly developed, to denote power and strength, showed at the same time a correct knowledge of the anatomy and form of the animal. Expanded wings sprung from the shoulders and spread over the back; a knotted girdle, ending in tassels, encircled the loins. As these sculptures were placed against walls forming a doorway or entrance, and thus only one side of the body was to be seen, they were carved partly in full and partly in relief. The head and forepart, facing the chamber, were in full; the rest of the figure was sculptured in high relief; and that the spectator might have both a perfect front and side view, it was furnished with five legs; four on the side forming the entrance, and an additional leg in front. The slab was covered, in all parts not occupied by the image, with inscriptions in the cuneiform character. Remains of colour could still be traced in the eyes – the pupils being painted black, and the rest filled up with a white pigment; but no other parts of the sculpture. . . .

I used to contemplate for hours these mysterious emblems, and muse over their intent and history. What more noble forms could have ushered the people into the temple of their gods! What more sublime images could have been borrowed from nature, by men who sought, unaided by the light of revealed religion, to embody their conception of the wisdom and power of a Supreme Being! They could find no better type of intellect and knowledge than the head of the man; of strength, than the body of the lion; of ubiquity, than the wings of the bird. These winged human-headed lions were not idle creations, the offspring of mere fancy; their meaning was written upon them. They had awed and instructed races which flourished 3,000 years ago. Through the portals which they guarded, kings, priests, and warriors had borne sacrifices to their altars, long before the wisdom of the East had penetrated to Greece, and had furnished its mythology with symbols recognised of old by the Assyrian votaries. They may have been buried, and their existence may have been unknown, before the foundation of the eternal city. For twenty-five centuries they had been hidden from the eye of man, and they now stood forth once more in their ancient majesty. But how changed was the scene around them! The luxury and civilisation of a mighty nation had given place to the wretchedness and ignorance of a few half-barbarous tribes. The wealth of temples, and the riches of great cities, had been succeeded by ruins and shapeless heaps of earth. Above the spacious hall in which they stood, the plough had passed and the corn now waved. Egypt has monuments no less ancient and no less wonderful; but they have stood forth for ages to testify her early power and renown; whilst those before me had but appeared to bear witness, in the words of the prophet, that once 'the Assyrian was a cedar in Lebanon with fair branches and with a shadowing shroud of an high stature; and his top was among the thick boughs . . . his height was exalted above all the trees of the field, and his boughs were multiplied and his branches became long, because of the multitude of waters when he shot forth. All the fowls of heaven made their nests in his boughs, and under his branches did all the beasts of the fields bring forth their young, and under his shadow dwelt all great nations'; for now is 'Nineveh a desolation and dry like a wilderness, and flocks lie down in the midst of her: all the beasts of the nations, both the cormorant and bittern, lodge in the upper lintels of it; their voice sings in the windows; and desolation is in the thresholds'.

Nineveh and its Remains, 1867

The Gilgamesh Epic is found

GEORGE SMITH

GEORGE SMITH (*1840–1876*) *was born in Chelsea, London. Lacking the advantage of extensive formal education, he began his professional career as a banknote engraver, but he spent so much of his spare time in the Assyrian Department of the British Museum that he attracted the attention of Sir Henry Rawlinson, who secured him a position in the Department. He shortly justified his appointment by the publication of an inscription fixing the date of the eclipse of the sun in 763* BC *and of another which fixed the date of the Elamites' invasion of Babylon in 2280* BC. *In 1872 he transcribed and translated the Gilgamesh epic, which was complete apart from seventeen lines. When this hiatus was discovered, the* Daily Telegraph *financed an expedition under Smith's leadership to find the missing lines, and almost unbelievably, these very lines were discovered on a tablet excavated early in the first season. The newspaper, considering that the purpose of the expedition was then fulfilled, declined further support and it was only by a fortunate chance that in its closing stages a group of tablets detailing the succession of the Babylonian dynasties was found. In 1874 and 1876 the British Museum financed two further expeditions under Smith's leadership, but he was not a man of strong constitution and the conditions of life and work in the desert proved too severe for his health. He contracted a fever and died at Aleppo in 1876.*

Turning from this I rode through the low ground by the side of the Tigris, and then along the face of the cliffs overhanging the water, and soon arrived at Mosul, from which I crossed over to Kouyunjik to see the progress of the excavations. My trenches in the palace of Sennacherib proceeded slowly and produced little result, the ground being so cut up by former excavations that it was difficult to secure good results without more extensive operations than my time or means would allow; inscriptions, the great object of my work, were however found, and served as compensation for the labour.

In the north palace the results were more definite. Here was a large pit made by former excavators from which had come many tablets; this pit had been used since the close of the last excavations for a quarry, and stones for the building of the Mosul bridge had been regularly extracted from it. The bottom of the pit was now full of massive fragments of stone from the basement wall of the palace jammed in between heaps of small fragments of stone, cement, bricks, and clay, all in utter confusion. On removing some of these stones with a crowbar, and digging in the rubbish behind them, there appeared half of a curious tablet copied from a Babylonian original, giving warnings to kings and judges of the evils which would follow the neglect of justice in the country. On continuing the trench some distance farther, the other half of this tablet was discovered, it having evidently been broken before it came among the rubbish.

On the 14th of May my friend, Mr Charles Kerr, whom I had left at Aleppo, visited me at Mosul, and as I rode into the Khan where I was staying, I met him. After mutual congratulations I sat down to examine the store of fragments of cuneiform inscriptions from the day's digging, taking out and brushing off the earth from the fragments to read their contents. On cleaning one of them I found to my surprise and gratification that it contained the greater portion of seventeen lines of inscription belonging to the first column of the Chaldean account of the Deluge, and fitting into the only place where there was a serious blank in the story. When I had first published the account of this tablet I had conjectured that there were about fifteen lines wanting in this part of the story, and now with this portion I was enabled to make it nearly complete.

After communicating to my friend the contents of the fragment I copied it, and a few days later telegraphed the circumstance to the proprietors of the *Daily Telegraph*. Mr Kerr desired to see the mound at Nimroud, but, as the results from Kouyunjik were so important, I could not leave the site to go with him, so I sent my dragoman to show him the place, remaining myself to superintend the Kouyunjik excavations.

The palace of Sennacherib also steadily produced its tribute of objects, including a small tablet of Esarhaddon, king of Assyria, some new fragments of one of the historical cylinders of Assurbanipal, and a curious fragment of the history of Sargon, king of Assyria, relating to his expedition against Ashdod, which is mentioned in the twentieth chapter of the Book of Isaiah. On the same fragment was also part of the list of Median chiefs who paid tribute to Sargon. Part of an inscribed cylinder of Sennacherib, and half of an amulet in onyx with the name and titles of this monarch, subsequently turned up, and numerous impressions in clay of seals, with implements of bronze, iron, and glass. There was part of a crystal throne, a most magnificent article of furniture, in too mutilated condition to copy, but as far as it is preserved closely resembling in shape the bronze one discovered by Mr Layard at Nimroud.

On the evening of Saturday, the 17th of May, after paying the workmen, I started to examine the mounds of Khorsabad. I crossed the Tigris, and passed through the ruins of Nineveh, by the side of the Khosr river, and went over the country to the mound of Kalata. From the lateness of the hour, I was unable to inspect Kalata, and put up in a village near that mound. Rising early next morning, I went to the mound of Kalata, a large, conical artificial elevation, which had been tapped by former explorers. The only thing that could be seen of any account was a chamber in the side of the mound, which appeared to me like a tomb. The vault had been recently rifled of its contents, and I was told several antiquities had been found there. From Kalata I went to Barimeh, a well-built village near the foot of the mountains of Jebel Maklub, and, passing through a beautiful country, rode to Khorsabad. A fine stream, a tributary of the Khosr, flows from Barimeh to Khorsabad. In one place there is a pretty waterfall, and signs of cultivation and fertility are visible in every direction. The neighbouring mountains and streams, the fields and flowers combine to make this district a contrast to the vast brown plains of most of Assyria, and fully justify the choice of Sargon, who fixed on the site of Khorsabad to build his capital.

The ruins of Khorsabad represent the old Assyrian city of Dur-sargina, and consist of a town and palace mound. The wall of the town is nearly square, rather over a mile each way, the angles of the square facing the cardinal points. On the south-west face of the wall there is the fortified enclosure of a citadel, and on the north-west face, along which runs the stream from Barimeh, stands the palace platform, somewhat in form of the letter T, the base of the letter being turned to the north-west, nearest to the stream. This part of the mound near the water is the highest, and covers the remains of the palace and a temple. The excavations here by M. Botta have been made in a systematic manner, and have laid bare a considerable portion of the palace, some of which can still be seen; but most of it has been covered again, to preserve it.

I spent some time in inspecting these ruins, and then returned to Mosul.

I have said I telegraphed to the proprietors of the *Daily Telegraph* my success in finding the missing portion of the deluge tablet. This they published in the paper on the 21st of May 1873; but from some error unknown to me, the telegram as published differs materially from the one I sent. In particular, in the published copy occurs the words 'as the season is closing', which led to the inference that I considered that the proper season for excavating was coming to an end. My own feeling was the contrary of this, and I did not send this. I was at the time waiting instructions, and hoped that as good results were being obtained, the excavations would be continued. The proprietors of the *Daily Telegraph*, however, considered that the discovery of the missing fragment of the deluge text accomplished the object they had in view, and they declined to prosecute the excavations further, retaining, however, an interest in the work, and desiring to see it carried on by the nation. I was disappointed myself at this, as my excavations were so recently commenced; but I felt I could not object to this opinion, and therefore prepared to finish my excavations and return. I continued the Kouyunjik excavations until I had completed my preparations for returning to England, and in the north palace, near the place where I found the tablet with warnings to kings, I disinterred a fragment of a curious syllabary, divided into four perpendicular columns. In the first column was given the phonetic values of the cuneiform characters, and the characters themselves were written in the second column, the third column contained the names and meanings of the signs, while the fourth column gave the words and ideas which it represented.

I searched all round for other fragments of this remarkable tablet, pushing my trench farther through the mass of stones and rubbish, the remains of the fallen basement wall of the palace. Large blocks of stone, with carving and inscriptions, fragments of ornamental pavement, painted bricks, and decorations, were scattered in all directions, showing how complete was the ruin of this portion of the palace. Fixed between these fragments were found, from time to time, fragments of terra-cotta tablets; and one day a workman struck with his pick an overlying mass of mortar, revealing the edge of a tablet which was jammed between two blocks of stone. We at once cleared away the rubbish, and then, bringing a crowbar to bear, lifted the upper stone block, and extracted the fragment of tablet, which proved to be part of the syllabary, and joined the fragment already found. The greater part of the rest of this tablet was found at a considerable distance in a branch trench to the right. It was adhering to the roof of the trench, and easily detached, leaving the impression of all the characters in the roof.

Two other portions of the sixth tablet of the deluge series also came from this part. They relate to the conquest of the winged bull, and will be given with the other portions of the Isdubar series.

On my left in this excavation stood a mass of solid rubbish, which had been undermined during the former excavations; and a crack having started between this and the mound at the back of it, it stood as if ready to fall into the trench. For some time the workmen were afraid to touch it; but I expected some fragments there, so I directed them to attack it from the top, and was rewarded by several parts of tablets. A second trench on the right yielded a good text, being a variant account of the conquest of Babylonia by the Elamites, 2280 BC. Most of the fragments from this part were obtained with considerable difficulty, on account of the masses of stone which had to be removed to get at the inscriptions.

In the northern part of Sennacherib's palace I made some excavations, and discovered chambers similar to those in the south-east palace at Nimroud. Here no inscriptions rewarded me; but in the part of the temple area near this I discovered a new fragment of the cylinder of Bel-zakir-iskun, king of Assyria, 626 BC. Farther to the south-east in this part of the mound I discovered brick inscriptions of Shalmaneser, 1300 BC, and his son, Tugulti-ninip, 1271 BC, both of whom made restorations and additions to the temple of Ishtar. Here was a later wall, in constructing which some fine sculptures of the age of Assur nazirpal, 885 BC, had been cut up and destroyed.

Such were my principal discoveries at Kouyunjik, and I closed the excavations there on the 9th of June. While I stayed at Mosul I made many friends among the Catholic missionaries and the merchants in the town, and in company with some of them, I paid a farewell visit to Nimroud on the 4th and 5th of June. On the 8th of June, as I was about to leave the country, I gave a farewell dinner to my friends, and next day we took leave of each other, I starting for Europe with my treasures.

Assyrian Discoveries, 1875

Early technical achievements

HERMAN HILPRECHT

HERMAN VOLRATH HILPRECHT (*1858–1925*) *was born in Hohenerxleben, Germany, and studied at the University of Leipzig. In 1886 he went to Philadelphia where he joined the staff of the University's department of Assyriology, and became curator of the Babylonian section of the University Museum. As a result of his excavations at Nippur he was invited to organize his finds, which were the statutory property of the Turkish government, in the Imperial Ottoman Museum at Istanbul, a job which occupied him from 1893 to 1909. His later years were clouded by his unjustifiable attempt to defend a mistake in his publication on the Nippur excavation, which ultimately led to his retirement, but the value of his work remains great.*

While examining the surroundings of this interesting edifice, Haynes came first upon the same gray or black ashes as are found everywhere in the court of the *ziggurrat* immediately below Naram-Sin's pavement, next upon 'lumps of kneaded clay', then upon several stray bits of lime mortar. All these traces of human activity were imbedded in the débris characteristic of the lower strata, which largely consist of earth, ashes, and innumerable potsherds. When he had reached a depth of nine feet from the top of the solid structure, – in other words, had descended about four feet below the bottom of the ancient curb on the south-east side of the stage-tower, – he found a large quantity of fragments of terra-cotta water pipes of the form here shown. Though the reports before me offer no satisfactory clue as to their precise use, there can be little doubt that they belong to the real pre-Sargonic period. I will try to explain their purpose later, Haynes' interpretation being better passed over in silence.

The explorer's curiosity was aroused at once, and having sunk his shaft a few feet deeper at the spot where the greatest number of these terra-cotta pipes were lying, he made one of the most far-reaching single discoveries in the lower strata of Nippur. After a brief search he came upon a very remarkable drain, reminding us of the advanced system of canalisation, as e.g. we find it in Paris at the present time.

It ran obliquely under the rectangular building described above, starting, as I believe, at a corner of the early sanctuary, but evidently having fallen into disuse long before the L-shaped building was erected. It could still be traced for about six feet into the interior of the ruins underlying the *ziggurrat*. But its principal remains were disclosed in the open court, into which it extended double that length, so that its tolerably preserved mouth lay directly below the ancient curb, – a fact of the utmost importance. For it constitutes a new argument in favour of the theory previously expressed that this curb marked the line of the earliest south-east enclosure of the *ziggurrat*, or whatever formerly may have taken the place of the latter. But it also follows that a gutter of some kind, which carried the water to a safe distance, must have existed in this neighbourhood outside the curb.

No sooner had Haynes commenced removing the débris from the ruined aqueduct, than he found, to his great astonishment, that it terminated in a vaulted section 3 feet long and was built in the form of a true ellipitical arch, – the oldest one thus far discovered. The often ventilated question as to the place and time of origin of the arch was thereby decided in favour of ancient Babylonia. The bottom of this reliable witness of pre-Sargonic civilisation lies fifteen feet below Naram-Sin's pavement, or ten feet below the base of the curb, which it probably antedates by a century or two. We may safely assign it, therefore, to the end of the fifth pre-Christian millennium. It presented a number of interesting peculiarities. Being 2 feet 1 inch high (inside measurement), and having a span of 1 foot 3 inches and a rise of 1 foot 1 inch, it was constructed of well baked plano-convex bricks laid on the principle of radiating *voussoirs*. These bricks measured 12 by 6 by 2½ inches, were light yellow in colour, and bore certain marks on their upper or convex surface, which had been made either by pressing the thumb and index finger deeply into the clay in the middle of the brick, or by drawing one or more fingers lengthwise over it. Primitive as they doubtless are, they do not (as Haynes inferred) 'represent the earliest type of bricks found at Nippur or elsewhere in Babylonia', – which are smaller and sometimes a little thicker, – though for a considerable while both kinds were used alongside each other and often in the same building. The curve of the arch was effected 'by wedge-shaped joints of the simple clay mortar used to cement the bricks'. 'On the top of its crown was a crushed terra-cotta pipe about 3 or 3½ inches in diameter', the meaning of which Haynes declares unknown. I cannot help thinking that it served a purpose similar to the holes provided at regular intervals in our modern casing walls of terraces, etc.; in other words, that the pipe was intended to give exit to the rain water percolating the soil behind and above it, and in this way to prevent the softening of the clay cement between the bricks of the arch, and the caving-in of the whole vault which would result from it. This explanation being accepted, it necessarily follows that the floor of the court surrounding the earliest sanctuary was not paved with burned bricks, an inference entirely confirmed by the excavations.

There is much to be said in favour of the theory that this skilfully planned tunnel was arched over originally along its entire length. Like its vault, the lower part of the aqueduct presented several most surprising features. 'Just beneath the level of the pavement and in the middle of the water channel were two parallel terra-cotta tiles, 8 inches in diameter, with a 6-inch flanged mouth'. Haynes, regarding this tunnel as a drain rather than the protecting structure for a drain, was at a loss to explain their presence and significance. They were laid in clay mortar and consisted of single joints or sections, each 2 feet long, cemented together by the same material. We may raise the question: Why are there two small pipes instead of one large one? Evidently because they carried the water from two different directions to a point inside the sacred enclosure, where they met and passed through the arched tunnel together. They surely testify to a most highly developed system of drainage in the very earliest period of Babylonian history. I have, therefore, no doubt, that the so-called 'water-cocks' previously mentioned serve some purpose in connection with this complicated system of canalisation, and that in all probability they are to be regarded as specially prepared joints intended to unite terra-cotta pipes meeting each other at a right angle.

The mouth of the tunnel was provided with a T-shaped construction of plano-convex bricks, which Haynes is inclined to consider as 'the means employed for centring the arch', or as 'a device to exclude domestic animals, like sheep, from seeking shelter within it against the pitiless sun's rays in midsummer', while the present writer rather sees in it a strengthening pillar erected to protect the most exposed part of the tunnel at the point where the arching proper begins and the side walls are most liable to yield to the unequal pressure from the surrounding mass of earth. That the last-mentioned view is the more plausible and the explanation of the single pipe placed over the arch as given above is reasonable, follows from what happened in the course of the excavations. A few months after Haynes had removed the brick structure with its two arms, he reported suddenly that the arch had been 'forced out of its shape, probably from the unequal pressure of the settling mass above it, which had been drenched with rain water'. Truly the original purpose of these simple means, which had secured the preservation of the arch for six thousand years, could not have been demonstrated more forcibly. At the same time, Haynes, who never thought of this occurrence as having any bearing upon the whole question, could not have paid a higher compliment to the inventive genius and the extraordinary forethought of the ancient Babylonian architects.

Like all other parts, the long side walls of this unique tunnel were built with remarkable care. They consisted of eleven courses of bricks laid in clay mortar – a sure indication that the tunnel itself was not intended to carry water. The six lowest courses, the eighth, the tenth and eleventh, were placed flatwise with their long edge presented to view, while the seventh and ninth courses were arranged on their long edges like books on a shelf with their small edge visible. Considering all the details of this excellent system of canalisation in the fifth pre-Christian millennium, which not long ago was regarded as a prehistoric period, we may be pardoned for asking the question: Wherein lies the often proclaimed progress in draining the capitals of Europe and America in the twentieth century of our own era? It would rather seem as if the methods of today are little different from what they were in ancient Nippur or Calneh, one of the four cities of the kingdom of 'Nimrod, the mighty hunter before the Lord' (Gen. 10:9), at the so-called 'dawn of civilisation', – a somewhat humiliating discovery for the fast advancing spirit of the modern age! How many uncounted centuries of human development may lie beyond that marvellous age represented by the vaulted tunnel with the two terra-cotta pipes imbedded in cement at its bottom, four feet below the former plain level of 'the land of Shinar'!

Explorations in Bible Lands, 1903

The royal graves of Ur

CHARLES LEONARD WOOLLEY

Sir Charles Leonard Woolley (1880–1960) was educated at St John's College, Leatherhead, and at New College, Oxford. Shortly after completing his studies at Oxford he was appointed an assistant curator at the Ashmolean Museum, and from this time the rest of his life was devoted to archaeology. He took part in many excavations; firstly he went to the Roman settlement at Corbridge, and then he joined the Oxford expedition to Nubia and then the British Museum excavation at Carcemish. The outbreak of war in 1914 found him in the Near East, where his local knowledge of Palestine and Egypt was invaluable when he joined Military Intelligence, but in 1916 he was taken prisoner by the Turks and held until the end of the war in 1918. The following year he returned to his excavations in Carcemish and in 1921 he spent a year at Tell el-Amarna. In 1922 he began the work which was to occupy him for the next twelve years and to produce the most spectacular and important discoveries since Schliemann's royal graves at Mycenae – the excavation of Ur of the Chaldees.

Just outside the wall which enclosed the Temenos of Ur, the Sacred Area within which stood the terraced tower of the Moon God and the main temples of his cult, lay an open space which three thousand years before Christ was the burial-place of the citizens of Ur. Later on, in the days of Sargon of Akkad (about 2560 BC), the area was used again for the same purpose and the gravediggers disturbed hundreds of the earlier tombs; later still, after 2000 BC, houses were built over the ancient cemetery, and the discovery of old graves containing treasure induced men to tunnel deep into the soil in search of plunder. Thus, most of the royal tombs we found had been robbed long ago, and the repeated working of the soil had confused the stratification; but none the less it was clear that the original cemetery was a little earlier in date than the First Dynasty of Ur, a dynasty of kings whose historical existence had first been demonstrated by the excavation of the temple at al 'Ubaid set up by A-anni-pad-da, the second of the royal line.

Of more than a thousand graves of the early period only sixteen were royal tombs: the rest were the graves of private citizens dug as near as might be to the resting-place of the semi-divine ruler, just as today in a Moslem cemetery the humble headstones cluster round the domed *turbeh* of a religious sheikh . . .

A great square pit was dug deep into the soil, approached by a downward-sloping ramp. In the pit was built a tomb, of stone or brick, vaulted or domed: it might be a single chamber or it might be a miniature house with three or four rooms and a connecting passage; the inner face of the walls and the chamber floors were smoothly plastered with white cement. This was the tomb proper. Into it the body was brought and laid upon a bier, surrounded by offerings that testified to the wealth of the ruler in his lifetime and might serve his pleasure hereafter; two or three of his more intimate attendants were killed and their bodies set alongside the bier; then the tomb door was walled up. Next, there came down the ramp into the pit, whose earth sides were masked by reed matting, the whole company of those who were to accompany their royal master to the other world; ministers of the household, musicians, dancing women, male slaves and soldiers of the guard, even the chariot drawn by oxen or by asses, with the drivers, the grooms and the animals, assembled in ordered ranks at the bottom of the pit. Presumably some kind of service was held (in Queen Shub-ad's grave the fingers of the girl harpist were still touching the strings of the lyre), and at its end each took a little cup, filled it might be from a great bronze vessel set in the pit's centre, and drank a draught of a narcotic and lay down in his place and slept. And, from above, the mourners threw in the earth of the pit's making and buried the sleepers and the tomb chamber, and stamped the earth down and made of it a level floor for the next stage of the ceremony. For the filling of the pit was a slow process, done in stages. On the floor, still deep below the ground's surface, there was held a funeral feast and then two or three more human victims were sacrificed and laid out, and more earth was flung in and trodden down, for the same ritual to be repeated two or three times until the shaft was filled up level with the surrounding soil; probably, though for this we have no certain evidence, a funerary chapel was built above-ground to mark the spot, a chapel in which offerings would be made to the memory of the dead and services conducted in his honour.

This generalised description is no flight of fancy: it is based throughout on evidence afforded by the tombs themselves. In the case of PG 1054 we dug down methodically through floor after floor in the filling of the pit, each with its votive deposits and subsidiary burials, till we reached the little domed stone chamber with its blocked door, against which had been put the bones of sacrificed animals, and found inside it the gold-bedecked body with its dead attendants. In Queen Shub-ad's grave the musician with her harp and the singers formed a group apart; the grooms were there with the gaily-adorned and inlaid sledge-chariot drawn by two asses; the Keeper of the Wardrobe lay beside the flat chest which had held the royal dresses. Inside the tomb chamber the ladies-in-waiting were crouched beside the bier on which their mistress lay shrouded in beads of gold and lapis lazuli and carnelian, wearing over her elaborately adorned wig the massive gold hair-ribbon, the gold chaplets and the five-flowered hair-pin of a queen, while on a shelf at her side was put another court wig bound by a broad fillet of lapis lazuli against which were set marvellously-wrought little gold figures of animals and fruit and ears of corn.

The queen's grave had been dug in the shaft of a slightly older tomb, perhaps that of her husband whose last resting-place she wished to share. The grave-diggers had hit upon the vaulted roof of the old king's chamber and, tempted too far, had broken in and plundered it of all its wealth, and had placed the queen's wardrobe chest over the hole to hide the evidence of their misdoing. But they had not disturbed the 'death-pit'. There we found all in order. Eight soldiers with spears and helmets lay in double rank at the ramp's foot. Facing the ramp (evidently it had been backed down the slope) was the heavy chariot drawn by oxen wearing silver collars, the reins, decorated with huge lapis lazuli beads, attached to silver rings in their nostrils. The drivers and soldier attendants were with the car. Against the wall of the tomb-chamber were the harpist and the singers; soldiers guarded the walled-up door and stood against the matting-draped sides of the pit; there were 63 persons gathered there to die. In another case, PG 1237, the floor of the death-pit was covered with bodies all in ordered rows: 6 men on the entrance side and 68 women in court dress, red coats with beaded cuffs and shell-ring belts, head-dresses of gold or silver, great lunate ear-rings and multiple necklaces of blue and gold. Amongst them was one girl who was not wearing her silver hair-ribbon, – it was in her pocket, tightly coiled up like a rounded tape, as if she had been late for the funeral and had not had time to put it on. Here there were four harpists with their lyres, grouped together, and by them in an open space lay a copper cauldron; it was difficult not to connect this with the little drinking-bowl found by every one of the 74 bodies in the pit.

None of the private graves in the cemetery had anything corresponding to this wholesale slaughter. Even the richest of them, the grave of Meskalam-dug, which contained a princely wealth of arms and vessels in gold, silver, bronze and stone, had in it no bodies other than that of 'the lord of the good land' himself, solitary in a wooden coffin. The built grave-chamber and the human sacrifice were a privilege reserved for kings. It seems to imply a belief that those kings were at least semi-divine beings for whom death was but a transition; and if we may judge from the fact that so many people died with them without violence, to the accompaniment of music made by themselves and by means of a narcotic voluntarily drunk, surely these people were buoyed up by the confidence that going thus in their lord's company they assured themselves of a continuance of their service and of an honourable place in that other world.

In all the Sumerian literature that we possess there is no hint of any such ritual forming part of the funeral of a king; and since the discovery at Ur was unique of its kind some scholars were loth to accept any such interpretation of the evidence. They pointed out that the few names recovered from the 'Royal Tombs' did not figure in the lists of kings recorded by Sumerian annalists. The facts of the burials were beyond dispute, but they preferred to see in them a sacrifice offered to the acknowledged gods, a 'Fertility rite' in which a mystic marriage symbolising the earth's fruitfulness culminated with the killing of the bride and bridegroom. The first point is true enough. But the Sumerian annalists enumerate only the kings of those dynasties which claimed to rule the whole land of Sumer. The occupants of our Royal Tombs make no such claim, but they do call themselves 'kings'. Their names are not unlike those of the First Dynasty kings – they might well belong to the family – but judging by the archaeological evidence they are older in date, and, if so, were necessarily not dynastic kings but vassals, lords only of a single city. If they were the chosen victims of a 'Fertility rite' they would scarcely call themselves kings at all.

Further, Sumerian literature, which is rich in liturgical and religious texts, gives no hint whatsoever that there was any killing of the protagonists of a 'mystic marriage' rite; no human sacrifice is suggested anywhere as part of the orthodox religion. The assumption of the 'Fertility rite' therefore does just as much violence to the literary evidence as does the assumption that these are royal burials – more, in fact, for there is no description of any royal burial anywhere in Sumerian literature. Again, the 'mystic marriage' involves two people, bride and bridegroom, and if they had to be killed surely they would be buried together. But each of the Royal Tombs at Ur contains only one principal body. Yet a further argument is this: the need for the fruits of the earth is constant, and if a 'Fertility rite' is practised at all it should be a yearly ceremony, as indeed it was in Sumer in historic times. But in the graveyard at Ur, which must have been in use for many generations, there are only 16 'Royal Tombs'. Did men only 16 times in all those years take steps to secure a good harvest? And now the evidence of the Royal Tombs no longer stands alone. At Ur we have found that a thousand years later the great rulers of the Third Dynasty at Ur had vast tombs just outside the Temenos wall wherein numerous people were buried with them, tombs surmounted by a palace-temple in which the eldest son of the house maintained the worship of the king, who was deified in his lifetime and counted as a god after his death. It was an enduring tradition, though literature is silent regarding it, whereby God's 'tenant farmer' partakes of his divinity and does not die but is translated to the heavens.

Here then, in this prehistoric cemetery at Ur, we have the graves of kings and commoners to teach us something of the thoughts and beliefs of a people who have left us no real written testimony of themselves, and to tell us very much about their arts and crafts and the material setting of their lives. Only in one respect does the evidence here compare poorly with that from other sites – we have not found such portrait statues as were unearthed in great numbers at Tell Asmar in northern Iraq in the course of the American excavations there. The reason is that at Ur the site is a cemetery, whereas the building at Tell Asmar was a temple. To the ancient Sumerians, a statue was the last thing one would think of putting in a tomb. A statue represented either a god, in which case the shrine was the obvious place for it, or the human worshipper, and the proper place for the worshipper too was in the temple, where he might stand day and night before his god in perpetual adoration and prayer. For a complete picture of Sumer as it was five thousand years ago we must collect our evidence not from one only but from many sources which in recent years archaeology has opened up to us; but none the less the objects from the ceremony of Ur bear full witness to the quality of the civilisation which had been developed in the Euphrates valley throughout the periods of al'Ubaid, Uruk and Jemdet Nasr and was flourishing at the dawn of the historic age.

Ur; the First Phases, 1946

Part Five

THE BOOK OF THE ROCKS AND VALLEYS

Staatliche Museen, Berlin

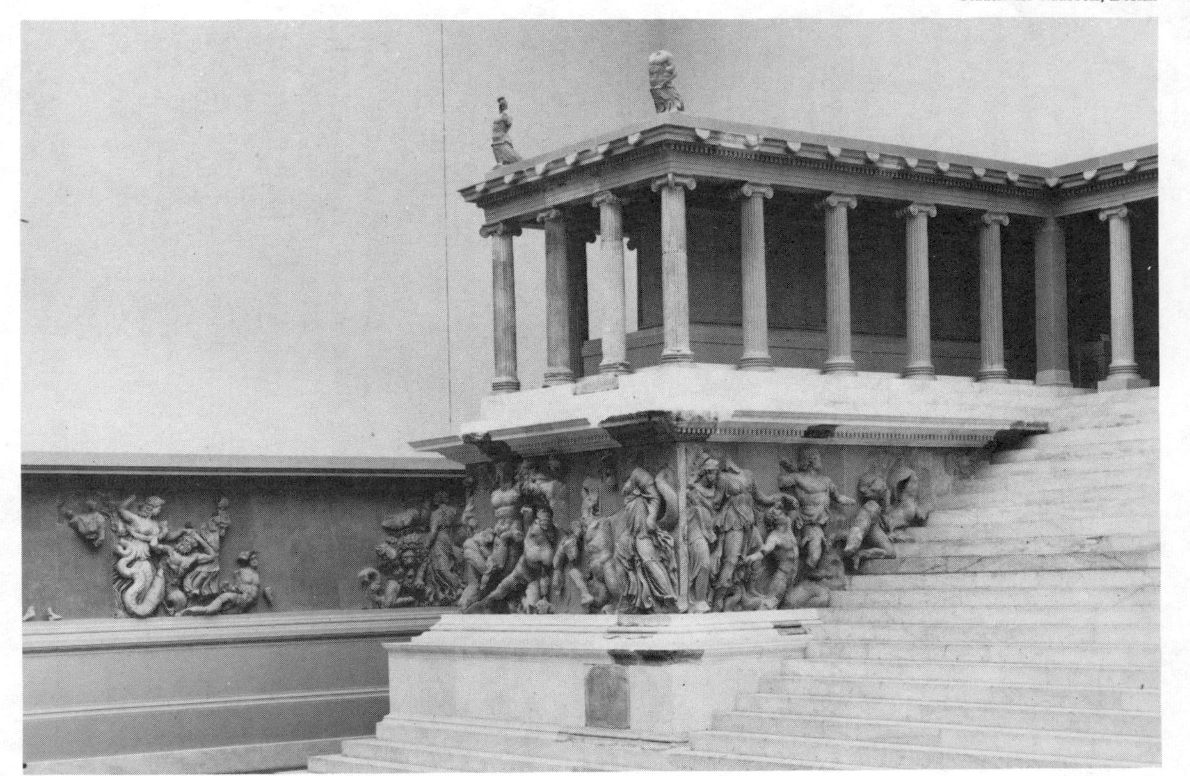

18. The Altar of Zeus at Pergamon, excavated by Carl Humann in 1884–6 and reconstructed in Berlin.

Digging up Pergamon

CARL HUMANN

Carl Humann *(1839–1896) was a railway engineer who in 1861 concentrated his activities in southern regions for reasons of health. He immediately showed, firstly on Samos, an interest in archaeology. He became famous through his excavation of the Altar at Pergamon (reconstructed in Berlin) which he concluded in 1886.*

Pergamon, 19 December 1871

My dear Mr Curtius,

Five weeks have passed since I last wrote and had I not then promised you to write again in 8–14 days to give you the results of the excavations and to send you the plan of Pergamon, I should have written again long ago.

Well, up to today I had neither of these, or, at any rate, not in their completed forms. It has been raining solidly here for five weeks, and only since new moon has there been a north wind and, as a superfluous addition, bitter cold. There you have my complete excuse – I have not been wasting time. I profited from every half day, if it was not raining, by climbing up to the Acropolis with my people, and am at last happy to tell you that I have really managed to get things moving.

Remember the high, thick wall up there in which I showed you the two sculptures projecting from underneath? I have now got these out and at home, on *Prussian* ground. . . .

No. 1: This is the stone which lay on the left; the chest was visible. When I had blasted the wall down so far that we were close up to it I personally carefully removed stone after stone and found the neck and chin, then the left cheek and the eye. When I saw the eye I cried out: '*That's a dead man!*' For this statue, although completely and beautifully sincere, definitely had the emaciated and stark look of death. I am telling you this because it shows that one can set no great store by my *artistic* critical faculty. Eventually the statue was completely excavated and turned out to be a beautiful youth with curly hair, stretched out, the breast high and drumlike (25 centimetres) the right arm, unfortunately broken, raised, the left hanging down, the head slightly inclined to one side, the mouth half open, not distorted by pain, but rather by fatigue, as though asleep; only the wide-open, rolled back eyes showed that we were looking at a man killed in battle. Strength and beauty were here united in most marvellous harmony. To the left a leg belonging to another statue is visible.

No. 2 in the drawing shows an aged, bearded man who, defeated in battle, looks on grimly; this head, also, although the chin and nose are missing, is beautifully carved. At first I took it to be a lion's head, before the left shoulder and the beautifully modelled sleeper had been dug out. The eyebrows are like thick rolls, but not exaggerated. A hand, most probably not his, for it would have to be the right one, holds a shield over his head. This shield is carved very thin, hardly a fingerswidth thick; and for this reason, mostly broken. Behind stands a man of whom only the right arm, the right breast, and a part of the back of the head are preserved, who is in the act of hitting the old man with a club. Over the left shoulder he wore a lion skin, a paw of which is still preserved. Head, left arm and left breast are unfortunately no longer in existence, as they probably stood out too far from the wall.

No. 3, a horse's foot, belongs to this category too. I've never seen a foot like it before! All the bones in the joint show through the skin. I don't know which I prefer, No. 1 or 3.

The three listed pieces are all made of the same bluish-white marble. The first two are both 89 centimetres high. As various blocks have previously been found here and have unfortunately been destroyed, it is certain, also taking these two into account, that they were part of a continuous frieze which showed a battle between men.

Years ago I saw a block which showed a man with a lion (at that time this was sent to Constantinople to Mr Karatheodoris): as well as this there is No. 3, the horse's foot, and so we have a whole battle with men, horses, wild animals. The frieze could only have been part of a very important building, e.g. the Temple of Minerva of the Acropolis. Then, to my joy, it turned out that all the architectural fragments of the building, whose foundations and lower vaulting you admired, were also made of the same pure bluish-white marble, which is furthermore in agreement with the diameter of the columns of this temple, which I have not yet been able to measure accurately, and agrees with the frieze's height of 89 centimetres.

I hope it is not just the ecstacy of discovering something oneself which leads me to say that we have here a masterpiece of sculpture. My sketches drawn in the courtyard with frozen fingers, can only give you inaccurate impression of the beauty of these pieces. On top of this, the stonehard limestone of the wall still lies between all the most delicate parts, as I have left it there for safety's sake. No. 1 and 2 are broken in two places, but so conveniently that none of the finest parts are cut through. The great expanse and uneven load of the wall seems to have broken them. One can hardly still call them *Haut-reliefs* as the figures are completely rounded and look as though they have been stuck on to slabs of 15-20 centimetres thick and are therefore almost statues. The chest of the young man taken together with the slab is more than half a metre thick. All the drawings are drawn to a scale of 1.10 so that the sizes can in all cases be calculated. The hatching indicates what is broken off.

No. 4 is a bas-relief and shows armour. On the left shoulder are fringes such as those worn by our drum majors; both sides carry figures of warriors, very lovely, but too small to be drawn in here.

No. 5 is an inscription on a white slab of marble; I pulled 4 and 5 out of the wall.

6a and 6b were given me by a Turk. It is the same frieze which you saw on the gateway of a Han, but in a better state of preservation. Were I to draw the small winged lion for you with all its muscles, it would take half a day and also I was no longer able to go on using the page of the enclosed drawing. Therefore I have indicated only size and colour.

As well as this I have in the house a bas-relief from a grave showing a rider, in front of him, a tree with a serpent, but everything rather blurred; also a small Ionic capital and base of about 1½ feet in diameter, so pretty and delicate that it will please any architect and that Mr Surveyor (Adler) will immediately want to have it measured. Also a stele with an inscription which I have no more time to copy today; the upper half is broken off, though I have just been told that it is preserved in a house, here. I shall annex it tomorrow. *Ischallah!* (God be willing!) Then I shall have the fragments of the broken man we discovered and various architectural fragments.

Then I dug out a seated robed female figure, in brilliant white marble, of the best period! – Head, arms, one breast and the feet are missing; she sits on a pillow. Drawing to follow soon; I hope that she will be coming down from the hill tomorrow. The one naked foot which projected from the wall was knocked off two years ago and sent to Constantinople to the Turkish Museum. That one was magnificent. I hope that they will allow it to be retrieved later on. *Bakshish!* With that, everything's possible.

The probable throne and a statue will appear tomorrow or the day after, for I've almost reached them. I bought a storage vessel, of fired clay, higher than a man and too large to be encompassed by three, in a village five hours from here. According to the description, it must be this shape; but because of the boggy roads it is at present impossible to bring it back here.

I have not yet been able to copy half a dozen inscriptions in the Turkish churchyards; they are still unknown; three more are coming off the walls this week. I have sent someone off to Kilise-Keni; they are asking 10 lire for the stone. I have offered 2 and hope to get it.

The Greeks don't want to give up the stone from the church, they consider this a sin, and furthermore they are not allowed to send their native tradition abroad. Those stupid Bulgarians just want to haggle and hope to gain a giant sum for it.

In a mosque I found a large stone fruit-motif carving, almost one metre square, beautifully executed, grapes, plums, laurel, acorns, figs, palms. Our governor, as you know, my intimate friend, is taking great pains to acquire it for me; but the damned Imam thinks it would be sinful to give Unbelievers something from the mosque, in spite of the fact that I offered them 10 lire for it; I shall have to give the Imam a few pounds. For the rest I have succeeded in getting the Mufti and Kadi to their feet to prove from the Koran that the mosque should engage in a deal if a profit is to be had. *Baccalym!* I shall not tell you about my coins and clay vessels; this letter is too long as it is.

As soon as I have got all the statues which are still visible out of the walls, I shall begin excavations on the ruins of the Temple of Minerva and without doubt find still more reliefs. All the heads which are to be seen in the museum here were also found there. From there I shall get very valuable architectural fragments. I possess a column *con verde antico* of about 1½ metres long at Dikeli on the coast. I have since stopped the work at the burial mound of the Eye or of Attalos because I wanted to be present, and this was impossible. It won't run away.

My plan of Pergamon has, of course, got delayed on account of the weather and the excavations; 3 or 4 days' work, and then it's finished. For your use for the present I am sending you herewith a rough copy.

I have discovered a great deal. I shall stay here over Christmas because of the excavations and shall probably not go to Smyrna until next week. I am bringing the slabs of marble down from the Acropolis on a large sledge, but shall have to take it apart at the bottom and take it back up piece by piece. You know how high it is. I have had specially tough carts built in which to take the things to Dikeli on the coast, from where I shall send them to Smyrna either by boat, or, should there by then be a great deal of stuff, perhaps the imperial ambassador will be able to transport them.

I am sending this letter to Dr Luhrsen for his information, partly for his private interest and partly for official reasons, so that he can, in case of need, help me verbally and practically, although up to now I have not encountered any difficulties at all.

Should, at some point or other, the matter of costs arise, I confirm herewith that up to the present moment no costs at all have been incurred for the Government, and yet, everything that I have collected was on the Government's behalf, and is its own property.

Well, that's enough. I wish you, dear Mr Curtius, a very happy Christmas and New Year, and hope that you will soon give me the pleasure of a few lines. I shall write again.

With best wishes, Yours very sincerely,

Carl Humann

Der Pergamon-Altar, entdeckt, beschrieben und gezeichnet von Carl Humann, 1959

Translated from the German by C. M. Kaine

The discovery of the Hamah stones

WILLIAM WRIGHT

WILLIAM WRIGHT *(1837-1899) was the son of a farmer and grew up in County Down, Ireland, but his academic abilities gained him scholarships to study at Queen's College, Dublin. Here he decided to enter holy orders and become a missionary, and with this in view he studied at the theological seminaries of Dublin and Geneva. In 1865 he went to Damascus and remained in this region for the next ten years. In addition to his religious work he devoted much time to travel, and to the study of antiquities, making journeys in Palestine and Syria and northern Arabia, and writing accounts for the* Pall Mall Gazette. *It was during this time that he became interested in the newly discovered Hittite civilization, and, hearing of the inscribed stones which had been reported at Hamah, he determined to secure and study them.*

On the 10th of November, 1872, I set out from Damascus intent on securing the Hamah inscriptions.

Sixty years previously Burckhardt, in his exploration of Hamah, had discovered, in the corner of a house in one of the Bazaars, a stone covered with figures and signs, which he declared to be hieroglyphics, but different from the hieroglyphics of Egypt. Every one who cared to know anything of Syria, read Burckhardt's travels. All admitted his accuracy of observation and truthfulness of description, yet so little interest was taken in his discovery, even by professional explorers, that Porter, in Murray's *Handbook*, so late as 1868, declares 'there are no antiquities in Hamah'.

At length, in 1870, Mr J. Augustus Johnson, the American Consul-General, and the Rev. S. Jessup, an American missionary, stumbled on the Hamah inscriptions, and from that moment a period of zealous effort to secure them succeeded the long period of apathy and neglect. The newly kindled enthusiasm with reference to the curious hieroglyphics, which had waited so long for an interpreter, seemed destined to endanger their existence, and from Damascus we watched, with almost breathless suspense, the various heroic but fruitless attempts to secure accurate copies.

The vague but much dreaded power of the American Consul, and the local knowledge and skill of an American missionary, availed not to enable them to make accurate transcripts of the re-discovered hieroglyphics.

In publishing a picture of one of the inscriptions, in the 'First Quarterly Statement of the American Palestine Exploration Society', in 1871, Mr Johnson says: 'We did not succeed in getting squeeze impressions, for fanatical Moslems crowded upon us when we began to work upon the stones, and we were obliged to be content with such copies of this and other inscriptions found on stones, *over* and *near* the city gate, and *in* the ancient bridge which spans the Orontes, as could be obtained by the aid of a native painter.' Mr Johnson must have been hard pressed, for he seems to have seen only one of the stones, as he describes the positions of the others incorrectly, doubtless having been led into error by the vague reports of the people; but his efforts were not in vain, and the imperfect facsimile of one of the inscriptions, published in the 'First Quarterly Statement of the American Palestine Exploration Society', did much to quicken interest in the new hieroglyphics, and stimulated others to succeed where he had partially failed.

The imperfect tracings of the 'native painter' were seen by Messrs Drake and Palmer, on their way home through Beyrout, from their wanderings in the Desert; and the Palestine Exploration Fund sent Mr Drake back to Syria, to examine and copy the inscriptions. By his great skill in dealing with natives, Mr Drake partly succeeded in taking photographs and squeezes of the most important, but gathering angry mobs obliged him to hasten his operations before he had effected his purpose.

Captain Burton, then Her Majesty's Consul at Damascus, also visited Hamah. He gives a good description of the stones, and points out accurately the places where they were to be found, but he also had to be content with the decipherings of one Kostatin-el-Khuri. These he published in *Unexplored Syria* with the following explanation. 'The ten sheets accompanying this article had been applied to the blackened or reddened faces of the four stones, and the outlines were afterwards drawn with a reed pen. In a few cases the fancy of the copyist had been allowed to run wild', &c.

Captain Burton suggested that the stone should be secured 'by means of a Vizerial order, intended to be obeyed', and he adds: 'When at Hamah, I began to treat with the proprietor of No. 1, the Christian Jabbour, who, barbarously greedy like all his tribe, began by asking a hundred napoleons'.

The publication of the rude tracings in *Unexplored Syria* increased still more the general interest in the inscriptions, and a very large sum of money was offered for the smallest stone, but the people of Hamah would not part with it at any price. Then a new and altogether different set of men began to bully and barter for the coveted curiosities, and we saw with dismay a commencement of the fussy peddling which, a short time before, had led to the destruction of the Moabite stone. At this juncture my opportunity arrived, not only of securing but of saving the precious inscriptions.

The Sublime Porte, seized by a periodic fit of reforming zeal, had appointed an honest man, Subhi Pasha, to be Governor of Syria. Subhi Pasha brought a conscience to his work, and not content with redressing wrongs that succeeded in forcing their way into his presence, resolved to visit every district of his province, in order that he might check the spoiler and discover the wants of the people. He invited me to accompany him on a tour to Hamah, and I gladly accepted the invitation. Mr W. Kirby Green, our excellent Consul at Damascus, was also to be his guest. I thought it best to join the party in the neighbourhood of Hamah, lest familiarity should breed contempt before the critical moment had arrived for asking permission to copy the inscriptions. This I was able to do after lingering on my way among the village schools in Jebel Kalamoun.

Having spent a few days in Saidnâya, M'alûla, Yabrûd, Nebk, and Deir Atîyeb, among the handsomest peasantry of Syria, some of them speaking a *patois* of Syriac, and all of them speaking Arabic with a Syriac accent, I struck north by Hasya, and joined the Pasha's cavalcade at Hums.

The following day we started for Hamah with an enormous following. Chiefs from all parts flocked in with their retainers to do honour to the Waly. Princelings, whose possessions had been reduced to a horse, a few arms, and a richly braided jacket, galloped over the plain, wheeling and tossing their spears in the air, and showing wonderful feats of horsemanship. Bedawin hostages from the Desert, white-turbaned Ulema, sugar-loaf-topped Dervishes, priests and peasants made up a procession, ten deep, more than a mile long, and surrounded by a picturesque army of skirmishers, who kept up their antics for miles all round the main body during the whole journey.

On the 25th of November we arrived in Hamah, late in the afternoon. During the day the Waly had consulted Mr Green and me as to his projects for ameliorating the condition of the people. We sat up late that night together, and I had an opportunity of asking his Excellency to aid me in getting perfect copies of the inscriptions. This he promised to do, and so gracious and kind was he, that he accompanied us to our beds to make sure that his guests were comfortable.

The next morning at an early hour Mr Green and I sallied forth in quest of the inscriptions. None of the books or articles referring to the inscriptions had reached us in Damascus before we set out, and we had to begin our operations without any advantage from the labours of our predecessors. Our first business was to find the inscribed stones, and this was not so easy as it might seem, for all whom we asked about them looked us steadily in the face, and swore vehemently that there were no stones such as we sought in Hamah.

In a large city of narrow crooked streets, it would have been a weary work to find the inscriptions for ourselves, and after so much disappointment we resolved to ask every person we met, in the hope that we might find some one not up to the plot of concealing the inscriptions from us. The first man we met after making this resolve proved to be Suliman-el-Kallas, in the wall of whose house was inscription H.1. The secret being out, we had no difficulty in finding all the stones, and they were also pointed out to the Waly.

Subhi Pasha, who was known in Europe as Subhi Bey before his appointment to Damascus, was descended from a noble Greek family. He was the most learned man among the Turks, and his private collection of coins and art treasures, the greater part of which has been since sold in London, brought him into scholarly relations with many of the *savans* of Europe. Subhi Pasha, who was the creator of the Constantinople Museum, recognised at a glance the great importance of the inscriptions, and sent a telegram to the Sultan asking him to accept the inscribed stones for the Museum.

I pointed out to His Excellency that such inscriptions ought to be the common property of all, that the scholars of Europe were waiting eagerly for accurate copies of them, and that they would doubtless open a new chapter in history which would show that a great people, called the Hittites in the Bible, but never referred to in classic history, had once formed a mighty empire in that region.

The Pasha not only consented to let me take copies of the inscriptions, but promised to bring the inscribed stones to the *Serai*, where I might copy them at leisure. Under other circumstances we should have experienced great difficulties in securing copies of the inscriptions, for the recent feeble attempts to get possession of the stones had brought the Hamathites to consider them of extraordinary value; and as we passed through the city to the baths with the Governor-General, we heard many expressions of muttered defiance, and threats of violence towards anybody that might venture to interfere with their sacred and venerable treasures.

Later in the day, when it became known that the Pasha would take the stones, we heard men vowing that they would destroy the inscriptions, as they have since done with that at Aleppo.

I saw now that a crisis was reached. For hundreds, perhaps thousands, of years these mute inscriptions had waited for some one to hear their story. Egyptian, Assyrian, Greek, Selucidae, Roman, Saracen, Crusader and Turk had passed them by as unworthy of even a passing notice; and now that travellers from the Isles of the Sea, eager to learn their secrets, had arrived, their voice was about to be hushed for ever. A greater calamity than that of the Moabite stone tragedy was imminent. A mighty Empire was about to claim its rightful position among the great nations of the ancient world, and a few fanatics were about to push it back into the outer darkness to which classic history had assigned it.

Mr Green and I saw that we must exert ourselves if we were to gain our purpose. We visited all the men in whose grounds or walls the stones were, and assured them, on the faith of a British Consul, that Subhi Pasha was altogether different from the other Pashas whom they had known; that he would pay full value, and more, for the stones; and now that the Sultan had replied by telegram accepting them, any one who interfered with the inscriptions would be most severely punished. We thus endeavoured to enlist the cupidity and fear of the Hamathites in favour of the stones.

We also laid the matter before the Waly, who placed the inscriptions under Ibrahim Pasha for the night, and he told off a number of soldiers for their protection. Hearing from some of our people that a formidable conspiracy was on foot for the destruction of the inscriptions, we told them candidly what we had heard, and assured them that dire punishment would fall on them if any mishap befell the stones. It was an anxious and sleepless night, and on the following morning the Waly, by our advice, paid sums varying from three to fifteen napoleons each for the stones, and the work of removing them to the *Serai* began.

The removal of the stones was effected by an army of shouting men, who kept the city in an uproar during the whole day. Two of them had to be taken out of the walls of inhabited houses, and one of them was so large that it took fifty men and four oxen a whole day to drag it a mile. The other stones were split in two, and the inscribed parts were carried on the backs of camels to the *Serai*. As the shrill-voiced Moslems were summoning from the minarets the faithful to prayer at set of sun, the last stone was to our great delight deposited in safety.

The removal of these mysterious relics produced a great commotion in Hamah. The fact of a British Consul and a Protestant missionary being the guests of the Waly of Syria, and accompanying him to mosques and baths, seemed strange and portentous in the eyes of fanatical Moslems, but was somewhat reassuring to the cringing native Christians. Celestial portents also combined to impress the Moslem mind; for on the night following the removal of the stones to the *Serai* a meteoric shower, in Eastern splendour, was seen by the Hamathites, who beheld in every brilliant sparkling train the wrath of Heaven fulminated against Hamah in the event of their sacred stones being taken away. The wrathful stars had appeared in accordance with an ancient prophecy.

There was much shouting and invoking the name of Mohammed and Allah during the night, and in the morning an influential deputation of green and white turbaned Moslems waited on the Waly to tell him of the evil omens, and to urge a restoration of the stones.

The Waly ordered coffee and cigarettes for all the members of the deputation, who squatted in solemn dignity around him. He listened patiently to all the speakers, several of whom spoke at great length and with much animation. When they had finished the Waly continued stroking his beard for some time. Then he asked, in a very grave manner if the stars had hurt any one. They replied they had not. 'Ah', said the Waly, brightening up and speaking with a cheery ringing voice that even the guards outside the door might hear, 'the omens were good. They indicated the shining approbation of Allah on your loyalty in sending these precious stones to your beloved Khalif, the Father of the Faithful'. The grave deputation rose up comforted. Each member kissed the Waly's hand and withdrew.

We had now got our hare, and we had to face the difficulty of cooking it. It was necessary to get transcriptions free from what Captain Burton called, in those which he reproduced, 'the vagaries of the native painter'. There was no photographer in Hamah, and we had no photographic apparatus with us, and we felt that it was of the greatest importance to secure exact facsimiles, as we knew not what might happen to the stones. I tried in vain to procure plaster of Paris in Hamah. I learned, however, that gypsum was found in the neighbourhood, and I sent two trusty men, well bribed, to search for it.

Then began the work of cleaning the inscriptions. The moss and dirt of ages had filled up the hollows between the raised characters. Lime mortar had been dashed into them, and during the lapse of ages it had grown almost as hard as the stone itself. It was a work that could be delegated to no one, and it required incessant scrubbing during the greater part of two days, with brush and water and pointed stick, to make the stones clean. Meantime the men had returned with a camel-load of gypsum in blocks. This had to be burnt, and pounded into powder.

Many attempts were made to decoy us from our labour to shoot woodcock, or to hunt wild boars, or to stalk gazelles and bustards; but we stuck to our task until we had two sets of perfect plaster casts of all the inscriptions. This work was fully shared in by Mr Green, who took my place at the inscriptions when I was obliged to be elsewhere, and who managed to make up for my absence from the Pasha's parties.

As soon as the casts were firm we despatched them by a safe man to Damascus, whence Mr Green sent one set to the Government for the British Museum, and at Mr Tyrwhitt Drake's request I sent the other set to the Palestine Exploration Fund. We had thus succeeded in placing within the reach of scholars exact facsimiles of the Hamah inscriptions, showing the actual lengths of lines and bars and characters and blanks, perfect even to the faults of the stone.

We now propose to investigate the records of Egypt and Assyria and the Hebrew Scriptures, with reference to the Hittites, before asking the question, Are these curious inscriptions Hittite remains?

The Empire of the Hittites, 1884

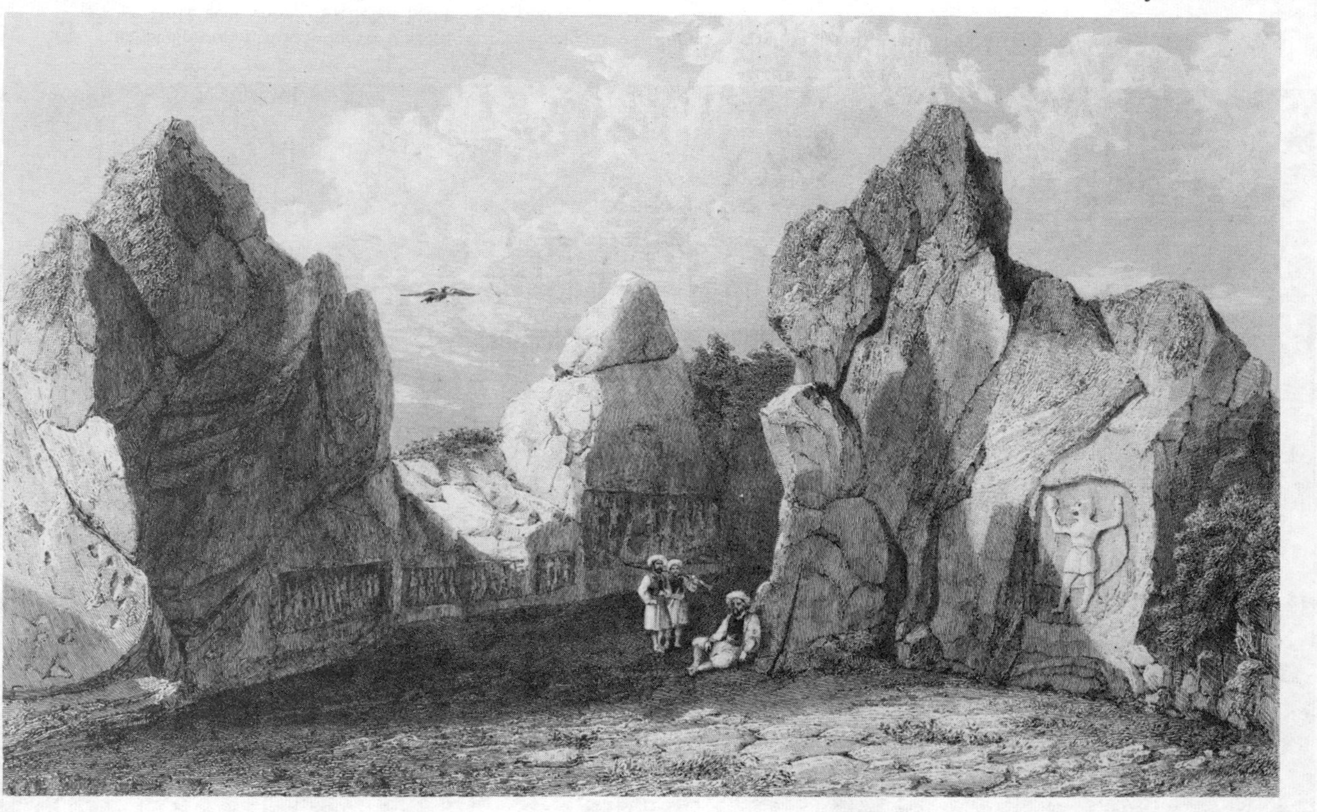

19. An early traveler's view of the Hittite rock sanctuary at Yazilikaya near Boghazköy, in what is today Turkey.

Courtesy, the Turkish Historical Society, Ankara

20. Sculpture and inscriptions of the Hittites from Karatepe. Three generations of scholars had tried in vain to decipher the writings of this people. Here at last the bilingual inscriptions were found that made decipherment possible.

To Boghazköy!

HUGO WINCKLER

HUGO WINCKLER (*1863–1914*) *was born in Saxony, and devoted all his academic career to the study of ancient texts. In 1904 he was appointed to the Chair of Oriental Languages at Berlin University, and contributed translations of the Amarna letters and the Code of Hammurabi, but he is better known for his findings at Boghazköy. Here his excavators discovered numbers of fine buildings and hoards of tablets, but unfortunately Winckler's interest was confined mainly to the subject-matter of the tablets and as a result much of the systematic recording of the excavation was neglected. Among the tablets he discovered and translated was a cuneiform version of the treaty between Ramesses II and the Hittites after the battle of Kadesh.*

The completion of this task was planned for the winter. An attempt was first made to obtain the relatively modest means needed for a preliminary expedition from influential sources who were actively concerned with the expedition. Meanwhile the scholars who had been consulted were of a different opinion on the subject of Boghazköy from my own, so I had to find another way of doing things. However, it turned out that the Near East Society and the Berlin Eastern Committee had limited funds obtainable. These could be made available for our purposes and the money, about the same amount again, which was missing was put at my disposal by my friends Dr Georg Hahn and the Military Chief Chaplain, Otto Strauss (Spendau). So by the summer we had the sum which we had estimated ready for our preliminary purpose and were in a position to prove who had been in the right about the potential prospects at Boghazköy.

On the seventeenth of July, early in the morning, we again rode into Zia-Bey's konak and were already greeted as old friends (with pleasant memories of Bakshish). As heir of an ancient race of princes, the Bey still enjoys a great deal of respect and one has to be sure of his influence if one wants to work in this district without difficulties. An expedition undertaken in the name of the Government would naturally not induce any obvious difficulties from anyone, but there are also others which are no smaller. And here the European is at a disadvantage because he has not the inexhaustible supply of time of the oriental. And the first requirement of this kind of warfare is time! We had stayed on very friendly terms with the Bey – he had made many requests, from a good bottle of cognac, to aid in a momentary difficulty – and for this in his own way he had also done us services. He supplied us, without any trouble at all, with a working party at his command – small services of friendship are well worth while in the Orient!

We were reckoning on about eight weeks' work and, as it was high summer, we wanted to spend them either in the tents or in huts made out of foliage. Memories of summer joys in the Lebanon were brought to my mind! Although here also in Asia Minor one goes higher up into the mountains in the summer to spend a summer holiday under canvas – which is what Zia-Bey did – I was bitterly disillusioned in my desire for warmth. We were able to camp at the foot of the actual peak of the Büyük Valley, at the source of an adequate spring. It is the place where, in the following year, our house was built. The modest tent which had to do for both of us offered us the kind of temperature, under the burning midday sun, which would have been not uncomfortable in a Turkish bath, but which was hardly refreshing for a midday nap. Soon after sunset the air cooled noticeably and with this drop in temperature a fierce evening wind blew down from the bare mountains, which led to a night in which there had to be good reason indeed to leave the warmth of the camp. So in the evening we sat in front of our tent in the howling wind to eat our evening meal, as our coats swelled with wind. Then, as a rule, one had cooled off enough to creep into one's tent, without all too many formalities, where there was just room enough for two men who were indefatigable at their work and between whom in this close contact there was never an irritated word or even an impatient thought, although at this time both had to suffer considerable physical hardship.

A bower of leaves accommodated the kitchen in which a cook of Bulgarian origin performed his duties in a pretty horrible fashion. He had recommended himself to my experienced friend on account of some knowledge of German, which should have made being here easier for me. The man had formerly been allowed to practise his art on the patients of a German hospital. I accepted his tricks with equanimity, for I set out on my travels with the idea that pleasure was not too eagerly to be sought. But my poor Macridi swallowed our anger twice and three times over for both of us and could not indemnify himself with clay tablets! A second arbour of leaves had to serve as shade for me in which to study the clay tablets and was soon ready to be put to extensive use. The whole camp was surrounded by a high fence woven of branches which at the same time acted as a badly needed windshield. Along a section of this, a bit lower down, a rather larger shelter made of branches had been erected which sheltered five beings who had never experienced better times in their whole lives – our horses! They earned their bread by doing almost nothing at all, whereas everyone else had more than enough to do. Their vicinity of course boasted a huge superfluity of flies, and for me this meant the pleasure of having to copy my clay tablets with covered head and neck and gloved hands, if I wanted to avoid stopping after each symbol to ward off the overpowering interest the friendly little animals took in my work. We are, of course, in our scholarship anxiously concerned to guard the spiritual right of the Firstborn.

From the camp sites (as now from the front of the house built in 1907) one looks out over the valley-bowl of Boghazköy and Jükbas to the chain of mountains which encloses it in the West. At the back lies the high Büyük Valley, which adjoins the eastern heights of the mountain basin.

So we had quickly settled ourselves in and my pencils were sharpened in readiness to record on paper the hoped-for treasured documents.

One should remind oneself of what had to be judged on the evidence of the facts known up to the present day with respect to what was expected to be discovered: the language of the lands which belonged to Arzawa, the land of the el-Amarna letters and the documents of the time of el-Amarna. The next step would therefore be to find information on Arzawa and to find its centre at Boghazköy. But already the size of the site of the town pointed to an especial significance of the place, and therefore of the country itself. We were not to be kept in suspense for too long. On 21st July the work on the Büyük Valley could be started and from the very first day onwards documents came to light. At first only small fragments. The ones which had been picked up earlier had been found on the slopes of the castle hill in the rubble which had rolled down, and inside a rather sharply defined strip. It therefore followed that the large expanse of mountainside had to be examined and in such a way that the rubble was cleared away from the bottom towards the top. It was work of not inconsiderable danger for the workmen, as an unwanted collapse of the overhanging earth and rock could at times be avoided only with the greatest precautions. The further into the mountain the work advanced, the larger became the fragments discovered. The productive strip narrowed a little towards the top, and our success showed that Macridi had from the start, with a lucky look, rightly gauged-round the actual site of the finds. Neither to the left or to the right of the strip was anything found and it was discovered in the following year that the actual source of the treasures had been at the edge of the mountain peak.

The majority of the pieces found this time showed the already familiar characters in the unknown language. The contents were varied, but at first too small to answer the problem which was primarily still unanswered: which part of the world we were in. That it had been a great centre was now quite clear and that it could not be the remains of the archives of an insignificant king, which came into our hands at the rate of 100-200 a day was also definite. The direction of Arzawa ... also had to be discounted after the first few days.

Soon a few pieces in Babylonian yielded the information. At first they were small fragments of letters, completely in keeping with the expected el-Amarna type, the remains of the diplomatic correspondence between two kings. These were the King of Egypt and the King of (C)Hatti. Therefore after a few days no doubt remained that we found ourselves on the site of the capital of the Kingdom of the Hittites (?) and that we had found the royal archives of the rulers of the Hittites at the time when they had been in contact with Egypt. This was at the time of el-Amarna and the period immediately following, that is 15-13 centuries BC. The first pieces did not yet contain the names of the kings in question. Also a fairly well preserved tablet, which spoke of a treaty between Egypt and (C)Hatti, did not name, as was usual, the kings concerned in the treaty, so that at first closer determination was not possible; that one had hoped to find something of the negotiations and treaties between Ramesses II and (C)Hatti referring to the big treaty between Ramesses II and 'Chetafar,' as he was then called, was self-evident, but to find something directly relevant to this, I had not dared to hope – being impermeated with the pessimism of experience, which showed that the facts never actually took the expected course.

This time, however, that which we did dare not hope for became fact. On the 20th August, after about twenty days' work, the trench which had been laid in the rubble of the mountain side had reached the first dividing wall. Under this was found a beautifully preserved tablet the appearance of which already gave a promising impression. One look at it, and all the experiences of my life paled into insignificance. Here was written what one had perhaps jokingly referred to as an idle wish: Ramesses wrote to Chattusil – *ci devant* Chetafar – of the two-sided treaty. Although during the last days more and more fragments were found concerning the treaty between the two states, only here was it actually confirmed that the famous treaty which one knew from the hieroglyphic record on the temple wall at Karnak had also been elucidated by the other side concerned in the treaty. Ramesses with his titles and his descent described in exactly the same words as those of the text of the treaty, writes to (C)hattusil, who is similarly recorded, and the contents of the writing follows word for word the paragraphs of the treaty. It is therefore not the actual final text of the treaty, but a letter written on this subject, perhaps the final version sent by the Egyptian side, which was used as a basis by the Hattians for the final treaty. As well as this a small fragment (of the beginning of the tablet in question) of a second copy of this letter was found. Like other important legal records it was therefore kept in duplicate in the archives.

They were strange feelings, those which I of all people experienced when I looked at such a document. Eighteen years had passed since I had got to know the Arzawa Letter of el-Amarna in the former Bulaq Museum and the language of the Mitanni in Berlin. At that time in consequence of the facts revealed by the find at el-Amarna I had ventured to suggest that also the Ramesses Treaty could originally have been written in cuneiform, and now I held in my hand one of the very letters which had been exchanged on this very subject – in the most beautiful cuneiform script and good Babylonian! It was truly a rare coincidence in the life of a man, how the first venture into oriental territory planned by the Egyptians had now found its confirmation in the heart of Asia Minor. As wonderful as a fairy story from the *1001 Nights* seemed such a coincidence – and yet the next year was to bring things even more fairy-tale-like, when all the documents were found in which those figures again reappeared who had so often occupied my attention in those eighteen years. As the King of the Mitanni, Tusratta, appeared in a Hattian elucidation and as even the Prince of Amuri, Arizu, the enemy of Rib-Addi of Byblos and the pike in the Phoenician goldfish pond, appeared in the documents, which must have acted as a commentary to his letters from el-Amarna! It was indeed a rare combination of circumstances in the life of one man . . . !

Nach Boghazköy, Der Alte Orient, vol. 14, part 3, 1913

Translated from the German by C. M. Kaine

Hrozný deciphers the Hittite cuneiform

L. MATOUŠ

FRIEDRICH (BEDRICH) HROZNÝ *(1879-1952) was born at Lysa nad Labem in Bohemia, and studied in Prague, Vienna, Berlin and London. In 1904 he took part in an expedition to northern Palestine, and in the following year he was appointed a professor of Prague University. He was attracted by the problem of the Hittite cuneiform and was immersed in his study of their decipherment when he was interrupted by the outbreak of the First World War, and conscripted into the army. Fortunately for oriental scholarship his commanding officer sympathized with his ambitions and understood the importance of his work, and he was excused from active duty in order to continue his researches. Basing his interpretation on his belief in the Indo-European origin of the Hittite language, he published his decipherment and translation of the cuneiform in 1915. Many and virulent attacks were made on his work by other scholars, but when his solution was applied to a large number of Hittite documents, including an extensive legal code, it was amply vindicated. During the remainder of his brilliant scholastic career he took part in several more expeditions and continued his work on decipherment problems, including an unsuccessful attempt on Cretan Linear B.*

The year 1913 marks the end of the first period in Hrozný's career. As has been stated before, the cultural history which he was planning, would – had he written it then – have left many aspects of the interrelations of the various Near Eastern cultures unexplained. The interruption in his plans which this year marks was only apparent, and actually to the advantage of his later work. He knew that more urgent tasks were calling him in other fields, that a whole complex of problems demanded elucidation, without the solution of which he would not be able to achieve the final synthesis he had in mind. It was characteristic of his mental quality never to lose sight of his appointed goal, never to be frightened from his path by even the most formidable obstacles he might encounter.

What were these pressing problems? Since the decipherment of cuneiform writing by Grotefend and Rawlinson, sufficient information had been gleaned from Sumero-Babylonian clay tablets to give a picture of the history and cultural life of the ancient Babylonians and Assyrians, but the history of Asia Minor remained a sealed book. The only sources of information available were indirect ones – Assyrian and Babylonian documents, Egyptian hieroglyphic texts, and the Bible, while the written documents of the nations of Asia Minor themselves remained incomprehensible. As early as 1906, the Berlin Assyriologist, Hugo Winckler (who had been Hrozný's teacher during the latter's stay in Berlin in the autumn of 1901), had succeeded in excavating near the Turkish village Boghazkeui in Asia Minor, some 145 km north of Ankara, the ruins of the ancient capital of the Hittite kingdom, Khattushash. These contained the archives of the Hittite kings on some 1,300 cuneiform tablets in the, as yet unknown, Hittite tongue. The archives of Boghazkeui, however, were not the first extant examples of the Hittite language. It was soon shewn that the language used in these inscriptions was identical with that of the country *Arzava* (i.e. western Cilicia), of which two examples had been found in letters discovered in 1888 in the archives of Tell el-Amarna, containing the correspondence of the Egyptian pharaohs, Amenophis III and IV, with contemporary kings and princes of Asia Minor. In view of the absence of contextual material, however, these letters continued to prove undecipherable. It was well known, from the cuneiform documents of Babylonia, that the Hittites had played an important part in the history of Mesopotamia. Hittite armies had been a source of constant anxiety to the mighty Babylonian empire from the first half of the second millennium BC onwards, and the fall of the great Khammu-Rabi dynasty is attributed to them by the Babylonian chronicles. According to the Bible, Heth was the son of Canaan, and the Old Testament always mentioned Syria as the home of the Hittites. These meagre biblical data had been somewhat improved upon by Egyptian sources, where the Hittites are mentioned in documents of the 18th to 20th dynasties, i.e. from 1500 to 1190 BC. It is quite clear, however, that on the strength of these indirect and fragmentary sources of information our ideas of the Hittites were incomplete and quite inadequate.

The task of elucidating the mysterious language of this unknown nation, which had lived in Asia Minor in the second millennium BC and which had left behind such vast numbers of cuneiform inscriptions in the Boghazkeui archives, can thus be seen as one of prime importance.

The work was facilitated somewhat by the fact that the cuneiform script could be read – though the language which it served to express had so far withstood all attempts at interpretation. Before Hrozný, the Berlin Assyriologist, Dr Weidner, Prof. Böhl of Gronhingen, and the discoverer of the archives, Hugo Winckler himself, had been working at this task. Hrozný offered to collaborate with the latter as early as 1910, but could not fully devote himself to this task, being engaged on his work on Babylonian wheat. It was only after this was completed and he had been officially commissioned (after Winckler's death in 1914) by the Berlin Oriental Society to publish the Hittite archives, that Hrozný really began his work of decipherment. Only the smaller portion of the inscriptions was in Berlin – the majority were kept at the Constantinople museum. In addition to the already mentioned Dr Weidner, Prof. Delitzsch had also been working on the Berlin inscriptions, as well as Dr O. Weber. Hrozný was not sent to Constantinople until April 1914, shortly before the outbreak of the Great War, in order to copy the inscriptions there together with the Berlin Assyriologist Dr Figulla, who had been working there since January 1, 1914. In order to make up for this delay, Hrozný did not lose a moment in copying inscriptions for the planned edition; at the same time he transcribed a number of tablets which he did not intend to publish, but which he required in connection with his work of decipherment. He spent his days copying tablets at the Ottoman Museum above the Golden Horn, and at night, often far into the early hours, he transcribed Hittite texts in his flat at Moda, on the Asiatic shore of the Marmorian Sea. The words thus transcribed he grouped into alphabetical dictionaries; not only by initials, but also by their endings, *a tergo* – this being an indispensable condition for the elucidation of unknown grammatical forms. The war caught him in the middle of this grinding labour, towards the end of August 1914, and necessitated his immediate return to Vienna. By then he had however already copied a sufficiently large number of inscriptions to continue his work, the fruits of which he presented to the public a year later.

The method which he adopted in deciphering this unknown tongue is not without interest. He chose for a starting point unilingual inscriptions which had to be elucidated on their own. There were, it is true, bilingual and even trilingual Hittite-Babylonian-Sumerian vocabularies, published in 1914 by Prof. Delitzsch, but their use offered too little opportunity of penetrating into the grammatical structure of the language. Hrozný found important aid, however, in proper names and

Sumero-Babylonian ideograms, i.e. cuneiform characters expressing complete words (word-pictures). It should be remembered that the Hittites, in taking over cuneiform spelling from the Babylonians, also adopted, not only ideograms, but entire words, which they spelt phonetically. Such word-pictures and loan-words often helped to elucidate the meaning of entire sentences. Adopting the method of combination, comparing phrases and meanings, progressing from the known to the unknown, Hrozný soon succeeded in understanding the structure of the tongue and in assigning it a place in the family of languages.

His starting point was the sentence: '*nu NINDA-an ezzateni vâdar-ma ekutteni*'. The only known factor here was the Sumero-Babylonian ideogram *NINDA*, meaning 'bread'. From examples in other places Hrozný established that the suffix *-an* was the termination of the Accusative Sing. Hrozný guessed correctly, as it turned out, that a sentence which gave emphasis to the word 'bread' might reasonably be expected to include the meaning 'to eat', which could be contained only in the word '*ezzateni*'. Since other passages had shown the suffix *-teni* to be the ending of the 2nd person pl. pres. or fut., he could venture a translation of the first half of the sentence: 'You (will) eat bread'. The structure of the second sentence was clearly parallel with the first, hence, if the noun corresponding the *NINDA* was *vâdar* – which might mean 'water', – then the verb on which the noun was dependent could only be '*ekutteni*' which in that case should mean 'drink'. Hrozný could now venture a reading of the entire sentence – '*Now you will eat bread, further you will drink water*'.

Hrozný at once identified the Hittite root '*ad-*', '*-ez*', contained in '*ezza-teni*', with the Latin '*edo*', the German '*essen*', the Old German '*ezzan*', i.e. with the roots of the Indo-European group, which included the family of Slav languages, the Germanic, Latin languages, etc. Similar affinities could be detected in the words of the second sentence also. The Hittite '*vâdar*' seemed related to the English 'water', the Czech '*voda*', and the root '*e(a)ku-*' contained in the word '*ekutteni*' – 'you (will) drink' revealed an affinity with the Latin '*aqua*'. The Indo-European character of the Hittite language was also shown clearly in its general structure, as in comparison of the personal pronouns – '*uga, ug*', 'I' and the Latin '*ego*', the Hittite '*kûish*', 'who', and the Latin '*quis*'. Another important characteristic was the declension of nouns and the conjugation of verbs, where especially the participles in '*-nt*' and the medio-passive forms in '*-ri*' point to the corresponding

Latin forms. Later detailed analysis showed that the general structure of the language placed it in the West Indo-European 'Kentum' group, i.e. in the same division as the Greek, Latin and Germanic languages.

Recognition that Hittite belonged to Indo-European stock was no mean surprise for Hrozný. That he had almost excluded this possibility is shown by the fact that among the books which he took to Constantinople, Indo-European philology was represented only by the small and quite inadequate manual by Meringer, from the Göschen collection. When Hrozný announced his conclusions for the first time at a meeting of the Near Eastern Society in Berlin, on November 24, 1915, they gave rise to a discussion lasting far into the night. In general, his conclusion that Hittite was an Indo-European language, was received with great scepticism. Attention was drawn in particular to the non-Indo-European physical character of the Hittite race, which, with its great curved nose and backwards sloping forehead seemed close to the 'Armenoid' type. The suggestion was made that Hittite was a Caucasian language, and Weidner even considered it closely related to Gruzinian. The most ferocious of Hrozný's opponents were Professors Bartholomae and Bork. On the other hand, Hrozný's lecture – repeated on November 16th at Vienna University under the aegis of the Eranos Vindobnensis Society, and published the same year under the title '*Die Lösung des hethitischen Problems*' (The solution of the Hittite problem) – was received by the press in Germany as well as in Austria with great respect, and commented upon as 'a milestone in the history of Indo-European philology and archaeology'. It must be admitted also that Hrozný's conclusions were often attacked on pettyfogging grounds. Thus, one comparative philologist refused even to consider his arguments, because Hrozný had claimed that the Hittite word '*vâdar*' was spelt with a long first syllable – which on the strength of the rules of comparative philology, he declared to be altogether inadmissible.

On December 1, 1915, Hrozný was called up for service with the Vienna Garrison Regiment, where, in view of his extreme shortsightedness, he served until the end of the war as a clerk. His superior officers showed unusual sympathy and understanding for his extramilitary interests and made it possible for him to devote several hours daily to his Hittitological studies. Thus Hrozný was able to publish even before the end of the war at Leipzig the first grammar of the Hittite language, under the title '*Die Sprache der Hethiter, ihr Bau und ihre Zugehörigkeit zum indogermanischen Sprachstamm*' (The language of the Hittite, its structure and its membership of the Indo-Germanic stock). In this for the first time he published his conclusions as a systematic grammar and defined the position of Hittite within the Indo-European group – surely a remarkable achievement, if we remember that he had succeeded, within a mere three years, in doing what so many before him had tried to do in vain. He had solved the mystery of this strange tongue, the oldest Indo-European language so far known.

In order to prove the truth of his theories, Hrozný at once began a systematic translation of Hittite religious and historical inscriptions, which appeared at Leipzig in 1919 as '*Hethetische Keilschrifttexte aus Boghazköi in Umschrift und Ubersetzung*' (Hittite cuneiform inscriptions from Boghazkeui in transcription and translation). The number of opponents and sceptics gradually grew smaller, and Indo-European philologists began to recognise the truth of his theories of Hittite as a Kentum language and of his readings and interpretations and of his view of Hittite grammar. The first to take Hrozný's side was the Norwegian philologist Marstrander in 1919. The following year, the German Indo-European philologist F. Sommer came to the conclusion, after many doubts, that Hittite was Indo-European in structure, but that its vocabulary was drawn mainly from indigenous Asia Minor sources. After this the number of Hrozný's followers grew steadily, and today there is not one among serious Indo-European scholars to doubt the truth of his interpretation. A just tribute was paid to Hrozný by the Professor of Hittitology at Leipzig University, Friedrich: '*Hrozný's name will always have an honourable place at the head of Hittitological studies. He saw and understood the basic characters of Hittite declension and inflexion so correctly that on the foundation laid by him others could build. It is not surprising in the work of a pioneer that he should occasionally make mistakes in the identification of forms. Hrozný, as the discovering genius, and Sommer as the careful methodician, are, as it were, the twin poles of Hittite philology*'. Thanks to Hrozný's brilliant pioneer labour, therefore, Hittitology quickly grew into an independent branch of philology and served to bring new light into the history of Asia Minor in the second millenium BC.

Bedrich Hrozný: The Life and Work of a Czech Oriental Scholar, 1949

Excavations at the Black Mountain

HELMUTH BOSSERT

HELMUTH BOSSERT (*1889–1962*) *was born in Landau and educated at the Universities of Heidelberg, Strasbourg, Freiburg and Munich. For some years he remained a private scholar, concentrating his interest upon Near Eastern studies, but in 1934 he accepted the appointment of Professor of Near Eastern languages and culture at the University of Berlin, and at the same time became Director of the Institute for the exploration of Near Eastern languages and culture at the University of Istanbul. He led many expeditions in the field and made extensive studies of the Hittite hieroglyphs. Since 1947 he directed the excavation of the Hittite remains at Karatepe.*

The exploration in Anatolia undertaken in summer 1945 by the Institute for Research in Ancient Oriental Civilisations of the University of Istanbul (the staff of the expedition, consisting of Prof. H. Th. Bossert, his assistants Dr Halet Çambel, Nihal Ongunsu and Muhibbe Darga, were accompanied by Bay Ali Riza Yalgin of the Direction of Antiquities from Ankara), led us along the road over the Taurus pass connecting Kayseri with south-eastern Anatolia and North Syria over Gezbel, Saimbeyll, Feke, Kozan and Ceyhan. Our aim was to determine as far as possible, the ancient Hittite road at the time of the New Hittite Empire. On our way we seized every opportunity of getting information from the inhabitants about possible Hittite monuments in the vicinity. In this way we collected a number of pieces of information which seemed worth while examining. Among others was a rumour about a supposedly Hittite lion-relief worked on the rock, somewhere in the mountainous region east of Kadirli. It being already very late in the season, we were unable to check this information right away and had to postpone the matter until the next year.

When, in February 1946, our group (composed of the same members) came into the same region – thanks to the helpfulness of Bay Hüsameddin Arkan, Director of Public Instruction in Adana – we felt it our duty to check the accuracy of this story; and in spite of the bad condition of the roads, impassable for motor-cars because of heavy rains during the past few days, we decided to set out for the mountainous region beyond Kadirli. Considering the difficulties of the trip under these conditions and the vagueness of our information, everybody tried to dissuade us from this undertaking and we ourselves were fully aware of the fact that though most rumours have some grain of truth in them, the whole matter could still prove to be a complete disappointment, for the relief in question might well be a Roman monument, especially since remains of this epoch are not at all rare in the region of Kadirli. After due deliberation we decided to continue our investigations in two different directions and to separate into two groups, of which one, consisting of Nihal Ongunsu and Muhibbe Darga, were to set out for Adana and thence to the Mersin region, while the other, consisting of myself and Dr Halet Çambel as well as Bay Naci Kum, Director of the Adana Museum, who had joined our group in the meantime and was kind enough to accompany us, were to set out for Kadirli.

On February 27 at 1 p.m. the three of us left Kozan in a horse-cart. At first the roads were fairly good and while we were crossing a not very high chain of hills no considerable difficulty was encountered. Having reached the village Koseli, in the plain east of this mountainous chain, however, we heard from the peasants that, owing to heavy rains, the road to Kadirli led through very swampy territory. We were therefore obliged to send back to Kazan our cart-driver who, besides not knowing the roads, had brought along horses in such poor condition that they could not be expected to overcome the difficulties of a march through swampy land; and we had to get a better one before it got too late in the day. With the kind assistance of the villagers this proved possible, and after a few minutes a new cart with strong horses was ready. A little beyond Koseli, after we had passed through the village Karaömerli and had inspected for pot-sherds the 'Mustafa Alinin Hüyüğü' which lies close to the road, we found that the main road had completely disappeared in swampy territory, and we were very glad that we had got this new driver, who, through a labyrinth of cart-tracks, brought us safe and sound to Kadirli, in spite of darkness having set in in the meantime and in spite of an accidental fall into a ditch.

It was after 7.30 p.m. when we pulled up before the municipal office of Kadirli, where the local authorities, who in the meantime had been notified by telephone of our arrival, were already expecting us. They very kindly invited us to dine with them, and during the excellent dinner that was served right there in the town hall, we had the opportunity of talking to the *kaymakam* of Kadirli Bay Münir Alkan, Bay Ibrahim Savrun (the head of the municipality), Bay Tevfik Coşkun (a member of the municipal council) and Bay Hilmi Inan, the headmaster of the primary school of Kadirli. We explained our plans to them and asked them to give us more information about the lion-monument in question, Unfortunately none of these gentlemen had ever seen or heard about it, so that at first we felt quite depressed and disappointed. But, not losing hope altogether, we asked if there was not anybody in Kadirli who knew the region well, who had wandered around and might thus have come across our monument. Bay Ekrem Kuşçu, teacher at the primary school of Kadirli for the last 20 years, who was said to have wandered more than once all around the region, was described as being such a man. He was sent for immediately, arrived after a short while, and could, to our great joy, give us very exact information about the monument, which, he said, he had visited four times in the course of the years 1927-44.

According to what he told us, the lion-monument was not a rock-relief but a sculpture in the round, a lion-base. On it had stood, originally, the statue of a man; but the statue had fallen down and lost its head in the course of the years. The body was covered with a cuneiform inscription all over. The monument, he said, was about 5-5½ hours on horseback to the east of Kadirli, on top of a wooded elevation which was part of a long, wood-covered mountain called Karatepe. All around were lying fragments of stones with remnants of writing and reliefs. All these were worked in a kind of black stone which was not naturally to be found in the vicinity, and the stones must have been brought from a pretty great distance. Besides this, a very great number of similar black stones lay dispersed on the opposite side of the Ceyhan river, which flows past the Karatepe; and these, surely, could be nothing but the remains of an ancient city belonging to the castle. Bay Ekrem told us further that, according to the information he had obtained from the peasants, the statue, including the head, was still standing 60 years ago. We were, of course, curious to know if the teacher had found this remote monument by chance or if he had heard about it through the peasants. Thereupon he told us that his attention had been drawn to the monument in 1927 by the then 80-year-old Abdullah (who died in 1932), son of Vahab and father of the actual *muhtar* of Kizyusuflu (a village lying between the Karatepe and Kadirli). He went on to tell us the following story: in 1915 a wise *hodja* came to Kizyusuflu and stayed for two months as a guest at Abdullah's house. Unable to pay back his host for his hospitality, he proposed to give him the benefit of his wisdom by helping him in the discovery of a treasure. 'Show me a place', he said, 'and I will find a treasure for you'. Abdullah thereupon led him to the lion-monument, but the *hodja* explained that this was the funeral monument erected by his men to a king torn to pieces on a lion-hunt by the lion, and therefore, he declared, no treasure was to be found there, Abdullah must lead him to another place. Thereupon he led him to Bodrum, lower down on the Ceyhan river; but whether they found the treasure or not we do not know.

Bay Ekrem told us further that, except for the peasants and himself and one man from Mersin whom he knew, nobody, and in particular no expert, had yet visited this ancient site. He himself had in his time told Bay Ali Riza Yalgin, then Director of the Adana Museum, about it, but had not led him there. Bay Ali Riza, with whom we discussed the matter later, confirmed what the teacher had said – Ali Riza had been to Kadirli in the spring of 1939 to study the habits of the Turcomans of the region and had met the teacher on that occasion. Bay Ali Rizi drew our attention to an article entitled 'The Turcomans of Kadirli' published in the Türksözü appearing in Adana of April 19, 1939, where, basing himself on the oral information of the teacher, he writes: '. . . With all this, Kadirli is capable of giving us monuments of older epochs too. But these are up in the mountains and in an untransportable state. The ruins of Karatepeli on the Ceyhan river in particular may be considered among the more important ones worth while examining.'

On the strength of all this information we decided to ride out to the monument the next day, and we asked the teacher to be so kind as to guide us, which he readily agreed to do. Thanks to the hospitality of Bay Ibrahim Savrun and Tevfik Coşkun and their families, we spent a very restful night at Kadirli.

The next day at 8.30 a.m. the necessary number of horses stood ready in front of the town hall and we set out without delay. On the map, which we owe to the courtesy of the foresters at the District Forest Department of Kadirli, our marching-route is indicated by a line of dots and dashes. It led us at first in roughly eastern direction through a valley and up into the mountainous region, and then, always following the crest of the mountainous range, turned southeastwards at Dögüşgedigi towards the Karatepe, a black mountain which could be seen in the distance. The way was quite practicable for the horses, though it consisted only of a narrow path. Favoured by the finest spring-weather we rode through budding shrubs, bushes, and low pines and after 3½ hours reached Kizyusuflu, a village of widely scattered houses. There we obtained receptacles to contain the water for wetting the squeeze paper. One of the villagers, Haci Aga, accompanied us on foot. Always following the crest of the hills, we rode happily on and on, with a marvellous view of the snow-covered heights of the Anti-Taurus on the east and, to the south, the Amanus, which we had crossed only a few weeks ago. Our path now gradually descended into a valley and, after passing over another elevation, led us down to the Akyol (pronounced Agyol by the peasants). This is a very old caravan route still used by the inhabitants of the region when moving to and from their summer pastures. Before us now lay a densely wooded long mountain with a maximum height of approximately 500 m. This was the Karatepe, on the northern-most but lower spur of which the lion-monument was to be found.

The ascent to this place on a narrow shepherd's path did not offer any difficulty. In 15 minutes' time we had reached the summit and before us lay the ruins of the destroyed royal Hittite castle.

II

Not far from the place where the shepherd's path had led to the summit of the hill, the lion-monument we had been searching for was lying, overthrown. This base, which showed a relief of two lions held by a standing man, seemed not to be *in situ* and had probably originally been standing on a level place worked into the natural rock, not far away. The human statue belonging to it lay overthrown near by. Its head was missing and no fragments that might have belonged to it were visible, at least in the immediate vicinity. The statue was lying on its face; the rather smooth back was covered with a 20-line Old Aramaic inscription. Beginnings of lines on the front side, visible even without turning over the statue, showed that here another inscription had been engraved. Taking into consideration the great weight of the statue and the fact that the ground underneath was very rocky, we did not think it advisable to try and turn it over, for the probability of damaging the excellently preserved back would have been too great. The front part of the statue had been damaged already, probably at the moment of being violently thrown down from its base; and it is even possible that a fragment bearing an Old Aramaic inscription, lying near by, is a part of it. The first question that arose now, was whether we should try to copy the inscription on the back or whether we should do better, taking into consideration that we had only three hours at our disposal, to start with the squeezes immediately after taking the necessary photographs. As the inscription was partly covered with algae, which would not have everywhere permitted a sure reading without previous cleaning, it seemed preferable to start right away with the squeezes, even at the risk that, owing to the season, they might not get completely dry.

While one of us (H. Çambel) got busy with the photos and squeezes, the other (H. Th. Bossert) started to look for more remnants of inscribed or sculptured stones. Though it was rather hard to search, because of the thorny thickets abounding all around, the fact that the stones used for inscriptions and sculptures were blacker in colour and harder than the natural stone of the Karatepe mountain, was of great help. First, the movable stones in the immediate vicinity of the lion-base, which had partly sunk into the ground, were turned and a number of inscribed and sculptured fragments were thus exposed. Though the sculptures were, with one exception, very badly smashed, some, at least, could still be identified as 'Hittite' reliefs, which seemed to be in a style even more rustic than that of the reliefs of Zincirli and Islahite. Most of them had probably been part of such orthostats as are known from other Hittite buildings. Such a representation, as the three birds placed one above the other, in spite of all its naïvity, seems to suggest that new designs may be found on this site too. Some of the most important finds were, however, the fragments of Hittite hieroglyphic inscription, for nowhere hitherto have Old Aramaic and Hittite hieroglyphic stone inscriptions been found side by side. While the Old Aramaic inscriptions of Karatepe are, as far as we know today, all incised, there seems to be at least one among the hieroglyphic inscriptions which shows very careful relief-work. As far as the character of the hieroglyphic incised inscriptions can be judged, they seem to belong approximately to the same epoch as the Old Aramaic ones. Another great surprise was the discovery of a very small inscribed fragment, which, though bearing only a very few letters, could be identified as of the *boustrophedon* type. No such Aramaic inscriptions have been recognised up to now and there is no reason to believe that any such existed. It is therefore very probable that this inscription was not written in the Old Aramaic language, but rather in some non-semitic language, using Old Aramaic characters. Still further, we found the breast-fragment of another statue (?) bearing an Old Aramaic inscription, which we did not deem necessary to depict in this preliminary report, as only a very few letters were left visible on it.

Most of the finds made in this short time were clustered round the lion-base. On the remaining parts of the hill-top a great many stone fragments of the same type were noticed, but these seemed not to bear any kind of inscription or decoration, though this of course may have been merely accidental. Owing to the shortness of the time and the thickness of the bushes, which made it difficult to move about, the slopes and the foot of the hill could not be examined thoroughly, though in all probability numerous inscribed and sculptured fragments are still to be found there. Nevertheless, a column-base, evidently not *in situ*, of the same type as those of Zincirli, but without any plastic decoration, was noticed on the slope; and remains of a violently destroyed citadel wall were encountered at different spots. It should moreover be noted, that, approximately at the centre of the hill-top, a rocky formation could still be seen, from which the stone for the building of the citadel had evidently been taken. Two ditches, one in the vicinity of the lion-base, the other one nearer the border of the hill-top, bore witness to the fact that peasants or shepherds had now and then searched for treasure on the Karatepe . . . Pot-sherds were also looked for, but since the natural rock is very near the surface on the hill-top, rains have probably washed most of the sherds down the slopes and only a very few small, weathered pieces of a buffish earthenware could be found, which gave no clue whatsoever as to shape, type or epoch.

The woodiness of the territory prevented us from getting a view of the city ruins on the other side of the river. These ruins probably belonged to the Karatepe citadel. It was only from the top of a tree that a photograph could be taken of the area where the ruins are said to lie. Time being short and the Ceyhan river being very wide at this time of the year, it was not possible to get across to inspect the ruins.

It was now gradually getting dark and our guides were in a hurry to leave. The squeezes were far from being dry and the only thing we could do was to take them down carefully and dry them over a fire. We then packed them into a tin case, loaded the smaller fragments into our saddle-bags for subsequent deposition in the Adana Museum, and, having made a last photo of our group, set out for night quarters at Molla Mehmet's house in Kizyusuflu, 1½ hours' ride away.

The remains of inscriptions, reliefs, statues and the citadel wall which we left behind and which slowly disappeared from view, were solid witnesses that a new Hittite site had been won for science.

Karatepe, 1946

The Royal Residence on the 'River of Nymphs' (Nymphaios)

FRIEDRICH DÖRNER

FRIEDRICH KARL DÖRNER *(1911–) was born in Gelsenkirchen in Germany, and educated at the University of Greifswald, where he specialized in ancient history, classics and archaeology. He travelled extensively in the eastern Mediterranean region, and first came to Kommagene in Syria in 1938. He is a member of the German Archaeological Institute at Berlin and Istanbul, and of the Austrian Academy of Sciences, and has taught at the University of Tübingen. Since 1950 he has held the post of Professor of Ancient History at the University of Münster. It was in 1951 that he discovered the royal palace of Arsameia at Kommagene, and has been digging there ever since.*

The discovery of the Kommagenian royal residence of Arsameia on the River of the Nymphs was not a chance find but is the result of a systematic examination of the Kommagenian cultural region on the Upper Euphrates in the magnificent mountain world of the Antitauros. There are only a few references to this region in ancient literature. It makes its first appearance in the annals of the Assyrian kings, in which it is recorded that the rulers of Kummhi (Kommagene) were to deliver tribute to Assyria, and above all, the valuable cedar tree-trunks, then much in demand. Apparently Kummhi was then, in the reign of Sarrukin (Sargon) II, who reigned from 721 to 705, annexed to the Assyrian Empire.

Although the land, on account of its important crossing-points of the Euphrates, must have played a great role in respect of the connections between North Mesopotamia and the coast of the Mediterranean, and although its position was also very important for the traffic to the land route to Asia Minor, we hear nothing more of its history in the course of the following centuries. Kommagene is not mentioned again in the historical records until the first century BC, when the Romans tried to push their eastern boundary towards their Parthian enemies. It is understandable that these sources – written from a Roman point of view – do not contain much favourable comment on a country whose rulers tried to uphold their political and cultural independence in the fight between the Roman Empire and the Parthian kingdom.

To these ancient records was added an unhoped-for, lively increase of information, the results of a German expedition which went to Kommagene in 1883 under the leadership of Karl Humann and Otto Puchstein. The two scholars had been commissioned by the Academy of Sciences in Berlin to investigate the necropolis of the Kommagenian king, Antiochus I, which this ruler had erected for himself on one of the peaks of the Antitauros. It was proved that the fantastic-sounding accounts which the German engineer, Karl Sester, had sent to Berlin before anyone else, had not been exaggerations. A Town of the Dead did indeed exist on Nemrud Dagh, more than 2000 metres up, built by Antiochus 'as near as possible to the Heavenly Thrones'. One special find was the discovery there of a monumental inscription, a unique contemporary record, in which Antiochus had let his religious ideas be recorded for posterity. It was no less astonishing to see the king as the creator of a religion whose elements were those of the religions of the Greek and Persian worlds. In front of the more than 50 metres high burial mound the king had had himself represented in the circle of native gods – in monumental proportions, which the rulers of the east loved, stern and immovable, like the lifeless chunks of cliff on the mountain landscape.

In the publication of the results of their journey Humann and Puchstein expressed the wish that an intensive exploration should be instigated. But the sensational excavations on the west coast of Asia Minor came overpoweringly to the fore. They were, above all, much more easily accessible than the lonely, impassable mountain region. So it was more than half a century before scholarly interest in Kommagene was again aroused.

My first expedition to Kommagene, which I undertook in 1938 together with R. Naumann, unfortunately remained no more than a short prelude. But during all the war years I never forgot the promise which I had made to myself and to my local companions to return for new research work.

In 1951 I actually got there, and immediately, in the first days of the exploration, I was lucky enough to find the royal residence of Arsameia on the River of the Nymphs. We had already struck camp before sun-up and reached, after a long ride over a sun-scorched treeless high plateau, the little village of Alut. How good it was to stretch out on the colourful, hand-woven carpets which had been laid out in welcome for us by the villagers next to an ice-cold spring under shady trees. Quickly we unpacked our provisions; added to these by our hosts were fresh yoghurt and marvellous grapes. Then began the usual oriental word-play of From where and Where to. When the villagers heard from me that I was searching for the sites of ancient ruins, the Turkish name for the mountain which lay near by was mentioned for the first time: Eski Kale (i.e. Old Castle) where a 'Picture Stone' had been dug out. I was eager to examine this locality more closely; but, as is so often the case in the East, I had to fight my impatience; for Nuri, who seemed to know most about Eski Kale, had no desire at all to play the guide in the scorching heat and to show me the narrow track up to the steep heights. He suggested that we should wait for the cool of the evening here at the spring. So I saw the legend-surrounded castle hill for the first time in the light of the setting sun. Its slopes fell down steeply and precipitously on all sides; only from the south was an approach possible. But where was the castle which had given its name to this bleak, bare slope? I looked round in vain for traces of walls or for the remains of the fortifications. When I asked Nuri why this mountain had been named 'Old Castle', he just shrugged his shoulders and said in a circumspect manner, 'That's what my grand-father already called it.'

All the same I was eager to have a look at the 'Picture Stone'. It must have quite recently been excavated and left lying where it was found by peasants who were looking for stone for house-building, because it had been too heavy to get down into the valley. A preliminary glance showed me that the piece in question was a fragment of a relief of Kommagene times showing the Persian god of light, Mithras, wearing a great crown of rays, the first important clue to the meaning of the 'Old Castle'!

With redoubled zest I searched further and soon discovered that the south flank had once been terraced and that when the walls had been destroyed they had buried all the buildings under them. An exposed, artificially flattened rock wall attracted my attention especially.

Could it be possible that the rock walls had not merely been worked but had also been covered with inscriptions? Momentarily it seemed as though this was so. In my excitement I came up closer to the rock and looked at it from the front, the light of the setting evening sun on my back; I could still see nothing more than a very cracked, shattered, grey wall of rock. Disillusioned, I turned away. It was obviously only my imagination which had been deceiving me. But then I suddenly saw something! In the slanting light, which came from the side, appeared the vertical and horizontal lines of letters, only very faintly recognisable, between the weatherbeaten marks of the stones. Excitedly I called for pick-axe and spade and there and then began to dust the lines of letters with my handkerchief and to clear away the earth from the wall of rock with my hands. Before the tools had been passed up to me I had already confirmed my guess: I stood before an inscription written in Greek letters.

The first blows of the pick-axe cleared away the rubble which had protected the letters on the lower level from destruction and weathering. More beautiful and undamaged than I had dared hope, the inscription emerged from the protecting soil. In the days which followed I tried to get rid of the rubble which had accumulated in front of the wall of rock. A first attempt at reading the letters showed that I had in front of me the end of an inscription arranged in several columns which, judging by the type of letters, belonged to the time of King Antiochus, i.e. the first half of the first century BC.

Of course I immediately tried to push forward to the beginning of the inscription. But this proved to be a difficult task because of the enormous amount of rubble. When eventually a third column followed the second, I was as happy about my discovery as I was despairing at the impossibility of penetrating any farther into the huge heaps of rubble of the terrace. But improvisation is the great art of every exploration! I therefore decided not to attempt a complete clearance but to grope my way along the rock wall along a tunnel. Luckily there was a bend in the wall after the fourth column, so that it now ran parallel with the slope. With the fifth column I had eventually found the beginning of the inscription.

Like the royal inscription on Nemrud Dagh, which it in many ways resembled, this inscription was also carved at the command of King Antiochus of Kommagene. In elevated language, beautifully written, the king here announced that his royal father, Mithradates Kallinikos, had chosen this place as his Hierothesion – i.e. as his sacred resting-place: he decreed that here a cult for both father and son should be practised, for which he was leaving exact instructions.

Luckily the king also makes reference to the site in the inscription. He praises the excellent location, for a fortification, which had led his ancestor Arsames to have a fortress built and a town founded, which in all times of need should be a reliable retreat for the royal house. Arsames had called the town Arsameia on the River of Nymphs in honour of himself and here 'in the suburbs of Arsameia' his father, in compliance with his own wishes, had been buried.

Had I not been firmly convinced that an excavation of the royal residence of Arsameia and the search for the royal tomb had great significance for our historical knowledge, and had I not had the confidence that we must succeed in the realisation of this plan, I would early have despaired of the immense difficulties. But where there is a will there is a way. It took two years until all the expert evidence had been given and the first excavation budget had been sanctioned by all the relevant parties. The Turkish Government had also given its permission for the excavations to be done at Arsameia on the River of the Nymphs, and so, in the autumn of 1953 and also 1954, I was able to carry out the excavation.

Of course our work was concentrated on the area of the Hierothesion of King Mithradates Kallinikos. The king's large inscription was completely uncovered; with this we found the magnificent relief with the scene of King Mithradates and the God Herakles greeting each other. Because of the quality of the work this find excels all other reliefs so far found in Kommagene and is of importance in the history of art as an excellent example of the reinterpretation which Hellenistic culture experienced in the oriental sphere.

But where was the king's tomb itself? Was it perhaps inside the castle hill? We had, in fact, beneath the third column, come up against a rounded arch hewn out of the rock which formed the entrance to a carefully worked rock passageway, within which a flight of rock steps led into the depths at an angle of inclination of 35-45 degrees.

The excavation of these presented us with a very difficult technical problem; for the entrance to the rock had been taken through serious fractures in the rock in a number of places, and the ancient builders had, unperturbed by the sequence of hard and soft parts of the rock, continued the stepped passage-way in the same direction as that taken at the start, even if in doing so, soft sections of varying depths had to be penetrated. Judging by the fragments we found, someone had, in ancient times, done exactly what we were doing and had propped up these very dangerous places with wooden supports. After each such disturbed section we always rediscovered the continuation of the rock passage and were eventually able to penetrate to a depth of 115 metres. But in the middle of a loamy layer we had to break work off, in autumn 1954, because of lack of the right technical equipment, so that the question of whether the passage really led to the tomb of King Mithradates or had served some other purpose within the sanctuary, still remained unanswered.

Simultaneously work on other parts of the southern slope was also in process, where we excavated a series of foundations of pedestals, some of which bore fragments of their reliefs. We also obtained important results from the excavation of the cultural levels on the heights of the mountain plateau. Here it was revealed that Eski Kale had also been inhabited in post-Kommagenian times until up to the middle ages, but, on the other hand, had also been inhabited, far before the Hellenistic foundation of Arsames, back in pre-historic times. So Eski Kale unexpectedly emerged from the darkness of history as a favoured settlement in Kommagene, and we can hope that by the exploration of the castle mound we may increase our knowledge about eastern Asia Minor in its role as a connecting link between the Mediterranean countries and the highly developed cultures of Asia.

Die Königsresidenz am Nymphenfluss, 1956

Translated from the German by C. M. Kaine

The discovery of Ugarit

CLAUDE SCHAEFFER

CLAUDE FREDERICK ARMAND SCHAEFFER (*1898–*) *was born in Alsace, studied archaeology at the Universities of Strasbourg and Paris, and married the daughter of an eminent archaeologist. He has not only worked in museums and on expeditions in the field, but has served as a consultant in the interests of antiquity to such government bodies as the* Commission des Fouilles et Missions Archéologiques *and the National Council of Scientific Research. He has made great contributions to Aegean archaeology in his work at Enkomi in Cyprus and his excavation of the site of ancient Ugarit, now called Ras Shamra, which he at first mistakenly identified as Sapuna.*

The excavations at Minet el Beida and Ras Shamra, begun in 1929 and continued in 1930, were undertaken at the suggestion of M. René Dussaud, Member of the Institute and Conservator at the Louvre. The natural harbour of Minet el Beida (the White Bay) lies facing Cyprus; and it was this fact which gave M. Dussaud the idea of a Mycenaean colony from Cyprus importing thither the copper which had to be disembarked for transport to the interior and to Mesopotamia. This theory was supported by the fact that 1000 metres from the bay is a huge *tell* (mound), called by the natives Ras Shamra (Cape Samphire), which might well hide the ruins of this assumed sea-port.

In 1928 there came the accidental discovery of a burial-vault at Minet el Beida, of corbelled construction and containing Mycenaean and Cypriote pottery dating from the 13th century BC. This was the first confirmation of the theories about the antiquity of Minet el Beida and Ras Shamra. The Académie des Inscriptions et Belles-Lettres, at M. Dussaud's suggestion, sent out an expedition to locate the ancient harbour, town and cemeteries of Minet el Beida. The direction was entrusted to the present writer, who chose as his assistant M Chenet, well known on account of his excavations of the Roman kilns and glass-factories of the Argonne.

Our excavations near the bay have revealed an important cemetery containing several large rectangular tombs with corbelled vaults, approached through a short vestibule or forecourt with stairway, the whole carefully built of well worked stone blocks. One of these tombs was hidden under a rather important building, to judge from the columns with attached walling which are all that remain of it today and which are not easy to explain. Directly communicating with the tombs were other still more important buildings, one of which was completely cleared this year; it contained thirteen halls, rooms and passages, without counting the upper story whose staircase with its landing are preserved. This building is generously provided with wells and water-channels, all of which have been rendered useless by artificial filling or concrete covers. Upon and beside these wells, along the passages, in the rooms and at the foot of nearly every column, were placed votive offerings of painted Mycenaean and Cypriote vessels, ordinary pots and objects of bronze, silver and gold, such as pins, lamps, knives and daggers. They prove that the building cannot have served a merely utilitarian purpose. Perhaps it may be regarded as one of those houses of the dead like those which some Egyptian pharaohs had built beside their funeral vaults. The comparison is strengthened by the fact that the civilisation of Ras Shamra, as we shall see presently, borrowed much from that of the Nile Valley.

A still more important series of discoveries awaited us to the north of the tombs, towards the sea. Here, at a depth of between 0 m. 50 and 1 m. 50, near a roughly built room, lay about 80 deposits consisting of Cypriote, Mycenaean and local pottery, bronze implements and weapons, stone weights conforming in part to the Egyptian mina of 437 grammes, shells or just plain pebbles from the shore close by. There were also curious stone tablets, pierced steles and stone phalli, large and very life-like. The richest deposit, near the centre of the group, contained two horus-hawks in the Egyptian style; one of them, of bronze, bore the double crown of Lower and Upper Egypt, the other, of bronze and gold, held the Uraeus between its feet. Not far off lay a statuette representing a seated deity with eyes of silver and enamel, giving a benediction with its outstretched hand, according to the manner of certain Syrian gods. The chief object of the group is the statuette (25 cm. high) of the Syrian god Reshef (sometimes identified with Baal); it is of silvered bronze, and the head and high coiffure are formed of a leaf of gold. The god is represented standing; formerly in his right hand he brandished a thunderbolt or battle-axe, while in his left he held a sceptre or spear, as he appears in other representations from Ras Shamra.

Not far from the majestic Reshef lay his colleague, the goddess Astarte with the Hathor coiffure, holding the lotus in her hands. Her fair, slender form is artistically wrought in gold leaf. A necklace of quartz and carnelian beads completed the hoard.

We must imagine that this hoard and those near it had been buried in honour of some great persons, probably the kings of the adjacent city of Ras Shamra, laid to rest in the vaults we found close by.

The first vault, whose covering-slabs were almost level with the surface, had been plundered by natives. In the debris from it was recovered Cypriote and Mycenaean pottery of the 13th century, an engraved spatula and a bronze bracelet.

Vault No. 2 had served as a quarry since ancient times. The three upper courses of the fine corbelled vault and that of the stairway had been carried away; the vault itself, the votive-niches in the walls, and the little recess alongside had all been robbed. Arrowheads, bronze spatulae and some pottery found on the floor of the tomb show that like the rest it belongs to the late Mycenaean period, and may be assigned to the 13th century BC.

The third vault, which is almost intact, was also visited by robbers in bygone times. They entered through a hole in the roof, carried off whatever valuable metal objects there may have been in the tomb, and blocked up the hole again after leaving. Happily their visit was clandestine, and in spite of the disorder they left behind them part of the grave-goods, which were very sumptuous, remained undisturbed and they did not even enter the passage. It was by this way through the entrance of the tomb we went in, collecting the native offerings of pottery which were placed in the corner of each step, leaving the middle of the staircase free. They consisted of Canaanite terra cotta lamps, small conical vases, a fine Mycenaean crater with overlapping ornament and a magnificent intact Egyptian two-handled vase of alabaster. On the threshold of the fine door of the vault lay a well preserved human skull; it is difficult to say whether it belonged to an attendant who was sacrificed and buried at the entrance of his master's tomb, or whether it had been thrown there by the robbers when they broke into the vault.

The skeletons – at least four in number – had suffered at the hands of the robbers, the bones were scattered and the skulls broken. But in their haste the robbers failed to search thoroughly the corners of the vault, where they missed finding rings and beads of gold or of silver and iron –

then regarded as a precious metal – haematite cylinder-seals, faience and alabaster vases and, above all, oval ivory boxes, one of which has a splendidly carved lid. It represents the Goddess of Fertility (the 'potnia theron'), seated on a throne flanked by two he-goats, and it is indisputably the finest Mycenaean ivory actually known. The pottery dates this vault too to the late Mycenaean (13th century BC).

Our excavations on the northern projection of the mound of Ras Shamra brought to light a large temple with two rectangular courts joined together and enclosed by thick walls. We found fragments of life-size granite statues of gods which had once stood on raised stone pedestals in the court; their style is that of the end of the 18th dynasty (1580-1350). From a stele dedicated by Mami, royal clerk of the Treasury, to Baal of Sapouna, we get the ancient name of the town. This large temple of Egyptian character reveals the strong influence exercised by the pharaohs or even their political control of the land of Sapouna in the 14th and 13th centuries BC. Beside it we found several shrines of lesser importance which appear to have been devoted to the cult of local divinities, two of whose images we found. One, female, was mutilated; the other, male, was fortunately intact. It represents a god in a standing posture, with an Egyptian coiffure of ostrich-plumes; on the forehead grows a spiral horn; in the left hand is a spear, and in the right the *hiq* – a kind of sceptre presented by the Egyptians to foreign rulers. The god is clothed simply in a loin-cloth kept in position by a belt with a big-pommelled dagger; he wears leather-thonged sandals with toes pointed after the Hittite style.

Beside the temple, as at Nippur, stood a school or seminary where the young priests must have learnt Sumerian – the Latin of those times – and the other languages used at Sapouna; where also they learnt the difficult profession of a scribe. We found their exercises in cuneiform writing, their lists of Sumerian and Babylonian (Accadian) words, as well as regular bilingual dictionaries intended to assist them in reading and composing religious and diplomatic documents. A letter quite in the style of the well-known Amarna correspondence refers to alterations of the frontier between three hitherto unknown Syrian towns – Halbini, Hazilu and Panashtai.

But what gives outstanding importance to the cuneiform tablets found at Ras Shamra is the fact that most of them contain a script that is wholly unknown and which had already become alphabetic. Professor Bauer of Halle and Father Dhorme of the Ecole Biblique at Jerusalem recognised a Semitic language in these documents; and they have put forward a preliminary explanation of it. The complete deciphering and first translation of the new writing are the work of M. Charles Virolleaud, the learned Assyriologist, to whom I entrusted the publication of the documents of Ras Shamra. He has just made a communication to the Académie des Inscriptions et Belles-Lettres concerning these texts, a portion of which is composed in almost pure Phoenician and whose contents are of capital importance for the religious history of the East. The principal document is a kind of epic poem in which the chief character is called Taphon, and which consists, in its present state, of nearly 800 lines. Chief among the divinities are the goddess Anat and the god Alein, son of Baal; but there are more than 20 others, among whom are Asharat, Astarte, Dagon, El-Hokmot the god of wisdom, and Din-el the Justice of God. The bilingual glossary contains a very complete list of words and some Sumerian phrases; but instead of the Babylonian which is usually employed in these glossaries to translate Sumerian, the glossary of Ras Shamra contains a language totally unknown up to the present. M. Thureau Dangin, the distinguished Assyriologist, will shortly make known its significance. The number of documents we found this year gives ground for supposing that the school of scribes possessed an important library, containing amongst other things large tablets of three or four columns each, which encourage us to expect a fine harvest of new historical knowledge.

Below the floor of the library and all around it we made numerous discoveries: – silver and bronze cups, copper ingots, a vase full of silver objects, and above all a splendid collection of 74 bronze implements and weapons in an exceptionally fine state of preservation. It consists of 4 swords, 2 daggers, 25 flat axes, 11 spearheads, 3 arrowheads, 6 chisels, 4 sickles, a fine tripod ornamented with pomegranate-flowers. The most valuable objects are 5 large implements of unknown use and 9 socketed adzes (herminettes), five of which have cuneiform inscriptions punched upon them, probably dedications. The presence of two cakes of metal and the fact that several of the weapons are unfinished show that the workshop where they were made cannot have been far distant.

At a lower level, clearly separated from the one above it, which belongs to the 14th and 13th centuries, we brought to light a cemetery of the 17th and 16th centuries completely free from Mycenaean influence. The pottery belongs to native Canaanite types, with blackish or reddish slip, unpainted.

Penetrating to a yet lower depth, at 7 metres down we found crude brick walls belonging to buildings that stood here long before the existence of the overlying cemetery; these must go back to the beginning of the 2nd or even to the 3rd millennium. The investigation of them must necessarily be postponed until the two upper levels have been cleared.

The French Excavations in Syria, Antiquity, vol iv, no 16, 1930

Solomon's foundries

NELSON GLUECK

NELSON GLUECK (*1900-*) *is a man whose life has always been directed by his undeviating devotion to scholarship. He took degrees in archaeological, oriental and Hebrew studies at the Universities of Cincinnati, Berlin, Heidelberg, Jena, and Hebrew Union College, and many other institutions have presented him with their highest academic honours. He first went to Jerusalem in 1928 as Fellow of the American School of Oriental Research, and from 1932 onwards he has pursued his explorations of Palestine with an enthusiasm which was undeterred by the harsh conditions of desert archaeology. For a long time he persistently ignored the dangerous political hostilities latent in the area, but by 1952 it was no longer possible for a leading Jewish scholar to live and work in the Arab states, so he turned his attention to the apparently empty and barren region of the Negev, where his explorations have made great contributions to Biblical and Oriental studies.*

We are of course speaking from hindsight about the copper and iron products of the Arabah and Ezion-geber. To our immense surprise, the excavations demonstrated that while Ezion-geber was undoubtedly a seaport, it was no less important as an industrial centre. There were nails and timbers and resin and ropes, which had undoubtedly been used to build and repair ships. There were fishhooks and net-weights and piles of sea shells related to the extensive fishing that had obviously been carried on in the rich waters of the eastern arm of the Red Sea, which is a fisherman's paradise even today. There were, to be sure, no traces of docks, but perhaps we should not have expected any. It is highly possible that the Tarshish ships were little more than small *dhows*, which were anchored offshore. And when, at times, a sudden storm blew up, and their mooring lines did not hold, they could be dashed to shore and broken to pieces on the rocks in the shallows. That is exactly what happened, as we have seen, to Jehoshaphat's fleet, about the middle of the ninth century BC.

What puzzled us greatly when we first commenced operations at Tell el-Kheleifeh was what seemed to us to be the particularly unfortunate location of the site. Situated in the centre of the Arabah rift, which is banked on either side by high hills leading, respectively, into Arabia and Sinai, it is open to the full fury of the almost constant winds that blow fiercely down the Wadi Arabah, as if forced through a wind tunnel. The result is an endless series of sandstorms, frequently so severe as to obscure vision. The architects of Ezion-geber could not possibly have chosen a more inclement site along the entire shoreline. It was understandable why they had not built farther to the west where the soil was poor and the water was worse, being completely undrinkable by either man or beast. But why, we asked ourselves at first in irritation at having to work eat and sleep in frequent sandstorms, had they not chosen a site farther to the east at Nabataean Aila or Arabic Aqabah, where the water is excellent, the soil is fertile and the winds are tempered by the hills? We began digging at the northwest end of Tell el-Kheleifeh, in order at least to have our backs and not our faces turned to the biting winds and blinding sandstorms. In the meantime, we fumed and fussed at what seemed to be the folly of Solomon's town planners. Their seeming madness, however, was soon explained.

The very first building brought to light at the northwest corner of the mound turned out to be the largest and most elaborate smelter ever discovered in antiquity. Each of the walls of its rooms was pierced by two rows of carefully constructed apertures, which could only be flues. The upper rows were intended to permit the gases formed in one chamber to penetrate into the second and so on and preheat its contents. It was easy to reconstruct the smelting process. The ores were given a preliminary 'roasting' at the individual mining sites in the Wadi Arabah, and then brought for further smelting and refining to Ezion-geber. Layers of ore were placed between layers of lime in large, thick-walled pottery crucibles.

Piles of charcoal from the wooded hills of Edom were packed all around them in the open furnace rooms of the smelter, with the fires being ignited in successive order at proper intervals of time. No hand-bellows system was necessary, because with brilliant calculation, Solomon's engineer had harnessed the winds to furnish a natural draft. The Bessemer principle of forced-air draft, discovered less than a century ago, was, in essence, already familiar some three millennia back. So well had the smelter been constructed that, when it had been completely exposed, we could place our hands on the flue holes in the wall at the south end of the structure and feel the air emerging, which had entered through the flue holes on the north side, a number of rooms away.

It became more apparent than ever, as a result of our excavations, why Edom and Judah had fought so long and so bitterly with each other over the Arabah and Ezion-geber although the Bible, however, as I have already pointed out, passes over in complete silence one of the main reasons for the prolonged warfare between them. The copper and iron mines of the Arabah and the control of access to the Red Sea were as much a cause of inextinguishable rivalry between them as oil in Arabia and along the Persian Gulf is a source of competition and conflict among many nations today. Both for Edom and Judah, the command of the resources of the Arabah and of the highway which led through it and the control of Ezion-geber:Elath, with its industries and access to the Red Sea, were indispensable to their safety, economic well being and potentialities of growth.

The turnabout ownership of Ezion-geber:Elath is illustrated by two names, one Edomite and the other Hebrew, which we came across in the excavations of the city of Elath. Built by the Judaeans on the ruins of Ezion-geber, it had been captured from them by the Edomites (II Kings 16:6), with whom it exited from history. The Edomite name occurred in seal impressions on the handles of a whole store-room full of fine pottery jars. On the handle of every one of them was stamped the following inscription: 'Belonging to Qausanal the Servant of the King.' We know that Qausanal is a typical Edomite name, the first part of which, Quas, is the designation of a familiar Edomite, Nabataean and Arabian deity. It seems likely that this Qausanal, who was undoubtedly an Edomite, was the governor of the district of Elath when it was under Edomite dominion. He acted as the personal representative, that is, the 'servant' of the Edomite king of the time.

The other inscription was found in an earlier level of Elath, when it was still in Judaean hands. It was part of what turned out to be the only seal signet-ring of a Judaean king ever discovered thus far. And thereby hangs a tale. At the last minute of the last day of the last of the three seasons of our excavations, I decided to make a final farewell tour of the site. Our Arabic foreman, Abbas, made the rounds with me. Yielding to a sudden impulse, I asked him to tear down with his pick-axe a bit of mud-brick wall that we had left standing until it was measured and photographed. As he pushed it over, he saw a tiny object that had lain underneath it, and quickly picked it up. 'What have you there, Abbas?' I asked him. Instead of replying, he asked me if the system of paying *baksheesh* for every object found still held good even though the expedition were formally over.

I must explain here that we paid our workmen a special reward for every object found, related to its market value, whether it was a broken bead or an ivory fragment or a piece of gold. This was necessary to ensure that every object got into our hands rather than into those of dealers, whose rates, incidentally, we were always prepared to match. Instead of keeping accounts, we would pay each workman immediately for the things he had found and had turned over to the staff member supervising the section he worked in as a pick-man, shovel-man or basket boy. By the time everyone concerned had looked carefully through the earth being dug up and removed, there was very little of value that escaped attention. In addition, we sometimes put the debris of entire rooms through sieves to make this assurance doubly sure.

I told Abbas that I would be delighted to pay him *baksheesh*, even at this stage of the game. He persisted and asked if I were willing to pay as much as a shilling or two for what he held in his closed fist. 'Hand it over, Abbas,' I said to him. He gave it to me. I took a hurried look, stuck it into an inner pocket, and told him to hold out his hands in cupped form. With that, I emptied into them all the silver and paper money in my pockets. It may have been the equivalent of fifty dollars. It was a lot of money for that part of the world. I could easily have engineered a minor revolution with it. He looked at the heap of shillings and pounds, which was indeed a veritable fortune to him, and, after a moment, said to me: 'Ya Mudir (O Master), but I can't possibly take all that money from you.' I assured him that I thought what he had found was worth a good reward, and that anyway I had intended giving him a parting gift. He had been most faithful and helpful during the years we had worked together, and we had become good friends. We embraced and took leave of each other, he back to Aqabah and the rest of us to our cars on the way to Amman and Jerusalem.

As soon as possible, I examined the find. It had been apparent immediately that it was some sort of a seal-signet ring, with an intact copper casing around a dirt-encrusted stone. It was the kind that was hung by a cord on the belt of a prominent person and served in effect as a badge of office (I Kings 21:8; Haggai 2-23). Cleaning it somewhat, I was able to make out what was engraved on the stone seal, which was stained green from the copper band around it. A horned ram, with a little man standing in front of it, was carved on it; and incised above it, in retrograde, in the clearest possible ancient Hebrew characters, was the inscription *LYTM*. The letter '*L*' means 'to' or 'belonging to'. And making allowance for the omission of vowels or vowel letters, which is characteristic of ancient Cannaanite writing, the three remaining consonants '*Y T M*' could signify nothing else than '*YOTAM*', which is the proper name of 'Jotham'. The translation of the entire inscription, therefore, is 'Belonging to Jotham'. This had to be a seal-signet ring of Jotham, King of Judah!

We know that a Jotham ruled Judah as regent during the last years of the reign of his father, Uzziah, who had been afflicted with leprosy, and that he succeeded him as king after his death. It was Uzziah who had built the new city of Elath on the sand-covered mound of the previously ruined and abandoned Ezion-geber. and it was during the reign of his grandson, Ahaz, the son of Jotham, that the Edomites drove out the Judaeans and established themselves firmly in Elath. It was, therefore, quite appropriate that the Qausanal impression should have been found in the Edomite stratum of Elath and the Jotham ring in the preceding Judaean one. There is little question but that this unique seal-signet ring lent royal authority to the governor, ruling the southernmost city of the kingdom of Judah, in the name of its king, Jotham.

Rivers in the Desert, 1959

The Dead Sea Scrolls

JOHN MARCO ALLEGRO

JOHN MARCO ALLEGRO (*1923-*) *was educated at Manchester University and after receiving an award for oriental research went to Magdalene College to study Hebrew dialects. He has conducted archaeological expeditions in Asia Minor, and published his results in lectures, broadcasts and television films as well as in print. In 1953 he was appointed British representative on the international team for editing the Dead Sea Scrolls, a task which called for the utmost skill and dexterity owing to the fragmentary condition of the material.*

The editing and publication of a complete scroll is a relatively simple task. The reading here and there may be difficult, but at least where the scroll is intact the position of the words and phrases is not in doubt. Very different is the preparation of hundreds of tiny fragments, many no bigger than a fingernail. All these must be laid out and minutely examined in the hope that they may connect with parent documents and be of use in reconstructing broken passages. The work of editing the fragments bought and excavated from the First Cave was entrusted to Fathers J. T. Milik and D. Barthélemy, both attached to the French School in Jerusalem. Starting work in 1952, the work appeared in 1955, having taken two full years to go through the Press. It is not surprising that the second-named collaborator was soon after flown home for extended medical treatment, although Milik has been able to continue on the work of preparing the Semitic texts of Murabba'at and, at the same time, by far the largest section of the fragments from the Fourth Cave. It is as well that the world should know the price in strained eyesight and mental fatigue which is being paid by scholars like these that it may have these priceless scroll fragments at the earliest possible moment.

As the Cave Four material flowed in, it became clear that its bulk was going to surpass by far anything found in the First Cave, and that it was beyond the capabilities of one or two scholars to edit in a reasonable time. De Vaux and Harding therefore decided that the work

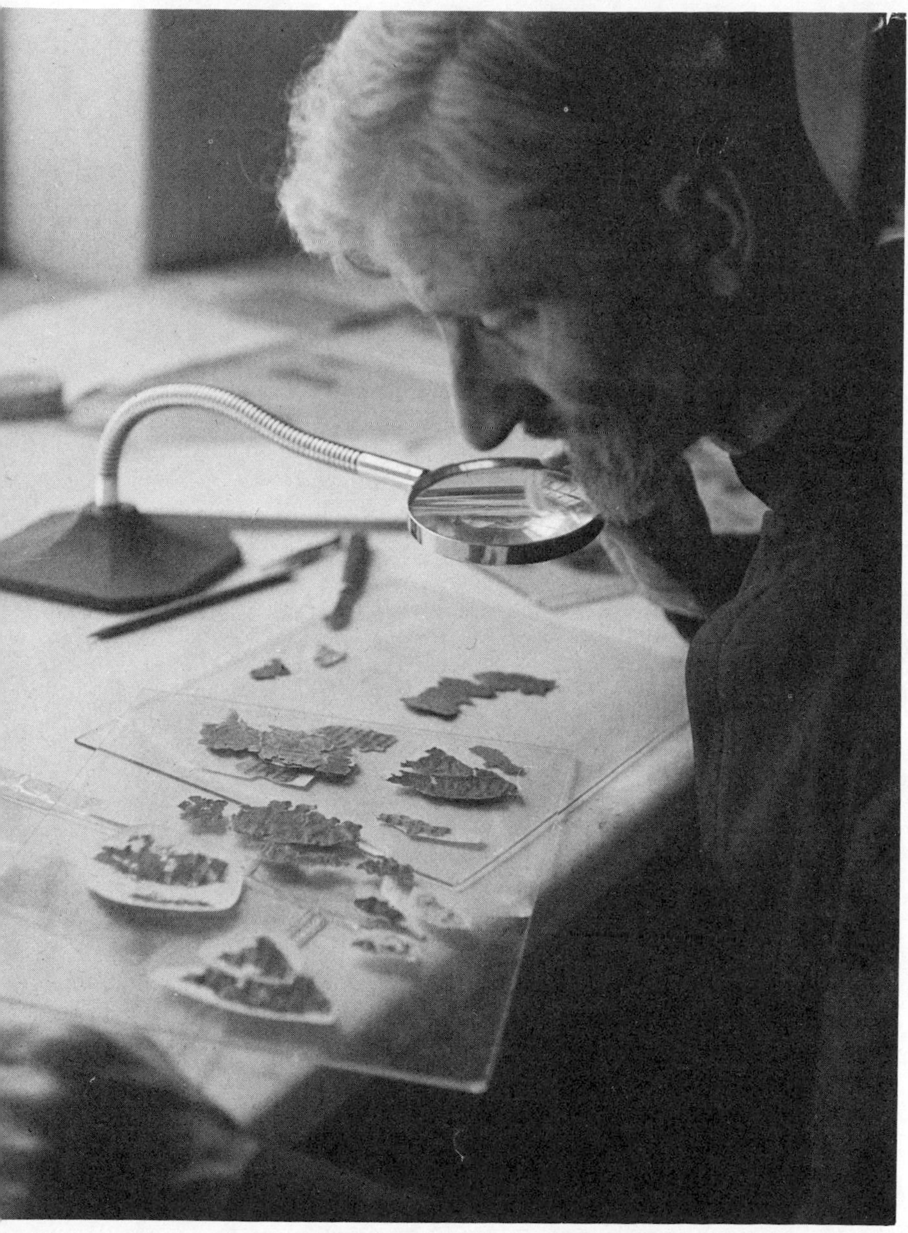

hn Allegro

21. Piecing together and deciphering the Dead Sea Scrolls.

should be shared by a team of scholars brought to Jerusalem and resident there for this purpose over several years, or at least for one year with return visits of several months each. Since the excavations have always been carried out by joint teams drawn from the French and American Schools, with the co-directorship of Lankester Harding, an Englishman, it was further decided that the Scrolls team should be of an international character. Thus there have been drawn to Jerusalem for this exciting work men from America, Britain, France, Germany, and Poland, eight of us in all. The whole project has been a happy example of close international collaboration, and a wonderful experience for all of us. The division of work has been roughly that the two American scholars, Dr Frank Cross and Father Patrick Skehan, have taken the biblical section, in all the remains of about a hundred different manuscripts, Father Jean Starcky the Aramaic works, Dr Claus Hunzinger the copies of the War Scroll and some papyrus manuscripts, Father Milik the apocryphal and pseudepigraphal works, the Manual and Damascus Documents manuscripts, and other sectarian works, Mr John Strugnell the hymn scrolls and other non-biblical works, and myself the Bible commentaries and some wisdom literature. The material from the other caves has been put in the care of Father Maurice Baillet of France. Even when we are not able to be in Jerusalem, much can be done on the photographs which we take to our home countries with us, but reference to the original pieces is absolutely essential to the work, and, all the time, examination of the unidentified fragments is continuing and pieces are being extracted for absent members of the team and put aside pending their return.

Naturally to bring out and keep a team of scholars for such work from the four corners of the globe is an expensive procedure. Some of the institutions to which the members are attached have financed their travel and residence, whilst for others it has been made possible by a generous grant from Mr John D. Rockefeller, under whose patronage the Museum in Jerusalem was first built and continues its work. The results of our labours will be published in a series of volumes, of which the first has been that of Barthélemy and Milik dealing with the Cave One fragments and excavations. Next will probably be the volume of the Murabba'at caves, then fragments from the minor caves, to be followed by the biblical volume of Cave Four, and the non-biblical volume(s). Again the cost of publication has been defrayed to a large extent by Mr Rockefeller's grant.

The fragments reach the Museum from Kando or the Bedouin in

cigarette cartons and the like, and are immediately stamped on the back with the code letters assigned to the various donors who have provided the money. Needless to say, that does not mean that those bodies will receive necessarily those pieces, for many will have been merged into their parent documents which may have been earmarked for elsewhere. In these cases as near an equivalent-sized fragment as possible will be allocated at the final distribution to replace the other. The fragments then have to be cleaned of the white dust with which most are covered. Sometimes this is so firmly engrained that no amount of brushing will remove it, and then we find that a very light brushing with a camel-hair brush touched with a non-acid oil, like castor oil, will make the marl translucent and bring up the writing very clearly. Very often it is not so much the dust that obliterates the writing as the colour of the leather itself, which has gone completely black from exposure to humidity and thus makes the writing indistinguishable from its surroundings. In these cases the process of infra-red photography has been particularly valuable in our work. We are very fortunate in having at the Museum a beautifully equipped photographic laboratory under the expert direction of Mr Nejid Anton Albina, who must by now be one of the world's foremost experts in this field. He used Kodak Infra-red plates and films, specially obtained from the United States, in conjunction with a red/violet, or a Red 3 filter fitted on to a Linhoff camera. Exposure at f.11 varies, of course, with the blackness of the subject and the distance from the lens, but to take our ordinary-sized glass plate of normally dark fragments (12 in. by 9½ in.) he sets his camera at about 32 in. from the subject, and gives exposures of six minutes between the hours of 8 and 10 a.m., and four between 10 a.m. and 2 p.m. A darker plate of fragments may need eight minutes, and exposures for particularly difficult pieces running over the hour are not uncommon. Such is the constancy of light in Jerusalem that he finds a light meter is unnecessary. Developing is done in ID 2 for five minutes and printed on soft or medium Bromide paper. The results on fragments where to the naked eye no writing at all was visible, are just amazing, and to this miracle we owe a very great deal of relief from serious eye-strain.

Very often the skin of the fragment is dry and brittle, sometimes tightly curled, and then it must undergo a process of hydration before it is safe to unroll it. The pieces requiring treatment are put into a glass vessel containing water at the bottom covered with a zinc perforated sheet and a sealed lid. After ten or fifteen minutes in hot weather the fragment is usually supple enough to allow gentle manipulation, but sometimes, with particularly coarse pieces, several hours of such treatment is necessary. If the piece is left too long, the result is a drop of liquid glue and one less epoch-making discovery. The clean fragments are laid out between the glass plates, several dozen or scores in each, and put out in the large room on trestle tables.

To the new collaborator entering the 'Scrollery' for the first time, the effect is rather shattering. He finds himself surrounded by about five hundred glass plates, packed with fragments of varying sizes, over which he will be the next year or two of his life crouching, trying to pick out pieces belonging to his documents, or seeking to identify new fragments. If he is a comparatively late-comer to the team, perhaps some of the results already obtained will strengthen his weakening resolve. In the corners of the room are the collected sections of other members of the team, and walking round he may see how pieces, no larger than the palm of the hand, have grown to cover complete volumes of text, and whose secrets will be proudly shown to him by the collaborator responsible. He may look wonderingly at a biblical text which is going to bring about a revolution in our ideas of text transmission, or on a commentary which throws new light on the messianic expectations of the time. He may find himself gazing at the Aramaic text of pseudepigraphal work never before seen in its original tongue, and all around him will be biblical texts older by a thousand years and more than Hebrew manuscripts of the Bible previously known. He will have walked into a new and exciting world, but the way to the revealing of its treasures is a hard one, and before he can be sitting down reading columns of text and preparing the transcriptions and translations for publication he has many months of extremely trying work ahead of him. Armed with one of his biggest fragments he will go slowly round those scores of unidentified plates seeking for the lost pieces. As he grows more proficient at the task he will be able to recognise a member of his flock from one letter or even part of a letter. One of the saving factors has been that of the four hundred or so manuscripts we have to deal with, surprisingly few have been written by the same scribe, so that by recognising the idiosyncrasies of one's own scribes you can be fairly sure that the piece belongs to his document. Of course, this is not always so, and often we may find, after some months of patient collecting, that we have more than one work on a plate, coming from the hand of the same scribe. However, besides the script there is the rather less dependable criterion for identification of the skin itself. Where this remains constant over the whole scroll, it can be a most useful means of quickly recognising parts from the same work. But, unfortunately, there are often extreme variations in colour and even texture where different skins have been sewn together to complete the work, or where disintegration of the scroll in antiquity has meant that different conditions have acted upon the pieces, so that one may be clean and supple, while its neighbour is darkened with moisture and warped completely out of shape. Warping is a major problem, for not only does it make pieces very difficult to join together even where the join is certain from the text, but it will distort the letters of the writing out of the true form, so that if there are only one or two letters on the piece, and the colour of the leather is changed from its parent document, it may be a long time before it is recognised as belonging to its own scroll.

Another cause of difficulty in joining is that worms or damp have often attacked the edges of fragments, so that real 'jig-saw puzzle' joins are no longer possible. This again is largely due to the scrolls having disintegrated in antiquity, and so frequently does this occur, and so often does one find tears which are certainly not new, that I am myself inclined to believe that the Fourth Cave was entered long ago and its contents maliciously damaged. Be that as it may, much of the relative positioning of the fragments in a document has to be done by 'dead reckoning' rather than edge-to-edge joins. This is not too difficult in the case of a biblical text where the order of the words is already known, although sources of trouble here are variant texts which we shall discuss in the next chapter. It is more difficult in the case of non-biblical works previously quite unknown or known only in translation.

An intriguing problem which has presented itself during the work has been the deciphering of a number of different secret codes in which several of the works were written. Happily they are nothing more complicated than new alphabets, which were composed by the Sectarians to keep certain works especially secret, and in one case they contrive to write most but not all of the words backwards, and use a mixture of four or five alphabets, including one or two of their own invention. Thus, for instance, one might come across a word written with a combination of alphabets in something after this fashion: X𐤄yיל FY κYOβ ϵ𐤄X. The reader might like to work that one out for himself, with the clue that the alphabets represented in this imaginary example are Latin, Greek, Phoenician, and Aramaic, and the principle of using ancient letters for their modern equivalents is precisely that used by the author of this Qumran document. Having deciphered one column including a particularly puzzling phrase, it was encouraging to find another piece in a further purchase which contained the same phrase written, rather carelessly for the coder, in 'clear' Hebrew, confirming the decipherment.

Another code used entirely letters of their own invention, and begins in 'clear' Hebrew: 'the wisdom which he spoke to the Sons of the Dawn', and then goes on into this unknown script, beginning 'Listen ye'. One day, when the three of us, who then constituted the team, were tired of cleaning the thousands of fragments in the boxes before us, we decided to enliven the proceedings by having a competition to see who could crack the code first. The main difficulty was that being very fragmentary there were very few complete words, so that determining the relative frequency of occurrence of letters, which would normally have given the answer in a very short time, would not work so easily in this instance. Some of the letters looked something like the proto-Hebraic writing, a derivation from the ancient Phoenician script, but they made no sense when given these equivalents. Whilst Cross and I were tearing our hair over it after lunch that day, Milik strolled in and informed us that he had done it, or at least got enough of the letters to make a full decipherment eventually possible. He had guessed the meaning of one of the few complete words, which had the pattern *ABCBAD*. Since Hebrew is based on the triliteral root system there are not a large number of words possible with this combination, and a common group *LHTHLK*, the infinitive of the reflexive form of the verb *HLK* with the prefix *L*, meaning 'to walk about', gave him enough letters to break other smaller words, and thence to work through the whole fragment until he had the alphabet, or as much of it as could be obtained from the evidence available. There are, however, other cryptic scripts which have been impossible to decipher so far for want of sufficient material.

I have said that a factor which is apt to give trouble is the changing of skins part way through a scroll. Just as at times like this one wishes there had existed animals with skins large enough to suffice for a complete scroll, we often wish they had invented the fountain pen in the first century BC. Some of our scribes seem to have had 'quill trouble', in that the instrument kept wearing down and giving the writing a quite different appearance from that presented when the scribe had newly sharpened his pen. I have one manuscript in my section, a commentary on Isaiah, whose writing changes startlingly in the first two columns, and fragments coming from later columns look different again. Of course, close examination shows the same basic characteristics are still there, but when one is looking through fragments of only one or two letters for pieces to match, these variations can be most puzzling. It is by no means unknown, also, for the Qumran Scriptorium to play a very mean trick on the Jerusalem Scrollery by changing horses in midstream, or rather scribes in mid-scroll. This is quite unforgivable, and most trying.

The Dead Sea Scrolls, 1956

Part Six

THE BOOK OF THE STEPS

The Pyramid of Cholula

ALEXANDER VON HUMBOLDT

ALEXANDER FRIEDRICH HEINRICH, BARON VON HUMBOLDT (*1769-1859*) *was a great scholar, explorer and savant. He was born in Berlin and after deep studies of many aspects of the natural sciences he was appointed Assessor of Mines in the government service. He quickly rose to a high rank, but, wishing to be free to travel, he then resigned. For the next five years after his resignation he explored Central America and collected so vast an amount of data on the geography, antiquities, meteorology and botany of the region that it took him twenty-one years to arrange it for publication after his return to Europe.*

The small city of Cholula, which Cortez, in his Letters to Charles V, compares with the most populous cities of Spain, contains at present scarcely sixteen thousand inhabitants. The pyramid is to the east of the city, on the road which leads from Cholula to Puebla. It is well preserved on the western side, which is that represented in the engraving. The plain of Cholula presents that aspect of barrenness, which is peculiar to plains elevated two thousand two hundred metres above the level of the ocean. A few plants of the agave and dracaena rise on the foreground, and at a distance the summit of the volcano of Orizaba is beheld covered with snow; a colossal mountain, five thousand two hundred and ninety-five metres of absolute height, and of which I have published a sketch in my Mexican Atlas, plate 17.

The teocalli of Cholula has four stories, all of equal height. It appears to have been constructed exactly in the direction of the four cardinal points; but as the edges of the stories are not very distinct, it is difficult to ascertain their primitive direction. This pyramidical monument has a broader basis than that of any other edifice of the same kind in the old continent. I measured it carefully, and ascertained, that its perpendicular height is only fifty metres, but that each side of its basis is four hundred and thirty-nine metres in length. Torquèmada computes its height at seventy-seven metres; Betancourt, at sixty-five; and Clavigero, at sixty-one. Bernal Diaz del Castillo, a common soldier in the army of Cortez, amused himself by counting the steps of the staircases, which led to the platform of the teocallis: he found one hundred and fourteen in the great temple of Tenochtitlan, one hundred and seventeen in that of Tezcuco, and one hundred and twenty in that of Cholula. The basis of the pyramid of Cholula is twice as broad as that of Cheops; but its height is very little more than that of the pyramid of Mycerinus. On comparing the dimensions of the house of the Sun, at Teotihuacan, with those of the pyramid of Cholula, we see, that the people, who constructed these remarkable monuments, intended to give them the same height, but with bases, the length of which should be in the proportion of one to two. We find also a considerable difference in the proportions between the base and the height in these various monuments: in the three great pyramids of Geeza, the heights are to the bases as 1 to 1·7; in the pyramid of Papantla covered with hieroglyphics, this ratio is as 1 to 1·4; in the great pyramid of Teotihuacan, as 1 to 3·7; and in that of Cholula as 1 to 7·8. This last monument is built with unbaked bricks (*xamilli*), alternating with layers of clay. I have been assured by some Indians of Cholula, that the inside is hollow; and that, during the abode of Cortez in this city, their ancestors had concealed, in the body of the pyramid, a considerable number of warriors, who were to fall suddenly on the Spaniards: but the materials with which the teocalli is built, and the silence of the historians of those times, give but little probability to this assertion.

It is certain, however, that in the interior of this pyramid, as in other teocallis, there are considerable cavities, which were used as sepulchres for the natives. A particular circumstance led to this discovery. Seven or eight years ago the road from Puebla to Mexico, which before passed to the north of the pyramid, was changed. In tracing the road, the first story was cut through, so that an eighth part remained isolated like a heap of bricks. In making this opening a square house was discovered in the interior of the pyramid, built of stone, and supported by beams made of the wood of the deciduous cypress (*cupressus disticha*). The house contained two skeletons, idols in basalt, and a great number of vases, curiously varnished and painted. No pains were taken to preserve these objects, but it is said to have been carefully ascertained, that this house, covered with bricks and strata of clay, had no outlet. Supposing that the pyramid was built, not by the Toltecks, the first inhabitants of Cholula, but by prisoners made by the Cholulans from the neighbouring nations, it is possible, that they were the carcases of some unfortunate slaves, who had been shut up to perish in the interior of the teocalli. We examined the remains of this subterraneous house,

22. Baron Alexander von Humboldt (1769–1859) in his study. He was the greatest explorer and natural scientist of his era.

Drawing by Alexander von Humboldt

23. Humboldt's sketch of the pyramid of Cholula in Mexico.

and observed a particular arrangement of the bricks, tending to diminish the pressure made on the roof. The natives, being ignorant of the manner of making arches, placed very large bricks horizontally, so that the upper course should pass beyond the lower. The continuation of this kind of stepwork served in some measure as a substitute for the Gothic vault, and similar vestiges have been found in several Egyptian edifices. An adit dug through the teocalli of Cholula, to examine its internal structure, would be an interesting operation; and it is singular, that the desire of discovering hidden treasure has not prompted the undertaking. During my travels in Peru, in visiting the vast ruins of the city of Chimu, near Mansiche, I went into the interior of the famous Huaca de Toledo, the tomb of a Peruvian prince, in which Garei Gutierez de Toledo discovered, on digging a gallery, in 1576, gold amounting in value to more than five million of francs, as is proved by the book of accounts, preserved in the mayor's office at Truxillo.

The great teocalli of Cholula, called also the *Mountain of unbaked bricks* (tlalchihualtépec), had an altar on its top, dedicated to Quetzalcoatl, the god of the air. This Quetzalcoatl, whose name signifies serpent clothed with green feathers, from *coatl*, serpent, and *quetzalli*, green feathers, is the most mysterious being of the whole Mexican mythology. He was a white and bearded man, like the Bochica of the Muyscas, of whom we spoke in our descriptions of the Cataract of Tequendama. He was high priest of Tula (Tollan), legislator, chief of a religious sect, which, like the Sonyasis and the Bouddhists of Indostan, inflicted on themselves the most cruel penances. He introduced the custom of piercing the lips and the ears, and lacerating the rest of the body with the prickles of the agave leaves, or the thorns of the cactus; and of putting reeds into the wounds, in order that the blood might be seen to trickle more copiously. In a Mexican drawing in the Vatican library, I have seen a figure representing Quetzalcoatl appeasing by his penance the wrath of the gods, when, thirteen thousand and sixty years after the creation of the World (I follow the very vague chronology computed by Rios) a great famine prevailed in the province of Culan. The saint had chosen his place of retirement near Tlaxapuchicalco, on the volcano Catcitepetl (*Speaking Mountain*), where he walked barefooted on agave leaves armed with prickles. We seem to behold one of those *rishi*, hermits of the Ganges, whose pious austerity is celebrated in the Pouranas.

The reign of Quetzalcoatl was the golden age of the people of Anahuac. At that period, all animals, and even men, lived in peace; the earth brought forth, without culture, the most fruitful harvests; and the air was filled with a multitude of birds, which were admired for their song, and the beauty of their plumage. But this reign, like that of Saturn, and the happiness of the world, were not of long duration; the great spirit Tezcatlipoca, the Brahma of the nations of Anahuac, offered Quetzalcoatl a beverage, which, in rendering him immortal, inspired him with a taste for travelling; and particularly with an irresistible desire of visiting a distant country, called by tradition Tlapallan. The resemblance of this name to that of Huehuetlapallan, the country of the Toltecks, appears not to be accidental. But how can we conceive, that this white man, priest of Tula, should have taken his direction, as we shall presently find, to the south-east, towards the plains of Cholula, and thence to visit this northern country, whence his ancestors had issued in the five hundred and ninety-sixth year of our era?

Quetzalcoatl, in crossing the territory of Cholula, yielded to the intreaties of the inhabitants, who offered him the reins of government. He dwelt twenty years among them, taught them to cast metals, ordered fasts of eight days, and regulated the intercalations of the Tolteck Year. He preached peace to men, and would permit no other offerings to the Divinity, than the first fruits of the harvest. From Cholula Quetzalcoatl passed on to the mouth of the river Goasacoalco, where he disappeared, after having declared to the Cholulans (Cholotecatles) that he would return in a short time to govern them again, and renew their happiness.

It was the posterity of this saint, whom the unhappy Montezuma thought he recognised in the soldiers of Cortez. 'We know by our books,' said he, in his first interview with the Spanish General, 'that myself, and those who inhabit this country, are not natives, but strangers, who came from a great distance. We know also, that the chief, who led our ancestors hither, returned for a certain time to his primitive country, and thence came back to seek those, who were here established. He found them married to the women of this land, having a numerous posterity, and living in cities, which they had built. Our ancestors hearkened not to their ancient master, and he returned alone. We have always believed, that his descendants would one day come to take possession of this country. Since you arrive from that region, where the Sun rises, and, as you assure me, you have long known us, I cannot doubt, but that the king, who sends you, is our natural master.'

Another very remarkable tradition still exists among the Indians of Cholula, according to which the great pyramid was not originally destined to serve for the worship of Quetzalcoatl. After my return to Europe, on examining at Rome the Mexican manuscript in the Vatican library, I found, that this same tradition was already recorded in a manuscript of Pedro de Los Rios, a Dominican monk, who, in 1566, copied on the very spot all the hieroglyphical paintings he could procure. 'Before the great inundation, which took place four thousand eight hundred years after the creation of the World, the country of Anahuac was inhabited by giants (tzocuillixeque). All those who did not perish were transformed into fishes, save seven, who fled into caverns. When the waters subsided, one of these giants, Xelhua, surnamed the architect, went to Chollollan; where, as a memorial of the mountain Tlaloc, which had served for an asylum to himself and his six brethren, he built an artificial hill in form of a pyramid. He ordered bricks to be made in the province of Tlamanalco, at the foot of the Sierra of Cocotl, and to convey them to Cholula he placed a file of men, who passed them from hand to hand. The gods beheld with wrath this edifice, the top of which was to reach the clouds. Irritated at the daring attempt of Xelhua, they hurled fire on the pyramid. Numbers of the workmen perished; the work was discontinued, and the monument was afterwards dedicated to Quetzalcoatl.' . . .

This history reminds us of those ancient traditions of the East, which the Hebrews have recorded in their sacred books. The Cholulans preserved a stone, which, enveloped in a ball of fire, had fallen from the clouds on the top of the pyramid. This aerolite had the figure of a toad. Rios, to prove the high antiquity of this fable of Xelhua, observes, that it was contained in a hymn, which the Cholulans sung at their festivals, dancing round the teocalli; and that this hymn began with the words *Tulanian hulutaez*, which are words belonging to no dialect at present known in Mexico. In every part of the Globe, on the ridge of the Cordilleras, as well as in the isle of Samothrace in the Egean sea, fragments of primitive languages are preserved in religious rites.

The size of the platform of the pyramid of Cholula, on which I made a great number of astronomical observations, is four thousand two hundred square metres. From it the eye ranges over a magnificent prospect; Popocatepetl, Iztaccibuatl, the peak of Orizaba, and the Sierra de Tlascalla, famous for the tempests which gather around its summit. We view at the same time three mountains higher than Mount Blanc, two of which are still burning volcanoes. A small chapel, surrounded with cypress, and dedicated to the Virgin de los Remedios, has succeeded to the temple of the god of the air, or the Mexican Indra. An ecclesiastic of the Indian race celebrates mass every day on the top of this antique monument.

In the time of Cortez, Cholula was considered as a holy city. Nowhere existed a greater number of teocallis, of priests, and religious orders (*tlamacazque*); no spot displayed greater magnificence in the celebration of public worship, or more austerity in its penances and fasts. Since the introduction of christianity among the Indians, the symbols of a new worship have not entirely effaced the remembrance of the old. The people assemble in crowds from distant quarters at the summit of the pyramid, to celebrate the festival of the Virgin. A mysterious dread, a religious awe, fills the soul of the Indian at the sight of this immense pile of bricks, covered with shrubs and perpetual verdure.

We have above remarked the great similarity of construction between the Mexican teocallis and the temple of Bel, or Belus, at Babylon. The analogy had already struck Mr Zoega, though he had been able to procure but very incomplete descriptions of the group of the pyramids of Teotihuacan. According to Herodotus, who visited Babylon, and saw the temple of Belus, this pyramidical monument had eight stories. It was a stadium high, and the breadth of its basis was equal to its height. The outer wall which surrounded it, the περιβολος, was two stadia square. A common olympic stadium was one hundred and eighty-three metres: the Egyptian stadium was only ninety-eight. The pyramid was built of brick and asphaltum. A temple (ναος) was erected on its top, and another at its basis. The first, according to Herodotus, was without statues; it contained only a table of gold, and a bed on which reposed a female chosen by the god Belus. Diodorus Siculus, on the other hand, asserts, that the upper temple contained an altar, and three statues, to which, according to notions taken from the worship of the Greeks, he gave the names of Jupiter, Juno, and Rhea. But neither these statues nor any part of the monument existed in the time of Diodorus and Strabo. In the Mexican teocallis, as in the temple of Belus, the lower *naos* was distinguished from the temple on the platform of the pyramid. The same distinction is clearly pointed out in the letters of Cortez, and in the history of the conquest written by Bernal Diaz, who dwelt several months in the palace of the king Axajacatl, and consequently opposite the teocalli of Huitzilopochtli.

Researches Concerning the Institutions and Monuments of the Ancient Inhabitants of America, 1814

Travels in the Yucatan

JEAN DE WALDECK

JEAN FREDERIC MAXIMILIAN, COMTE DE WALDECK (*1766–1875*) *was the descendant of a noble German family who had settled in France. Like Denon, he started his career as an art student under the tuition of the painter David, and he too followed Napoleon's army to Egypt. When the army withdrew, he remained in Egypt and travelled on his own initiative up the Nile as far as Aswan. Encouraged by the success of this trip, he next organized an expedition to cross the Sahara, but it ended in disaster with the deaths of all the participators except himself. In 1821 he made his first journey to Guatemala and in the next year he went to London to help with the illustrations of a book on Palenque; there he met Lord Kingsborough, who financed several of his expeditions to central America. After Kingsborough's death, Waldeck found that he could not raise sufficient funds to publish the results of his investigations, but an appeal to Prosper Mérimée and the French Academy was finally successful and, at the age of one hundred, he was able to publish his account of Palenque. His report on his earlier journeys in Yucatan had been published in 1838 but, before the discoveries of John Lloyd Stephens roused public interest in pre-Columbian archaeology, it attracted little attention.*

Prior to my expedition, the ruins of Uxmal had been visited only by the owners of the neighbouring farm, worthy people for whom a shattered city is no more than a quarry for building materials; but these ruins, described with such poverty by Cogolludo and his successors, are the remains of a powerful city, comparable in size with our greatest European capitals. What name can we give them? Could they be part of Mani, even Itzalana perhaps? There are no historical records to shed light on this important question; but I believe there are certain reliable indications which can lead us to discover the truth.

In the first place, it is impossible that the dwellers in this city were of a minor order; if it were so, what could we make of Mani, Mayapan,

Tichualajtun and other great cities whose ruins still stand? So there existed here a vast and powerful centre, a people great enough to give rise to an immense capital. We can dismiss the theory that these ruins belong to an outpost of another ancient city near by, for their position on a high mountain plateau is sufficient indication of an isolated city. On these two points, then, there can be no argument. If, further, we remember that Itzalana is known to have been near Mani, traces of which bestrew the plain; that those latter ruins and the ones on the mountain summit are very close together; that there are no others in the vicinity; we can rest assured that the precincts I explored were indeed Itzalana. Finally, we know that the Itaexes were the cruellest of all the peoples in this region; the only teocalli in the whole of the Yucatan is in these ruins. This problem, which may not prove too weighty, has absorbed me for some time, and will no doubt be resolved when men skilled in deduction in this field follow my researches with their own, and dispel the gloom amidst which I hope to light a feeble candle.

The structures at Palenque are, with the exception of the palace, on a small scale; those at Uxmal are of colossal dimensions, and are all constructed of dressed stone. Four great principal buildings, separated by open spaces, enclose an area of 57,672 square feet. The longest side of this rectangle is 227 feet 8 inches long, the shortest 172 feet 9 inches, not counting the double gaps we see at each end of the structure, which are 20 feet long. The teocalli is built on a pyramid; its principal staircase has 100 steps, 1 foot high by 5 inches broad. This is the only known sacrificial temple in all Mexico. I should say that even this was not recognized, for the local people had nicknamed it the Tower of the Wizard, a name which bears no relation whatever to the function of a teocalli. As this monument is the highest and most singular of the five I saw, and the first I set eyes on, I followed my examination of it by naming it after my generous patron, Lord Kingsborough.

Asiatic influence can easily be discerned in the architecture of these monuments. The symbol of an elephant occurs on the rounded corners of the buildings, the trunk uplifted on the East side and lowered on the West. It is disappointing, however, that no whole figures remain; generally the legs are missing. These sculptures are life-size reliefs; their delineation is extraordinarily accurate in some places, yet poor in others. It is chiefly in the ornaments that we can admire the patience of the craftsmen employed on these buildings, and perceive the taste of these ancient peoples for monumental splendour.

The building which forms the North face of the structure and closes in the area I have described has a double gallery and measures 227 feet 8 inches long by 27 feet 8 inches wide; it contains 16 small rooms, 11 feet across and varying in depth from 22 feet to 26 feet 6 inches. I cannot tell whether this irregularity is significant, or merely the result of the builders' whim. Each room has an entrance, and we notice, on the inside, stone rings fixed at the height of the joist which forms the top of these doorways. These rings served doubtless to support the rod which held the tapestry or curtain which closed off each opening; we do not see here, as at Palenque, the stone hinges which are evidence of the firm seal which closed the doors of the edifices there. Above the doorways of these 16 rooms on the outside we see an enlarged version of the *calli* sign. There are 18 such signs, and we can guess that they were intended to mark a certain period of time which elapsed before the construction of the building. Equally, it might be that, as well as the katuns by which they marked the divisions of their era, the Mayas had another method of reckoning time, a symbolic system connected with their religious rites which is found in these calli. The age of the building is thus found to be 832 years; what is certain is that it existed a century before the conquest; since we can go back no farther, let us rest on this reliable evidence. Here, then, is an antiquity of 932 years up to the arrival of the Spaniards; moreover, since the invasion of the Yucatan took place in 1519, it follows that the Mayas were a nation, and had reached a high level of civilization, in AD 587. The plague which decimated the Toltecs did not, according to all the chronologies and dates we have collected, prolong its ravages beyond the year 1050. So we are left with a gap of 567 years between the period of Mayapan's magnificence and the plague which devastated Tula; it is therefore true to say, as I had always believed before this irrefutable proof, that it was the Mayas who passed on to the Toltecs and Aztecs their civilisation and part of their culture. Add the fact that we find not a single Aztec word in the Yucatec language – an impossibility if the Mayas were the last comers. The Mayas could be descended from the Palenqueans, and the lawgiver of Tula, Quetzalcoatl, could have been a grandson of Zamna, or descended from those who formed this leader's entourage when he came to civilize the Yucatan.

The ruins of Itzalana have one important difference from those of Palenque. Although the single or double galleries of Itzalana end pyramid fashion, we see no openings linking one gallery to another; nor are there any giving access from the interior to the outside. At

Palenque, by contrast, we find numerous high windows in the shape of the Greek *tau* (T) which served to admit air and light to the chambers. The only apertures in the rooms of the Uxmal buildings are a mere 6 inches deep, and are set opposite one another; from this arrangement it is clear that they were intended to support cross-beams from which hammocks were slung; so these rooms were bed-chambers. The absence of windows indicates, as I have said above, that the doorways were closed only by curtains; otherwise, in these completely sealed rooms, the heat would have been intolerable. The doors of the buildings at Palenque were wooden and turned on stone hinges, necessitating vents to the interior, and it was by means of the *tau* openings that light and air reached the galleries. These *tau* shapes were the symbol of the Lingam cult, in so far as it played a part in the religion of Palenque, where Buddhism seems, for the rest, to have been extremely pure.

The glyphs of Itzalana which are indisputably connected with those of the Toltecs and Aztecs are: *cohuatl*, *calli*, *miquiztli*, *atl* and *quiahuitl*, which can be identified with a *cipactli*. A representation of Tonatiuh in a mask is repeated seven times on the facade of one most remarkable edifice. These are the only signs in the ruins which show any kinship with those of Mexico; the rest are totally different; nor did I find there so much as one hieroglyph like those on the Toltec remains at Xochicalco.

The dress of the Itzalana statues is closer to the Palenquean style than to any other. The headdress worn by one sacrificer . . . occurs in a bas-relief at Ototiun; likewise with the same personage's cape. This correspondence points to a Palenquean tradition, an assumption which is supported by the close similarity of the Palenquean and Maya methods of building.

Between the construction of Maya buildings and Mexican – the sole example of which is Xochicalco – there is an important difference. The Toltecs first raised the main structure of their building, and carved the ornaments afterwards *in situ*. The Mayas followed the reverse procedure. If they wished to cover a façade with ornaments or symbolic figures, they began by painting the whole wall in the chosen colour; this background was almost always red, as with the structures at Palenque. This first task completed, they stuck on the painted wall the stone marquetry which would provide the decoration, colour-washing it with somewhat more care than the background. Blue was used here, for we can still see traces of this colour in the grooved lines of the squares which frame a type of small turned cross. Red and blue are the only colours I could distinguish on the sacrificial temple at Itzalana. However, yellow and white must also have been used, for these two tints are still visible on other buildings. . . . We notice that even tiny stones are shaped with enormous care, and the whole is an assemblage as perfectly fitted as a joiner's.

The boxes or coffers which adorn the façades of the buildings at Itzalana must draw the attention of artists and scholars. No one who makes a close examination of the cubes which compose this attractive decoration can doubt that the authors of this astonishing piece of cutting thoroughly understood the principles of geometry. I have measured every line, slid the lead over every join, and I have never found the slightest deviation beneath the cord. The native inhabitants of the country continually affirm that the Indians of old were barbarians. This ludicrous assertion, fostered by the Spaniards, who had a motive for spreading the belief that there had been nothing here before their arrival but misery and gloom, this assertion, I say, is proof that we need not hesitate to turn upon the modern people of the Yucatan their own reproach of barbarism. If they do not know how to appreciate the splendour and beauty of the ruins which bestrew their country's soil, it is because they themselves sleep in the profoundest ignorance. This truth needs no further demonstration.

Voyage Pittoresque et Archéologique dans la Province d'Yucatan et aux Ruines d'Itzalane, 1838

Translated from the French by V. M. Conrad

The purchase of a city

JOHN LLOYD STEPHENS

JOHN LLOYD STEPHENS (*1805–1852*) *was born in Shrewsbury, New Jersey, and studied law, but his greatest interest was always the study of archaeology. He travelled extensively in the eastern Mediterranean area, and there he met Mr Frederick Catherwood, who had been attached to the unsuccessful Robert Hay expedition in Egypt. On his return to the United States he began to study the existing documents relating to the great Central American civilizations, which convinced him that surviving remains of extensive cities must await discovery in the jungles. His appointment to a diplomatic mission in the area gave him the opportunity he needed, and he secured the cooperation of Mr Catherwood to draw anything he might find and set off in search of ruins. His search was dramatically rewarded, and his account of his journey is lively and humorous as well as informative.*

All day I had been brooding over the title-deeds of Don Jose Maria, and, drawing my blanket around me, suggested to Mr Catherwood 'an operation'. (Hide your heads, ye speculators in up-town lots!) To buy Copan! remove the monuments of a by-gone people from the desolate region in which they were buried, set them up in the 'great commercial emporium', and found an institution to be the nucleus of a great national museum of American antiquities! But query, could the 'idols' be removed? They were on the banks of a river that emptied into the same ocean by which the docks of New-York are washed, but there were rapids below; and, in answer to my inquiry, Don Miguel said these were impassable. Nevertheless, I should have been unworthy of having passed through the times 'that tried men's souls' if I had not had an alternative; and this was to exhibit by sample: to cut one up and remove it in pieces, and make casts of the others. The casts of the Parthenon are regarded as precious memorials in the British Museum, and casts of Copan would be the same in New-York. Other ruins might be discovered even more interesting and more accessible. Very soon their existence would become known and their value appreciated, and the friends of science and the arts in Europe would get possession of them. They belonged of right to us, and, though we did not know how soon we might be kicked out ourselves, I resolved that ours they should be; with visions of glory and indistinct fancies of receiving the thanks of the corporation flitting before my eyes, I drew my blanket around me, and fell asleep.

At daylight the clouds still hung over the forest; as the sun rose they cleared away; our workmen made their appearance, and at nine o'clock we left the hut. The branches of the trees were dripping wet, and the ground very muddy. Trudging once more over the district which contained the principal monuments, we were startled by the immensity of the work before us, and very soon we concluded that to explore the whole extent would be impossible. Our guides knew only of this district; but having seen columns beyond the village, a league distant, we had reason to believe that others were strewed in different directions, completely buried in the woods, and entirely unknown. The woods were so dense that it was almost hopeless to think of penetrating them. The only way to make a thorough exploration would be to cut down the whole forest and burn the trees. This was incompatible with our immediate purposes, might be considered taking liberties, and could only be done in the dry season. After deliberation, we resolved first to obtain drawings of the sculptured columns. Even in this there was great difficulty. The designs were very complicated, and so different from anything Mr Catherwood had ever seen before as to be perfectly unintelligible. The cutting was in very high relief, and required a strong body of light to bring up the figures; and the foliage was so thick, and the shade so deep, that drawing was impossible.

After much consultation, we selected one of the 'idols' and determined to cut down the trees around it, and thus lay it open to the rays of the sun. Here again was difficulty. There was no axe; and the only instrument which the Indians possessed was the machete, or chopping-knife, which varies in form in different sections of the country; wielded with one hand, it was useful in clearing away shrubs and branches, but almost harmless upon large trees; and the Indians, as in the days when the Spaniards discovered them, applied to work without ardour, carried it on with little activity, and, like children, were easily diverted from it. One hacked into a tree, and, when tired, which happened very soon, sat down to rest, and another relieved him. While one worked there were always several looking on. I remembered the ring of the woodman's axe in the forests at home, and wished for a few long-sided Green Mountain boys. But we had been buffeted into patience, and watched the Indians while they hacked with their machetes, and even wondered that they succeeded so well. At length the trees were felled and dragged aside, a space cleared around the base, Mr C.'s frame set up, and he set to work. I took two Mestitzoes, Bruno and Francisco, and, offering them a reward for every new discovery, with a compass in my hand set out on a tour of exploration. Neither had seen 'the idols' until the morning of our first visit, when they followed in our train to laugh at los Ingleses; but very soon they exhibited such an interest that I hired them. Bruno attracted my attention by his admiration, as I supposed, of my person; but I found it was of my coat, which was a long shooting-frock, with many pockets; and he said that he could make one just like it except the skirts. He was a tailor by profession, and in the intervals of a great job upon a roundabout jacket, worked with his machete. But he had an inborn taste for the arts. As we passed through the woods, nothing escaped his eye, and he was professionally curious touching the costumes of the sculptured figures. I was struck with the first development of their antiquarian taste. Francisco found the feet and legs of a statue, and Bruno a part of the body to match, and the effect was electric upon both. They searched and raked up the ground with their machetes till they found the shoulders, and set it up entire except the head; and they were both eager for the possession of instruments with which to dig and find this remaining fragment.

It is impossible to describe the interest with which I explored these ruins. The ground was entirely new; there were no guide-books or guides; the whole was a virgin soil. We could not see ten yards before us, and never knew what we should stumble upon next. At one time we stopped to cut away branches and vines which concealed the face of a monument, and then to dig around to bring to light a fragment, a sculptured corner of which protruded from the earth. I leaned over with breathless anxiety while the Indian worked, and an eye, an ear, a foot, or a hand was disentombed; and when the machete rang against the chiselled stone, I pushed the Indians away, and cleared out the loose earth with my hands. The beauty of the sculpture, the solemn stillness of the woods, disturbed only by the scrambling of monkeys and the chattering of parrots, the desolation of the city, and the mystery that hung over it, all created an interest higher, if possible, than I had ever felt among the ruins of the Old World. After several hours' absence I returned to Mr Catherwood, and reported upward of fifty objects to be copied.

Courtesy, Trustees of the British Museum

24. Frederick Catherwood's engraving of a fallen Maya stele at Copan in Honduras. Nothing was known to the civilized world of the vanished Maya culture. Catherwood's drawings in 1844 were the first pictures of its relics seen in the Western world.

Courtesy, American Museum of Natural History, New York

25. Stucco head of a Mayan noble found in the crypt underneath the Temple of Inscriptions at Palenque, Mexico.

I found him not so well pleased as I expected with my report. He was standing with his feet in the mud, and was drawing with his gloves on, to protect his hands from the moschetoes. As we feared, the designs were so intricate and complicated, the subjects so entirely new and unintelligible, that he had great difficulty in drawing. He had made several attempts, both with the camera lucida and without, but failed to satisfy himself or even me, who was less severe in criticism. The 'idol' seemed to defy his art; two monkeys on a tree on one side appeared to be laughing at him, and I felt discouraged and despondent. In fact, I made up my mind, with a pang of regret, that we must abandon the idea of carrying away any materials for antiquarian speculation, and must be content with having seen them ourselves. Of that satisfaction nothing could deprive us. We returned to the hut with out interest undiminished, but sadly out of heart as to the result of our labours.

Our luggage had not been able to cross the river, but the blue bag which had caused me so many troubles was recovered. I had offered a dollar reward, and Bartolo, the heir-apparent of lesseeship of our hut, had passed the day in the river, and found it entangled in a bush upon the bank. His naked body seemed glad of its accidental washing, and the bag, which we supposed to contain some of Mr C.'s drawing materials, being shaken, gave out a pair of old boots, which, however, were at that time worth their weight in gold, being waterproof, and cheered Mr Catherwood's drooping spirits, who was ill with a prospective attack of fever and ague or rheumatism, from standing all day in the mud. Our men went home, and Frederico had orders, before coming to work in the morning, to go to Don Gregorio's and buy bread, milk, candles, lard, and a few yards of beef. The door of the hut looked toward the west, and the sun set over the dark forest in front with a gorgeousness I have never seen surpassed. Again, during the night, we had rain, with thunder and lightning, but not so violent as the night before, and in the morning it was again clear.

That day Mr Catherwood was much more successful in his drawings; indeed, at the beginning the light fell exactly as he wished, and he mastered the difficulty. His preparations, too, were much more comfortable, as he had his water-proofs, and stood on a piece of oiled canvass, used for covering luggage on the road. I passed the morning in selecting another monument, clearing away the trees, and preparing it for him to copy. . . . Mr Catherwood went to the ruins to continue his drawings, and I to the village, taking Augustin with me to fire the

Balize guns, and buy up eatables for a little more than they were worth. My first visit was to Don Jose Maria. After clearing up our character, I broached the subject of a purchase of the ruins; told him that, on account of my public business, I could not remain as long as I desired, but wished to return with spades, pick-axes, ladders, crowbars, and men, build a hut to live in, and make a thorough exploration; that I could not incur the expense at the risk of being refused permission to do so; and, in short, in plain English, asked him: What will you take for the ruins? I think he was not more surprised than if I had asked to buy his poor old wife, our rheumatic patient, to practise medicine upon. He seemed to doubt which of us was out of his senses. The property was so utterly worthless that my wanting to buy it seemed very suspicious. On examining the paper, I found that he did not own the fee, but held it under a lease from Don Bernardo de Aguila, of which three years were unexpired. The tract consisted of about six thousand acres, for which he paid eighty dollars a year; he was at a loss what to do, but told me that he would reflect upon it, consult his wife, and give me an answer at the hut the next day. I then visited the alcalde, but he was too tipsy to be susceptible of any impression; prescribed for several patients; and instead of going to Don Gregorio's, sent him a polite request by Don Jose Maria to mind his own business and let us alone; returned, and passed the rest of the day among the ruins. It rained during the night, but again cleared off in the morning, and we were on the ground early. My business was to go around with workmen to clear away trees and bushes, dig, and excavate, and prepare monuments for Mr Catherwood to copy. While so engaged, I was called off by a visit from Don Jose Maria, who was still undecided what to do; and not wishing to appear too anxious, told him to take more time, and come again the next morning.

The next morning he came, and his condition was truly pitiable. He was anxious to convert unproductive property into money, but afraid, and said that I was a stranger, and it might bring him into difficulty with the government. I again went into proof of character, and engaged to save him harmless with the government or release him. Don Miguel read my letters of recommendation, and re-read the letter of General Cascara. He was convinced, but these papers did not give him a right to sell me his land; the shade of suspicion still lingered; for a finale, I opened my trunk, and put on a diplomatic coat, with a profusion of large eagle buttons. I had on a Panama hat, soaked with rain and spotted with mud, a check shirt, white pantaloons, yellow up to the knees with mud, and was about as outré as the negro king who received a company of British officers on the coast of Africa in a cocked hat and military coat, without any inexpressibles; but Don Jose Maria could not withstand the buttons on my coat; the cloth was the finest he had ever seen; and Don Miguel, and his wife, and Bartalo realised fully that they had in their hut an illustrious incognito. The only question was who should find paper on which to draw the contract. I did not stand upon trifles, and gave Don Miguel some paper, who took our mutual instructions, and appointed the next day for the execution of the deed.

The reader is perhaps curious to know how old cities sell in Central America. Like other articles of trade, they are regulated by the quantity in market, and the demand; but, not being staple articles, like cotton and indigo, they were held at fancy prices, and at that time were dull of sale. I paid fifty dollars for Copan. There was never any difficulty about price. I offered that sum, for which Don Jose Maria thought me only a fool; if I had offered more, he would probably have considered me something worse.

Incidents of Travel in Central America, 1842

The palace at Palenque

JOHN LLOYD STEPHENS

In the mean time work went on. As at Copan, it was my business to prepare the different objects for Mr Catherwood to draw. Many of the stones had to be scrubbed and cleaned; and as it was our object to have the utmost possible accuracy in the drawings, in many places scaffolds were to be erected on which to set up the camera lucida. Pawling relieved me from a great part of this labour. That the reader may know the character of the objects we had to interest us, I proceed to give a description of the building in which we lived, called the palace.

A front view of this building is given in the engraving. It does not, however, purport to be given with the same accuracy as the other drawings, the front being in a more ruined condition. It stands on an artificial elevation of an oblong form, forty feet high, three hundred and ten feet in front and rear, and two hundred and sixty feet on each side. This elevation was formerly faced with stone, which has been thrown down by the growth of trees, and its form is hardly distinguishable.

The building stands with its face to the east, and measures two hundred and twenty-eight feet front by one hundred and eighty feet deep. Its height is not more than twenty-five feet, and all around it had a broad projecting cornice of stone. The front contained fourteen doorways, about nine feet wide each, and the intervening piers are between six and seven feet wide. On the left (approaching the palace) eight of the piers have fallen down, as has also the corner on the right, and the terrace underneath is cumbered with the ruins. But six piers remain entire, and the rest of the front is open.

The building was constructed of stone, with a mortar of lime and sand, and the whole front was covered with stucco and painted. The piers were ornamented with spirited figures in bas-relief, one of which is represented in the engraving opposite. On the top are three hieroglyphics sunk in the stucco. It is enclosed by a richly-ornamented border, about ten feet high and six wide, of which only a part now remains. The principal personage stands in an upright position and in profile, exhibiting an extraordinary facial angle of about forty-five degrees. The upper part of the head seems to have been compressed and lengthened, perhaps by the same process employed upon the heads of the Choctaw and Flathead Indians of our own country. The head represents a different species from any now existing in that region of country; and supposing the statues to be images of living personages, or the creations of artists according to their ideas of perfect figures, they indicate a race of people now lost and unknown. The headdress is evidently a plume of feathers. Over the shoulders is a short covering decorated with studs, and a breastplate; part of the ornament of the girdle is broken; the tunic is probably a leopard's skin; and the whole dress no doubt exhibits the costume of this unknown people. He holds in his hand a staff or sceptre, and opposite his hands are the marks of three hieroglyphics, which have decayed or been broken off. At his feet are two naked figures seated cross-legged, and apparently suppliants. A fertile imagination might find many explanations for these strange figures, but no satisfactory interpretation presents itself to my mind. The hieroglyphics doubtless tell its history. The stucco is of admirable consistency, and hard as stone. It was painted, and in different places about it we discovered the remains of red, blue, yellow, black, and white.

The piers which are still standing contained other figures of the same general character, but which, unfortunately, are more mutilated, and from the declivity of the terrace it was difficult to set up the camera lucida in such a position as to draw them. The piers which are fallen were no doubt enriched with the same ornaments. Each one had some specific meaning, and the whole probably presented some allegory or history; and when entire and painted, the effect in ascending the terrace must have been imposing and beautiful.

The principal doorway is not distinguished by its size or by any superior ornament, but is only indicated by a range of broad stone steps leading up to it on the terrace. The doorways have no doors, nor are there the remains of any. Within, on each side, are three niches in the wall, about eight or ten inches square, with a cylindrical stone about two inches in diameter fixed upright, by which perhaps a door was secured. Along the cornice outside, projecting about a foot beyond the front, holes were drilled at intervals through the stone; and our impression was, that an immense cotton cloth, running the whole length of the building, perhaps painted in a style corresponding with the ornaments, was attached to this cornice, and raised and lowered like a curtain, according to the exigencies of sun and rain. Such a curtain is used now in front of the piazzas of some haciendas in Yucatan.

The tops of the doorways were all broken. They had evidently been square, and over every one were large niches in the wall on each side, in which the lintels had been laid. These lintels had all fallen, and the stones above formed broken natural arches. Underneath were heaps of rubbish, but there were no remains of lintels. If they had been single slabs of stone, some of them must have been visible and prominent; and we made up our minds that these lintels were of *wood*. We had no authority for this. It is not suggested either by Del Rio or Captain Dupaix, and perhaps we should not have ventured the conclusion but for the wooden lintel which we had seen over the doorway at Ocosingo; and by what we saw afterward in Yucatan, we were confirmed, beyond all doubt, in our opinion. I do not conceive, however, that this gives any conclusive data in regard to the age of the buildings. The wood, if such as we saw in the other places, would be very lasting; its decay must have been extremely slow, and centuries may have elapsed since it perished altogether.

The building has two parallel corridors running lengthwise on all four of its sides. In front these corridors are about nine feet wide, and extend the whole length of the building upward of two hundred feet. In the long wall that divides them there is but one door, which is opposite the principal door of entrance, and has a corresponding one on the other side, leading to a courtyard in the rear. The floors are of cement, as hard as the best seen in the remains of Roman baths and cisterns. The walls are about ten feet high, plastered, and on each side of the principal entrance ornamented with medallions, of which the borders only remain; these perhaps contained the busts of the royal family. The separating-wall had apertures of about a foot, probably intended for purposes of ventilation. Some were of this form ✢, and some of this T, which have been called the Greek Cross and the Egyptian Tau, and made the subject of much learned speculation.

The ceiling of each corridor was in this form ⏢. The builders were evidently ignorant of the principles of the arch, and the support was made by stones lapping over as they rose, as at Ocosingo, and among the Cyclopean remains in Greece and Italy. Along the top was a layer of flat stone, and the sides, being plastered, presented a flat surface.

The long, unbroken corridors in front of the palace were probably intended for lords and gentlemen in waiting; or perhaps, in that beautiful position, which, before the forest grew up, must have commanded an extended view of a cultivated and inhabited plain, the king himself sat in it to receive the reports of his officers and to administer justice. Under our dominion Juan occupied the front corridor as a kitchen, and the other was our sleeping apartment.

From the centre door of this corridor a range of stone steps thirty feet long leads to a rectangular courtyard, eighty feet long by seventy broad. On each side of the steps are grim and gigantic figures, carved on stone in basso-relievo, nine or ten feet high, and in a position slightly inclined backward from the end of the steps to the floor of the corridor. The engraving opposite represents this side of the courtyard, and the one next following shows the figures alone, on a larger scale. They are adorned with rich headdresses and necklaces, but their attitude is that of pain and trouble. The design and anatomical proportions of the figures are faulty, but there is a force of expression about them which shows the skill and conceptive power of the artist. When we first took possession of the palace this courtyard was encumbered with trees, so that we could hardly see across it, and it was so filled up with rubbish that we were obliged to make excavations of several feet before these figures could be drawn.

On each side of the courtyard the palace was divided into apartments, probably for sleeping. On the right the piers have all fallen down. On the left they are still standing, and ornamented with stucco figures. In the centre apartment, in one of the holes before referred to of the arch, are the remains of a wooden pole about a foot long, which once stretched across, but the rest had decayed. It was the only piece of wood we found at Palenque, and we did not discover this until some time after we had made up our minds in regard to the wooden lintels over the doors. It was much worm-eaten, and probably, in a few years, not a vestige of it will be left.

At the farther side of the courtyard was another flight of stone steps, corresponding with those in front, on each side of which are carved figures, and on the flat surface between are single cartouches of hieroglyphics. . . .

The whole courtyard was overgrown with trees, and it was encumbered with ruins several feet high, so that the exact architectural arrangements could not be seen. Having our beds in the corridor adjoining, when we woke in the morning, and when we had finished the work of the day, we had it under our eyes. Every time we descended the steps the grim and mysterious figures stared us in the face, and it became to us one of the most interesting parts of the ruins. We were exceedingly anxious to make excavations, clear out the mass of rubbish, and lay the whole platform bare; but this was impossible. It is probably paved with stone or cement; and from the profusion of ornament in other parts, there is reason to believe that many curious and interesting specimens may be brought to light. This agreeable work is left for the future traveller, who may go there better provided with men and materials, and with more knowledge of what he has to encounter; and, in my opinion, if he finds nothing new, the mere spectacle of the courtyard entire will repay him for the labour and expense of clearing it.

The part of the building which forms the rear of the courtyard, communicating with it by the steps, consists of two corridors, the same as the front, paved, plastered, and ornamented with stucco. The floor of the corridor fronting the courtyard sounded hollow, and a breach had been made in it which seemed to lead into a subterraneous chamber; but in descending, by means of a tree with notches cut in it, and with a candle, we found merely a hollow in the earth, not bounded by any wall.

In the farther corridor the wall was in some places broken, and had several separate coats of plaster and paint. In one place we counted six layers, each of which had the remains of colour. In another place there seemed a line of written characters in black ink. We made an effort to get at them; but, in endeavouring to remove a thin upper stratum, they came off with it, and we desisted.

This corridor opened upon a second courtyard, eighty feet long and but thirty across. The floor of the corridor was ten feet above that of the courtyard, and on the wall underneath were square stones with hieroglyphics sculptured upon them. On the piers were stuccoed figures, but in a ruined condition.

On the other side of the courtyard were two ranges of corridors, which terminated the building in this direction. The first of them is divided into three apartments, with doors opening from the extremities upon the western corridor. All the piers are standing except that on the northwest corner. All are covered with stucco ornaments, and one with hieroglyphics. The rest contain figures in bas-relief.

The first was enclosed by a border, very wide at the bottom, part of which is destroyed. The subject consists of two figures with facial angles similar to that in the plate before given, plumes of feathers and other decorations for headdresses, necklaces, girdles, and sandals; each has hold of the same curious baton, part of which is destroyed, and opposite their hands are hieroglyphics, which probably give the history of these incomprehensible personages. The others are more ruined, and no attempt has been made to restore them. One is kneeling as if to receive an honour, and the other a blow.

So far the arrangements of the palace are simple and easily understood; but on the left are several distinct and independent buildings, as will be seen by the plan, the particulars of which, however, I do not consider it necessary to describe. The principal of these is the tower, on the south side of the second court. This tower is conspicuous by its height and proportions, but on examination in detail it is found unsatisfactory and uninteresting. The base is thirty feet square, and it has three stories. Entering over a heap of rubbish at the base, we found within another tower, distinct from the outer one, and a stone staircase, so narrow that a large man could not ascend it. The staircase terminates against a dead stone ceiling, closing all farther passage, the last step being only six or eight inches from it. For what purpose a staircase was carried up to such a bootless termination we could not conjecture. The whole tower was a substantial stone structure, and in its arrangements and purposes about as incomprehensible as the sculptured tablets.

Left of the tower is another building with two corridors, one richly decorated with pictures in stucco, and having in the centre the elliptical tablet represented in the engraving opposite. It is four feet long and three wide, of hard stone set in the wall, and the sculpture is in bas-relief. Around it are the remains of a rich stucco border. The principal figure sits cross-legged on a couch ornamented with two leopards' heads; the attitude is easy, the physiognomy the same as that of the other personages, and the expression calm and benevolent. The figure wears around its neck a necklace of pearls, to which is suspended a small medallion containing a face; perhaps intended as an image of the sun. Like every other subject of sculpture we had seen in the country, the personage had earrings, bracelets on the wrists, and a girdle round the loins. The headdress differs from most of the others at Palenque in that it wants the plumes of feathers. Near the head are three hieroglyphics.

The other figure, which seems that of a woman, is sitting cross-legged on the ground, richly dressed, and apparently in the act of making an offering. In this supposed offering is seen a plume of feathers, in which the headdress of the principal person is deficient. Over the head of the sitting personage are four hieroglyphics. This is the only piece of sculptured stone about the palace except those in the courtyard. Under it formerly stood a table, of which the impression against the wall is still visible, and which is given in the engraving in faint lines, after the model of other tables still existing in other places.

At the extremity of this corridor there is an aperture in the pavement, leading by a flight of steps to a platform; from this a door, with an ornament in stucco over it, opens by another flight of steps upon a narrow, dark passage, terminating in other corridors, which run transversely. These are called subterraneous apartments; but there are windows opening from them above the ground, and, in fact, they are merely a ground-floor below the pavement of the corridors. In most parts, however, they are so dark that it is necessary to visit them with candles. There are no bas-reliefs or stucco ornaments; and the only objects which our guide pointed out or which attracted our attention, were several stone tables, one crossing and blocking up the corridor, about eight feet long, four wide and three high. One of these lower corridors had a door opening upon the back part of the terrace, and we generally passed through it with a candle to get to the other buildings. In two other places there were flights of steps leading to corridors above. Probably these were sleeping apartments.

In that part of the plan marked Room No. 1, the walls were more richly decorated with stucco ornaments than any other in the palace; but, unfortunately, they were much mutilated. On each side of the doorway was a stucco figure, one of which, being the most perfect, is given in the engraving opposite. Near it is an apartment in which is marked 'small altar'. It was richly ornamented, like those which will be hereafter referred to in other buildings; and from the appearance of the back wall we supposed there had been stone tablets. In our utter ignorance of the habits of the people who had formerly occupied this building, it was impossible to form any conjecture for what uses these different apartments were intended; but if we are right in calling it a palace, the name which the Indians give it, it seems probable that the part surrounding the courtyards was for public and state occasions, and that the rest was occupied as the place of residence of the royal family; this room with the small altar, we may suppose, was what would be called, in our own times, a royal chapel.

With these helps and the aid of the plan, the reader will be able to find his way through the ruined palace of Palenque; he will form some idea of the profusion of its ornaments, of their unique and striking character, and of their mournful effect, shrouded by trees; and perhaps with him, as with us, fancy will present it as it was before the hand of ruin had swept over it, perfect in its amplitude and rich decorations, and occupied by the strange people whose portraits and figures now adorn its walls.

Incidents of Travel in Central America, 1842

The elephant in America?

GRAFTON ELLIOT SMITH

SIR GRAFTON ELLIOT SMITH (*1871–1937*) *was born in Grafton, New South Wales, and studied medicine at the University of Sydney. In 1894 he began his research career in anatomy, specializing in the structure of the human brain, and in 1896 he came to England to continue his studies at Cambridge. In 1900 he accepted the post of Professor of Anatomy in the Government Medical School at Cairo, and during his stay in Egypt he developed an interest in the possibilities of applying his work to the study of archaeology and anthropology. He joined with a team of archaeologists in a survey of 20,000 Nubian burials and made extensive contributions to the science of palaeopathology. Throughout his further career as Professor of Anatomy at Manchester University and University College, London, he continued to preserve a lively interest in all aspects of magic and religion, early emigrations and diffusions of culture, and propounded a theory about the possible Egyptian origin of the Central American civilization which has many supporters today.*

The discussion of representations of the elephant has played an exceptionally prominent part in the interpretation of man's achievements in the past, so that the identification of conventionalised elephants has become one of the deciding issues in the great problem of the reconstruction of the early history of civilisation.

In his *History of New France*, published in 1744, Father Charlevoix gave an account of a tradition, that still survives among the North-American Indians, of a great elk, concerning which the late Sir Edward Tylor made the comment: 'It is hard to imagine that anything but the actual sight of a live elephant would have given rise to this tradition.' In 1813 Baron von Humboldt described the picture . . . of a creature with the head of an elephant, human hands, the feet of a bird, and, as Professor Seler pointed out some years ago, the wings of a bat, concerning which Humboldt made the following remarks: 'The disguise of the sacrificing priests presents some remarkable and apparently not accidental resemblances with the Hindoo Ganesa (the elephant-headed god of wisdom)'. One seems to recognise in the sacrificer's mask the trunk of an elephant. The snout of the tapir no doubt protrudes a little more than that of our pigs, but it is a long way from the tapir's snout to the trunk figured in the 'Codex Borgianus'.

During the intervening period there has been considerable controversy concerning these and many other pictures and sculptures. For instance, there is a picture in the 'Codex Cortes' . . . representing a human figure with an elephant's head. The identity of this elephant-headed god is obvious, because he carries thunderbolts, and is associated with a serpent coiled round so as to retain the water that should fall as rain. In other words, it is a child-like representation of an episode in the *Rig-veda*, in which the god Indra, who is associated with an elephant and with thunder, has a combat with the serpent Vritra, who is described in the Indian epic as holding up the water in precisely the same way as the Maya artist depicts the episode.

In another Maya Codex . . . the elephant-headed god is represented pouring out the rain from a vase, and putting his foot upon the head of the serpent so as to prevent the rain from reaching the earth. This again is another incident in the mythology of India, and one might collect scores of other pictures from these early American manuscripts which might serve as a child's guide to the *Rig-veda*. If it be objected that the *Rig-veda* was written perhaps twenty centuries before the American artist drew these pictures, it is important not to forget that the ancient Indian stories were still current in Java, Cambodia, and elsewhere in the neighbourhood of the south-east corner of Asia, at the time when the American artist on the opposite side of the Pacific was drawing his illustrations of the story.

During the last century there has been a great amount of controversy concerning certain architectural embellishments of the corners of Mayan buildings in Central America, which have been compared – and rightly compared – with similar adornments of Asiatic buildings, particularly those of Indo-China and Java, and have been claimed to represent the trunks of elephants. Anyone who studies the Asiatic evidence, however, will realise that these adornments do not usually represent elephants' trunks at all, but highly specialised and diverse forms of the makara, the Indian capricorn.

The upper end of a stela at Copan (eighth century AD) in Central American is shown in the photograph . . . of Dr Maudslay's drawing. The peculiar headdress of the central figure presents features distinctive of Java and Indo-China. Both in the ancient sculptures of Boro-budur, in Java, and in the Cambodian temples, a headdress such as is shown here is worn, as it still is by the Emperor of Annam. The most distinctive feature of this particular stela is the upper left-hand corner, which seems to be a conventionalised picture of an Indian elephant with a rider bending forwards on it, and also wearing an Indian turban. The mode of conventionalising the ear is found also in Asia, from India to Java; and the peculiar method of conventionalising the tusk and the under-surface of the trunk by two areas with cross-hatching, introduces exactly the methods employed by the Eastern Asiatic artists – in particular, those of China – at a time corresponding to that in which these American sculptures were made. These and many other representations of the elephant have been discussed for more than a century, but several new bits of information have come to light recently, which, as it seems to me, settle the question definitely once for all.

The elephant-like forms at the upper corners of Mayan buildings in Central America have been the subject of controversy for more than eighty years (see my book, *Elephants and Ethnologists*, 1924), but new evidence has just come to light to settle the matter once for all.

Mr J. Eric Thompson has just discovered in the Ayer Collection of the Newberry Library in Chicago the hitherto unpublished water-colour sketches (of which photographic copies are reproduced on page 85) made about ninety years ago by M. Frédéric de Waldeck, a French artist who has been described (by the historian Bancroft) as 'the most indefatigable and successful explorer of Palenque'. No one is likely to doubt the accuracy of the representation of the elephant's head, either in the profile views or in the front view with the mouth widely opened in the 'bun-catching' attitude. The lozenge-shaped form of the open mouth, the cut stumps of the tusks, and the markings of the under-surface of the trunk are all quite distinctive of the elephant.

Waldeck writes that the four strips (bas-reliefs in stucco) were found by himself on the floor of a subterranean room in the Palace at Palenque (of which Dr Alfred P. Maudslay, in *Biologica Centrali-Americana*, has given full information with exceptionally beautiful photographs and plans), and the photographs reproduced on page 85 were made from his water-colour sketches. The other photograph reproduces Waldeck's drawing (the shaded parts are restorations) of part of the wall in the same room.

My colleague, Professor Collie, has called my attention to the fact that the very un-Maya-like floral pattern intertwining both the elephants' heads (and their anthropomorphised derivatives on the second slab) suggest well-known Chinese motives of the T'ang period, which points to the eighth or ninth century AD – a date that seems to be appropriate for the Maya building in which the slabs were found. The third slab is of special interest because it represents a conventionalised tapir – the form of the ear, mouth, and snout being characteristic.

The design upon the wall is peculiarly interesting. The elephant's head is set upon the entwined snake, as so often happens in the Maya codices. But the Maya sculptor, unwittingly anticipating the controversies that were to develop ten centuries after him, has placed as heraldic supporters of the elephant two of the rival claimants put by modern ethnologists, the macaw on the right, and on the left a highly conventionalised tapir (compare the stucco slab) borne upon a bird's body. Here, then, is decisive evidence that ought to settle the elephant controversy once for all.

Other representations of elephants have been brought to light in San Salvador and Panama. In 1916 Dr Thomas Gann found in a mound at Yallock in Guatemala a cylindrical vase (now in the Bristol Museum) with polychrome paintings of two elephants, shown in the correct colour. . . . The form of the head, body, and legs does not admit of any doubt as to their identity as elephants; and the peculiarities of the lower jaw and teeth can be explained by studying the mode of conventionalising elephants in Java and elsewhere in the Eastern Asiatic area. During the centuries when the Indian Gupta phase dominated artistic expression in Indo-China and Indonesia, China also came under the sway of its influence. It is not a mere chance that Chinese art attained the zenith of its accomplishment during the T'ang period (AD 602-907). The influence of India left its mark upon Chinese Buddhistic art, and probably also upon that of the Nara period in Japan. But the great wave of culture that flowed over Eastern Asia and the Malay Archipelago in the eighth century swept out into Oceania also, and was carried to Central America. The Palenque bas-reliefs represent the elephant in association with floral designs suggestive of the T'ang period because they belong to that period and were expressions of the same inspiration.

The Elephant Controversy Settled by a Decisive Discovery
Illustrated London News, 15 January, 1927

The temple pyramid of Tepoxtlan

EDUARD SELER

EDUARD SELER (1859–1922) was born in Germany and planned to become a schoolmaster. A serious illness obliged him to seek a more sedentary occupation, so he turned to work as a translator. A book on pre-Columbian America aroused his interest in the subject, and he obtained an appointment in the Americanist department of the Berlin Ethnological Museum. By this time his health had substantially improved and in 1887 he left on an expedition to Central America. He made great contributions to the study of Maya and Aztec writings and expounded the complicated Aztec calendar system in addition to his field-work on the monuments of the area.

The causeway leading from the City of Mexico, which runs southward, formerly through the waters of the salt lake itself, now through meadow land, to Churubusco, the ancient Uitzilopochco, where the road branches off to Chalco, and to the margin of the great lava stream, which extends from a little volcano below the lofty Cerro de Ajusco to the plain lying 2,300 meters above the sea. A traveller leaving the city by this road sees before him a high mountain range, which connects the towering Ajusco with the snow-capped cone of Popocatepetl and in this direction forms the termination of the undrained basin of Mexico. This mountain range is crossed from Xochimilco by a long, gradually ascending path, which finally leads into extensive pine forests covering the whole breadth of the ridge. Another road, from Chalco, runs in the valley of Amecameca, immediately at the western base of Popocatepetl, to a less elevated path. In both places the mountain slopes on the south quite precipitously to the valleys below, the streams of which flow into the Rio de las Balsas. These are the valleys of Cuernavaca, situated about 1,600 meters above the sea, and of Yautepec, lying about 500 meters lower. They have been celebrated from ancient times for their mild climate. Here the Mexican kings had their pleasure gardens, in which they cultivated plants of the tierra caliente that did not thrive in Mexico itself. Cortes did not fail to include this district within the limits of his marquesado, and the viceroys, and also the unfortunate Maximilian, loved to sojourn in this favoured vale. Midway between Yautepec and Cuernavaca, directly at the foot of the lofty mountain range towering on the north, on a riblike spur at the upper end of a range of hills and ridges which divides the valleys of Yautepec and Cuernavaca, in the centre of a small plain forming the extreme northwestern extremity of the valley of Cuernavaca, lies the small town of Tepoxtlan. Although but three miles distant from each of the cities previously named, this place, because it is situated quite away from the great highroads radiating from the capital and at the foot of the mountain, has remained until very recently little known or investigated. The ancient inhabitants, who undoubtedly were of the same race as the Tlalhuies of Cuernavaca, have in the main shared the history of the latter. Cuernavaca, the ancient Quauhnauac, was the first territory which fell into the hands of the Mexicans when they began to spread beyond the limits of the valley. In the reign of the third Mexican king, Itzcouatl, who reigned in the second quarter of the fifteenth century, the siege and subjugation of Cuernavaca is reported, and under Motecuhzoma Ilhuicamina, the king succeeding Itzcouatl, Tepoxtlan is named in the Mendoza codex, together with Quauhnauac, Uaxtepec, and Yautepec, among the conquered cities. The Historia Mexicana of the year 1576 (Aubin-Goupil codex) reports in connection with the accession to the throne in the year 1487 of King Ahuitzotl, which was celebrated with great sacrifices of captives, that new kings had been installed in Quauhnauac, Tepoxtlan, Uaxtepec, and Xiloxochitepec.

In the tribute list (Mendoza codex, page 26, no. 13) Tepoxtlan, the 'place of the axe', is again put with the same towns in the Uaxtepec group. Cortes came into contact with Tepoxtlan in the year 1521 on his march from Yautepec to Cuernavaca, when, because the inhabitants did not voluntarily surrender, he burned the town. Bernal Diaz extols the fine women (*muy buenas mugeres*) and the booty which the soldiers obtained here. After the establishment of Spanish rule Tepoxtlan, with Cuernavaca, was included in the principality, which, with the title Marques del Valle de Oxaca, was awarded Cortes as recompense for his distinguished services. A manuscript Relacion of the year 1582, which is preserved with others of like character in the Archivo General de las Indias in Sevilla, refers to the place as Villa de Tepoxtlan, and mentions six estancias subordinate to it. In the same Relacion it is also stated that the Mexican language was spoken by the inhabitants, both by those who still lived in the place and those who, having become disgusted with the country, had emigrated to the neighbourhood of Vera Cruz. Through incorporation into the marquesado the town was doubtless saved from oppression and vexation by lesser encomenderos. In their isolated mountain home the people have been able to preserve their language and their old customs. The place has now a population numbering from 5,000 to 6,000 souls of fairly pure Indian descent, who speak pure, uncorrupted Mexican, are proud of their descent, and cling tenaciously to the ancient traditional customs. It is deserving of mention as an interesting fact that since last year a newspaper has been published here with the title El Grano de Arena, which, besides the Spanish text, always contains several columns of matter in the Mexican language.

As we passed through the town of Cuernavaca in December, 1887, on the return from our expedition to Xochicalco we were told that there was a pyramid in Tepoxtlan as interesting as that of Xochicalco. We wished to visit it, but the governor of the state of Morelos told us at that time – whether correctly I leave undecided – that he could not permit it, for 'these Indians are terrible'. As we had still so much else to see we did not insist upon it. Beyond this general report nothing has been known until very recently of the pyramid of Tepoxtlan, but two years ago, when the extraordinary session of the Americanist Congress was about to be held in Mexico and an effort was being made throughout the whole country to furnish something fresh in the nature of relics and finds for the scholars attending this meeting, the thought arose even in Tepoxtlan of freeing the pyramid of that locality from the rubbish hiding it from view and of opening up its interior chambers and outer walls. A young engineer, Francisco Rodriguez, a native of Tepoxtlan, followed out this idea with enthusiasm and strove to carry it into execution. He was able to induce the people of his district to furnish volunteer labour, and thus in the months of August and September, 1895, the pyramid was uncovered, a result of which the Tepoxtecs themselves are now quite proud. A description of the pyramid, including a plan of the structure, was submitted by Mr Rodriguez to the congress assembled in October of the year 1895. It has now been published in the proceedings of the congress. Later, accompanied by Mr Rodriguez, Mr Marshall II Saville visited the pyramid and took several photographs of it. In August, 1896, Mr Saville read a report on this pyramid before the American Association for the Advancement of Sciences, convened in Buffalo, which was published in volume 8 of the bulletins of the American Museum of Natural History, and again later in the journal Monumental Records. From this and from Mr Rodriguez's report I gathered the information which appears below:

The pyramid is situated about 2,000 feet above the town, on a cliff detached from the ridge of the mountain range, which north of the town rises rugged and precipitous above the level plain. The pyramid itself is not visible from the plain, but its approximate location is marked by huge crags which on the left project above the mountain ridge. From the foot of the precipice the road ascends through a small canyon. Several long flights of steps are encountered, some of them cut into the rock, others built of masonry. Carved inscriptions are to be seen here and there on the perpendicular walls of the ravine. About halfway to the top the road emerges from the canyon and winds aloft on the very face of the cliff. For nearly 100 steps, according to Saville's statement, the ascent is almost perpendicular. Steps are hewn into the rock or supported by masonry. When Rodriguez began his excavations here he was obliged to use ladders in two places, because the way was obstructed by fallen rock fragments. When the top of the cliff is finally reached it is seen to consist of two separate plateaux which are connected by a narrow neck. On the western one of these two plateaux is the temple pyramid; the eastern one is almost completely covered with foundation walls of buildings of different kinds and sizes, which probably were the dwellings of priests, and other buildings adjoining. Behind rises a rocky cliff covered with pine woods, which can only be reached from this spot, and here Mr Rodriguez found running water.

Viewed from the east side, the pyramid is seen to rise in three terraces over a rough substructure that forms a horizontal base on the uneven, rocky ground. . . . A flight of steps on this side leads up to the top of the first terrace, which, rising to a height of 9·5 meters above the rock foundation, forms the broad base of the building proper, formed by the two other terraces. A second stairway on the south side near the entrance of the temple leads to the top of the lower terrace. . . . On the west side, which is the front of the temple, this first terrace forms a small platform . . ., and in the centre of this there is a low rectangular bench, with serrated corners, up which flights of steps probably led on all four sides. The location of this little structure corresponds to the spot where, in the great temple of Mexico, stood the two round stones, the quauhxicalli and the temalacatl, and it was probably used for similar sacrificial purposes. I also found a very similar structure in Quiengola in the middle line of the platform of the east pyramid, whose front likewise faced the west. From this platform a stairway leads to the top of the second terrace and to the entrance of the temple itself, which the third terrace forms. This temple is formed of walls 1·9 meters thick, constructed of blocks of red and black tezontle (porous volcanic rock) with copious mortar of lime and sand, and reaching to a height of 2·5 meters. The roof has fallen in. From the ruins Mr Rodriguez was still able to determine that it had been a flat arch, with a maximum rise of 0·5 meter, a span of 5 meters, and a thickness of 0·7 meter, formed of pieces of tezontle and a great quantity of mortar, the use of which in thick layers made the construction possible. On the site of the front wall are to be seen the remains of two rectangular masonry columns, which left a wide central doorway with a narrow one on each side. The interior space is divided by a wall, 0·9 meter thick, pierced by a doorway, into two rooms, of which the front one runs back 3·73 and the inner one 5·2 meters, with a width of 6 meters. In the middle of the front room Rodriguez found a rectangular depression, and in it remains of charcoal and a couple of well-preserved pieces of copal. This was probably, therefore, the hearth where the sacred fire burned and whence, perhaps, glowing coals were obtained with which to burn incense to the god.

In the axis of the inner chamber against the rear wall stood the idol. The doorway connecting the two rooms has a width of 1·9 meters. It is flanked by two pillars, which are covered with stucco and richly ornamented. At the bottom there is a sort of fluting; above this a grecque in relief, like those in the palaces at Mitla, and at the top a picture of the sun, only the lower part of which is still preserved. All are painted in colour, and the colours are still tolerably fresh. In the place where the idol stood, in the rear room, Rodriguez found remains of a sub-structure among which were two sculptured fragments, one of them, according to his account, containing a bas-relief, of what character is not stated, painted in a deep red colour; the other, the relief picture of a Mexican royal crown (xiuh-uitzolli). Both pieces are now preserved in the cabildo of Tepoxtlan, in a room transformed into a museum. The most interesting feature of the inner apartment are the benches, ornamented on the front with carved stones. These run round a part of the front room and along the rear and both lateral walls of the back room. They display at the upper part a narrow, somewhat projecting frieze, on which, it seems, the twenty characters for the days are represented. Beneath this, on each lateral wall, there are placed four large slabs, with symbols in relief, apparently relating to the four cardinal points. On the south side we see what seem to be the four prehistoric ages; on the north side the gods corresponding to the four cardinal points are represented by their symbols. I must forgo attempting to explain these more exactly until casts or good photographs are submitted for study. The reliefs on the rear wall are, perhaps, of a still more interesting nature, but unfortunately here a portion of the bench is destroyed. It is to be hoped that Mr Saville, who has now started again for Tepoxtlan and Xochicalco, will bring home satisfactory casts and make known these representations.

Finally, in addition to the above, two stone tablets, which were found built into the south wall of the lower terrace of the pyramid, are of special importance. One contains the hieroglyph of King Ahuitzotl, who derived his name from a small ghostlike water animal, which, according to Mexican tales, played the rôle of a sort of nixy and was represented in this form. On the other slab a rabbit is depicted, and beside it are 10 circles, which would indicate the year 10 Tochtli, corresponding to the year 1502 of the Christian chronology, the last year of Ahuitzotl's reign, or the year of his death. Saville has interpreted these two tablets quite correctly, and he concludes that the year of the erection of the temple and its builder were thus immortalised. This is probably correct, in which case, in truth, 'the ancient temple of Tepoxtlan would be the only aboriginal structure still standing in Mexico to which we can with probability assign a certain date'.

It would next be desirable to know to which god sacrifices were offered in this place. Neither Rodriguez nor Saville have attempted to answer this question. I am fortunately in a position to be able to decide this matter beyond dispute. There was a class of deities among the Mexicans which excited the special wonderment and abhorrence of the monks and the Spaniards generally. These were the pulque gods, or the gods of drunkenness. As we say (in German) of a drunken man that 'he has got an ape', so the Mexicans, of course, with a doubtless wholly different train of thought, spoke of a rabbit (tochtli), under whose influence the intoxicated person acted. They said he had 'rabbited himself' (omotochtili), when anyone drank to insensibility and in this condition came to any harm. Hence the gods of drunkenness were also called Totochtin, 'rabbits'. The day ome Tochtli, '2 rabbits', was under their influence. Whoever was born on that day, if he did not take special precautions, seemed inevitably doomed to become a drunkard. Since there were different kinds of drunkenness, intoxication manifesting itself with different people in very different ways, the

'400 rabbits' (centzon totochtin) were spoken of 'as though one intended to say that pulque made innumerable kinds of drunkards'. Hence the pulque gods were also designated as centzon Totochtin, the '400 rabbits', and a large number of them were specified by particular names. Concerning the significance of these deities, this one fact is of primary importance, that they are all closely related to the earth goddess. Like her, they wear the golden Huaxtec nose ornament, shaped like a crescent, which was called yacametztli. This ornament is so characteristic of them that it is usually marked on all objects dedicated to the pulque gods. A second characteristic of these deities is the bi-coloured face, painted red and black. The two colours, in many parallel red and black longitudinal stripes, likewise served to denote an object as consecrated to the pulque gods. Thus, in the picture manuscript of the Biblioteca Nazionale in Florence, the *manta de dos conejos*, 'blanket of the 2 rabbits' (ome-tochtilmàtli), the shoulder covering of the pulque gods, and, in the same manuscript, the shield of Macuil-Xochitl, are marked in this way. These gods are characterised by a remark which occurs above them in the picture manuscript of the Biblioteca Nazionale in Florence still more exactly than by their relation to the earth goddess. The pulque gods in this manuscript are represented after or among the *fiestas móbiles*, immediately after the feast of flowers (chicome xochitl and ce xochitl), and it is stated in this place that 'when the Indians had harvested and gathered in their maize, then they drank to intoxication and danced while they invoked this demon and others of these four hundred'. It seems, therefore, that here we have to do with gods of husbandry, who were to impart virtue to the soil as the pulque – and this is always brought out – imparts courage and strength and was the drink of the fearless and strong, the eagles and jaguars (quauhtli and ocelotl), that is, the warriors.

Among the names by which these gods were known, in addition to ome Tochtli, '2 rabbits', which refers directly to their nature as pulque gods, we meet almost exclusively such as are derived from place names, or at least are formed in a similar manner to those derived from place names as Acolhua, Colhuatzincatl, Toltecatl, Totoltecatl, Izquitecatl, Chimalpanecatl, Yauhtecatl, Tezcatzoncatl, Tlaltecayoua, Pahtecatl, Papaztac, Tlilhua: and a pulque god Tepoxtecatl, a god of Tepoxtlan, is repeatedly and prominently mentioned.

If the fact is taken into consideration that the temple which I have described above is still called by the people 'casa del Tepoxteco', then the supposition is not far to seek that it is our Tepoxtlan from which the pulque god Tepoxtecatl derived his name, and this supposition is confirmed by two good witnesses. In the Relacion that I already mentioned at the beginning, which was the reply to an inquiry blank, dispatched under King Philip II with the same wording to all towns of the Spanish colonial territory, the question concerning the name of this place and the meaning of the name is answered thus: 'They say that the place is named Tepoxtlan because, when their ancestors settled this land, they found this name already in use, for those who settled there before (or first) said that the great devil, or idol, which they had, was called Ome tuchitl, that is, '2 rabbits', and that he bore the surname Tepoxtecatl'. The other testimony is furnished by the often-mentioned picture manuscript of the Biblioteca Nazionale in Florence, which, besides various other pulque gods, represents Tepoxtecatl in full figure and in hieroglyph and remarks concerning him: 'This is the representation of a great iniquity which was the custom in a village named Tepoxtlan; namely, when an Indian died in a state of intoxication the others of this village made a great feast to him, holding in their hands copper axes which were used to fell wood. This village is near Yautepeque. They are vassals of the Lord Marques del Valle'. . . .

It is to be hoped that the interest once aroused among the patriotic inhabitants of Tepoxtlan will continue, and that further investigation will produce other important material for the study of the ancient civilisation and history of these regions.

The Temple Pyramid of Tepoxtlan,

Bulletin of the Bureau of American Ethnology, No. 28, 1904

A royal tomb at Palenque

ALBERTO RUZ

ALBERTO RUZ (*1906–*) *was educated at the Universidad Nacional in Cuba, then at the School of Anthropology and History in Mexico, and has devoted many years to his researches in archaeology and anthropology at the Universidad Autonoma of Mexico and in Paris. He has held progressively important posts in the National Institute of Anthropology and History of Mexico, and was finally appointed Director. In this capacity he has conducted many valuable investigations into the history of Central America, with particular emphasis on the civilization of the ancient Maya.*

When in the spring of 1949 the National Institute of Anthropology and History of Mexico appointed me Director of Research at Palenque, I fully appreciated that this was the most important event in my professional life.

I knew that my predecessors had been explorers, artists, scientists, distinguished men, and that marvellous sculpture had been discovered there during the course of 150 years; but I was convinced that many other archaeological treasures still lay hidden in the rubble of the palaces, temples, and pyramids, and beneath the dense and mysterious Chiapas jungle which had been their jealous guardian.

A feature of my working plan was one which should always be present in the plans of archaeologists working in Mexico and Central America; to seek for architectural structures of an earlier date and lying beneath the actually visible building. It has, in fact, been proved that the ancient inhabitants of Central America were in the habit of building on top of older constructions, more with the object of increasing their height and bringing them closer to the heavens in which the gods lived than for any practical purpose.

For various reasons I decided to make such a search in the Temple of the Inscriptions. First, because it was the tallest building in Palenque and therefore the most likely to have been built on top of something older; secondly, because of its importance and its containing some fine, large, sculptured panels and one of the largest Mayan hieroglyphic inscriptions; and thirdly, because it had never been explored and its flooring was more or less intact – owing to its being made of great slabs instead of the more usual simple levelled plaster.

This temple is composed of a portico leading to a sanctuary and two lateral cells; and in the central room of the temple one of the slabs of the flooring caught my eye, as it had done with my predecessors on the site. This slab has round its edges two rows of holes provided with stone plugs. After thinking for some hours on its possible purpose, I came to the conclusion that the answer would be found underneath the stone; and accordingly I began to clear the floor beside it, in a place where the slabs had been already removed or broken by treasure-seekers, who had been discouraged from going on by meeting with a heavy filling of large stones.

Quite soon after beginning to remove the rubble I noticed that the temple's walls were prolonged under the floor instead of stopping at its level – a sure sign that there was 'something' to be found underneath. Elated by this prospect, I began excavating and on the next day – May 20, 1949 – there appeared that stone which in Mayan buildings is always used to close up a vault. The Mayans did not build a true arch, their vaulting being simply the result of bringing walls closer together by means of inclined facings which converge until there remains only a very small space to be closed with a single flat stone. A few days later I found a step, and then more and more steps. What had been found was an interior staircase descending into the pyramid and which for a reason which we then did not know, had been made impracticable by a filling of large stones and clay.

Four spells of work – each two-and-a-half months long – were needed before we were able to clear the filling from this mysterious staircase. After a flight of 45 steps, we reached a landing with a U-turn. There followed another flight, of 21 steps, leading to a corridor, whose level is more or less the same as that on which the pyramid was built – i.e., some 22 metres under the temple flooring. In the vaulting of the landing two narrow galleries open out and allow air and a little light to enter from a near-by courtyard.

Above one of the first steps we reached we found a box-shaped construction of masonry containing a modest offering: two ear-plugs of jade placed on a river stone painted red. On reaching the end of the flight we found another box of offerings, backing on to a wall which blocked the passage. This time it was a richer offering: three pottery dishes, two shells full of cinnabar, seven jade beads, a pair of circular ear-plugs also of jade, the plugs of which were shaped like a flower, and a beautiful tear-shaped pearl, with its *lustre* pretty well preserved. An offering of this kind, at such a depth, told us without any doubt that we were approaching the object of our search.

And, in fact, on July 13, 1952, after demolishing a solid obstruction some metres thick, made of stone and lime – this was very hard and the wet lime burnt the hands of the workmen – there appeared on one side of the corridor a triangular slab, 2 metres high, set vertically to block an entrance. At the foot of this slab, in a rudimentary stone cist, there lay, mixed together, the largely destroyed skeletons of six young persons, of whom one at least was a female.

At noon on the 15th of the same month we opened the entrance, displacing the stone enough for a man to pass through sideways. It was a moment of indescribable emotion for me when I slipped behind the stone and found myself in an enormous crypt which seemed to have been cut out of the rock – or rather, out of the ice, thanks to the curtain of stalactites and the chalcite veiling deposited on the walls by the infiltration of rain-water during the centuries. This increased the marvellous quality of the spectacle and gave it a fairy-tale aspect. Great figures of priests modelled in stucco a little larger than life-size formed an impressive procession round the walls. The high vaulting was reinforced by great stone transoms, of dark colour with yellowish veins, giving an impression of polished wood.

Almost the whole crypt was occupied by a colossal monument, which we then supposed to be a ceremonial altar, composed of a stone of more than 8 square metres, resting on an enormous monolith of 6 cubic metres, supported in its turn by six great blocks of chiselled stone. All these elements carried beautiful reliefs.

Finest of all for its unsurpassable execution and perfect state of preservation was the great stone covering the whole and bearing on its four sides some hieroglyphic inscriptions with thirteen abbreviated dates corresponding to the beginning of the seventh century AD, while its upper face shows a symbolic scene surrounded by astronomical signs.

I believed that I had found a ceremonial crypt, but I did not wish to make any definite assertions before I had finished exploring the chamber and, above all, before I had found out whether the base of the supposed altar was solid or not. On account of the rains and the exhausting of the funds available for this phase of the exploration, we had to wait until November before returning to Palenque. I then had the base bored horizontally at two of the corners; and it was not long before one of the drills reached a hollow space. I introduced a wire through the narrow aperture and, on withdrawing it, I saw that some particles of red paint were adhering to it.

The presence of this colouring matter inside the monolith was of supreme importance. The offerings found at the beginning and the end of the secret staircase had borne red paint; and the sides of the great stone showed traces of having been painted red all over. This colour was associated in the Mayan and Aztec cosmogony with the East, but also it is nearly always found in tombs, on the walls or on objects accompanying the dead person or on his bones. The presence of red in tombs came, therefore, to indicate resurrection and a hope of immortality. The particles of cinnabar adhering to the wire inserted into the centre of the enormous stone block was therefore unquestionable evidence of burial: and our supposed ceremonial altar must therefore be an extraordinary sepulchre.

To prove this it was necessary to lift the sculptured stone, which measured 3·80 metres by 2·20 metres (some 13 by 7 ft.), weighing about 5 tons and constituting one of the most valuable masterpieces of American pre-Hispanic sculpture. The preparations lasted two days in the midst of feverish tension. It was necessary to fell in the forest a hard-wood tree of the kind called in that region 'bari', and to cut it into sections of different lengths, lift these along a greasy path to the lorry, convey them by motor to the pyramid, move them by manpower to the temple, lower them by cables through the interior staircase and introduce them through the narrow aperture of the crypt.

The four major sections of the trunk were placed vertically under the corners of the stone and on top of each was placed a railway or motor-car jack. On November 27, at dusk, after a twelve-hour working day, the soul-shaking manœuvre took place. Every kind of precaution was taken to prevent the stone tipping up or slipping, and, above all, to prevent its suffering any damage. Handled simultaneously and without any jerking, the jacks lifted the stone millimetre by millimetre, and while this was happening slabs were placed underneath it to hold it up. When the jacks reached the limit of their extension, other sections of the tree were inserted and the operation was repeated. A little before midnight the stone was resting intact 0·60 metre above its original level on six robust logs of 'bari' and a few days later it was lifted to a height of 1·12 metres.

Once the stone left its seating and began to rise it could be seen that a cavity had been cut out of the enormous block which served it as a base. This cavity was of an unexpected shape, oblong and curvilinear, rather like the silhouette in schematised form of a fish or of the capital letter Omega (Ω), closed in its lower part. The cavity was sealed by a highly polished slab fitting exactly and provided with four perforations, each with a stone plug. On raising the slab which closed it we discovered the mortuary receptacle.

This was not the first time during my career as an archaeologist that a tomb had been discovered, but no occasion has been so impressive as this. In the vermilion-coloured walls and base of the cavity which served as a coffin, the sight of the human remains – complete, although the bones were damaged – covered with jade jewels for the most part, was most impressive. It was possible to judge the form of the body which had been laid in this 'tailored' sarcophagus; and the jewels added a certain amount of life, both from the sparkle of the jade and because they were so well 'placed' and because their form suggested the volume and contour of the flesh which originally covered the skeleton. It was easy also to imagine the high rank of the personage who could aspire to a mausoleum of such impressive richness.

We were struck by his stature, greater than that of the average Mayan of today; and by the fact that his teeth were not filed or provided with incrustations of pyrites or jade, since that practice (like that of artificially deforming the cranium) was usual in individuals of the higher social ranks. The state of destruction of the skull did not allow us to establish precisely whether or not it had been deformed. In the end, we decided that the personage might have been of non-Mayan origin, though it is clear that he ended in being one of the kings of Palenque. The reliefs, which we have still to uncover on the sides of the sarcophagus and which are now hidden under lateral buttresses, may tell us before long something of the personality and identity of their glorious dead.

Even if he had not been buried in the most extraordinary tomb so far discovered in this continent of America, it would still be perfectly possible to assess the importance of this personage from the jewels which he wore – many of them already familiar in Mayan bas-reliefs. As shown in some reliefs, he was wearing a diadem made from tiny disks of jade and his hair was divided into separate strands by means of small jade tubes of appropriate shape; and we discovered a small jade plate of extraordinary quality cut in the shape of the head of a Zotz, the vampire god of the underworld and this may have been a final part of the diadem. Around the neck were visible various threads of a collar composed of jade beads in many forms – spheres, cylinders, tri-lobed beads, floral buds, open flowers, pumpkins, melons, and a snake's head. The ear-plugs were composed of various elements, which together made up a curious flower. From a square jade plate with engraved petals, a tube, also of jade, projected and this ended in a flower-shaped bead; while on the back of the square plate (which carries a hieroglyphic inscription) a circular plug was fitted. All these elements would be united by a thread and it would seem that there hung as a counterpoise to them, behind the broad part of the ear, a marvellous artificial pearl, formed by uniting two perfectly cut pieces of mother-o'-pearl, polished and adjusted to give the impression of a pearl of fabulous size (36 mm). Over the breast lay a pectoral formed of nine concentric rings of twenty-one tubular beads in each. Round each wrist was a bracelet of 200 jade beads, and on each finger of both hands a great ring of jade. We found these still fixed on the phalanges, and one of the rings was carved in the form of a crouching man, with a delicate head of perfect Mayan profile. In the right hand he held a great jade bead of cubical form, and in the left, another, but this one spherical, the two being perhaps symbols of his rank or magical elements for his journey to another world. Near his feet we found another two great jade beads, one of them hollow and provided with two plugs in the shape of flowers. A jade idol of precious workmanship stood near the left foot and is probably a representation of the sun god. Another little figure of the same material must have been sewn above the breech-clout. From the mouth cavity we extracted a beautiful dark jade bead, which, according to the funeral rites of the Mayans, was placed there so that the dead person should have the means to obtain sustenance in the life beyond the tomb. At the moment of burial, the personage wore over his face a magnificent mask made of jade mosaic, the eyes being of shell, with each iris of obsidian, with the pupil marked in black behind. Of the hundreds of fragments, some remained on the face, adhering to the teeth and the forehead, but the greater part were lying on the left side of the head, clearly as the result of the mask's slipping off during the burial. The corpse must have been set in the sarcophagus entirely wrapped in a shroud painted red, and the same cinnabar colour adhered to the bones, the jewels and the bottom of the sarcophagus when the cloth and the flesh decomposed. The mask was fitted directly on the dead man's face, the fragments being stuck in a thin coating of stucco, the remains of which fitted to the human face. Nevertheless, the mask had to be prepared beforehand and may perhaps have been kept on a stucco head. It is perfectly possible that its main traits, realistic as they are, represent more or less those of the actual dead man. After the burial the sarcophagus was closed with its lid and covered with the enormous sculptured stone. Some jewels were thrown upon this – a collar with slate pendants and what was probably a ritual mask made of jade mosaic – and there were placed underneath the coffin various clay vessels, perhaps containing food and drink, and two wonderful human heads modelled in stucco, which had been broken from complete statues. At the closing of the crypt six young persons, perhaps sons and daughters of important persons at Court, were sacrificed to act as companions and servants of the dead man in the other world. In the best preserved of their skulls could be noted the cranial deformation and the mutilation of the teeth which were customary in the nobility alone. A serpent modelled in lime plaster seems to rise straight out of the sarcophagus and ascend the steps which lead to the threshold of the room. Here it is transformed into a tube, running as far as the flooring of the corridor and after this, it leads on to the temple, in the form of an echeloned moulding, hollow and superimposed on the steps. This amounts to a magical union, a conduit for the spirit of the dead man to ascend to the temple in order that the priests might continue to be in contact with his deified being and able to explain his mandates. Our search for an older building under the Temple of the Inscriptions could therefore not lead to the expected result, but in exchange, it revealed a tomb whose discovery leads to considerable modification of certain established concepts concerning the function of the American pyramid. It was formerly thought that this was solely a solid base for supporting a temple, unlike the Egyptian pyramids, which are vast mausoleums. Palenque's 'Royal Tomb', as it is now popularly called, with a certain intuitive propriety, perhaps – brings us a great deal closer to the Egyptian concept once we grant that the pyramid which hid it, although supporting a temple, was also constructed to serve as a grandiose funeral monument. The monumental quality of this crypt, built by thousands of hands to challenge the centuries and enriched with magnificent reliefs; the sumptuousness of the tomb itself, a colossal monument weighing 20 tons and covered all over with bas-reliefs of stupendous quality; the rich jade finery of the buried personage; all this expensive toil and this magnificence suggest to us the existence in Palenque of a theocratic system similar to that of Egypt, in which the all-powerful priest-king was considered during life or after death to be a real god. This Palencan Royal tomb also leads us to suppose that the attitude towards death of the Mayan *halach uinic* was very close to that of the pharaohs. The stone which covers the tomb appears to confirm this obsession and synthesises in its reliefs some essentials of the Mayan religion. The presence here, in a sepulchral slab, of motives which are repeated in other representations, gives perhaps the key to interpret the famous panels of the Cross and the foliated Cross (in Palenque) and also some of the paintings in the codices. On the stone in question we see a man surrounded by astronomical signs symbolising heaven – the spatial limit of man's earth, and the home of the gods, in which the unchanging course of the stars marks the implacable rhythm of time. Man rests on the earth, represented by a grotesque head with funereal traits, since the earth is a monster devouring all that lives; and if the reclining man seems to be falling backwards, it is because it is his inherent destiny to fall to the earth, the land of the dead. But above the man rises the well-known cruciform motif, which in some representations is a tree, in others the stylised maize plant, but is always the symbol of life resurgent from the earth, life triumphing over death.

Illustrated London News, 29 August 1953

Machu Picchu, the sacred city

HIRAM BINGHAM

HIRAM BINGHAM (*1875–1956*) *was born in Honolulu and educated at the Universities of Yale, California and Harvard. He also held the degree of Litt.D. from the University of Cuzco in Peru and had a distinguished political career in addition to his academic achievements. Shortly after graduating, he joined an expedition to South America, and since 1906 he made five trips devoted to exploration and research. His work brought to light much information about the splendid civilization of the Incas, and perhaps his most spectacular success was the discovery, during the campaign of 1911, of a magnificent stone-built Inca city in the mountain region of Machu Picchu.*

The ruins of what we now believe was the lost city of Vilcapampa the Old, perched on top of a narrow ridge lying below the peak of Machu Picchu, are called the ruins of Machu Picchu because when we found them no one knew what else to call them. And that name has been accepted and will continue to be used even though no one now disputes that this was the site of ancient Vilcapampa.

The sanctuary was lost for centuries because this ridge is in the most inaccessible corner of the most inaccessible section of the central Andes. No part of the highlands of Peru is better defended by natural bulwarks – a stupendous canyon whose rock is granite, and whose precipices are frequently 1,000 feet sheer, presenting difficulties which daunt the most ambitious modern mountain climbers. Yet, here, in a remote part of the canyon, on this narrow ridge flanked by tremendous precipices, a highly civilized people, artistic, inventive, well organized, and capable of sustained endeavour, at some time in the distant past built themselves a sanctuary for the worship of the sun.

Since they had no iron or steel tools – only stone hammers and little bronze crowbars – its construction must have cost generations, if not centuries, of effort. To prevent their enemies or undesirable visitors from reaching their shrines and temples, they relied, first, on the rapids of the Urubamba, which are dangerous even in the dry season and absolutely impassable during at least half of the year. On three sides this was their outer line of defence. On the fourth side the massif of Machu Picchu is accessible from the plateau only by a narrow razor-like ridge less than 40 feet across and flanked by precipices, where they constructed a strong little fort – a veritable Thermopylae. No one could reach the sacred precincts unless the Inca so decreed, as Friar Marcos and Friar Diego found to their cost.

While the lower slopes of Huayna Picchu are relatively easy of access in the dry season, the mass of Huayna Picchu is separated from the ruins by another razor-like ridge impassable on the east side and having only a footpath for sure-footed Indians on the west side. This trail passes for more than a hundred yards along a horizontal cleft in an overhanging precipice of sheer granite. Two men could defend it against an army and it is the only route by which Machu Picchu may be reached from Huayna Picchu.

So much for the northern approach. The east and west side of the ridge are sufficiently precipitous for fifteen hundred feet to be well-nigh unassailable. Rocks could easily have been rolled down upon invaders in the manner referred to by the conquistadors as a favourite method of Inca soldiers. If a path was maintained on each side, as is the case today, these paths, in turn, could easily have been defended by a handful of men. Wherever breaks in the precipices would give a foot-hold to intruders they were walled up and the natural defence strengthened.

On the southern side rise the precipitous cliffs of Machu Picchu Mountain. In ancient times they were flanked by two Inca roads. The road on the west side of the peak ran along another horizontal cleft or fault in the very face of a magnificent precipice. Traces can still be seen but rock slides have destroyed it. On the opposite side of the mountain the Inca road climbed the abrupt declivity by means of a stone stairway and circumvented the mountains by a trail which only goats could have followed with ease. Both of these roads led to the little ridge on which was the aforementioned Thermopylae, and which alone gave access to Machu Picchu Mountain from the plateau and the southern rim of the canyon. Both of them could have been readily defended in various places.

In accordance with their well-known practice, we found on top of both neighbouring peaks on Machu Picchu and Huayna Picchu the ruins of Inca signal stations, from which it was possible for messages to be sent and received across the mountains. The arrival of unwelcome visitors or even the distant approach of an enemy could have been seen and instantly communicated to the city. That on top of Machu Picchu was necessarily the more important. No pains were spared to make it safe and convenient. Its construction required great skill and extraordinary courage. It is located on top of one of the most stupendous precipices in the Andes. If any of the workmen who built the retaining wall on the very edge of the signal station slipped he must have fallen 3,000 feet before striking any portion of the cliff broad enough to stop his body. I do not mind admitting that when I took pictures from it I not only lay flat on my stomach, I had two trusty Indians hang on to my legs. It really was a dizzy height. But imagine building a wall on it!

The Sanctuary of Vilcapampa was regarded as so sacred that in addition to the outer defences and the reinforced precipices which protected the city against enemies, two walls were built to keep out visitors or workmen who had been allowed to pass the mountain Thermopylae. On the south side of the city are an outer wall and an inner wall. The outer runs along the ends of a magnificent tier of agricultural terraces. Near by are half a dozen buildings which may have been intended as barracks for the soldiers whose duty it was to protect the city on the only side where it could be reached by the ancient roads, and was comparatively vulnerable. There was still an inner line of defence. At the narrowest part of the ridge, just before one reaches the city from the south, a fosse, or dry moat, was dug, its sides faced with stone. Above it the wall of the city proper extends across the top of the ridge and down each side until it reaches precipitous cliffs which make the wall no longer necessary.

On the very top of the ridge the wall was pierced by a large gateway built of massive stone blocks. The gate itself, probably a screen of heavy logs lashed together, could be fastened at the top to a large ring-stone or eye-bonder firmly embedded above the lintel and underneath 6 or 8 feet of masonry. At the sides, the door could be fastened by a large cross-bar whose ends were tied to powerful stone barholds, stone cylinders, firmly anchored in holes left in the doorposts for that purpose. Such a door might, of course, have been smashed in by an attacking force using a large log as a battering ram. To avoid the likelihood of this the engineer who constructed the fortifications brought forward a salient from the wall at right angles to the doorway. By this means the defenders standing on top of the salient could have rained down a lateral fire of rocks and boulders on the force attempting to batter down the gate.

The walls of the city were too high to be scaled with ease. In fact, an attacking force which had been so fortunate as to overcome all the natural defences of this powerful stronghold and had circumvented the defenders of the several Thermopylae-like passes would have found themselves in a very bad situation when rushing along the terraces towards the inner fortifications. At the end of the terraces they would have found it necessary to jump down into the dry moat and scale its farther side as well as the city wall, all the time subjected to a shower of stones from the slings of the defenders. It is difficult to imagine that any attacking force could possibly have been large enough to overcome a vigorous defence even if the city were held by only a few score determined soldiers. Of course the walls served equally well in peace time to keep intruders from entering the sacred precincts of the sanctuary. In the *accla-huasi*, or houses of the Chosen Women of the Sun, no men were permitted to enter except the Emperor, his sons, the Inca nobles, and the priests.

The city gate shows evidences of being repaired. The top of the narrow ridge is at this point occupied by a large granite boulder which was worked into the fortifications, or, rather, the walls were strengthened by its being used as a member. As a result, the outer gatepost of the massive entrance rests on an artificial terrace. This terrace has settled a few inches, owing to erosion in the steep hillside. Consequently the wall has been thrown out of the perpendicular and has started to destroy the fine old gateway. It will not be long before the great lintel will fall and carry with it the repaired part of the wall which is superimposed above it. One clearly gets the feeling, in looking at the entrance to the citadel, that it was rather hastily repaired at a period long subsequent to its original construction, probably by Manco II.

Space was limited and the houses were crowded closely together, but an extensive system of narrow streets and rock-hewn stairways made inter-communication within the walls of the city comparatively easy. In fact, perhaps the most conspicuous feature of Machu Picchu is the quantity of the stairways, there being over one hundred, large and small, within its limits. Some of them, to be sure, have but three or four steps, while others have as many as a hundred and fifty. In several cases the entire flight of six, eight or even ten steps was cut out of a single boulder. The stairways which connect the various agricultural terraces follow the natural declivity of the hill even where it is so steep as to make them seem more like a ladder than a flight of stairs. In several places a little garden plot was tucked into a terrace less than eight feet square behind and above a dwelling house. In order to make little garden terraces like these accessible the Incas constructed fantastic stairways scarcely wide enough to permit the passage of a boy. Within the city, however, and particularly in the narrow streets or alleyways, the stairs were constructed on a comfortable grade.

The stairway or flight of steps as an ornamental or ceremonial motif in Inca architecture does not seem to occur here, although it might well have originated in this locality. In the ruins of a monolithic gateway at Tiahuanaco, Bolivia, in a curiously carved rock called Khenko, near Cuzco, are little flights of stairs which were carved for ceremonial or ornamental purposes and which serve no useful object as far as one can see. The stairways of Machu Picchu, on the other hand, with possibly one exception, all appear to be available for reaching locations otherwise difficult of access. While they are more numerous than was absolutely necessary, none of them appears useless, even today. The longest stairway, which may properly be described as the main thoroughfare of the city, commences at the top of the ridge at the terrace by which the highway enters the walls, and, roughly dividing the city into two parts, runs all the way down to the impassable cliffs on the north-eastern slope.

The central thoroughfare in the heart of the city consisted in part of this granite stairway of one hundred and fifty steps, and was the site of the principal waterworks. As usual, the Incas took great pains to do everything possible to provide adequate water.

There are several springs on the side of Machu Picchu Mountain, within a mile of the heart of the city. The little *azequia*, or conduit, which brought the water from the springs, may still be followed along the mountain side for a considerable distance. It has been partly destroyed by landslides but may be seen where it runs along one of the principal agricultural terraces, crosses the dry moat on a slender stone aqueduct, passes under the city wall in a groove less than 6 inches wide, and is carried along one of the terraces to the first of the series of fountains or little stone basins which are located near the principal stairway. The first four are south of the stairway. Near the fourth the stairway is divided into two flights. At this point there begins a series of twelve. The *azequia* runs south from the last fountain and empties into the moat.

The basins of the Stairway of the Fountains are usually cut out of a single block of granite placed on a level with the floor of the little enclosure into which the women came to fill their narrow-necked jars.

Frequently one or two little niches were constructed in the side walls of the enclosure as a shelf for a cup or possibly for the stoppers of the bottles, made of fibre or twisted bunches of grass. Sometimes a small lip was cut in the stone at the end of the conduit so as to form a little spout, thus enabling the water to fall clear of the back wall of the fountain. In other cases the water would usually pass through the narrow orifice with sufficient force to reach the opening of the jar without the necessity of the carrier dipping the water from the basin. In times of water scarcity, however, we may be sure that the latter method was followed, and that the reason for the sixteen basins was not only in order to permit many jars to be filled at once but to keep the all too precious fluid from escaping. The *azequia* is narrower than any I have seen elsewhere, being generally less than 4 inches in width.

The stone basins are about 30 inches long by 18 inches wide and from 5 to 6 inches in depth. In some places both the basin and the entire floor of the fountain enclosure are made of a single slab of granite. Sometimes holes were drilled in one corner of the basin to permit the water to flow through carefully cut underground conduits to the next basin below; in case of necessity these holes could easily have been plugged up to permit the basin to fill. The conduits run sometimes under the stairway and sometimes at its side. It is perhaps worth noting that the modern Peruvians call these fountains *baños*, baths, but it does not seem to me likely that they were used for this purpose. On account of the rarefied air, the cold, and the rapid radiation, even Anglo-Saxons do not bathe frequently in the Peruvian highlands, and the mountain Indians of today never bathe. It is hardly to be supposed, therefore, that the builders of Machu Picchu used these basins for such a purpose. On the other hand, the Incas were fond of making easy the work of the water carriers and providing them with nicely constructed fountains.

Possibly one reason for abandoning Machu Picchu as a place of residence was the difficulty of securing sufficient water. In the dry season the little springs barely furnished enough water for cooking and drinking purposes for the forty or fifty Indian workers and ourselves. In the earliest times, when the side of the mountain was forested, the springs undoubtedly did better; but with the deforestation which followed continued occupation and the resultant landslides and increased erosion of the surface soil, the springs must at times have given so little water as to force the city dwellers to bring the water in great jars on their backs for considerable distances.

It is significant that the sherds found near the city gate represent forty-one containers of liquid refreshment as compared with only four cooking pots, nine drinking ladles, and not a single food dish. Evidently the dispensers of *chicha* were stationed here. The results are the more striking when compared with the finds in the south-eastern quarter, where almost as many food dishes were found as jugs.

The largest flat space within the city limits lies in a swale at the widest part of the ridge. This was carefully graded and terraced, and at the time of our visit had recently been cultivated by Richarte and his friends. In fact, one would have to go a good many miles in the canyon of the Urubamba to find an equally large 'pampa' at an elevation of not less than 7,000 nor more than 10,000 feet. In other words, this little pampa offered an unusual opportunity to a people accustomed to raising such crops as flourished in Yucay and Ollantay-tambo. The fact that it was possible for them also to cover the adjacent hillside with artificial terraces which would increase the potentiality of the region as a food producer was doubtless as important a factor in the selection of this site as the ease with which it could be made into a powerful citadel or a very sacred sanctuary. One of the most carefully constructed stairways leads directly from the chief temples to the little pampa itself. It may have been the pampa where the *huilca* tree grew – the *huilca-pampa*.

There is only one city gate. The Northern, or Huayna Picchu side, was not defended by a transverse wall but by high, narrow terraces built on little ledges which would otherwise give a foothold on the precipices. Near these terraces there is a broad saddle connecting Machu Picchu with a conical hill that is part of a ridge leading to the precipitous heights of Huayna Picchu. South of the saddle, which was once covered with a dense forest, is a rude amphitheatre. It had been terraced and there are five or six different levels, recently used for the small plantations of the Indians. This might very well have been the special garden plot for raising food for the rulers. On the surface of the ground, among the cornstalks, pumpkin vines, and onion patches, we found occasional pieces of pottery.

Lost City of the Incas, 1951

I. Mann

26. The Inca's sacred city of Machu Picchu.

John R. Freeman

27. The centuries-old "Bridge of San Luis Rey," on the Apurímac River, Peru. Though suspended by ropes "the thickness of a human body," it collapsed one day. Thornton Wilder made this catastrophe the basis of his world-famous novel.

The bridge of San Luis Rey

VICTOR VON HAGEN

VICTOR WOLFGANG VON HAGEN (*1909-*) *was born in St Louis, Missouri, and the list of the explorations he has undertaken seems too many for one man's lifetime. In the Americas alone they include Mexico, Ecuador, the Upper Amazon, the Galapagos, the Honduras, Guatemala, North Panama, Columbia, the Amazon, Peru, the West Indies and Bolivia. He has not confined his journeys exclusively to the New World; in 1959 he undertook to trace the Imperial Roman road system from the Rhine to North Africa, and went on to visit Italy, Yugoslavia, Greece and Turkey. One of the most important assignments he has carried out was that of Director of the Inca Highway for the American Geographical Society when he traced the great post-road of the Incas from end to end.*

The walls of the tunnel, which was 250 yards long by actual measurement, were pierced with openings to allow in the light and air. Through these 'windows', into which I climbed, I could see the snow-topped peaks of Mt Marcani beyond us. The tunnel had been fashioned by the Incas much as the Romans mined rock. After a fierce fire had been built against it, water was thrown on the hot rock, splitting the friable lime and sandstone. The Incas, with their knowledge of working stone with stone, were presented with no problem. Their daring techniques in engineering were something else. At the end of the tunnel, which had once been connected with a stone stairway cut and built into the rock, we eased across that dangerous cleft and, gaining the circular stairway, went very slowly down the step-road. Cieza de Leon back in 1543 had had trouble with these same stairways, even when they were in good repair: 'Here the road is so rugged and dangerous, that some horses laden with gold and silver, had fallen in and been lost, without any chance of saving them.' Several hundred feet below, we came to what had been the platform, on which we found the remains of two enormous stone towers or pillars supporting the cables of the bridge. Two hundred feet directly in front of us, across the stygian gap of the river, we could clearly see the other side of this 'bridge of the . . . Apurimacchaca'. Cieza had written that it 'was the largest bridge encountered from Cajamarca . . . with the road well built along the sides of the mountains. . . . The Indians who built it must have performed herculean labour. . . .'

No precise data can be given for the bridge's construction. After the year 1300 the Incas expanded their realm, to the edge of the Apurimac and about this time, according to their chronicles, Inca Roca, then chieftain, finished the bridge. This would have been *circa* AD 1350. The detailed description of its structure is given by the Cuzco-born historian Garcilaso de la Vega, surnamed 'The Inca':

> The Apurimac bridge which lies on the royal road from Cuzco to Lima has its pillar support (he called it stirrup) made up of natural rock on the Cuzco side; on the other side (where we were now standing trying to figure it all out) was the stone tower, made of masonry. Under the platform that held this tower, five or six large wooden beams were inserted as thick as oxen – they stretched from one side to another. They were placed one higher than the other like steps. Around each of these beams, each of the suspension cables is twisted once so that the bridge will remain taut and not slacken with its own weight, which is very great.

Until nineteenth-century technology ushered in the use of iron chains for suspension cables, this Bridge of San Luis Rey, hanging by enormous rope-cables across the Apurimac, was one of the largest bridges of its type known. The Incas had no knowledge of the arch, nor, for that matter, did any other of the preliterate peoples in America. Depending as it does upon the principles of gravity, pressure and weight, the arch is yet earthbound and passive and therefore could not have been used here even had the Incas been familiar with it. Instead, they perfected the principles of the suspension bridge by reversing the arch-curve and giving it wings.

The Bridge of San Luis Rey, like all suspension bridges on the Royal Road, hung from rope cables hand-twisted from the fibres of the maguey plant. Those of this bridge, of 'the thickness of a man's body', were just laid over the high stone towers for their 'suspending' and then buried in the thick masonry on the platform of the towers. From the suspended cables, supports hung down, and to these the bridge platform made of wood planking was attached. Cables attached to the main bridge served as wind bracing.

Although the materials were primitive, the essential nature of the technology of the Inca suspension bridge is, in principle, the same as the best-constructed suspension bridges of today. Rope bridges have been built since immemorial times, but few other cultures before the advent of recent eras built so well as the Inca. This particular bridge indeed was so well made that it lasted for five hundred years, the cables, of course, being renewed every two years as a part of their work-service by Indians living at the *tampu* of Cura-hausi. This system of maintenance, so efficacious that the Spanish conquerors maintained it throughout the colonial period, disappeared only after the 'wheel' conquered the Andes, and the bridge which had served as a highway for foot and mule traffic for a period of five hundred years was allowed to fall into slow decay.

The Incas built for eternity; performance was to them, as it was with the Romans, the base of all their construction. If the Inca road system is here occasionally compared with the Roman road system, it is because, until very recent times, there have been no other communication systems that can be compared with either. Other civilizations had, of course, their highways, but until the advent of the Romans none maintained a road system.

However, structurally an Inca road differed greatly from a Roman road. The Romans employed heavy-wheeled carts with rigid front axles which necessitated a deep roadbed. The Incas, since their roads were travelled only by those on foot and by llama herds, had no need for the roadbed. But apart from this the two civilizations, Inca and Roman, were amazingly similar in their concept of road engineering. While there is no denying Rome's place in civilization's sun, the Incas, living on a neolithic cultural horizon tied to stone tools, still conceived a communication system that stands extremely high in comparison with the Roman.

The Romans had three thousand years of experience to draw on. The facets of Old World thought and techniques regarding the building of roads are a vast web stretching from the first wagon ruts of ancient India to the stoneways of the Persians. Remote as certain of these areas were, and removed from each other by time and space, the Romans had all these centuries of cultural heritage on which to draw. The Inca had none of these, yet an Inca road is in many aspects superior to a Roman road. Every feature of a Roman road is paralleled in an Inca road except that, for the most part, the Incas built – literally – in the clouds. The Apurimac Bridge, for example, was part of a highway which came from heights the like of which no Roman had ever seen. The passes the Romans conquered were as nothing compared to these in the Andes; Mont Blanc, the highest peak in Europe, is 15,800 feet high; yet here in Peru we have walked over Inca roads *built* at this height. The old Roman roads which crossed the spine of the Italian promontory of the Apennines were no higher than the city of Cuzco, which is 10,200 feet above the sea. Again we turn to our Cieza. As a boy in Spain, he knew the Roman Road. He had walked between Tarragone and Cadiz over the Via Augusta, built in the first century BC and rebuilt every quarter of the century by the Caesars. He drove his mules over the Via Argenta, which ran between Merida and Salamanca – a road which was started by Tiberius, continued by Nero and fully repaired by Caracalla in AD 214 – so he and others like him knew what they were saying when they wrote as a general rule that there is 'nothing in Christendom that equals the magnificence of the Inca roads.'

The remarkable thing is the similarity in approach to the 'idea' of roads between the Inca and the Roman. Both civilizations were of the land. Both had land armies, and land armies need roads; and since a road is only a road if one can go back over it, both believed that the road must be well built and well maintained. The Romans, it is true, ruled the straight line into civilization's thinking, whereas the Inca's road *surmounted* obstacles rather than avoided them, and as a general rule their engineers employed what I will call 'directional straightness' – that is, between two given points their road ran unerringly straight. Caius Caesar personally laid down vast stretches of road and the Claudian family, when public funds were not available, defrayed expenses for road-building out of its own privy purse. In Peru the road-building programme was also identified with the rulers and the roads were called after the Inca who built them. For example, one 2,500-mile-long road than ran to Chile was known as the Huayna Capac Nan, or the Road of Huayna Capac. Often an Inca would order a road to be built for himself grander than that of his predecessor. The Romans put up milestones as markers, while the Incas built their *topus* 'with the distance between them a Castilian league and a half'. Along their road, the Romans placed night quarters or *mansiones*; in Peru, the Incas erected and maintained *tampus* every four to eight or twelve miles (according to the difficulty and arduousness of the terrain) along the entire route of their roads. Roman couriers had a change of horse-mounts at *mutationes* to hurry up messages along the Imperial Way; the Incas, depending on foot, had their *chasqui* stations every two and a half miles as way stations for the trained runners who carried messages over the most terrifying terrain in the world.

The bridge, 'the little brother of the road', was ever an important link in the great Inca road system. How many of them there were along the length and breadth of the Andes we cannot be sure. But of them all, the Apurimac-chaca, the Bridge of San Luis Rey, was the greatest. Few who passed over it did so without pausing to wonder at this miracle of engineering. As to its length, the Inca historian, Garcilaso de la Vega, guessed it to be 200 paces long – 'although I have not measured it, I have asked many in Spain who did'. Cieza, that most accurate of observers, thought it was 'fifty estados' or about 85 metres (250 feet) in length. Sir Clements Markham, who crossed it in 1855, estimated the Apurimac-chaca at 90 feet and its elevation above the river's surface at 300 feet, while Lieutenant Lardner Gibbon, who made a survey of the Amazon for the United States Government in 1817, estimated its length at 324 feet.

When Squier came to the bridge in the summer of 1864, he and his companions lost no time extracting the measuring tapes and sounding lines. They found that the bridge was 148 feet long from end to end and that it was suspended 118 feet above the surging river. That was the first and last time this famous bridge was exactly measured, for although it was still hanging in 1890 it was no longer used and the cables, unreplaced, curved dangerously downward into the gorge and were slowly decaying with time. Squier also made several daguerreotypes of it, which he used in a somewhat dramatized and heightened version as a woodcut illustration in his book, *Peru, Land of the Incas*. Of the bridge, he wrote:

> Between the precipices on either side, looking wonderfully frail and gossamer-like, was the famed bridge of the Apurimac. A steep, narrow path following for some distance a natural shelf, formed by the stratification of the rock, for the rest of the way hewn in its face, led up for a hundred feet to a little platform also cut in the rock where were fastened the cables supporting the bridge. On the opposite bank was another and rather larger platform roofed by rock where was the windlass (a feature added by the Spaniards) for making the cables taut and where, perched like goats on some mountain shelf, lived the custodians of the bridge. . . . It was a memorable

incident in my travelling experiences – that crossing of the great swinging bridge of the Apurimac; I shall never forget it.

Later, in the beginning of the present century, Hiram Bingham, in speaking of the origins of his interest in Peru, said that this illustration of the bridge 'was one of the reasons why I decided to go to Peru'.

It is known that this dramatic picture of the bridge inspired Prosper Mérimée to use it as a literary device in a fictional piece on Peru, and that Thornton Wilder later, inspired both by the suggestions of the French writer and by the great span that crossed the Apurimac, and fascinated by its picturesque remoteness, wrote his literary masterpiece, *The Bridge of San Luis Rey*. With this book in hand I now stood looking down on the hiatus between the walls where the bridge once hung. Later I wrote Thornton Wilder from La Estrella hacienda. I knew that he regarded the bridge as a literary device, but so well had he described it that I felt that he must have seen, perhaps in some old issue of *Harper's Magazine*, a reproduction of Squier's stirring woodcut of this ancient bridge, which was in fact the actual hero of his novelette. 'It is best, von Hagen', he answered me, 'that I make no comment or point of it. . . . I wish I were with you and could see the great river and the gorge.'

The afternoon wind came up loud and shrill as we were standing on the platform that once held the great suspension cables of the bridge to set the foliage that clung to the rock walls rustling. We knew now that an old adage about the wind and the bridge was true, and that when the afternoon winds blew even the wind-braced cables could not hold the bridge steady and it would swing like a hammock.

It was late afternoon by the time we regained the boulder-strewn shores of the river. The sun was lighting the snow peaks while the shadows of the mountains fell across the canyon. A long shadow falling across the vertical cliffs gave a curious illusion of a hanging bridge. At that moment I must have been very close to the spot where Fra Juniper had stood looking upward at the bridge when a 'twanging noise filled the air . . . and he saw the bridge divide and fling the five people into the river below.'

' "Why did this happen to *those* five?" ' the Fra asked himself. 'If there were any plan in the universe at all, if there were any pattern in a human life, surely it could be discovered mysteriously latent in those lives so suddenly cut off. *Either we live by accident and die by accident* or we live by plan or die by plan.' With that soliloquy Wilder began his story. It is an ironic truth that if this tragic story had not been written, this wondrous bridge built in 1350 by the Inca Roca, which was to endure for five centuries as one of the greatest tributes to man's domination of wild nature, would have been lost to memory.

With the dying sun now playing fully on the glaciers, the river canyon became as bright as if it were full day. The shadows were gone and, with them, the illusion of the hanging bridge. When I next looked back, there was again only emptiness between the two vertical walls.

Highway of the Sun, 1956

A problem of Tihuanacu

ARTHUR POSNANSKY

ARTHUR POSNANSKY *was the Royal Bavarian Professor and Civil Geodetic Engineer, and for many years held the post of Professor of archaeology and physical anthropology at the University of La Paz. For more than fifty years he studied the antiquities of Tihuanacu in the High Andes of Bolivia, which many scholars claim to be the earliest civilization of the Western Hemisphere. The city reached its zenith long before the emergence of the empire of the Incas, and showed an astonishingly high standard of development at a time comparable to that of the earliest settlements of the Old World.*

For many, the group of ruins found 246 metres to the east of the Temple of the Sun, Kalasasaya, is a real mystery, and many investigators, including Squier, hold the opinion that it is a spot used for blood sacrifices. After long and conscientious studies we have come to the conclusion that what today is called 'Kantataita' is a model of a building of Tihuanacu, perhaps similar to the one which from the time of the French Mission (1903) has been called the 'Temple of the Sarcophagi', described in one of the previous chapters.

Now, of course, from the point of view of the modern engineer, to make a construction, no matter how large or small, the first thing that is done is to make a drawing, a plan, in which there are co-ordinated the ideas of form and appearance that will be given to the building, the accessories that it will have on the inside, and its exterior appearance and configuration. And since in our time one works on a dwelling or public building from say six months to a maximum of three years, and the one who plans it usually finishes it, a plan like the one described above is sometimes sufficient. But in the case of Tihuanacu, when the idea of 'time is money' did not exist, because there was more than enough time and the means, resources and systems of construction were still very rudimental – to such a degree that to move the surface of a stone a metre square they took months – a construction job might in spite of the many hands last a century or more, and even then not be finished. On this account, during the construction of a temple or palace of a public nature, it is unquestionable that the architects, and the directors of the work, were changed many times. Since there were no drawings or plans to which those who were continuing the work might refer, they would have needed something else to perpetuate the constructive idea, something which would incorporate the primitive concept and plan of the building on which they were working. This is why they adopted a system which is used in modern times to give a picture of the form and perspective of a building or monument which is to be constructed – in other words, a 'model'. In this era, the building is constructed on a small scale of stucco or some other material, in which one can see the perspective and main form of the building better than in a drawing. This is not only for the use of the architect of the project but especially for those untrained in this sort of material and unversed in the 'reading' of an architectonic plan with its different projections. It seems that this system of models is the one that was used in the Third Period of Tihuanacu to carry out a magnificent construction and, in our opinion, that which is today called Kantataita, is a horizontal model of a sumptuous construction. Also, a block near Puma-Punku, which the common people call 'the writing desk of the Inca', is nothing more than the vertical model of a façade, possibly of a building set to be constructed in the group now known as Puma-Punku and which actually is the Temple of the Moon of Tihuanacu.

With regard to Kantataita, this group of ruins is also completely destroyed. Everything that could be used in the way of slabs and finely carved stones, with and without figures, was carted off by both cultured and uncultured iconoclasts from Tihuanacu, the 'quarry of carved stones', long before the Conquest. Thus it is that considerable study, fancy and imagination are required to reconstruct in one's mind the form and appearance of this architectural group, which, like all in Tihuanacu, was not finished during its time. This group of buildings is apparently 40 m. long on the axis and perhaps 30 m. wide. But it is logical to suppose that a great number of the blocks found on the extreme western part belong rather to the sculptural atelier and would possibly have formed, when finished, a part of the great model or a part of another splendid building around this group. The principal part of the whole construction seems to be a slab of great dimensions which has caused some people to presume and still insist that this building was planned for 'blood sacrifices', the famous *Wilancha*, which the author has considered in other works. In the slab there is a square incision with a balcony on which it can be seen that there descend from the upper platform to the bottom, five little stairs composed of three steps. The idea of those who think that this was a sacrificial stone has its origin in the six holes carved on the upper platform of the block where, according to this opinion, there were six square columns which supported a flat stone to hold the sacrifice. The little steps served, according to those who hold the above opinion, to measure the amount of blood which ran from the chests or throats of the propitiatory victims.

Any person who studies Tihuanacu with care, rejects this idea at once. For example, in order to measure the blood, a single little step would have been sufficient, since the slab was level. What this slab actually represents is the model of a typical and genuine building of Tihuanacu. When the French Mission excavated the building called the 'Palace of the Sarcophagi', considered in a previous chapter, the section that was discovered then also had its balcony part, and showed exactly, even to the smallest details and with its little steps, the form seen in the slab that we are considering. Just as the last part of the balcony section of the model which is found to the east is broken, there is also broken the last but most marvellous stair which formed the entrance to the miniature building. This, without the least doubt, was in its turn also no more than a miniature of the three-coloured perron with three steps which gave access to the 'Palace of the Sarcophagi', of which, as well as of other details, we still have good photographs. Unfortunately, it was not possible to photograph the excavation of the French mission immediately, because of a lack of 24 × 30 plates and for other reasons. We say 'unfortunately' since on the following nights the oft-mentioned iconoclasts had already destroyed practically everything and carried off to the village tons of finely carved stones and beautiful slabs of all sizes. When we returned a few days later, there remained only the large blocks which could not be moved and transported. The two photographs (24 × 30) of this material, the only existing documentation, show the remains of what was probably one of the most artistic buildings, of a rare and magnificent architectonic work of the prehistoric Americans. In the light of the foregoing discussion, we have no doubt that what is now popularly called 'Kantataita', is nothing more than a model of a building in construction in the Third Period. This structure was undoubtedly a semisubterranean building with an external platform at a greater height than the ordinary level of Tihuanacu. The slab which we have described and which is the principal part of the model, is 4·05 m. wide by 4 m. long, 30 cm. deep and the part to the west is somewhat sunken in. It is composed of hard andesitic material, which was employed in the most select constructions of the Third Period. On the west side of this group there is found in a great heap a quantity of blocks, some in the form of steps and others with typical staircase ornaments and we again emphasize that it is very difficult to decide whether they were all destined for the model or miniature building, or whether a portion of them was for other buildings and whether, finally, the model occupied a square of only thirty metres per side or whether it was larger. Future studies carried out on the basis of methodical excavations and reconstructions, will supply the last word on the subject of this mysterious construction, whose secret, as well as many others in Tihuanacu, may never be revealed to the man of today. The aforementioned topographical map which accompanies this volume will give the student a full idea of what still remains of this work on the surface of the ground.

Tihuanacu: Cradle of American Man, 1945

Part Seven

NEW METHODS IN ARCHAEOLOGY

Archaeology from the air

OSBERT CRAWFORD

Osbert Guy Stanhope Crawford (1886–1957) was born in Bombay and came to England as a child. He was educated at Marlborough and Keble College, Oxford, where he read classics, but soon began to turn to the more technical aspects of archaeology. In 1914 he secured a place on an expedition to the Sudan, but this was cancelled on the outbreak of war. He joined the army and shortly transferred to the Royal Flying Corps, where he made many surveying flights. After the war he dug in Wales until 1920 when he was appointed Archaeological Officer to the Ordnance Survey. This work suited his tastes and talents to perfection, and he continued in this post until the first appearance of the periodical 'Antiquity', which he founded and continued to edit until his death.

We now come to the discovery of a technique which revolutionized field archaeology, that of air-photography. I have given elsewhere the main facts of its history and need not do so again. I would merely point out that the advantages of the vertical view of earthworks was fully realized by both Dr Williams-Freeman and myself long before we had either of us ever seen an air-photograph, and before our time by Colonel Sir Charles Arden-Close and by the late Sir Henry Welcome, who actually had vertical photographs taken from a box-kite of his excavations in the Sudan in 1913. What neither Dr Williams-Freeman nor I realized was the extraordinary clarity and sharp definition that would be given to earthworks by air-photographs. We were accustomed to look at them at close range; we used occasionally to see in the corn the track of a ploughed-up ditch showing as a broad greener band; but seen from near by from the opposite hill the outline was rather blurred. We longed to see it, not obliquely but in plan, as would be possible in an aeroplane, but we did not then realize that the greater distance given by the height would so greatly improve its appearance. It is exactly the same thing as the reduction by photography of a coarsely-drawn plan; the rough edges disappear, and what looked coarse becomes fine and pleasing.

I made several unsuccessful efforts after the 1914-18 war to get hold of some British air-photographs, and tried to interest the Earthworks Committee, also without success. Through the failure of their then honorary secretary to do anything the Committee lost the chance of its life-time. My expectations were at last satisfied when Dr Williams-Freeman asked me to come over to Weyhill and see some air-photographs with curious markings on them that had been shown to him by Air Commodore Clark Hall, then in command of the R.A.F. station there. What I saw far surpassed my wildest dreams, and I felt much the same excitement as, according to the poet, did stout Cortez on a memorable occasion. Here on these photographs was revealed the accurate plan of field-systems that must be at least 2,000 years old, covering hundreds of acres of Hampshire. There followed a period of intensive field-work over the area, supplemented by fresh air-photos taken in Hants and Wilts. The results were announced at a meeting of the Royal Geographical Society on 12th March 1923. The paper which I then delivered was published in the *Geographical Journal* for May of that year, and subsequently reissued with some alterations as an Ordnance Survey monograph (*Air Survey and Archaeology*, 1st edn. 1924, 2nd edn. 1928). In 1929, after we had had time to study air-photos more thoroughly, I wrote another monograph (*Air Photography for Archaeologists*) dealing not so much with the new discoveries themselves as with the ways in which they were revealed by photography. There was not, as some were almost inclined to think, any magic power in the camera; as a matter of fact it sees no more than does the naked eye. What it does is to make a document, the photographic print, which has all the properties of an original historical manuscript except its uniqueness – for it can be replaced if lost. This document can be studied at leisure in the home or office, and compared with others and with maps of the region – things that are impossible when observing from a fast-moving aeroplane. In this second monograph I classified the ancient sites revealed by air-photography into three groups: (1) shadow-sites; (2) soil-sites; (3) crop-sites; and that classification has been found adequate and still holds good, not only in this country, but all over the world.

During this same decade I took some air-photographs myself, working in collaboration with Mr Alexander Keiller in a specially chartered aeroplane from a base near Andover. The results were published in a joint book, *Wessex from the Air* (Oxford, 1928). Soon after this, I think about 1930, a private flier, Major George Allen, happened to pick up one of my Ordnance Survey monographs in a hotel at Southampton, and was immediately interested. He wrote to me about it, and began work on his own account. Having his own aeroplane he was a free agent and could go where he wished and take his own photographs. For a decade he continued to explore the country round Oxford and sometimes farther afield, and gradually accumulated a magnificent collection. The majority of his sites were crop-sites and new discoveries. He did more than anyone else to advance the new technique; and his untimely death by accident in 1940 was a very severe loss. He bequeathed his collection of photographs and records to the Ashmolean Museum at Oxford, where they are now available for the use of students. Comparable with Major Allen's work is that of Father Poidebard in Syria, where with the co-operation of the French Air Force he has surveyed the Roman frontier defences and discovered an enormous number of new Roman forts and roads. He has also succeeded in adding a fresh triumph, the photography of ancient remains beneath the sea (at Tyre) both from the air and below the water. (I tried out the possibilities of this myself in December 1928, when I flew over the harbour of Alexandria looking for the submerged quays there; but the sea was rough and muddy and I could see little or nothing.)

To return to the technique of air-photography, however. Shadow-sites are those whose surface is irregular, consisting of banks, mounds, ditches, and terraces whose presence is revealed by the shadows they cast when seen in the low light of the rising or setting sun. There is of course nothing at all mysterious about this process, which can be observed (though far less effectively) on the ground. Exactly the same principle is employed in photographing inscribed stones and carvings in low relief, where a side-light is necessary to bring out the detail. In explaining by examples how the shadow technique works I am necessarily anticipating somewhat, for I have to assume a familiarity with certain types of remains which I have not yet described; but it will be quite enough if for the moment they are regarded simply as banks (or whatever they may be) without worrying about their archaeological significance, which will appear later. The simplest and most familiar examples of banks are the ramparts of prehistoric hill-forts like Maiden Castle or Badbury Rings, or to take examples from Hampshire, St Catherine's Hill at Winchester, Tachbury Mount and Toothill near Romsey. These are all shadow sites of the most obvious kind. An observer visiting these hill-forts sees of course the shadows on the slopes away from the sun, but he gets no clear view of the hill-fort as a whole nor of its plan, for he is too near it. Returning to my analogy of the carved stone he is in the position of a fly on its surface. It is unnecessary to labour this point further; the basic principle is very easy to grasp.

Under the head of shadow-sites must also come, rather paradoxically, those where there are no shadows at all. When the land slopes towards the sun the banks on it reflect the light at a different angle and appear as brighter lines than the rest of the terrain. The light thus reflected is fore-shortened and condensed and therefore brighter. The banks of prehistoric fields show up in this way.

Shadow-sites can all be seen by an observer on the ground. Many of them were already known before they were photographed from the air; but even so air-photography has often revealed new features which had not been observed before. The classic example is the Trundle, a hill-fort near Worthing, where an air-photograph revealed within the ramparts a hitherto unnoticed circle which Dr Cecil Curwen subsequently excavated and proved to be the rampart of an earlier neolithic habitation-site. This led to a re-examination of other well-known hill-forts in some of which similar remains were found.

When taken in a good low light an air-photograph will reveal undulations in the surface so slight and broad that they might, and often did, escape the notice of a field archaeologist. When, however, with his attention thus drawn to them, he goes over the ground (as he always should) with the air-photograph in his hand, he can generally see something of them, however faintly. One of the chief services of air-photography has been to sharpen our eyes so that we can see these faint undulations. To the inexperienced eye they seem so slight as to be negligible; but no clue, however faint, should be neglected. Others brush them aside as products of the imagination, but air-photography has vindicated them, and their observers. It must be remembered, because it is a fundamental axiom of field archaeology, that in the chalk regions and in some (but not all) others, every irregularity of the surface is of human origin and demands an explanation. Broad low banks may seem trifles, but every gardener and every farmer knows that they are not. The cubic content of a bank that, though now only a few inches high, is several yards broad, represents long hours of human labour; and people do not undertake that for no purpose, or merely to mislead field archaeologists. The same remarks apply conversely to a silted-up ditch whose present depression may be a matter of a few inches only. Its original depth is probably not far short of its present width; the ditch of a levelled hill-fort may appear as a depression of a foot only with a width of fifteen feet representing perhaps a depth of ten feet. That is quite a formidable affair.

Soil sites are those which are revealed by disturbance and consequent discoloration of the surface. Except in deserts (where the few human sites are mostly shadow-sites) soil-sites usually occur on cultivated land when it is not bearing a crop. The marks are usually caused by the dispersal of the soil of banks and mounds and of the causeways of Roman or other made roads. In the chalk country such banks will have been made by digging a ditch and piling up the white chalk, which causes the resulting bank to remain visible even after many years of ploughing. Ditches and pits are sometimes revealed in bare soil even when they have become completely filled in and invisible as surface irregularities because their filling retains more moisture and thus has a darker appearance. For the same sort of reason a wet towel is darker than a dry one. Soil-sites are more common in winter and early spring, especially in a dry spring, than at other times of year. In the case of hill-forts it is usually the bank, or what remains of it, which shows up a soil-mark, and the ditch as a crop-mark. It is therefore a good thing to photograph such sites more than once at different times of the year and under the different conditions of moisture.

Crop-sites are perhaps the most important and the most numerous of all. Most of those known represent completely new discoveries. A crop-site is one that is revealed by the differential growth of a crop; the causes are excess and defect of moisture; ditches, pits, and post-holes, when they silt up, remain soft spots whose filling is of a different composition from that of the ground in which they are dug, whether that be chalk, sand, gravel, hard rock or even clay. When a crop of corn (and some other plants) is sown in a field containing such silted-up holes, the corn will grow better in the moister, more fertile soil of the silting, and will therefore be of a darker green colour. When seen from above those patches of darker green corn stand out in sharp contrast to the rest; and a vertical photograph of them gives an accurate plan of the bands or spots, which appear on it of course in black. No matter how long the holes have been filled up, the pattern is sharp and precise. The ditches of barrows that were ploughed flat in the Iron Age, some 2,000 years ago, have come to light again in this way as perfectly sharp, clear circles.

Even to give a list of the important discoveries of crop-sites made during the last quarter of a century would be impossible here, and I must confine myself to mentioning a few of them. The first and one of the most famous was the continuation of the avenue leading to Stonehenge. I saw it first in 1923, not on a print but on a negative that was taken in 1921 by the R.A.F. at Old Sarum, in the ordinary routine of practice. The existence of the ditches of the avenue was proved by excavation the same year. A little later, in 1926, Squadron Leader Insall, V.C., discovered not far away the timber circles which have been called Woodhenge, whose post-holes showed up as concentric ovals of dark spots enclosed within a dark ring marking the ditch. It was excavated later by the Cunningtons, who published their report in book form. One of the most striking crop-sites was that of Woodbury. I found this myself in 1924, but was unable to photograph it, and it was rediscovered independently and a remarkably good photograph taken of it by a member of the R.A.F. photographic staff at Old Sarum in 1929. The site was selected for excavation by the Prehistoric Society, and two seasons' work were done there in 1938 and 1939, under the direction of Professor Bersu. It proved to be an Early Iron Age habitation-site. It was very well reconstructed by Jacquetta Hawkes in consultation with Professor Bersu, at Denham, and used in the film of prehistoric life. Major Allen discovered innumerable crop-sites in the Oxford district; and during the 1939-45 war Flight-Lieutenant D. N. Riley found more both in the same region and in the Fenland and other parts of East Anglia. Since the war Dr St Joseph has discovered many important crop-sites, including dozens of new Roman forts and marching camps.

In Iraq, Squadron Leader Insall discovered the site of Seleucia, the Hellenistic capital of Mesopotamia, by observing the rectangular lay-out, revealed partly by vegetation and partly by soil discoloration.

The remains of ancient irrigation-systems provide ideal subjects for both crop- and soil-sites. Those of Iraq can generally be seen as shadow-sites, for the ancient canals silted up their beds till they grew into great embankments. But there is a very good silted-up canal to be seen (as a soil- or crop-site) near Ur, complete with its distributary channels. The Romano-British drainage channels and associated field-systems and tracks are revealed in copious detail by air-photography, but remain for the most part unpublished. Extinct irrigation systems have been reported from Nubia, Turkmanistan and Soviet Azerbaijan, but neither Egyptologists nor apparently Soviet archaeologists have published any air-photographs of them.

ourtesy, Dr. C. M. Lerici

28. An aerial view of an Etruscan necropolis. The hidden tombs show as patches of light. Both as an instrument of large-scale reconnaissance of extensive and difficult terrain and as a means of spotting buried ruins, graves, walls, streets, and canals, aerial photography has become a vital aid to archaeology.

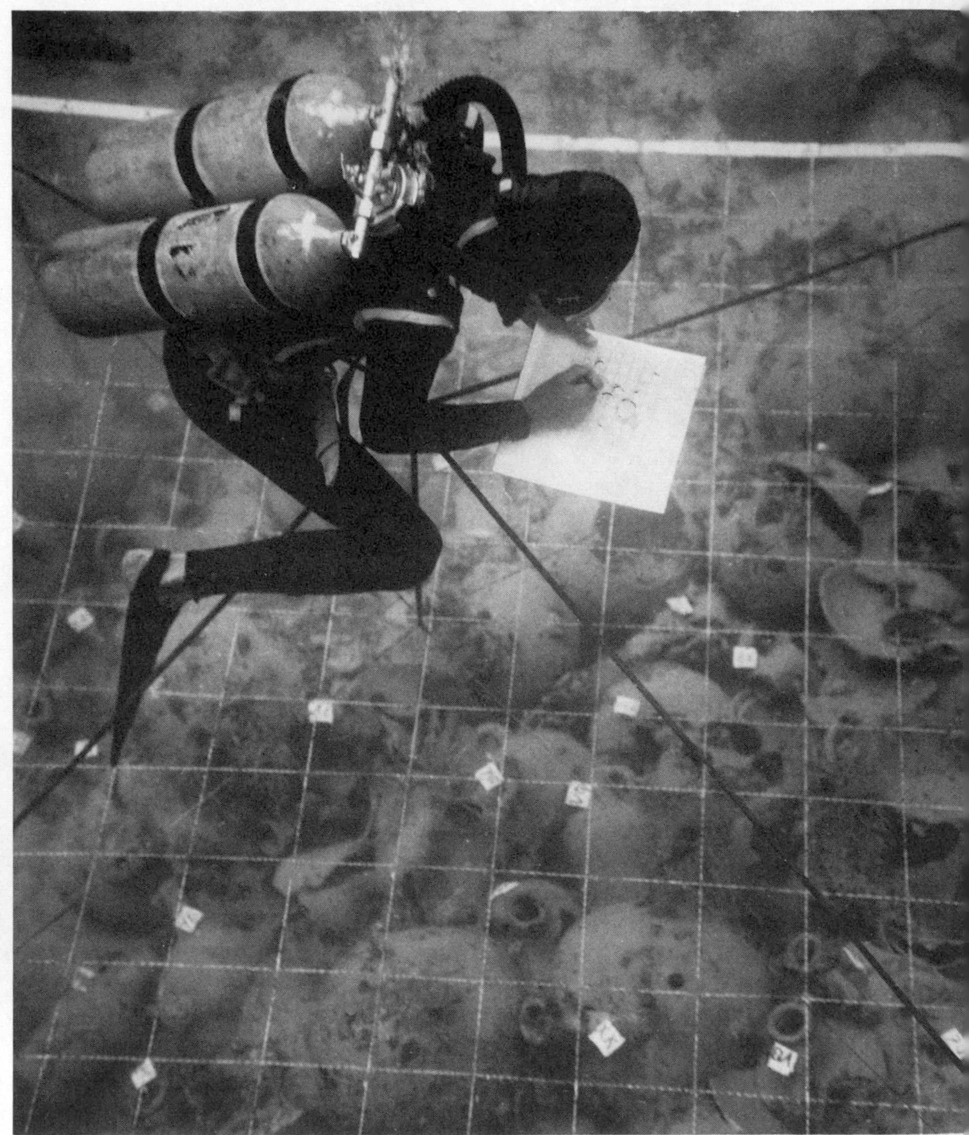

George F. Bass, by courtesy of the Pennsylvania University Museum

29. Underwater exploration, one of archaeology's oldest dreams, began to come true when Captain Jacques-Yves Cousteau developed the aqualung. It has now become possible to locate by relatively simple means the innumerable shipwrecks of classical antiquity along the Mediterranean seacoasts and to salvage their treasures.

One of the most important discoveries of crop-sites was made in Italy at the end of the last war by Mr John Bradford. Here turned up a wholly unsuspected group of Neolithic or Early Bronze Age hill-forts whose encircling ditches can be seen with astonishing sharpness and accuracy of outline on some air-photos taken partly during the war and partly on special archaeological reconnaissances undertaken by Mr Bradford immediately after it.

Crop-sites as yet unpublished have been recorded by photography in Siam and French Indo-China; and they have been seen also in North America by Dr St Joseph.

There are therefore crop-sites to be found in every continent (except, up to the present, Australia), and it is evident that we are merely at the beginning of discoveries. There is no reason to doubt that in favourable regions whole epochs of lost history may be recovered by air-photography followed up by scientific excavation. Obviously not all can be excavated; but when some have been and the plan-type thus securely established, air-photography will provide the data for distribution-maps of these types.

If one were to attempt to indicate where the most abundant harvest of crop-sites was likely to be gathered, one would find it difficult to exclude any country in the world outside the Polar Regions and the tropical forests and deserts. I did in fact intend at this point to make such an attempt, but on getting out my atlas and looking through it I gave it up. There are so few regions that are likely to be completely barren, and so many that will almost certainly be rich and productive. The harvest is indeed ready but the labourers are few, and often frustrated by official apathy or by their own lack of enterprise and initiative. I will confine myself to a bare list of some obviously promising regions: China, Indo-China and Siam, northern India, western Turkey, Thessaly and Thrace, central Europe from the Russian steppes (which must abound in crop-sites) to Hungary (where I have seen them myself), Nigeria, the corn-lands of North and South America. One would not look for crop-sites except where large level areas are under cultivation and where prehistoric man has been busy digging holes and ditches. The former considerations exclude many Mediterranean and most mountainous lands, and the latter such regions as Australia and parts of Central Asia where existence has been chiefly nomadic. But there is quite enough left to keep archaeologists busy for many centuries.

Archaeology in the Field, 1953

The blue museum

JACQUES-YVES COUSTEAU

JACQUES-YVES COUSTEAU (*1910-*) *was born in the Gironde and educated at naval college. During World War II, in which he served with such distinction as to be awarded the Croix de Guerre, he realized the need for a form of under-water movement more free than traditional helmet diving, and after much experimentation and some personal hazard he developed the aqualung. After the war he recognized the possibilities of his invention as an aid to oceanographic research, and since then his work in marine biology, exploration and archaeology has won for him many international honours.*

There are finer treasures in the Mediterranean, waiting within range of the lung. She is the mother of civilization, the sea girt with the oldest cultures, a museum in sun and spray. The grandest of undersea discoveries, to our taste, are the wrecks of pre-Christian ships on the floor. Twice we have visited classic wrecks and recovered riches beyond gold, the art and artifacts of ancient times. We have located three more such vessels which await salvage.

No cargo ship of antiquity is preserved on land. The Viking ships that have been found buried in the earth and the Emperor Trajan's pleasure barges which were recovered by draining Lake Nemi in Italy, are splendid examples of non-commercial vessels of ancient times, but little is known of the merchant ships that brought nations together.

My first clue to the classic ships appeared in the Bay of Sanary, where forty years ago a fisherman brought up a bronze figurehead. He died before I came to Sanary, and I have never been able to learn where he found it.

Years later Henri Broussard, leader of the Undersea Mountain-climbing Club of Cannes, came up from an aqualung dive with a Greek amphora. The graceful two-handled earthenware jar was the cargo cask of antiquity, used for wine, oil, water, and grain. The cargo ships of Phoenicia, Greece, Carthage, and Rome carried thousands of amphoras in racks in the hold. The bottom of the amphora is conical. On land it was punched into the earth. On shipboard it probably fitted into holes in the cargo racks. Broussard reported that he saw a pile of amphoras in sixty feet of water. He did not guess that it indicated a wreck, because the ship was completely buried.

We dived from the *Elie Monnier* and found the amphoras tumbled and sharded on a bed of compacted organic matter in a dusty grey landscape of weeds. With a powerful suction hose we tunnelled down to find the ship. A hundred amphoras came out of the shaft, most of them with corks still in place. A few had well-preserved waxen seals bearing the initials of ancient Greek wine merchants.

For several days we siphoned mud and amphoras. Fifteen feet down we struck wood, the deck planking of a freighter, one of two ancient cargo vessels that have been found. We were not equipped to carry out full-scale salvage and our time was limited. We went away with amphoras, specimens of wood, and the knowledge of a unique hydro-archaeological site which awaits relatively simple excavation. We believe the hull is preserved and could be raised in one piece. What things that wreck might tell of the shipbuilding and international commerce of the distant past!

Of ancient ships we know a smattering from murals and vase paintings, and can make fairly sound guesses at the science of their navigators. Their cargo ships were short and broad and probably could not work to windward. The few existing light-houses were fires kept burning on shore and there were no beacons or buoys on rocks and shoals. The skippers must have hated to lose sight of land and always tried to moor at night. The pilots must have inherited a knowledge of generations to risk voyaging a ship. Sentenced to skirt the shore, the ships were prey to sudden Mediterranean storms and treacherous rocks. Most of them that foundered, therefore, must have gone down in relatively shallow littoral waters, within diving range. Naval battles and piracy added to the toll of wrecks in shallow depths. I believe there are hundreds of ancient hulks preserved in accessible mud.

A ship that settled in less than sixty feet of water has probably vanished in the scattering action of tide and current, but if it landed deeper it lies in the calm museum of the floor. If the ship fell on rock bed and could not be wholly swallowed, it was overcome by the intense life of the sea. Algae, sponges, hydrozoa, and gorgoniae enveloped it. Hungry fauna sought food and shelter in the wreck. Generations of shellfish died and were crunched by other animals that rained excremental sand and mud which mounted as the wreck broke down. After centuries the simultaneous enveloping and consuming actions reached a common level and the sea bottom healed, leaving perhaps a scar.

A diver needs trained eyes to find the signs of such a wreck – a slight anomaly of the bottom contour, a odd-shaped rock, or the graceful curve of a weed-grown amphora. Broussard's amphoras must have been deck cargo. Amphoras in the hold would have been covered with the ship. Many ancient ships would have been lost beyond trace when coral or sponge divers ignorant of the probability that amphoras point to a ship beneath, removed the jars without noting their location.

Unmistakable were the signs of the only other classic cargo vessel ever found, the galley of Mahdia. The designation is, however, a misnomer; the ship had no tiers of oars; it was a pure sailing vessel which was specially designed to carry an incredible load for its day, at least four hundred tons. The argosy of Mahdia was built by the imperial Romans nearly two thousand years ago for the express task of looting the art treasures of Greece. Our finding of the argosy was the climax of an archaeological detective story.

In June 1907 one of the gnomelike Greek divers who roam far and deep in the Mediterranean was prospecting for sponges off Mahdia on the Tunisian east coast, when he found one hundred and twenty-seven feet down row after row of huge cylindrical objects, half-buried in the mud. He reported that the bottom was covered with cannon.

Admiral Jean Baehme, in command of the French Tunisian naval district, sent helmet divers to investigate. The objects consisted of sixty-three cannon lying in apparent order in a scattered oval on the sea plain, along with other large rectangular forms. All were heavily encrusted with marine life. The divers raised one of the cylinders. When the organisms were removed, marble fluting was revealed. The 'cannon' were Greek Ionic columns.

Alfred Merlin, the Government director of antiquities in Tunisia, sent the news to the famous archaeologist and art historian, Salomon Reinach. Reinach aroused art patrons to finance a salvage effort. Two Americans subscribed, an expatriate who styled himself the Duke of Lubar, after a Papal patent, and James Hazen Hyde, who gave $20,000. Reinach guaranteed no results, but Hyde was willing to back the effort. The expedition was in charge of a Lieutenant Tavera, who engaged experienced civilian divers from Italy and Greece, equipped with the latest helmet diving suits.

The depth was a serious problem at that stage of diving technique. That year the Royal Navy Deep Diving Committee was working out the first tables of stage decompression for operations to one hundred and fifty feet, of which Tavera did not yet have knowledge. Several divers were so heavily stricken with the bends that they could never work again. The difficult and dangerous operation was pursued for five years.

The argosy was a museum of classic sculpture. It held not only capitals, columns, plinths, and horizontal members of the Ionic order, but carved *kraters*, or garden vases, as tall as a man. The divers found marble statuary and bronze figures scattered across the floor as though they had been deck cargo, strewn as the ship side-slipped down like a falling leaf.

Merlin, Reinach, and other experts attributed these treasures to Athens of the first century BC. They believed that the argosy had foundered about 80 BC while carrying the loot systematically gathered by the Roman dictator Lucius Cornelius Sulla, who had sacked Athens in 86 BC. The evidence was that the architectural members constituted a complete temple or sumptuous villa which Sulla's art commissioners had taken apart in Athens for shipment to Rome. The ship was right off course for a journey from Greece to Rome, but that was a not uncommon dilemma for the clumsy sailing ships of that era. Enough *objets d'art* were brought up to fill five rooms of the Alaoui Museum in Tunis, where they may be seen today. In 1913 the salvage operation was broken off when financial aid ran out.

We first heard of the argosy in 1948, when we made an undersea archaeological investigation of the supposed sunken commercial harbour of ancient Carthage. The summer before, Air General Vernoux, commanding in Tunisia, had personally taken some curious aerial photos of the shallow water off Carthage. Through the clear sea were seen distinct geometrical forms that startlingly resembled the moles and basins of a commercial harbour. The photographs were examined by Father Poidebard, a Jesuit scholar, who was also an Air Force chaplain. He had found underwater remains of the ports of Tyre and Sidon in the early twenties and was eager to look into the Carthage discovery.

Father Poidebard came abroad the *Elie Monnier* and we took a ten-man diving team to examine the harbour. We found no trace of masonry or man-made construction, and to check our conclusions we had a powerful dredge cut trenches through the 'harbour' features. The dredgings held no traces of building material.

Then in the Tunisian archives and in the Alaoui Museum we came upon the story of the argosy of Mahdia. Merlin's monographs and Lieutenant Tavera's report led us to believe there were many treasures still left in the wreck. I had a thrill when I came across the name of Admiral Jean Baehme: he was my wife's grandfather. When we found Tavera's clear detailed sketches, showing the bearings of the wreck, we went after it.

We lay off shore in dazzling Sunday morning sunlight, studying the sketches. There were three drawings of landmarks which could be aligned to bring us over the argosy. The first alignment was a castle sighted past a stone butress in a ruined jetty. We saw the castle immediately, but there were four piers of the fallen jetty which could be lined up on it.

The second bearing was to bring a small bush on the dunes in line with the crest of a hill. In the thirty-five years since Tavera had drawn the lonely bush, a veritable forest had grown up around it. The last clue was a change in colour of a distant olive grove with a windmill in the foreground. We squinted through the glasses until our eyes wavered but saw no windmill. We made disparaging remarks about Lieutenant Tavera, now a deceased admiral, and wished he had studied treasure-map cartography from Robert Louis Stevenson.

We went ashore to look for the ruins of the mill. We loaded a truck with wooden beams and muslin to construct a signal beacon on the site. Up and down the dusty road we went, questioning the natives. No one remembered the mill, but someone suggested the old eunuch might know. We found him hobbling down the road, a withered octogenarian with a bald head and fluffy white side-whiskers. It was difficult to imagine him as he once must have been, the sleek and proud factotum of an Arabian Night's harem. His blank eyes lighted encouragingly. 'Windmill? Windmill?' he squeaked. 'I'll take you to it'. Carrying our gear we followed him several miles across country to a pile of rubble. We hurried to build the beacon. The ancient looked worried and mumbled to me 'I remember another mill further on'. He took us to a second heap of stones. As we regarded it with pain, he thought of still another ruined mill. The coast of Mahdia seemed to be a graveyard of windmills.

We returned to the *Elie Monnier* and held council. We decided to exert the maximum possibilities of aqualung search technique to rediscover the wreck as though we knew nothing of its location. That was not greatly exaggerating the situation. We had two facts – the, wreck was somewhere near and it was in one hundred and twenty-seven feet of water. Echo sound established that the floor was nearly level with slight variations in depth. We cruised until we found the depth area closest to Tavera's sounding.

On the sea floor we laid a steel wire grid covering one hundred thousand square feet, with fifty feet between each cross-line. The divers could then swim to and fro along the strips, surveying the terrain right and left for signs of wreck. It took us two days to canvass the grid. We would have found a watch dropped on the field. There was no Roman freighter in our web.

Lieutenant Jean Alinat proposed that he should go down on the undersea sledge. We towed him round the outskirts of the grid, but he found nothing. So passed the fifth fruitless day of our argosy hunt. That night we indicated our desperation by deciding to search closer to shore.

Next morning Commandant Tailliez waved the sledge aside and elected to be towed on a shotline by an auxiliary tender. In our campaigns against the unmanageable sea, I believe I felt the low point that morning, the sixth day of failure. I mentally composed a report to my superiors in Toulon explaining why I had had to work two naval vessels and thirty men for a week on a wreck that had been salved in 1913. Father Poidebard was beginning to remind me of an angry admiral.

A look-out shouted. Out on the sunny water bobbed a tiny dot of orange plastic, the personal signal buoy which Tailliez carried on his belt. When the little buoy comes up, the diver has marked something important. Tailliez broke water, tore out his mouth grip, and yelled. 'A column! – I've found a column'.

The old records indicated that one pillar had been dragged away from the wreck and abandoned when operations were terminated. The argosy was ours. We ran into Mahdia for the night and ordered champagne for all hands. What occurred in the bistros that night illustrates the problem of a crew that has found undersea treasure. The town buzzed with the news that we had found the galley's fabled golden statue, a mythological object locally venerated for a third of a century. Philippe's mollusc-eaten pillar became a fortune of gold. Admirers thronged abroad to congratulate us.

We began work at daybreak. Dumas and I went down and found the main wreck site. It looked nothing like a ship. The fifty-eight remaining columns were vague cylinders covered with thick blankets of vegetation and animals. They lay pounded, flattened into the muddy basement. We called on our imaginations to conjure up a picture of the ship. She must have been a whale of a vessel in her day. Tape measurements on the distribution of the columns outlined a ship perhaps one hundred and thirty feet long by forty feet wide, twice the displacement of the *Elie Monnier*, hanging in the sky above.

The argosy was lost in a bare prairie of mud and sand that spread beyond sight into the clear depths. It was an oasis for fish. Big rock bass swam in the drowned museum. We noticed there were no commercial varieties of sponges growing on the columns. The thoroughgoing Greek sponge divers of our day had apparently gleaned them all. Perhaps they had also removed some small *objets d'art* as a belated patriotic recovery of the Roman pillage.

We were confronted with a semi-industrial salvage operation. We were heirs of the great advances in diving science since Tavera's brave men had dared the wreck, and we had, in fact, a set of unique diving tables newly worked out under Lieutenant Jean Alinat's direction. They were designed for aqualung work, in which men could go down and come back quickly in a series of short dives, without building up the nitrogen saturation of prolonged single plunges. The latest helmet diving tables for a man who was to work forty-five minutes at a depth of the argosy required him to return by stages to decompress. He had to halt four minutes at a depth of thirty feet, proceed to twenty feet and spend twenty-six minutes, and halt for another twenty-six minutes at ten feet, before surfacing.

It cost him almost an hour to return from a three-quarter-hour dive. Alinat's schedule, in contrast, sent a man down for three fifteen-minute dives, alternated by three-hour rest periods. The independent diver needed only five minutes of stage decompression at ten feet after the third dive, one-twelfth of the helmet diver's decompression wait.

To make Alinat's theories work for an efficient attack on the Roman ship, the two-man team had to go down and come up on a rigid timetable. They could not be expected to consult their own wrist-watches. We devised a 'shooting clock', a rifle-man on deck, who fired into the water five minutes after they gone down, again at ten minutes, and discharged three rounds at fifteen minutes as the imperative signal to surface. The shock impact of bullets could be heard distinctly in the wreck.

On the first day I saw a diver surface, holding up a small glittering object, and my heart leaped, for we had hoped to find Greek bronzes. It was merely a bullet from the shooting clock. The floor had become covered with them. It would have been fun to have been hiding behind a column when the next sponge diver sneaked down and saw the bottom gleaming with gold.

The timetable was also threatened by the fact that in wind and current the *Elie Monnier* swung wide off its anchor, so that the divers had long unpredictable diagonals to swim on their way to work, a drain of time and energy. Dumas hoisted out on deck a sling-load of miscellaneous dockyard scrap he had foraged, such as rusted girder bolts and hunks of plate. The divers laughed at the boyish simplicity of Didi's solution. Holding a fifteen-pound scrap iron against his belly, a diver could go sailing down, using his body as a hydrofoil to control his slanting glide. He could come on the wreck from any approach by adjusting his ballast. He could drag, side-slip, or plunge; arrive rested; and drop his iron season ticket.

Didi dutifully obeyed the shooting clock, until one day he spied something fascinating as he climbed from his third dive. The sun was still aglow on the floor. Dumas could not resist a lighting dive at it. He found nothing of interest and returned. At dinner he remarked on a twinge in his shoulder. We grabbed him instantly, locking him in the recompression chamber on deck, and dialled the inside pressure to four atmospheres. We could not take the chances on the bends, which can hit a diver some time after he surfaces. There was a phone from the recompression chamber to a loudspeaker in the divers' ready room. After we had eaten, Dumas took the microphone and broadcast a diatribe against the shipmates who starve a friend. We let him cool off for an hour. It was the only time we have used the recompression chamber on our dives.

The world of the argosy was twilight blue in which flesh became a greenish putty colour. The far-off sun gleamed on the chromed regulators, winked on the frames of the masks, and ensilvered our exhaust bubbles. The light-coloured sea-bed suffused a reflected light strong enough to make a colour movie of the divers at work. I believe it was the first colour film made at such a depth.

The Athenian marbles were dark bluish shapes, blurred with blankets of marine life. We dug under with our hands, dog-fashion, to pass cargo slings under them. As the stones were raised by a winch, colour grew on the crust and at the surface they swung into the air ablaze with life. As they lay draining on deck, the many-coloured coat of flora and fauna faded. We scraped, scrubbed, and hosed the snowy marble volutes and bared them to their first sun since ancient Athens.

Of the stones on the floor, we took four columns, two capitals, and two bases. We raised two mysterious leaden parts of ancient anchors, which were found near the supposed outlines of the ship in positions that indicated the anchors had been stowed when the vessel sank. She must have met her fate suddenly. The anchor parts, each weighing three-quarters of a ton, were oblongs with reinforced holes in the middle, obviously to take wooden posts that had rotted away. Such straight metal shapes could not have been the arms or hooks of the anchors. We dug around for the arms and found none. The finds could only have been the stocks, or top cross-bars. The rest of the anchors must have been made of wood. Here was a puzzle. Why did the ancients put the greatest weight at the top of the anchor?

We argued over evidence and supposition and formed a possible explanation. The ancient ships did not have anchor chain, but used rope. A modern anchored ship driven by wind or current keeps its hook fast by means of the horizontal stress on the lower end of the anchor chain. The Roman anchor rope drew taut in such conditions and would have lifted the wooden hooks if the top had not been weighted with a leaden stock, which provided the horizontal stress.

We worked six days in the Roman argosy, increasingly absorbed with its clues to original seamanship. We wanted to dig for the ship itself. Tavera's records indicated that the helmet divers had excavated extensively in the stern. I selected marbles from a compact area on the starboard ship amidships and sent them up to clear an area for excavation. We lowered a powerful water hose to blow away the earth. A slight current conveniently carried off the mud we raised. We supposed that the heavily laden vessel had burst her top framing outward in the crash and that the main deck had been hammered in by the deck cargo. The theory seemed to be borne out.

Two feet down we stubbed our fingers on a solid deck covered with leaden plates. The sea washed mud into the hole almost as soon as we clawed, but we felt enough of the sturdy deck to estimate that the Roman ship is two-thirds intact. We dug up an Ionic capital which was encased entirely in mud. No molluces or plants had reached it. It scrubbed down to the pristine beauty of the days when it was carved, before Christ was born.

I am confident that amidships there is unbreached cargo. I am certain that then as now the crew lived in the forecastle, the least desirable place of a ship, and that there are intimate possessions and tools buried there that could tell us about what kind of men sailed the Roman ship.

We were merely scratching at history's door in our few days in the huge argosy. We found iron nails corroded to needle thicknesses and bronze nails worn to bright threads. We turned up a millstone, with which the sea cooks had ground grains carried in amphoras. We brought up yard-long pieces of Lebanon cedar ribs covered with the original yellow varnish. (It would be useful to know how to make marine varnish that will survive twenty centuries of immersion.) I dug down five feet at the prow against the sliding sands and embraced the cedar stempost. I could barely touch fingertips round it.

Four years later in New York, I met the president of the French Alliances of the United States and Canada, a lively old gentleman named James Hazen Hyde, and linked his name with that of the patron who had helped salve the treasure of Mahdia. It was the same man. He invited me to dinner at the Plaza and I showed him the colour film of the divers in the wreck. 'Fascinating' he said 'You know I've never seen the things that were brought up. In those days one had a lot of money and a steam yacht. I was cruising in the Aegean while they were diving. I never got to the museum at Tunis. Salomon Reinach sent me photographs of the kraters and statues, I got a nice letter from Merlin, and the Bey of Tunis gave me a decoration. It is interesting indeed to see it after forty-five years'.

The Silent World, 1953

Atomic physics in archaeology

THOMAS GEOFFREY BIBBY

THOMAS GEOFFREY BIBBY (*1917-) was born in Westmorland and educated at Caius College, Cambridge. From 1947 to 1950 he was employed by the Iraq Petroleum Company, but since 1950 he has devoted himself exclusively to his work on archaeology. He now lives in Denmark, where he holds the post of Keeper and head of the Oriental Department of the Forhistorisk Museum.*

Once again the new method clears away a misconception. Just as De Geer showed that a year was a concept independent of man, so Professor Willard F. Libby of the University of Chicago, the inventor of the radio-active-carbon technique, has shown that time is a concept independent of years. The age of an object is not basically the number of years but rather the length of time which it has existed. Years, though not man-made, are man-employed as a unit for measuring time. But time goes on, regardless of whether man measures it in years or not.

Carbon is the basic ingredient for all organic matter, the major constituent of animal and vegetable life, and at the same time, in the form of carbon dioxide, one of the principal ingredients of the air. Carbon is absorbed from the carbon dioxide of the air by plants which release the surplus oxygen; and this assimilated carbon in the plants is in turn consumed by animals and by man. Both in plants and in animals the carbon is partly used to replace structural wastage and to build up new structure, the process we call growth. There is a constant influx of new carbon to any living growing organism, and a constant, though lesser, outflow of the old.

Now, carbon is not the simple element that it was believed in pre-atomic times to be. It consists of three isotopes, three distinct substances which are chemically indistinguishable but which have different physical characteristics, the most obvious being a different in atomic weight, 12, 13 and 14. Ordinary everyday carbon is of atomic weight

12. But C-12 is mixed with one part to several million of C-13 and C-14. These tiny proportions of the heavier carbon are manufactured in the upper levels of the atmosphere. There the carbon dioxide of the air is exposed to bombardment by cosmic rays, the unexplained streams of ionized particles which shower down upon the earth from outer space. When such a particle strikes an atom of carbon in the carbon-dioxide of the atmosphere, sufficient of the energy, or matter, of the particle is absorbed to convert the C-12 into C-13 or C-14.

This 'heavy carbon' is like the ordinary carbon, absorbed from the atmosphere, at first or second hand, by every living thing.

This process would be of only academic interest were it not for a very important fact. Carbon 14 is radio-active.

Now, radio-active materials do two things. They emit particles, the rate of emission of which can be measured on a Geiger counter, and in the process they break down into other normally non-radio-active substances. They break down at a fixed rate for each radio-active substance, so that it is possible to state that after a definite length of time the amount of radio-activity in a quantity of material will be reduced to half, and after the same period again to a quarter, and so on. This fixed period is known as the 'half-life' of the substance.

Libby, a gangling six-foot atomic chemist, first became interested in Carbon 14 in 1946, after an exciting four years on the Manhattan Project. And he reasoned out that, once the proportion of C-14 in the carbon of the atmosphere is kept constant by the continual streams of cosmic rays, and since every living creature keeps renewing its C-14 by absorption of the atmospheric carbon, then every living creature is radio-active, and to exactly the same degree.

This rather disturbing thought was still not of immediate concern to the prehistorian interested in determination of chronology. But in 1947 Libby took his reasoning a step further. When an organism dies, it ceases to absorb new carbon from the air. From that point the natural breakdown of its C-14 is not counter-balanced by new intake. Therefore its proportion of C-14 to C-12 will slowly drop – *and drop at a fixed rate*. The half-life of Carbon-14 was found to be 5,568 years, to an accuracy of 0·54 per cent. So that a tree cut down 5,568 years ago would produce only half as many clicks on a Geiger counter as a tree cut down yesterday.

Now the prehistorians woke up. For the reverse was also true. If a piece of wood gave only half the number of clicks given by a modern piece, then that piece of wood was 5,568 years old. And any other proportion of clicks could likewise be converted into a date, as far back as the limits of accuracy of the machine. A method of dating any prehistoric material containing carbon had suddenly appeared out of the blue.

And so it proved. A committee of four archaeologists was set up by the American Anthropological Association in February of 1948 and proceeded to submit samples of every conceivable type of prehistoric material containing carbon to Libby and his battery of Geigers. The first samples were objects of known date – wood from the graves of Egyptian Pharaohs and from Hittite palaces, ashes from Roman encampment and cloth from the Dead Sea scrolls. Libby was able to indicate a date conforming to within ten per cent with the date already known. This new method had proved itself.

Now the impossible could be attempted. The objects that were, by axiom, undatable could be tested. The embers of a fire from the cave at Lascaux dated the Stone Age habitation of the cave to 15,516 years ago; birchwood from the edge of the ice cap in northern Germany determined the retreat of the ice from that point as occurring 10,800 years ago; shells from one of the earliest agricultural settlements in the world, Jarmo in Iraq, gave a reading of 6,707 years.

We should not be misled by the apparent exactitude of the number of years resulting. In each case the number was accompanied by a statement of the permissible error, and which was usually up to, and sometimes over, ten per cent. But even a ten per cent inaccuracy is many times better than the highly subjective estimates previously possible. And better shielding of the Geigers from stray cosmic rays, better preparation of the samples, and greater care in their collection and transport have already resulted in a significant drop in the margin of error.

It is with the Geiger counter that the future of archaeological dating rests – until an even better method is found. Libby's machine has been duplicated at all the major centres of anthropological study in America, and a number have been erected in Europe, the first being at Cambridge and Copenhagen. And now, in the museum that Thomsen founded, only a short way from the rooms in which he first displayed his collection arranged by the system of three chronologically successive ages, a lead-shielded apparatus clicks busily, measuring out with increasing accuracy the age of the objects that he first dared to suggest were prehistoric.

The Testimony of the Spade, 1957

The Lerici Periscope

CARLO MAURILIO LERICI

CARLO MAURILIO LERICI (1890–) was born in Verona and studied industrial and mechanical engineering at Turin Polytechnic. During the early part of his life he achieved considerable success as an industrial engineer, pioneering new geophysical methods of prospecting for oil and water, but his interest began to turn towards antiquity when his relatives asked him to design a suitable family mausoleum. With characteristic thoroughness he undertook a study of ancient models upon which to base his design, and his attention gradually became absorbed by the monuments of the fascinating and little-known civilization of the Etruscans. He is deeply concerned for the threatened safety of the Etruscan remains, and has devoted all the resources of his scientific training and archaeological knowledge to their discovery and preservation. His geophysical techniques, which he was the first to apply to archaeological problems, have achieved remarkable results; in the following passage (written in 1961) he quotes the discovery of 600 tombs at Cerveteri and 2,600 at Tarquinia, but by June 1964 these figures had risen to 950 at Cerveteri and 5,250 at Tarquinia.

A few months ago the Lerici Foundation of the Milan Polytechnic was asked to organize an archaeological survey of the ancient city of Sibari and of other interesting remains in the area round the rivers Crati and Coscile in Calabria.

This is a large area, extending over several tens of square kilometres, so that emphasis was on the development of apparatus which would enable a small group of people to work very much faster than large teams using traditional methods.

That these new methods have proved themselves remarkably successful can be seen by the following list of discoveries made in five years by two people, with subsidiary labour recruited on the spot.

At Fabriano a necropolis.

At Cerveteri 600 tomb chambers containing 6,500 excavated objects.

At Vulci numerous structural remains of the ancient city, including the Tomb of the Inscriptions, with a large sculptured sarcophagus.
At Tarquinia, 2,600 tomb chambers, 20 of them painted.
At Sibari various remains of ancient buildings.

For comparison with previous work, it is sufficient to record that in the Tarquinia region it had previously taken the whole of the nineteenth century to record as many painted tombs as we have recorded in five years; that since 1892, i.e. during sixty-six years, not a single painted tomb had been discovered, and that during the last fifteen years an average of one tomb a year had been discovered in the Cerveteri region. A comparison with the records shows that our discoveries at Tarquinia which are still proceeding with success, will soon double the heritage of Etruscan pictures. The Polytechnic group has accomplished in five years what would previously have taken more than a century.

THE METHODS

The methods found to be most successful are: (1) measurement of the *electrical resistance* of the ground, by which changes under the surface are revealed, and (2) the use of *exploratory probes* at points indicated by resistance measurement. These probes can be used, either to bring up a complete sample of the soil strata as a core, or, if a tomb is pierced, to allow visual and photographic examination of the interior.

These methods have proved of outstanding value, and will be described in a section below. But other methods have also been used to gather useful information.

First among these is *aerial photography*. This is regularly used in our work. But two points should be noted. Firstly, the usual survey photographs are not the best for our purpose, since light and other factors should be so chosen as to emphasize archaeological detail. Also infra-red photographs are of particular value. Secondly, we have shown in the sites so far surveyed that archaeological detail is not likely to appear if the remains are below 1·5–2 metres from the surface. In the Latium region, for instance, details of necropolises at Cerveteri and Tarquinia, and of inhabited settlements at Vulci, are only visible when closer to the surface. Thus about 50 per cent of the formations at Cerveteri and 75 to 80 per cent at Tarquinia are not visible in aerial photographs, while at Sibari aerial photographs are of very little value.

With these reservations, aerial survey offers an indispensable beginning to every large-scale archaeological project.

In cases where moisture in the soil renders resistance measurement less effective, this method may be supplemented by seismic recordings. Here, a small explosive charge is detonated at one point in the ground, and the multiple echoes at various receiving points are recorded.

ARCHAEOLOGICAL SURVEY BY MEASUREMENT OF THE ELECTRICAL RESISTANCE OF THE GROUND

If two metal rods (the electrodes) are pushed into the ground and a current passed between them, we can measure the electrical resistance between them in the normal way. The resistivity of a material is the resistance of a block of unit length and cross-section, in this case a cubic metre, and we can obtain the resistivity of the earth approximately from the resistance reading. As we move the electrodes farther apart, the resistance will increase, but if the earth is uniform the resistivity will remain constant. The farther apart the electrodes are placed, the more the current will travel to deeper layers as it passes from one electrode to the other. Thus if there is a lower layer of earth through which the current passes more easily (i.e. a lower resistivity), this will eventually start to contribute to the result, and the overall resistivity will fall. If the electrodes are over an empty tomb, the reverse may happen, since air has a very high resistivity, and the resistivity will rise, as the electrodes are moved apart. . . .

It can now be seen that any buried structures, such as tombs or buildings, can be detected and their depth estimated.

There are two methods of resistance survey: vertical and horizontal electrical soundings.

Vertical Electrical Soundings

The two middle electrodes are kept fixed, and the two outer electrodes are moved apart in stages. Thus we get a picture of the vertical structure of the soil below the apparatus.

Horizontal Electrical Soundings

To explore the nature of the ground at a fixed depth below the surface, we fix the distance between all four electrodes, and move the whole set together along the ground.

It is our common practice to determine first of all the layer structure of the ground with a few vertical soundings, and then to survey along a line with horizontal, and finally to confirm any discovery with a vertical sounding.

Equipment for Resistance Measurement

The portable apparatus for the surveys described above consists of two parts. The lower part is the power pack, which converts the current from a 12-volt battery to values suitable for the recording devices housed in the upper part. Readings can be taken in a few seconds. This apparatus has been developed by the Foundation. In use, it is mounted in the back of a jeep.

THE PROBES

The MacCullogh Motor-probe

This portable motor drill, weighing 40 kg., can be used in two ways. (A) With a twist-drill bit, holes may be bored up to 12 cm. in diameter. (B) With a core sampler in place of the twist-drill, a core of soil up to 40 cm. long may be withdrawn so that all the strata down to this depth are revealed.

Thus, when the resistance survey indicates a likely archaeological formation, the motor-probe may be used, either to bring up a sample of the soil, or to pierce a tomb-chamber.

The Periscope

When a tomb-chamber has been located and pierced by the motor-probe, the periscope can be lowered so that the interior of the chamber may be studied and photographed. This device was developed in the Polytechnic for our work. It consists of a compound tube from 3 to 5 metres long, with two windows at its lower end, the upper for viewing and photographing, and the bottom window for illumination of the chamber. A sequence of 12 photographs, with the periscope turned through 30 degrees after each exposure, will record the complete tomb.

In this way the periscope enables the tomb to be examined in all detail without entry. Thanks to this instrument the Milan Polytechnic now has archives of unprecedented scope covering the tombs of the seventh-third centuries BC. Some of these tombs must wait many months before they are opened.

A complete documentation in colour of all the new discoveries will be published in 1961 under the auspices of the Lerici Foundation of the Milan Polytechnic.

SOME PROBLEMS

The aim of the work described above is to defend and conserve our buried archaeological inheritance.

Fondazione Lerici

30. C. M. Lerici's periscope camera at work. The camera-eye explores the inside of an Etruscan grave: is it worth while to open it?

Fondazione Lerici

31. Objects inside an unopened Etruscan tomb, photographed by the periscope camera.

It has been argued by our critics that these rapid methods do not allow the thorough and detailed examination that is required by archaeology today. This criticism can best be answered by stating the following facts.

1. Our survey leaves the tombs undamaged in every way, and located for subsequent detailed investigation, the probe hole being plugged.

2. Extensive cultivation in the last ten years is frequently preceded by deep-ploughing, using bulldozers. On several occasions these have irreparably damaged archaeological material near the surface. Furthermore, owing to the subsequent enrichment of the soil with fertilizers, salt-enriched water seeps into the buried remains and causes further damage. The Etruscan necropolis at Tarquinia offers an impressive example of this destruction. Deterioration is proceeding at such a rate that in a few years there will be very much less to recover.

3. Illegal research. Today illegal research in the archaeological zones of Italy forms the *larger part* of all excavations, because it is many times superior in efficiency of discovery to that carried out by the Administration of Antiquities and other authorized bodies. The damage caused by this robbery, either through the dispersal of unrecorded material or through negligent treatment, can be valued in billions of lire every year. The Milan Polytechnic has in its records examples of impressive gravity, such as the destruction of certain painted walls in the Tarquinia necropolis in order to penetrate the adjacent spaces and steal the antiquities. These facts must fully justify a rapid and careful survey of existing archaeological formations, with a view to their subsequent protection and conservation.

The speed of our discoveries has found the authorities unprepared; and in fact sufficient personnel and funds are simply not available in Italy to cover even the most important works of conservation.

As we work, we know very well that illegal excavators are carefully observing our survey. In many cases the Milan Polytechnic has had to provide day and night guards at its own expense. Notwithstanding, where the Polytechnic squad works, there the illegal excavators concentrate their work. There have even been attempts to export whole fragments of walls.

Conservation Required

After a tomb has been entered, it is most important to ensure that it remains so isolated that temperature and humidity remain as before, and fairly constant. Measures may then be taken to remove incrustations of salts and to prevent further seepage. Some paintings, however, must be removed to stable environments. Here the methods of the Instituto Centrale at Rome have proved invaluable, and should be extended.

Methods used in the Archaeological Prospecting of Etruscan Tombs,
Studies in Conservation, vol. 6, no. 1, 1961

Photogrammetry

Archaeology, which has for so long depended upon the interpretive eye and mind of the scholar, is now beginning to take its place among the exact sciences, where the use of complex technical devices is gradually cutting down the possibility of error. As we have seen, machines can be used to locate the position of underground chambers, to ascertain the date of ancient artifacts, to trace the outline of earth-works invisible from ground level. They can also reproduce exact copies of carved or moulded surfaces, and may even one day help us to unravel forgotten languages.

The Documentation Centre was set up in May 1955 by the Antiquities Service of Egypt with the direct co-operation of Unesco. It is an Egyptian body, financed by the government of the United Arab Republic. Unesco has a representative on the Board of Directors of the Centre and provides technical aid in the form of international specialists.

From the days of Champollion – the founder of scientific Egyptology – the work of preserving monuments, organizing excavation work, research and documentation studies has been carried out by a great many foundations, museums and universities in Egypt, Europe and America. It has often been done most successfully, but almost inevitably in a piece-meal fashion. Never until now has so systematically organized a body as the Cairo Centre been at work in this field. Its operations have called for powerful resources and the services of large teams of full-time specialists working in a synchronized operation.

Originally, the Centre had chosen as its first task to make systematic surveys of the Necropolis of Thebes where the tombs, once well preserved, had shown signs of deterioration. The announcement of the High Dam project changed the order of priorities and began the race against time in Lower Nubia. In the next five years something like one hundred missions are planned with a clear-cut programme of work relating to the monuments threatened by the Aswan High Dam.

The archaeologists and philologists attached to the Centre co-ordinate all operations, taking into account existing documentation and data. They direct work in the field and then record the results of every mission on card indexes.

Facts needed to complement copies and descriptions are assembled by the technical section. Architects prepare plans, sections and elevations, complete to the most minute detail – every brick, every flagstone and even the smallest hole in a wall is marked in. Experts in architectural drawing trained at the Centre use photographs to prepare exact plans of groups of monuments. The old method of making tracings from actual monuments is no longer used except for small details, or in cases where monuments are too closely hemmed in or in too bad a state of preservation for satisfactory photographs to be taken. Copies of those reliefs which are renowned for their beauty or historical interest and of any hieroglyphic inscriptions likely to provoke controversy, are made by moulders, who also prepare architectural models.

Photographers find themselves working closely with many of the other specialists. Following details of the master plan, they develop their test film each day on the spot before sending the negatives to the developing laboratory in Cairo. At the same time they take identical photographs on colour film. Yet even all this work is not enough.

The photographic reproduction of works of art, and of sculpture in particular, is – as André Malraux has termed it – a phenomenon of recreation. Freed from the recesses where they were hidden away, sculptures seem to spring into life again when viewed in this new light, becoming familiar and acquiring fresh significance.

Photography, like drawing and even architectural plans, contains a certain element of subjectivity which can produce various degrees of distortion. To obtain the absolute accuracy demanded by scientific recording, use has been made of photogrammetry, a process that has been employed for the past forty years in the preparation of geographical maps.

This method was first used to survey a monument in 1850 and today provides invaluable documentary material for archaeologists. The stereoscopic photographs, taken with the aid of a phototheodolite, give precise information down to the smallest detail of a relief and thus make possible the creation of an absolutely faithful copy in reproductions, models and casts.

Photogrammetry opens up new horizons in the knowledge of forms and techniques. It may even make possible the discovery of architectural laws as yet undisclosed by Egyptologists, and may add to our knowledge of sculptural techniques. For instance, the contour lines taken on the face of the North-West Osirian colossus (23 feet) in the inner court of the Great Temple of Abu Simbel, and those taken on the face of the South colossus (65 feet) on the façade, show some striking resemblances between the two even down to the modelling of the cartilage of the nose.

When all the survey programmes are completed, the Documentation Centre of Cairo will be a rich, permanent source of information both for Egyptological studies and for works destined for the man in the street. As a safety measure, all the archives are to be microfilmed and one copy of every document will be given special security treatment to guard against any possible destruction or deterioration.

Thanks to the international action undertaken by Unesco there is now reason to hope that these majestic monuments will be saved from the encroaching waters and that present and future generations will still be able to visit the giant statues of Rameses II and the island temples of Philae. Furthermore, the extensive work undertaken by the Documentation Centre on Ancient Egypt will give the world's Egyptologists the possibility of adding to our knowledge of one of the areas of the Ancient World which has by no means finished yielding up its secrets.

Unesco Courier, February 1960

Computer decipherment?

In the latter half of 1960 a group of workers at the Institute of Mathematics of the Siberian Division of the USSR Academy of Sciences undertook an experiment in deciphering the Maya language with an electronic computer. The results of this work were reported at the Conference on Information Processing, Machine Translation and the Automatic Reading of Text, held at Moscow, January 21–30, 1961.

This was accompanied by publication of a reading (to be more precise – transliteration without translation) of fragments of Maya texts.

The value of the work of the Institute of Mathematics personnel lies in the fact that this was the first practical proof of the possibility of successful study by computer of ancient systems of writing. Theoretically this problem arose some years ago, after statistical methods had been successfully employed by 'manual' means for deciphering ancient systems of writing (by M. Ventris for the syllabic Cretan script, and by the present author with respect to the hieroglyphic Maya script). Thus, the use of computers for decipherment was a logical consequence and capping of a new stage in the development of the theory of decipherment characterized by large-scale employment of statistical methods.

In posing the general objective of investigating 'the possible applications of computers to solution of problems in ancient systems of writing and in developing a technique for effective employment of electronic computers towards this end' (Evreinov I, p. 3) the authors of these papers had the goal, with respect to Maya hieroglyphic texts, 'of establishing the relationship between the words of the lexicon and the manuscript texts, and of determining by this means the nature of the employment of the hieroglyphs and their meanings' (Evreinov I, p. 4). From the published materials it follows that, in fact, a somewhat narrower objective was posed – that of providing a transliteration of the hieroglyphic texts into Latin script (or, to be more exact, into the so-called 'traditional' Maya alphabet) with no effort at translation.

The authors were, of course, familiar with 'manual' decipherment of Maya writing and with the technique employed in it.

The Institute of Mathematics workers selected the Dresden and Madrid Maya codices for study. Palaeographic work (such as identification of symbols un-clearly written, discovery of errors in writing etc.) was not undertaken, as the workers used the present author's texts of all the manuscripts and certain Maya inscriptions in numeral coding (a three-digit number for each symbol), as well as a catalogue of the symbols with denotation of allographs. Omission of the Paris Codex from consideration was unfortunate inasmuch as the Madrid Codex is in considerably worse condition. Moreover, limitation of the raw material complicates the investigation. The major sources employed on the Maya language of the colonial period were the Motul Dictionary, the *Book of Chilam Balam of Chumavei* and the Codex Perez. . . .

The processing of the lexical data took place parallel to the processing of the hieroglyphic texts: the frequency of syllables and words was computed and, in addition, lists of words were compiled in accordance with their meanings (the animal and vegetable world, various trades, objects of daily life, gods, rituals, sacrifices, astronomical and calendrical terms, and the most commonly used words). In view of the substantial difference in the vocabulary of the Maya language during the colonial period and that of the hieroglyphic texts, these lists proved to be essentially useless.

In comparisons of the processed data, the symbols were compared with the syllables in frequency, the number of symbols in the hieroglyph was compared with the number of syllables in the word. ('The most efficient method was the so-called "rebus" method, based upon seeking points of correspondence between complexes containing specific numbers of symbols, and words containing the corresponding number of syllables' (Evreinov I, p. 10); in another paper we read that the 'rebus' method 'consists of the hieroglyphs being identified with words against the background of the subject of the section being dealt with, the meaning of symbols formerly defined, and the methods by which the symbols are employed in the given hieroglyph' (Ustinov, p. 15).) For hieroglyphs whose meaning was determined on the basis of the drawings, appropriate synonyms were chosen in accordance with lists by subject matter, and then one of them was chosen in accordance with conditions of the criteria of accuracy.

It must be noted that the authors developed no new methods whatever, but employed those long since utilized in the study of Maya codices, for the most part as far back as the last century. Uncoordinated employment of all these various methods is responsible for the confusion in the results and led to elementary errors and, in addition, changed the problem posed. In its final form the task undertaken proved to be the following: to provide a transliteration without translation of a text consisting of phrases accompanied by illustrations and written in unknown symbols in a known language. In this extremely simplified form, the problem has little in common with that of deciphering ancient systems of writing. Nevertheless the authors regard it as being 'similar in nature to the problems of machine translation and problems of study of signal systems', and compare the research process to translation of creative writings (Evreinov I, p. 11). The extensive employment of supplementary methods demonstrates that the authors were unable to employ statistical methods with satisfactory effect.

For the reasons detailed above, the results following twenty hours of computer processing of the data proved to be very modest. The authors themselves assert that they had read 'approximately forty per cent' of the Madrid and Dresden Maya codices (Ustinov, p. 25). What they probably meant is that they had succeeded in duplicating approximately forty per cent of the published 'manual' decipherment. This is approximately correct. The published 'Preliminary Results' (Predvaritel'nye rezul'taty) (Evreinov III) adduces transliterations of eight paragraphs (of 170) in the Dresden Codex and 27 (of 250) of the Madrid. A transliteration is provided of 367 hieroglyphs, including repetitions (all told, the codices contain about 5,300 differentiable hieroglyphs). If we eliminate repetitions, the authors provide a transliteration of sixty-seven hieroglyphs (representing words or combinations thereof). The so-called 'readings' (i.e. transliterations) of hieroglyphs – both by the Novosibirsk team, and in general in the literature of deciphering of the Maya script – are by no means of equal value throughout. . . .

For all practical purposes, this exhausts the results of decipherment in the true meaning of the term, i.e. determination of the phonetic reading of the symbols. The 'machine' decipherment yielded considerably fewer readings than the 'manual' and provided no correct new readings whatever (whereas in the incorrect readings it essentially repeated the early results of 'manual' decipherment). . . .

The authors assert that the results of their work confirm the assumption on which it was based. If, as the result of the 'machine' decipherment of the Maya script, confirmation was obtained of the author's 'hypothesis' of identity of the language of the hieroglyphic texts and the language of the 16th century Maya, this would mean that 'machine' decipherment is an absurdity. In reality this 'hypothesis' is wholly refuted by the results of the 'machine' decipherment (as otherwise it would not have been necessary to substitute the conventional names for the hieroglyphs in place of true readings).

The authors' papers contain a number of erroneous propositions that tend to mislead the reader. It is impossible to examine them all in the present article, but it is necessary to pause to consider at least a few. The authors assert, for example, that 'investigation of the script of the ancient Maya was performed by mathematical methods and with an electronic computer. The processing of informational data of such great volume and diversity in any form of notation is virtually impossible without the employment of modern methods of research. So is disclosure of all the connections and laws of quantitative and qualitative aspects of the problem capable of shedding light on determination of the precise sense and phonetic significance of the symbol and hieroglyph' (Ustinov, pp. 12-13; compare also Evreinov II, p. 4). This assertion does not correspond to the facts. It is common knowledge that an increase in the amount of data does not complicate but facilitates decipherment, be it 'manual' or 'machine'. On the other hand, a reduction in the amount of material increases the volume of work required for decipherment to astronomical dimensions. It is when the volume of data is small (i.e. the inscription on a clay vessel from the Slavic burial ground in Alekonovo village, or the inscription on the Phaistos disk) that virtually insuperable difficulties for deciphering arise.

Further, the authors assert that 'in analysis of the archaic script of the Maya, in which heterogeneous material must be studied, it is impossible to limit oneself to some single method' (Evreinov I, p. 8). This assertion is not only untenable as theory, but has now since been refuted in practice by the fact of 'manual' deciphering which, as is well known, was accomplished exclusively by statistical means.

The problem before the writers was to employ modern computer equipment for an experimental decipherment of an ancient script. It was completely unimportant whether this script had already been deciphered or not, although for control purposes it made sense to start with an analysis of a script already deciphered. This was the reason for selection of the Maya script for the first effort (it would have been just as possible to employ Egyptian hieroglyphics, the cuneiform writing, etc.). The work carried out by the writers under review demonstrated in practice that modern computer technology can be employed in deciphering ancient systems of writing. The 'machine' deciphering confirmed the fact that when a script is studied objectively the results certainly agree. It must be observed that if the results of 'machine' decipherment had not coincided with those of the prior 'manual' work, it would have been necessary to review the 'machine' (and not the already proved 'manuai') deciphering, as must actually be done with respect to that portion of the work in which obviously erroneous phonetic readings are adduced (although they, too, repeat previously published work). The 'machine' deciphering was successful only in part in duplicating the 'manual' work and added nothing to our knowledge of Maya script. In order to achieve results of practical significance for American studies, the authors will have to re-examine their theoretical postulates and considerably improve the methods of programming.

Soviet Anthropology and Archaeology, vol. 1, no. 3 Winter, 1962/3

SOURCES

J. M. Allegro: *The Dead Sea Scrolls*. London: Pelican Books; 1956. By permission of Penguin Books, Ltd.

G. B. Belzoni: *Narrative of Operations and Recent Researches in Egypt and Nubia*. London: John Murray; 1820.

Geoffrey Bibby: *The Testimony of the Spade*. New York: Alfred A. Knopf; 1956. By permission of the publishers.

Hiram Bingham: *Lost City of the Incas*. New York: Appleton-Century; 1951. By permission of J. M. Dent & Sons Ltd.

Helmuth Bossert: *Karatepe*. Istanbul: Istanbul University; 1946. By permission of Dr. E.-M. Fischer-Bossert.

P. E. Botta: *Letters on the Discoveries at Nineveh*. London: Longman, Brown, Green and Longmans; 1850.

R. L. S. Bruce-Mitford: *Recent Archaeological Excavations in Britain*. New York: Macmillan; 1957. By permission of Routledge & Kegan Paul, London.

E. A. W. Budge: *By Nile and Tigris*, Vol. I. London: John Murray; 1920. By permission of the publishers.

J. L. Burckhardt: *Travels in Nubia*. London: John Murray; 1819.

Howard Carter: *The Tomb of Tut-ankh-Amen*, Vol. II. London: Cassell and Company Ltd.; 1927. By permission of Curtis Brown Ltd.

J. F. Champollion: *Lettre à M. Dacier Relative à l'Alphabet des Hiéroglyphes Phonétiques*. Paris: Academie Royale; 1822.

Jacques-Yves Cousteau: *The Silent World*. New York: Harper and Row; 1953. By permission of Hamish Hamilton, London.

O. G. S. Crawford: *Archaeology in the Field*. New York: Frederick Praeger; 1953. By permission of J. M. Dent & Sons Ltd.

E. Curtius: *Archaeologische Zeitung*, Vol. XXXV, Part I. Berlin, 1877.

——— and F. Adler: *Olympia*, Vol. I. Berlin: A. Asher & Co.; 1870.

G. Dennis: *Cities and Cemeteries of Etruria*, 3rd edn., Vol. II. London: John Murray; 1883.

D. V. Denon: *Travels in Upper and Lower Egypt*. London: James Ridgway; 1802.

F. K. Dörner: "Die Königsresidenz am Nymphenfluss," *Kosmos*, Vol. LII. Stuttgart: Franck'sche Verlag; 1956. By permission of Professor Dr. F. K. Dörner and Franck'sche Verlag, Stuttgart.

Amelia Edwards: *A Thousand Miles Up the Nile*. London: George Routledge and Sons; 1889.

Earl of Elgin: *Memorandum on the Subject of the Earl of Elgin's Pursuits in Greece*. London: William Miller; 1811.

Arthur J. Evans: *The Palace of Minos*, Vol. III. London: Macmillan & Co. Ltd.; 1930. By permission of Agathon Press, Inc. *The Palace of Minos* was reprinted in 1964 by Biblo & Tannen, Inc., in co-operation with Agathon Press.

Fouilles de Delphes, Vol. 4, Part 5. Paris: École française d'Athènes; 1890.

Nelson Glueck: *Rivers in the Desert*. New York: Farrar, Straus & Giroux; 1959. By permission of Weidenfeld and Nicholson, London.

Augustus Goldsmidt: "The Plaster Corpses of Pompeii": see *Proceedings of the Society of Antiquaries of London*.

M. Zakaria Goneim: *The Lost Pyramid*. New York: Holt, Rinehart and Winston; 1956. By permission of Longmans, Green & Co., London.

Victor W. von Hagen: *Highway of the Sun*. New York: Duell, Sloan and Pearce; 1955. By permission of Mr. V. W. von Hagen.

H. V. Hilprecht: *Explorations in Bible Lands*. Edinburgh: T. and T. Clark; 1903.

C. Humann: *Der Pergamon-Altar*, ed. E. Schulte. Dortmund: Ardey Verlag; 1959.

Alexander von Humboldt: *Researches Concerning the Institutions and Monuments of the Ancient Inhabitants of America*. London: Longman, Hurst, Rees, Orme & Brown, J. Murray and H. Colburn; 1814.

Athanasius Kircher: *Lingua Aegyptiaica*. Rome: Hermann Scheus; 1643.

Robert Koldewey: *The Excavations at Babylon*. New York: Macmillan; 1915.

Henry A. Layard: *Nineveh and its Remains.* London: John Murray; 1867.

C. M. Lerici: Lecture to the Rotary Club of Rome. Milan Polytechnic, Lerici Foundation, 1958. By permission of Professor C. M. Lerici.

———: *Methods Used in the Archaeological Prospecting of Etruscan Tombs.* London: *Studies in Conservation,* Vol. 6, No. 1; 1961. By permission of Professor C. M. Lerici.

Paul MacKendrick: *The Mute Stones Speak.* New York: St. Martin's Press; 1962. By permission of Methuen & Co. Ltd., London.

A. E Mariette: *Monuments of Upper Egypt.* London , 1877.

Gaston Maspero: *Institut Egyptien Bulletin,* Series 2, No. 2. Marseilles, 1881.

L. Matous: *Bedrich Hrozny: The Life and Work of a Czech Oriental Scholar.* Prague: Orbis; 1949. By permission of Professor L. Matous.

Memorandum on the Subject of the Earl of Elgin's Pursuits in Greece: *see* Elgin.

Napoleon I: *Correspondance de Napoléon,* Vol. I. Paris: Imprimerie Impériale; 1858.

W. M. Flinders Petrie: *Ten Years' Digging in Egypt.* Edinburgh: Religious Tract Society; 1892. By permission of Miss A. Petrie.

Arthur Posnansky: *Tihuanacu: Cradle of American Man.* New York: J. Augustin; 1945.

Proceedings of the Society of Antiquaries of London, Series 2, Vol. II. London, 1863.

Henry Rawlinson: "The Persian Cuneiform Inscriptions at Behistun," *Journal of the Royal Asiatic Society,* Vol. 10. London, 1846.

Claudius Rich: *Second Memoir on Babylon.* London: Longman, Hurst, Rees, Orme and Brown, J. Murray; 1818.

Alberto Ruz: "An Astonishing Discovery," *Illustrated London News,* 29 August 1953, pp. 321–3. By permission of the publishers.

C. F. A. Schaeffer: "The French Excavations in Syria," *Antiquity,* Vol. IV, No. 16. London, 1930. By permission of Professor C. F. A. Schaeffer.

Heinrich Schliemann: *Ilios.* London: John Murray; 1880.

———: *Mycenae.* London: John Murray; 1878.

———: *Troy and its Remains.* London: John Murray; 1875.

Eduard Seler: "The Temple Pyramid of Tepoxtlan," *Bulletin of the Bureau of American Ethnology*, No. 28, pp. 341–52. Washington, 1904. By permission of the Smithsonian Institution, Washington.

George Smith: *Assyrian Discoveries*. London: Sampson Low, Marston, Low & Searle; 1875.

George Elliott Smith: "The Elephant Controversy Settled by a Decisive Discovery," *Illustrated London News*, 15 January 1927, pp. 86, 87, and 108. By permission of the publishers.

Charles Piazzi Smyth: *Our Inheritance in the Great Pyramid*. London: Charles Nisbet & Co.; 1890.

Sir Hans Sloane: *Printed Will and Codicils of Sir Hans Sloane, Bart.* London: John Virtuoso; 1753.

Soviet Anthropology and Archaeology, Vol. I, No. 3, Winter 1962/3, pp. 43–50. New York: International Arts and Sciences Press. By permission of the publishers.

John L. Stephens: *Incidents of Travel in Central America*. New York: Harper and Brothers; 1842.

Claude Tarral: "The Discovery of the 'Venus de Milo,' " *Revue Archéologique*, Series IV, Vol. VII, pp. 193–9. Paris, 1906.

Lord William Taylour: *The Mycenaeans*. New York: Praeger; 1964. By courtesy of Lord William Taylour.

General Sir Tomkyns H. Turner: "How the Rosetta Stone Came to the British Museum," *Archaeologia*, Vol. XVI, pp. 212–14. London, 1812.

Vittorino Veronese: "An Appeal" (by the Director-General of UNESCO), *UNESCO Courier*. Paris, February 1960.

Von Hagen, V. W.: *see* Hagen, V. W. von.

Von Humboldt, Alexander: *see* Humboldt, Alexander von.

J. F. M. Waldeck: *Voyage Pittoresque et Archaéologique dans la province d' Yucatan et aux ruines d'Itzalanes*. Paris: Dufour; 1838.

Horace Walpole: *The Letters of Horace Walpole*, Vol. III, ed. Mrs. Paget Toynbee. Oxford: Clarendon Press; 1903. By permission of the publishers.

Johann J. Winckelmann: *A Critical Account of the Situation and Destruction of Herculaneum and Pompeii*. London: T. Carnan and F. Newbery; 1771.

Hugo Winckler: "Nach Boghazköy," *Der Alte Orient*, Vol. 14, Part 3. Berlin: Vorderasiatische Gesellschaft; 1913. By permission of J. C. Hinrichs Verlag, Leipzig.

William Wright: *The Empire of the Hittites*. London: James Nisbett; 1884.

C. Leonard Woolley: *As I Seem to Remember*. New York: Praeger; 1962. By permission of George Allen & Unwin, London.

———: *Digging Up the Past*. New York: Crowell; 1955. By permission of Ernest Benn Ltd., London.

———: *Excavations at Ur*. New York: Barnes and Noble; 1955. By permission of Penguin Books, London.

INDEX

(N.B. The names of the principal archaeologists, scholars, authors, etc., are given in capitals and small capitals. An asterisk denotes that a biographical note is to be found on that page. Alternative spellings are given in brackets.)